INFORMATION MANAGEMENT: SETTING THE SCENE

PERSPECTIVES ON INFORMATION MANAGEMENT SERIES

Series Editor: **Rik Maes**

Published:

Power Laws in the Information Production Process: Lotkaian Informetrics
LEO EGGHE

Looking for Information
DONALD CASE

Understanding Reference Transactions: Turning Art Into a Science
MATTHEW LOCKE SAXTON & JOHN V. RICHARDSON

Models for Library Management, Decision-Making, and Planning
ROBERT M. HAYES

Text Information Retrieval Systems, Second Edition
CHARLES T. MEADOW, BERT R. BOYCE & DONALD H. KRAFT

Communicating Research
A. J. MEADOWS

Automated Information Retrieval: Theory and Methods
V. FRANTS, J. SHAPIRO & V. VOTSKUNSKII

Biomedical Information Technology: Global Social Responsibilities for the Democratic Age
HAROLD SACKMAN

Implementation of Organizational Innovation: Studies of Academic and Research Libraries
PETER CLAYTON

Information Tasks: Toward a User-Centered Approach to Information Systems
BRYCE L. ALLEN

Advances in Strategic Management Serial
JOEL BAUM (SERIES EDITOR)

Related Journals
International Journal of Information Management
International Journal of Accounting Information Systems
Journal of Strategic Information Systems
The Encyclopaedia of Information systems (4 Volumes)

INFORMATION MANAGEMENT: SETTING THE SCENE

16040/

EDITED BY

ARD HUIZING

Universiteit van Amsterdam Business School, The Netherlands

ERIK J. DE VRIES

Universiteit van Amsterdam Business School, The Netherlands

ELSEVIER   Amsterdam • Boston • Heidelberg • London • New York • Oxford
Paris • San Diego • San Francisco • Singapore • Sydney • Tokyo

Elsevier
Linacre House, Jordan Hill, Oxford OX2 8DP, UK
Radarweg 29, PO Box 211, 1000 AE Amsterdam, The Netherlands

First edition 2007

Notice
No responsibility is assumed by the publisher for any injury and/or damage to persons
or property as a matter of products liability, negligence or otherwise, or from any use
or operation of any methods, products, instructions or ideas contained in the material
herein. Because of rapid advances in the medical sciences, in particular, independent
verification of diagnoses and drug dosages should be made

British Library Cataloguing in Publication Data
A catalogue record for this book is available from the British Library

Library of Congress Cataloging-in-Publication Data
A catalog record for this book is available from the Library of Congress

ISBN: 978-0-08-046326-1
ISSN: 1755-3512 (Series)

For information on all Elsevier publications
visit our website at books.elsevier.com

Printed and bound in The Netherlands

07 08 09 10 11   10 9 8 7 6 5 4 3 2 1

Working together to grow
libraries in developing countries

www.elsevier.com | www.bookaid.org | www.sabre.org

ELSEVIER   BOOK AID
International   Sabre Foundation

Contents

Section VI: Designing Information and Organizations

Book Series Perspectives on Information Management

The book series *Perspectives on Information Management* is dedicated to creating and disseminating academic knowledge on information management that opens new avenues for academic research and is relevant to practitioners in the field.[1] Our central mission is to enhance the profession of information management by advancing scholarship and by enriching the professional development of our audience in a way that is relevant and makes valuable contribution to society and its institutions. The book series provides a high-quality international forum for researchers, practitioners and policy makers to exchange ideas on information management.

The series is motivated by developments in the field of information management. Information management nowadays is focussed on the *management of information* instead of the management of ICT[2] or the management of the business–ICT relationship.[3] As information is primarily a social construct and subject to interpretation, information management is about the construction of meaning for the organization and, derivatively, the construction of the organization's meaning for its environment. Information management deals with the identity of organizations.[4] Information management is about organizing information and communication processes and media around the construction of meaning for the organization and its environment and around identity development of organizations and organizational members. Information management is about decisions connecting organizational structures and technological infrastructures to facilitate such processes. Information governance and superior information use are more important than increasingly sophisticated data production. Understanding organizational ambiguity has become more important than understanding technical complexity. In our vision information management is a discipline not necessarily executed in a separate organizational function or profession; it is the aspect of general management where information is

---

[1]Like (Chief)Information Officers (CIOs), Information Managers, policy makers and general managers who work for information-intensive organizations in which the management of information has become core business as for instance in the financial service industry, the travel industry, government or the health care industry.

[2]Over the last two decades information management was completely absorbed by ICT management and hence non-existent. The CIO, if in function, was more a Chief Technology Officer (CTO), responsible for ICT and, derivatively, for its link with business departments.

[3]In the sense of a liaison function to bridge gaps between business departments and ICT suppliers/departments.

[4]Maes, R. (2004). Information management reconstructed, PrimaVera Working Paper 2004–19, Universiteit van Amsterdam.

consciously and knowledgeably dealt with. Information management is not restricted to intra-organizational issues: information management questions are also about supply chains, networks of organizations, networks of professionals, social networks, and societies at large. Hence, advancement of the information management field asks for multiple perspectives; we therefore encourage contributions from multiple disciplines and industries and welcome inter-disciplinary work.

Besides this vision on developments in the information management discipline, the book series is further motivated by a vision on the relationship between academic research and practice. In recent years there has been a debate in the academic literature on the topic 'rigor versus relevance'.[5] It is our intention to be *rigorously relevant* by emphasizing relevance in our choice for themes and topics to be included into the book series. As research in the field matures, there is an increasing need to carry its results into practice and to align research with practice. We do so by choosing topics in which enduring organizational problems and timely business issues are addressed.[6] The book series further contributes to linking research with practice and policy by targeting a mixed audience of people working at universities, research institutes, governments and the private sector. The series focuses on relevance by providing incentives to apply research methods that make sense to practitioners, to produce policy research and to write papers that are consumable for practitioners[7]; and by welcoming thoughtful practitioner reflections on action[8] and case studies.

---

[5]This debate evolves around the idea that research in our field is in crisis because academics are unable to target the practitioners audience due to an overemphasis on quantitative rigor, irrelevant topics, unreadable papers and long lead-times for publication, as stressed in: Robey, D., & Markus, M. L. (1998). Beyond rigor and relevance: Producing consumable research about information systems. *Information Resources Management Journal*, 11 (1), 7–15.

[6]As has been suggested in: Benbasat, I., & Zmud, R. W. (1999). Empirical Research in Information Systems: The Practice of Relevance. *MIS Quarterly*, 23(1), 3–16.

[7]As has been suggested in: Robey, D., & Markus, M. L. (1998). Beyond rigor and relevance: Producing consumable research about information systems. *Information Resources Management Journal* 11(1), 7–15.

[8]Meant as in: Schön, D. A. (1983). The reflective practitioner. How professionals think in action. New York: Basic Books.

Chapter 1

Information Management: Setting the Scene

Erik J. de Vries and Ard Huizing

ABSTRACT

Is information management in need of a new identity? Now that ICT has become ubiquitous and many technology-related activities are sourced from outside companies, the emphasis of information management shifts to what its name implies: the management of information as a business and societal resource. Because of the many ICT and market-related management notions involved in today's information management, the field struggles with its identity. This chapter presents an outline of the book. Several authors pinpoint the roots of information management's identity crisis, but most contributors focus on providing alternative notions, perspectives and vocabulary to set the scene for tomorrow's information management. In reviewing the different book sections and their chapters, we highlight a number of themes and relevant questions that emerge from all contributions. We end this chapter with our rationale explaining how the book has been composed and by describing its main characteristics.

Information Management's Struggle with Identity

The central question in this book is: what is the identity of information management now that ICT is ubiquitous and increasingly sourced from independent, specialized ICT services and software companies?

In the next chapter of this volume, Maes argues that information management struggles with its identity because it is rooted in different disciplines. Maes further argues that ICT experts have assumed responsibility for many of the issues related to the management of information in the recent past, approaching the issue primarily from a technological perspective. By using notions such as business–ICT alignment, ICT strategy, architecture and sourcing, the management of information technology has become almost synonymous with the management of information. Now that ICT is increasingly sourced from specialized ICT service and software companies, the lack of information-related notions and the over-emphasis on technological notions have become apparent. Furthermore, the key concept to managing ICT in relation to business needs — *strategic alignment* — perceived by many people as the central issue in information management, has also been heavily criticized. In the next chapter, Maes asserts that alignment is a misleading term and in the book section on ICT, strategy and identity, Brigham and Introna (Chapter 12) then challenge the basic assumptions underlying alignment and finally, Introna proposes an autopoietic approach as an alternative view in Chapter 11.

In many organizations, information management struggles with a legacy of technology-related notions and language. Information management is approached by general management in that language and is still being held responsible for ICT performance. Assuming that identity is set by notions of oneself in relation to one's social environment, getting expressed and reinforced in the language spoken, information management is in a *genuine identity crisis*.

This crisis is further reinforced by a strong tendency among general, information and ICT management to think in market terms, as Huizing points out in Chapter 6. Take, for instance, the traditional definition of information management: 'the gathering, storage, refining, and distribution of information'. It is supply-driven and appears to stop at 'information distribution', metaphorically understood as throwing the information over the wall to the eager information users. As Huizing states, the combination of such market terminology with technological notions further commoditizes the concept of information, such that it degenerates into only a marketable product. Bryant warns us in Chapter 5 that such terminology also gives rise to ideas like the mechanical transfer of information between anonymous senders and receivers. In organizations where general management has taken such an operational, technological and instrumental vision on information-related issues, information management runs the risk of being viewed by the organization as merely the functional management of information systems responsible for the operational control of change requests and ICT procurement.

The problem is that such a view conceals information usage related issues such as the following:

- The role and function of information in social processes;
- The centrality of information and communication in establishing the identity of organizations and its strategic positioning;
- The relation between information and communication processes and the division of labor (in and between organizations), specialization and resulting coordination and contracting needs;
- The role and function of information in innovation processes and the fact that information and communication processes themselves are subject to innovation;
- And the design of organizational or technological structures in which people have to live and work and of which they become inseparable parts.

Setting the Scene for Future Information Management

As articulated by the editorial board, the central mission of the book series *Perspectives on Information Management* is to enhance the profession of information management by advancing scholarship and by enriching professional development in a way that is relevant and that makes valuable contributions to society and its institutions. This vision becomes operational in this first volume by setting the scene for the IM discipline given its current situation in the broader domain of management and organization.

In Chapter 2, Maes provides us with an integrative framework for information management in which we can position issues that are central to the field. He defines information management as the management discipline concerning strategic, structural and operational information-related issues, and relates the (external and internal) information and communication processes and their supporting technology to general business aspects. His framework explicitly acknowledges issues related to information and communication and of (infra) structural arrangements, such as business processes, infrastructure, architecture, etc. The structure of this volume is inspired by the actual and emergent issues Maes describes and summarizes in Figure 3 in the next chapter: identity, sourcing issues, customer focus and flexibility of systems and design. These issues are taken as the most prevalent ones in the field for the coming years and together with two sections on information management in general, these issues set the context for the remaining sections of the book.

The volume is divided into this introductory chapter, Chapter 2 in which Maes puts forward his integrative framework, two sections on information management in general, followed by four sections on the actual and emergent issues in information management: ICT, strategy and identity; ICT (out)sourcing; customer-oriented innovation; and design. All members of the Editorial Board of the new book series *Perspectives on Information Management* have contributed chapters to this volume and all sections have been coordinated by Editorial Board members. Every section starts with a short introduction in which the section coordinators introduce the section topic, they note how these topics are relevant to the information management field, and they introduce the individual chapters in these sections.

This introductory chapter addresses themes that recur in different sections and overall arguments on how the sections contribute to the changing identity of information management.

The first section on information management in general provides a more general historic context to the field, reminding us of what information management was before ICT. Black (Chapter 3) recognizes three different occupations that have been involved with information management in the past: the managers of mechanization (leading to centralized departments as early as 1935, which could be viewed as the predecessors of current ICT departments); the librarians (who have lost the battle with their successors, the information officers (who are the third group). The information officers defined themselves as managers, abstractors and communicators of information that was packaged in a variety of formats, stressing the importance of their subject knowledge and taking an activist approach to users. Brunt (Chapter 4) describes the work of these professionals in central registries in the British intelligence service during the period of the two world wars. He shows how the purpose of the intelligence service and 'the aspects of the world' which needed to be reflected in their (index) systems, determined the intelligence work.

From this historic context it seems that the rapid advances of technology over the last decades and its associated specialization have forced managerial attention on the mechanization part of the field. It should be acknowledged, however, that the contemporary content structuring work we now see in the field of content management systems and databases resembles the work of central registries and information officers as described by Brunt and Black. The components of information work (e.g. the work of the information officer and later, the information scientist) as described by Black, reminds us of what information management could be if we put less emphasis on its technological aspects. Moreover, Bryant (Chapter 5) reminds us of the 'actual behavior' of managers and employees toward information and the limitations of 'engineering models' when it comes to understanding such behavior.

In the second section on information management in general, Huizing discusses the disadvantages of the generally accepted objectivist and market notions on information (in Chapter 6) and provides us with an alternative perspective on information from subjectivist sociology and anthropology (in Chapter 7). Applying microeconomics to deepen our understanding of objectivism and applying practice-based social theory to do the same for subjectivism, he poses the question of whether or not a sound and solid basis for information management can be found in either perspective. In both cases, the answer is negative leading us to the inescapable assertion that both objectivism and subjectivism are needed for an integrative approach to information management — one is better off when informed by the other. Choo (Chapter 8) adds to this by examining a number of subjective psychological processes that negatively affect the sharing and processing of information in organizational groups, such as management or project teams. He also indicates how information management can help reduce such subjectivity in group discussions and improve intersubjective information use in organizational teams.

Chapter 2 and the first two sections on information management in general add to our search for a new identity of information management by providing a framework to position the field and its main subjects of interest; by historical contextualization and by a critical examination of the assumptions underlying the central notions of information management, contrasting these core notions with alternative ones. The chapters jointly provide a vocabulary to discuss the current state of information management and the need to search for and develop a new identity for information management that better fits current times. This vocabulary is enhanced in the next four sections, which are more focused on current central issues in the field: ICT, strategy and identity; ICT (out)sourcing; customer-oriented innovation; and design.

In Chapter 5, Bryant recalls an important question from Beer (1981) that is highly relevant to information management, which could be reframed in current terminology as: '*Given ICT; what is the nature of our enterprise?*' This question addresses a central issue in information management and answering this question will direct a search for this field's new identity. The question resonates in different sections and contributions throughout the book.

The underlying theme of the third section is that ICT, strategy and identity should not be viewed as separate phenomena but as phenomena mutually constituting each other; that is, as phenomena that are inseparably interwoven, making each other possible. When ICT, strategy and identity are mutually constitutive, alignment becomes an impossible issue. How could inseparable phenomena be aligned? Consequently, the notion of alignment, which is considered by many to define information management's identity, is at stake in this section. Furthermore, despite the popular view of Carr (2003), ICT *does* matter because it constitutes us and our organizations, as argued by Introna (Chapter 9). This view is illustrated in Wigand (Chapter 19) and Slagter et al. (Chapter 20) in the section on customer-oriented innovation where they describe how people express and reinforce their identities in Web 2.0 and how they become 'Cyborgian' in Second Life. The section on ICT, strategy and identity continues with Chapter 10 by Ilharco in which strategy is understood as choosing to choose, to take a stand. Strategic changes are seen as both ambiguous and paradoxical, creating hospitable or hostile relations between the new and the existing practices instead of being seen as the result of strategic alignment or top-down planning (Brigham and Introna, Chapter 12). New technology, for example, is thought of as an ambiguous stranger, an image which is so aptly illustrated by the way companies react to Web 2.0, as described by Wigand. The real work of strategizing then is not top-down alignment but the continual questioning and interpreting of the relationship between 'the guest' (the new technology) and 'his host' (the organization).

Bryant's question also resonates in the book's final section. Using the case of 3D technology in the construction industry, Boland (Chapter 21) demonstrates that the relationship between information systems and the organization, in which these systems are conceptualized, is mutual. The organization imposes its structure upon the technological system, but new technologies provide opportunities for restructuring as well, making former, traditional organizational arrangements obsolete. Gal et al. (Chapter 22) provide a similar logic in showing that technology as a boundary object is influenced by the identities of the organizations using these objects, and that these identities are also influenced through these boundary objects. Like Boland, they base this assertion on a case study conducted in the same construction industry. The idea in both contributions could be interpreted using Ciborra's (1993) idea that technology enables other contractual arrangements. As organizations can be seen as contractual arrangements and ICT can be perceived as one of the ways to arrive at new contractual arrangements (according to institutional economics (Wigand, Picot, & Reichwald, 1997)), implementing new ICT requires that organizations reconsider how they are organized.

Another central theme in information management that spans various sections and chapters of this book is the transformation of organizations and systems into *customer-oriented* ones. This theme is central to information management because it assumes that organizations establish mechanisms for information sharing and sense making with their external partners, customers and partners in demand-driven supply chains. Terms that are associated with customer orientation are market intelligence and research, customer/user requirements, (mass) customization, customer-centered innovation, blurring boundaries between production and consumption, prosumer, user-generated content, user communities, human-centered design, etc. The main idea behind all of these terms is that customers have *information about their use context*, which needs to be shared with producers' *information on production contexts* (von Hippel, 2005). Combining both types of information is by no means trivial. This challenge is readily apparent when we reflect, for example, on the inevitable problems in information systems development, and on new product or new service designs. The consequences of this combining are twofold. First, the producer is compelled to become actively involved and to become more familiar with the world of the customer or *vice versa*. Second, the producer can never meet the demands of all customers and therefore he has to restrict himself to a particular amount of flexibility in offering products and services.

Both consequences are dealt with in the fifth section on customer-oriented innovation. De Vries (Chapter 18) illustrates that service innovation is interactive (with customers and business partners) and he further illustrates that service positioning in the market can be strengthened by ad hoc innovations that respond to customer specific requests. De Vries also demonstrates that management trade-offs need to be made between the degree to which one is willing to service the customer and the service positioning strategy of the business unit to avoid 'strategic drifting'. Finally, he shows that through innovations companies could migrate from one positioning strategy to another, but that this is not without its consequences and management trade-offs. In the same section, Segers et al. (Chapter 17) reinforce De Vries' idea of service innovation being interactive and show its interdisciplinary nature, its lack of clear organization such as, for example, R&D in the manufacturing sector, and its lack of cooperation with academia and governmental agencies. Moreover, this section illustrates that information management should anticipate drivers for service innovation that are different from technological advances. The contributions of Wigand on Web 2.0 in general (Chapter 19) and of Slagter et al. on Second Life in particular (Chapter 20) pinpoint current trends that are by no means merely technological but are also social and economical. Both chapters indicate the interesting phenomenon of citizens already possessing information on the use context of a new trend where companies have yet to find out what to do with it.

The theme of customers having to share information on their use context with producers bringing to bear their information on production contexts is revisited in the section on design. Hovorka and Germonprez (Chapter 23) articulate design principles to design flexible, tailorable systems that could be adopted by users to different use contexts. Conceptually, at least, several of their design principles are quite similar to the ones that are used in service development, suggesting that a set of universal principles is actually available. Avital (Chapter 24) goes one step further in proposing design principles for generative systems, systems that are conducive to innovative processes. The chapters of Hovorka and Germonprez, and that of Avital both deal with design exercises in which the designer tries to anticipate use contexts, which are unknown at the moment of design. As service delivery becomes increasingly dependent on ICT systems and infrastructures, empirical grounding of these design principles might lead to interesting new avenues in service delivery design and innovation.

So, one theme addressed in this volume is that ICT *does* matter because it is mutually constitutive with strategy and identity. A second theme is the problematic nature of the exchange of information on use and production contexts. These two themes also play an important role in sourcing relationships. The degree to which strategy, identity and technology are mutually constitutive determines whether the technology can be outsourced and if so what kinds of contracts and organizational arrangements should be used to govern it. In the section on ICT (out)sourcing, Hirschheim and George, Willcocks et al. and Cumps et al. discuss some of the considerations that are needed, using the language of the resource-based view or transaction costs economics. Based on their 17 years of research, Willcocks et al. additionally indicate which contractual arrangements and management practices are appropriate under which circumstances. Hirschheim and George have an intriguing parallel with the contributions of both Boland and Gal et al. in the designing information and organizations section. One wonders how sophisticated ICT-based outsourcing relationship management tools can provide new contracting opportunities which alter organizational arrangements in outsourcing relationships, as Boland and Gal et al. discuss for the construction industry. In this case, Bryant's question could be reframed as follows: 'Given this technology, what could be the nature of our outsourcing arrangements?' The second theme, the sharing of information in use contexts with that of production contexts, is important in sourcing relationships as well. In sourcing relationships, information managers, now being part of the use context, need to share their information with ICT service suppliers, to enable these ICT service suppliers to make sense of how technology is used in their company. Cumps et al. describe this need to share information between the outsourcing organization and technology service providers. They demonstrate for two typical outsourcing situations how information management could be organized to increase the likelihood that outsourcing becomes a success.

Conclusion and Outlook

Information management means that superior information use rather than sophisticated data production is recognized as the predominant source for increasing the value information management adds to the business. Consequently, information management needs to focus on information and communication processes, within organizations, between organizations in supply chains, with customers, in professional communities and in social networks. It further acknowledges that information and communication processes could be enabled or limited by (infra)structural arrangements, which implies that information management must assume responsibility for this topic as well. Having knowledge of ICT is not sufficient anymore, but it is still indispensable because technology, identity and strategy are so tightly interwoven. Information management deals with questions such as:

- Given this technology; what is the nature of our enterprise or of myself?
- Given this technological design how could we design relationships between organizations?
- How does my company or this group of citizens share information between use contexts and production contexts?
- How to design systems, infrastructures or service concepts that provide enough flexibility to anticipate unknown future usage?

- How could we share information about use contexts with our ICT provider's production contexts and how do we govern sourcing relationships?

These issues and questions *set the scene* for information management for the coming years. We need a language that is bound to these issues and questions, not one that is linked to the management of ICT. With such a language we can build a new identity.

What is interesting about these issues and questions is that many of these cross different departments and even organizations, indicating that information management is a shared responsibility of many (line) managers in similar ways as HRM, financial management or marketing are. Those who have job titles such as CIO, information officer or information manager should anticipate being responsible for areas that are beyond their direct control and that of their teams or departments. This responsibility is far-reaching, and impacts a variety of stakeholders including citizens, clients, employees, shareholders, the Board, technology providers, governing institutions, the environment/ecology or society at large; on a wide range of issues such as privacy, business continuity, (interorganizational) infrastructure, sustainability, projects and programs, budgets, ethical and legal issues, technology assessment, governance and quality. We expect that subsequent volumes in this series would take a close look at several of these responsibilities, against the background of the scene set in this volume.

This volume has been edited in close cooperation with the Editorial Board of the book series *Perspective on Information Management*. To set the scene according to ideas shared by the Editorial Board, all Board members contributed chapters to this volume and all sections have been coordinated by Editorial Board members. The introductions to each chapter have been written by one of the coordinators. The coordinators were:

Section I: The CIO Before ICT — Tony Bryant.
Section II: Rising Above Objectivism and Subjectivism — Chun Wei Choo and Ard Huizing.
Section III: ICT, Strategy and Identity — Lucas Introna.
Section IV: ICT (Out)sourcing — Guido Dedene and Rudy Hirschheim.
Section V: Customer-Oriented Innovation — Erik de Vries.
Section VI: Designing Information and Organizations — Michel Avital and Kalle Lyytinen.

From the early start, the Editorial Board took a Kantian approach to this volume, as is also taken in the chapter of Hovorka and Germonprez to which we refer for further explanation. Our idea was to approach the topic of the identity of information management from different angles and disciplines to come to an overall picture consisting of some core issues and intriguing questions. Contributions to this volume have been made not only from disciplines which information management traditionally builds on such as information systems, computer science, information science/library science, economics and management, but also from less adjacent disciplines such as philosophy, sociology, anthropology, history, technology studies, architecture and design and even music. Part of this approach has been to involve CIOs of international companies and governmental organizations in the development of the ideas. First ideas on this volume have been discussed with 20 CIOs from several large European companies and governmental organizations, out of which several of the topics discussed in this volume emerged. We intend to continue this close cooperation with practice for future book volumes.

The sections are self-contained and can be read independently. We used two chapter formats: full papers and short papers. Short papers were meant to be cases, illustrations or positioning papers. As a result, the nature of the chapters differs. Some provide overviews (like the ones of Maes, Huizing, Hirschheim and George or Willcocks et al.). Other chapters are built on cases (like Brigham and Introna, de Vries, Dedene and Heene or Gal et al.). Black and Brunt are typical historical studies. Hovorka and Germonprez base design principles on a literature study. Introna's chapter on becoming technological has a contemplative character and Avital's chapter is a typical positioning paper. When it comes to methodology, we have deliberately chosen not to include extended methodological paragraphs in the chapters to keep the book accessible to practitioners. In some chapters some methodological specifics are outlined in appendices. As the topic is approached from different angles, methodology is pluralistic as well, ranging from analytical research to archival research, qualitative methods (mainly case studies) and quantitative research.

References

Beer, S. (1981). *The brain of the firm: Managerial cybernetics of organization*. Chichester: Wiley.

Carr, N. G. (2003). IT doesn't matter. *Harvard Business Review, 81*(5), 41–49.

Ciborra, C. U. (1993). *Teams, markets and systems, business innovation and information technology*. Cambridge: Cambridge University Press.

von Hippel, E. (2005). *Democratizing innovation*. Cambridge, MA: MIT Press.

Wigand, R., Picot, A., & Reichwald, R. (1997). *Information, organization and management, expanding markets and corporate boundaries*. West Sussex, England: Wiley.

Chapter 2

An Integrative Perspective on Information Management

Rik Maes

ABSTRACT

Information management (IM) is an integrative discipline, connecting all information-related issues of an organization. Its integrative nature is investigated through a generic framework linking strategy and operations as well as business and technology. The main activities and topical burning questions of IM are discussed. Future perspectives on IM are delineated and an appeal is made for responsible IM in organizations as well as in society in general.

Problems are solved, not by giving new information, but by arranging what we have always known.

Ludwig Wittgenstein, Philosophical Investigations

Introduction

Despite the fact that information has always been a primary organizational resource and even been called "the unique feature of the market economy" (Drucker, 1993), information management (IM) is still a rather indistinct discipline, both in academic research and in practice. It deals with the management of information as a business resource and, hence, encompasses all the processes and systems within an organization for the creation and use of information. Further, given the ubiquitous nature of information and communication technology (ICT), the business — ICT relationship has traditionally been a point of particular interest in IM.

The indefinite identity of IM is reinforced by reminiscences from the past, where the term IM was claimed by the library sciences[1] (see e.g. Macevièiūtè & Wilson, 2002), and by the advent of adjacent and even partially overlapping disciplines such as knowledge management.[2] This struggling with its own identity is also due to the handover of the discipline to ICT people, who approached the organizational use of information in a one-sided "technocratic utopian" (Davenport, Eccles, & Prusak, 1992) way. Facetiously spoken, IM resembles a discipline in its puberty: it is reacting against its technology-coloured interpretation, but at the same time has difficulties in finding its own identity and its right place in the organization.

Notwithstanding this disorientation, the importance of IM has only increased. Reasons for this are numerous, but can be brought back to the following:

- By ICT becoming more mature, transaction costs associated with information have substantially decreased. Because of this, organizations are more and more information-dependent; they are at the same time struggling with information overload and with information underuse. The combination of these seemingly contradictory effects is a serious motive for managing information as a resource.
- The maturity of ICT makes it possible to exploit scale. ICT can be managed as a normal resource, i.e. based on its output, and can eventually be put at a distance from the organization (hence outsourcing and off-shoring). Contrary to the information supply side, its demand side is highly immature: organizations all over the globe are struggling with a serious lack of deep understanding of their information processes, apart from their technical components. Reasons enough to look after targeted IM.

Visions on IM are too often first and foremost based on the underlying technologies (the "how?"), whereas one simultaneously continues to stress the importance and strategic impact (the "what?") of information. The aim of this article is to discuss IM in an integrative way and, because of this, to cover the full scope of the management of information as an (inter)organizational resource. To this end, we first ponder its fields of influence, after which we present an integrative framework that enables us to discuss the main constituents of as well as the actual and emerging issues in IM as part of an advancing discipline. We conclude with a view on future developments in the field of IM.

Information Management: Between the Devil and The Deep Blue?

IM has traditionally been a discipline in between business and ICT, in academic terms in between the management discipline and information systems, if not

---

[1]Information management is in this discipline nowadays quite often equivalent to "content management".

[2]A discussion on the differences between both disciplines can be found in Bouthillier and Shearer (2002). An extremely critical review of what is new in knowledge management compared to IM is offered by Wilson (2002).

computer science. The image of the business–ICT relationship has been that of "a troubled marriage in need of guidance" (Ward & Peppard, 1996). I prefer René Magritte's painting *Les Amants* (*The Lovers*) as a metaphoric representation, where both lovers are dying to kiss each other on the mouth but are severely obstructed by their heads being fully wrapped up. Similar distressing remarks have been made regarding the relationship between the business and ICT *departments*, where miscommunication and even non-communication are said to be the main source of misalignment (Coughlan, Lycett, & Macredie, 2005). It has, however, been emphasized that creating value out of these relationships is basically a general management responsibility, exceeding IT management (Tiernan & Peppard, 2004).

"Strategic alignment", prominently introduced by Henderson and Venkatraman (1993), has since been the key word to open up and manage the business–ICT relationship (Hirschheim & Sabherwal, 2001; Avison, Jones, Powell, & Wilson, 2004), though it has been criticized as being only a purely rational top-down approach (Simonsen, 1999) and hence only partially effective (Chan, 2002), lacking practical handles and therefore in large measure irrelevant (Sauer & Burn, 1997) and even inconvenient and harmful (Ciborra, 1997). Despite all this, it is still high on the hit parade of any chief information officer (CIO) survey of pressing questions. I believe, in line with Hussain, King, and Cragg (2002), that strategic alignment is used to mean a variety of things and is consequently a misleading term, as it implies, e.g. both the ultimate destination and the road leading to it (though driving this road is pretended to be badly understood, Smaczny, 2001; Sabherwal & Chan, 2001). What's more, it suggests that a perfect alignment is ideal. Therefore, I will argue in the next section in favour of "managing in mutual accordance" without any direct connotation of equilibrium, purposiveness, etc.

An imminent gap much less noticed and discussed in the scientific literature than that between business and ICT, but mentioned by leading practitioners,[3] is the one between strategy and operations. This phenomenon might be partially due to the growing disinterest of the board for ICT in general, in resonance with Nicolas Carr's "IT doesn't matter any more" (Carr, 2003), or to their disenchantment with the ICT department's inability to deliver the pretended "motor for innovation". ICT is, in that case, a cost factor and a candidate for savings. Another, in many instances, a more evident explanation has to do with the general economic climate where boards of large organizations are operating in a context far away from day-to-day operations, the latter being only of strategic (i.e. related to the stock prices of the company or, in the case of governmental agencies, to the political impact) importance when confronted with emergencies catching external attention. IM is, in that respect, caught between delivering effective and efficient support for the existing and new businesses and the pending requests originating from strategic moves such as mergers, acquisitions, etc. Many years' investments in streamlining the organization's ICT along a certain ERP software package, might, e.g. be overruled by the acquisition of an overseas competitor.

---

[3]One of the outcomes of a number of explorative meetings with leading Dutch CIO's.

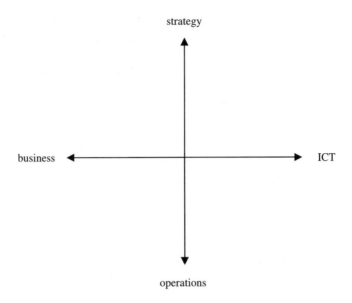

Figure 2.1: IM's double splits.

The resulting view on IM is shown in Figure 2.1. We will argue in what follows that full IM operates in each of the four resulting quadrants and derives its identity precisely from its integrative nature. The relative importance of each individual aspect is context-dependent and, as a consequence, the interpretation as well as the realization of the concept of IM is subject to contingency factors.

An Integrative Framework

Departing from Figure 2.1, IM can tentatively be circumscribed as the integrative discipline connecting business, ICT, strategy and operations. Along these lines, the four quadrants, business strategy, ICT strategy, business operations and ICT operations are its obvious areas for special attention. A company confronted with a myriad of overlapping information systems, e.g. might opt for a short-term, almost exclusive concentration on its ICT strategy,[4] whereas a company struggling with its turning over towards a customer-oriented organization might temporarily focus on streamlining and reorienting its business operations. As a matter of course, all four quadrants will, generally speaking, be part of an organization's IM orientation. Not surprisingly, these quadrants coincide to a large extent with the building blocks of the strategic alignment model of Henderson and Venkatraman (1993).

---

[4]This particular ICT strategy, involving dramatic reductions in systems in existence, was called by one of the CIO's a "surgical strategy" as opposed to an often more comforting "homoeopathic" one.

The most intriguing part of this rather classical interpretation of IM is what is not explicitly addressed, particularly the vital role of the factor information as the linking pin between the four components of Figure 2.1. Indeed, ICT is only *indirectly* influencing the business, *viz.* by the information generated, the communication supported, etc. The quality of information *use* is seriously filtering the impact of ICT and, as a consequence, is a key control lever to be taken care of in any serious attempt to delineate IM in its full amplitude. Similarly, the information *infrastructure*, in Henderson and Venkatraman's model part of the internal, operational domain, is the linking pin par excellence between strategy and operations; this structural variable is responsible for the flexibility or the rigidity of the organization and its services.

The resulting integrative framework, represented in Figure 2.2, is in itself the outcome of a long process of elaboration and validation (Maes, 1999, 2003, 2004) and has favourably been compared with other alignment models (Avison et al., 2004), despite the fact that it is only meant to be an integrative *positioning* framework, allowing to frame and discuss the different aspects of IM in their mutual dependence without any reference to full alignment or whatsoever managerial imperative.

Based on this framework, we can describe IM as the integrative, balanced management of the different domains represented in Figure 2.2. It concerns strategic, structural and operational information-related issues (the vertical dimension of the enneahedron of Figure 2.2) and relates the (external and internal) information and communication processes and their supporting technology to general business aspects (the horizontal dimension). The central axes of this figure do not correspond

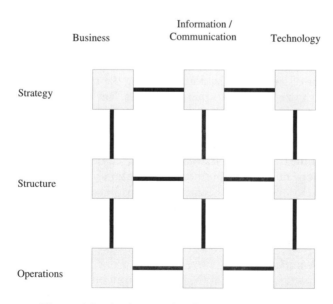

Figure 2.2: An integrative framework for IM.

to subordinate or even disregarded aspects of IM, as the latter is the case in Henderson and Venkatraman's model, *yet to the core itself of IM.*

A number of elucidating interpretations and similarities can be derived from Figure 2.2, referring to its three columns:

- From right to left, we *produce, interpret* and *use* information. In the right column, we call it *data*, in the middle one *information* and in the left one *knowledge.* IM has to do with all three of these designations.
- For each of the columns, clearly distinct expertise is needed: from left to right, respectively, domain expertise, information expertise and technology expertise (distinction taken from Choo, 1998). IM is concentrating on information expertise, without neglecting the other two.
- Technology (right column) can be considered as introducing a new *syntax*, while business (the left column) constitutes the *pragmatics* of a given problem. As a consequence, the very heart of IM (the middle column) is dealing with sense making, *semantics.*
- There is a striking similarity with the concept of "information orientation" as introduced by Marchand et al. (Marchand, Kettinger, & Rollins, 2000, 2001) in order to indicate an organization's quality of dealing with information. They subdivide this standard in three sub-standards: "information technology practices", "information management practices" and "information behaviours and values". These sub-standards coincide, respectively with the right, the middle and the informational aspects of the left column.

IM is supporting the primary identity and activities of an organization; therefore, the natural *scope* of the framework will, generally spoken, be the corporate or (strategic) business unit level. As a matter of fact, assuring the integrity of IM at different organizational levels is one of the essentials of IM; it can be done with the assistance of the framework at each of these levels, including, if relevant, at the level of inter-organizational networks.

A vast number of large organizations are using the framework as a guideline for analysing and organizing their information services. The framework has proven to be a practical instrument for general managers, information managers and ICT managers, specifically in sharing their mutual understanding of the situation. It helps them in evaluating the current situation and in steering future developments through mapping both on the framework. Indeed, a completed framework details the position of the organization, in terms of business, information and technology, from a strategic, structural and operational perspective. Gaps in some of the domains indicate either a poor understanding of these parts of the organization or an effective lack of provisions, often leading to re-allocation of project resources.

More in detail, the framework is used as follows:

- *Descriptive/orientating*: In this case, the framework is functioning as a "lingua franca" for all parties involved in IM (ranging from business people to information systems (IS) people). The different information-related problem areas are indicated on the framework. Experience shows that especially the differentiation between information/communication and IT (the latter one inclusive of information systems), but also between (infra)structure and operations are fruitful to consider. The framework is stimulating the participants to converse about information services without recurring to technical jargon and to position the areas for special attention in their mutual relationship.

- *Organizing/designing*: A number of organizations, e.g. the Dutch Police Services, are using the framework to redesign their overall IM, especially in the case where the IT facilities themselves are concentrated or outsourced. Used in this way, the framework is useful in delineating the areas of concern and responsibility of the CIO and the information managers. Remark that the framework is not a diagram of the organization, but an indication of the domains of attention and their interrelationships.
- *Prescriptive/normative*: Yet other organizations (including their consultants) are using the framework as a diagnosis tool, e.g. to define and further investigate the "blind spots" in their information services. Traditionally and dependent on the "information maturity" of the organization, the central axes of the framework are serious candidates for this. Giving harmonious and mutually aligned attention to the different domains of the framework, including the links between the domains, is raised to a rule in these organizations.

The Constituents of IM

The integrative framework of Figure 2.2 allows us to expand the constituents of IM in an interdependent way (Maes, 1999). Basically, each constituent (each of the nine domains of the generic framework) is made up of its own area of concern, taking into account its connections with the adjacent constituents in the framework. In what follows, we restrain ourselves from a discussion in full detail of each of the constituents; rather, we present a point-by-point survey of the domains and for each of these one or two examples. Two important restrictions have to be made at this instant:

1. IM is an important sub-discipline, but nothing more; the pretension to cover, e.g. business strategy is only true to the extent that IM (and the CIO) is contributing to it in terms of the opportunities and challenges (*viz.* threats) the factor "information" and ICT are offering
2. the intertwining of the constituents might heavily restrain the degrees of freedom within a single domain; IM then becomes the management of the network of relationships between the constituents, including these between different organizational levels as has been indicated in the previous paragraph.

Strategy Level

The strategic level of the generic framework recognizes the need of modern organizations to address information and communication processes and the underlying technology in relation to their overall business strategy. According to Henderson, Venkatraman and Oldach (1996), decisions on *scope, core capabilities* and *governance* are key at this level.

Business Strategy

- Business scope
  - To determine the organization's product/service–market-channel combinations
  - To create strategic alliances rendered possible and advantageous through information sharing in the value chain
- Business core capabilities
  - To determine the differentiating core capabilities of the organization
- Business governance
  - To determine the business risks involved in strategic ICT projects

I/C Strategy

- I/C scope
  - To determine the organization's generic external (e.g. what kind of information do we want to share with customers?) and internal (e.g. who owns the data?) I/C strategy
  - To assess societal evolutions in the use of information, e.g. the advent of communities, the application of social software, etc.
- I/C core capabilities
  - To determine the organization's overall strategy regarding knowledge management
  - To determine the differentiating capabilities for using and sharing information
- I/C governance
  - To develop guidelines for the appropriate use of information
  - To decide on strategic partnerships for information procurement

Technology Strategy

- Technology scope
  - To determine the organization's overall ICT strategy
  - To assess emerging technologies
- Technology core capabilities
  - To determine the organization's differentiating ICT capabilities
  - To define rules for innovation *versus* legacy replacement issues
- Technology governance
  - To decide on sourcing and strategic partnerships with key technology providers
  - To determine the policy regarding strategic ICT standards

Structure Level

The structure level of the generic framework emphasizes the significance of tuning the organizational, informational/communicational and technological architectures and capabilities. Its importance has significantly increased due to the emergence of resource-based thinking. The integrated information infrastructure, defined as the generic, relatively permanent basic facility for the purpose of developing and using information services and encompassing technological, informational and organizational components (Maes, 1990), is recognized as the managerial instrument *par excellence* in this respect (Weill & Broadbent, 1998).

The main decision areas at the structure level concern the *architecture* of the information infrastructure and the establishment of *capabilities* (Henderson et al., 1996); the latter are derived (in essence: generalized) from work practices at the operations level. Information infrastructure and capabilities constitute the substantiated capacity of the organization to realize its goals.

Business Structure

- Business architecture
  - To develop the organization's business architecture
  - To determine and (re)design the critical business processes
- Business capabilities
  - To select and develop promising business capabilities (e.g. to work in mixed teams)
  - To transform a product-centred organization into a customer-centred one

I/C Structure

- I/C architecture
  - To develop the organization's information/communication architecture (in essence: who should inform/communicate with whom?)
  - To determine and (re)design the critical information and communication processes
- I/C capabilities
  - To select and develop promising information and communication capabilities (e.g. to share information over departmental borders)
  - To combine information on customers from different sources

Technology Structure

- Technology architecture
  - To develop the organization's technology (data, systems, configuration and the supporting ICT organization) architecture (the technology "blueprint")
  - To determine and (re)design the critical ICT processes
- Technology capabilities
  - To select and develop promising technology capabilities (e.g. knowledge about XML)
  - To develop an ICT staffing and recruitment plan

Operations Level

For a lengthy period, strategists have distanced themselves (and still do) from operations on the work floor, as has been explained in second paragraph: *operational effectiveness is not a strategy* (Porter, 1996). However, the strategic importance of excellent operations has been (re)discovered in the context of customer-oriented thinking. The contribution of accurate information and communication processes and technology to operational excellence is addressed at the operations level of the generic framework. This level deals primarily with *work processes* and *skills* (Henderson et al., 1996).

Business Operations

- Business processes
  - To install and monitor new business processes
  - To monitor customer satisfaction on a permanent basis
- Business skills
  - To develop and monitor a customer-centred attitude

I/C operations

- I/C processes
  - To install and monitor I/C processes (e.g. the exchange of information between different departments)
  - To install integrated and easily manageable information about the customer
- I/C skills
  - To train people in the use of integrated customer information

Technology Operations

- Technology processes
  - To (re)design, perform and monitor ICT processes (development, maintenance, ...)
  - To develop operational ICT management (e.g. ITIL)
- Technology skills
  - To acquire new ICT people and train the skills of the existing ICT professionals

Actual and Emerging Issues in IM

IM entails the balanced management of the domains represented in the enneahedron of Figure 2.2, as has been worked out in the previous paragraph. The same framework allows us to arrange the hot issues in IM anno 2007,[5] as is done in Figure 2.3.

---

[5]These issues originate from ample survey sessions with CIO's and information managers, e.g. in the context of the Executive Master in Information Management program of the University of Amsterdam.

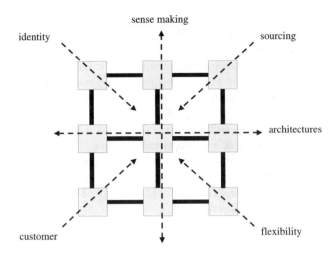

Figure 2.3: Actual and emerging issues in IM.

These issues, though inherently interrelated as is indicated in the framework, require some separate reading.

Organizations, companies and governmental institutions alike, are confronted with their very *identity*, mainly but not only under the influence of major macro-economic shifts: globalization, virtualization, socialization, customization etc. are only a few of the highbrow terms wandering around to indicate a common phenomenon: organizations are no longer the centre of their own world, as they used to perceive. The advent of Internet was one of the determining sources of this revolution. More and more organizations are judged on (and eventually punished for) the quality of their information resources. Housing cooperatives, e.g. are supposed to play a major role with regard to safety in the neighbourhoods, but discover much to their surprise that they have almost no useful information on their tenants.

Similarly, many organizations are confronted with the value and costs of their ICT. This is partly due to the economic squeeze in which they are supposed to operate and partly to the advent of alternatives, e.g. in offshore countries. *Sourcing* issues, whether in the form of shared services or of outsourcing, are still high on the agenda of many a CIO. Outsourcing as part of inter-organizational IM practices is discussed by Cumps, Dedene and Viaene (2007).

Organizations are further supposed (and even obliged) to deliver customized products and services, even in business sectors as power supply, post delivery, etc. Transforming their product-oriented systems and databases into integrated *customer*-focused ones, including the business intelligence needed, but even more the transformation of the organization as a whole into full customer-orientation, is a major operation and a hot issue in many of them. As a matter of fact, organizational agility is a major asset for organizations operating in volatile environments, as almost all do; it requires continuous devotion to the *flexibility* of the systems base.

These hot issues, connected to the four vertices of Figure 2.3, are interrelated through the topics covered by the central axes of the framework, in themselves at the same time instruments and points of particular interest for CIO's. The structure-related horizontal axis, is the natural playground of the enterprise architect. The use of the term *architecture* here is rather confusing, as almost everything is called a, preferably, *service-oriented* architecture nowadays, and to a great extent still dominated by technological thinking: the logic of ICT architectures is easily extended into the direction of organizational architectures. The result is remaining and even rising misunderstanding between the ICT division and the rest of the organization. What is basically missing in many organizations is a clear vision on their information and communication architecture, i.e. on the (preferred) information exchange patterns inside the organization and between the organization and its environment. Social network analysis is a more effective technique to support this than the traditional data modeling techniques taken from database design.

The latter omission has to do with the underestimation and neglect of the world behind the central, information/communication-related column of the framework. The interpretation of reality, and hence *sense making*, is at the heart of this column. It links the objectivistic ("data") view on information, coinciding with the management of the supply side, with the inherently subjectivistic ("knowledge") view of the business. Information governance, i.e. care for the appropriate use of information based on a deep understanding of the information culture (Choo et al., 2006), is the instrument par excellence in this area. These ideas will be worked out in "Future Perspectives", where I deal with future developments in IM, as they are still embryonic in their practical application.

Future Perspectives

In the past decades, IM has grown as an integrative discipline linking business and ICT as well as strategy and operations. It has become a core activity in information-based organizations and in the information society in general. Its future will be determined by the evolving vision on the role and position of ICT and, to an even larger extent, on the very nature of its basic ingredient, information itself.

The perception of ICT is rapidly developing from a product into a service, as is proven by the advent of the service-oriented architecture (SOA) movement (Allen, 2006; Marks & Bell, 2006). ICT is getting a more and more facilitating and hidden character, thereby becoming transparent. The emphasis is shifting into the direction of the former "user" now becoming a "consumer" of ICT (Dahlbom, 2003). In terms of Marchand et al. (2000, 2001): "information technology practices" are asking less and less managerial attention for the benefit of "IM practices" and "information behaviours and values". This evolution is illustrated and accentuated by the concentration of ICT in (if so desired: outsourced) shared service centres. Metaphorically speaking, the right column of the framework of Figure 2.2 is shifting away from the other two columns and, as a result, information/communication is becoming more a general management concern than it used to be in the past, covered as it was by the ICT department.

A further shift in the perception of ICT is determined by its infrastructural nature. Many information processes are crossing the borders of organizations; we call it supply/value chain integration, process integration, etc. The information infrastructure involved is supposed to support these interdependencies (Wisse, 2007). The likely consequence is to start from an inherently inter-organizational and even societal view on infrastructures. Despite this clear trend, we naturally continue to define IM within the boundaries of a single organization; inter-organizational IM is generally limited to cooperation at project level, a concise system of understanding and if necessary a club of information managers meeting on an occasional basis. I foresee a situation where we define IM at the level of society or at least at that of a broad common area of attention and where IM at the level of an individual organization is fitting in (instead of the opposite situation nowadays).

In addition, I am convinced that our vision on *information* is still in its preliminary phase.

The vision presupposed in IM is that of a business resource. This is basically an economic perspective: information can be traded (and becomes more and more tradable through digitalisation) and complies with specific economic laws (Shapiro & Varian, 1998). More generally speaking, this is the underpinning of the so-called information economy. A distinctive feature of this type of economy is that organizations, but sectors and economies as well, derive value from the *immaterial* aspects of their activities. Terms like knowledge economy, experience economy, attention economy, etc. refer to this phenomenon.

In addition to this exclusively economic perspective, one can study information also from a socio-constructivistic point of view — here, information is a social construct that derives its value from and gives value to the (subjective) context in which it is used — *Information is not just affected by its environment, but is itself an actor affecting other elements in the environment*; hence, information has *an enormous power in constructing our social (and ultimately physical) reality* (both citations: Braman, 1989). As a consequence, information could be considered as a design variable both at the level of organizations and of society. From this angle, information is a source of continuous interpretation and sense making. Here too, dematerialisation plays an important role, but now pointing to a growing significance of sense making, interpersonal communication, learning processes, emotional interpretation, trust (Nevejan, 2007), etc. The management of information, once in essence a management of facts, is becoming the management of mechanisms that give meaning to these facts (Introna, 1997). In other words, IM can no longer concentrate itself on the delivery of data (the right column in the framework), but is becoming the management of their interpretation. IM is transforming into *management of meaning*.

Both perspectives, extensively elaborated on by Huizing (2007) in this volume, are complementary, but at this moment apparently incompatible. Information, e.g. in the economic perspective has high fixed costs and variable costs tending to zero, whereas about the opposite is true in the socio-constructivistic perspective. When to apply which perspective is not at all an open-and-shut case, as is not the role of ICT in this respect: too often the ICT world is pushing an objectivistic world view which can then be bought in one or another software package. Maybe we cannot solve this dichotomy at the level of an individual organization as we ultimately need "IM for society", as is also alluded to by the growing interrelationships between organizations and between their infrastructures. Indeed, *the first decision that must be made is about the shape of the society that is desired* (Braman, 1989).

Conclusions

The integrative perspective presented in this article is a (possibly necessary) stepping stone for a more comprehensive view on IM. Ultimately, IM is more than the integrative discipline linking business and ICT, respectively, strategy and operations of an organization. Not only has it, in its very essence, to do with the construction of meaning for an organization, but it also contributes to the meaning of the organization for its environment — IM is about the identity of an organization (Maes, 2005).

If information is as important as we pretend it to be, then the IM community cannot limit its span of attention on the one hand to the organizational level, and on the other, the way in which we produce information. Knowledge regarding information, communication and ICT must be brought together in harmony with sense making, societal and ecological visions in order to be able to clarify the question of acceptability of business practices. One important step in this achievement could be the combination of the economic and socio-constructivistic perspectives on information. For this to happen, researchers and reflective practitioners should fully cooperate; together, they can devise a common frame of concepts, not only bridging the gap between both perspectives, but also between theory and practice.

Knowledge of ICT is, given the ubiquitous character of ICT, absolutely indispensable for CIO's and information managers alike, but as absolutely insufficient. After all, information governance is more important for their success than ICT governance, superior information use more important than increasingly sophisticated information production and understanding organizational and societal ambiguity more important than understanding technical complexity. Still, their attitude and their behaviour are more vital than their knowledge: successful information managers are "infopreneurs", hypersensitive to the disclosive nature of human activity, contributing to the reconfiguration of their organization's and society's practices and embodying this in their professional and personal life (Maes, 2005).

Sensitivity to contexts, to relationships and to consequences are key aspects of the transition from mindless development to design mindfulness (Thackara, 2005). Mindful IM should be responsive to the justified aspirations of all parties involved, mindful information managers should feel responsible for the outcomes of their interventions. The aim of IM is to deliver value to people, not to deliver people to systems. This appeal for mindful IM may sound naïve and for some even illusory, but hasn't CIO for a long time been the acronym of "chief imagination officer"?

References

Allen, P. (2006). *Service orientation, winning strategies and best practices.* Cambridge, UK: Cambridge University Press.

Avison, D., Jones, J., Powell, P., & Wilson, D. (2004). Using and validating the strategic alignment model. *Journal of Strategic Information Systems, 13,* 223–246.

Bouthillier, F., & Shearer, K. (2002). Understanding knowledge management and information management: The need for an empirical perspective. *Information Research, 8* (1), available at: http://InformationR.net/ir/8-1/paper141.html

Braman, S. (1989). Defining information: An approach for policymakers. *Telecommunications Policy, 13*(3), 233–242.

Carr, N. (2003). IT doesn't matter anymore. *Harvard Business Review, 81*(5), 41–49.

Chan, Y. E. (2002). Why haven't we mastered alignment? The importance of the informal organization structure. *MIS Quarterly Executive, 1*(2), 97–112.

Choo, C. W. (1998). *The knowing organization: How organizations use information to construct meaning, create knowledge, and make decisions.* New York: Oxford University Press.

Choo, C. W., Furness, C., Paquette, S., Van den Berg, H., Detlor, B., Bergeron, P., & Heaton, L. (2006). Working with information: Information management and culture in a professional service organization. *Journal of Information Science, 32*(6), 491–510.

Ciborra, C. (1997). De Profundis? Deconstructing the concept of strategic alignment. *Scandinavian Journal of Information Systems, 9*(1), 67–82.

Coughlan, J., Lycett, M., & Macredie, R. D. (2005). Understanding the business–IT relationship. *International Journal of Information Management, 25,* 303–319.

Cumps, B., Dedene, G., & Viaene, S. (2007). ICT-outsourcing: A resource-based information management perspective. In: A. Huizing, & E. J. de Vries (Eds.), *Information Management: Setting the Scene* (Vol. 1). Book Series Perspectives on Information Management. Oxford: Elsevier Scientific Publishers.

Dahlbom, B. (2003). From users to consumers. *Scandinavian Journal of Information Systems, 15*(1), 105–108.

Davenport, T. H., Eccles, R. G., & Prusak, L. (1992). Information Politics. *Sloan Management Review, 34*(1), 53–63.

Drucker, P. (1993). *Post-capitalist society.* New York: HarperBusiness.

Henderson, J. C., & Venkatraman, N. (1993). Strategic alignment: Leveraging information technology for transforming organizations. *IBM Systems Journal, 32*(1), 4–16.

Henderson, J. C., Venkatraman, N., & Oldach, S. (1996). Aligning business and IT strategies. In: J. N. Luftman (Ed.), *Competing in the information age: Strategic alignment in practice* (pp. 21–42). Oxford: Oxford University Press.

Hirschheim, R., & Sabherwal, R. (2001). Detours in the path toward strategic information systems alignment. *California Management Review, 44*(1), 87–108.

Huizing, A. (2007). The value of a rose: Rising above objectivism and subjectivism. In: A. Huizing, & E. J. de Vries (Eds.), *Information Management: Setting the Scene* (Vol. 1). Book Series Perspectives on Information Management. Oxford: Elsevier Scientific Publishers.

Hussain, H., King, M., & Cragg, P. (2002). IT alignments in small firms. *European Journal of Information Systems, 11,* 108–127.

Introna, L. (1997). *Management, information and power: A narrative of the involved manager.* London: Macmillan.

Macevièiūtė, E., & Wilson, T. D. (2002). The development of the information management research area. *Information Research*, *7*(3), available at: http://InformationR.net/ir/7-3/paper133.html

Maes, R. (1990). Infrastructuur: een sleutelbegrip voor het plannen, ontwikkelen en gebruiken van informatiesystemen. In: J. Truijens, A. Oosterhaven, R. Maes, H. Jägers & F. van Iersel (Eds.), *Informatie-infrastructuur, een instrument voor het management* (pp. 58–77). Deventer: Kluwer Bedrijfswetenschappen.

Maes, R. (1999). *Reconsidering information management through a generic framework*. PrimaVera Working Paper 1999-15, University of Amsterdam.

Maes, R. (2003). On the alliance of executive education and research in information management at the University of Amsterdam. *International Journal of Information Management*, *23*(3), 249–257.

Maes, R. (2004). *Information management: A roadmap*. University of Amsterdam, PrimaVera Working Paper 2004-13. Presented at the 1st European Conference on IS Management, Leadership and Governance, Reading, 2005.

Maes, R. (2005). Information management reconstructed: The real meaning of the role of the CIO. *Journal for Convergence*, *6*(1), 10–11.

Marchand, D. A., Kettinger, W. J., & Rollins, J. D. (2000). Information orientation: People, technology and the bottom line. *Sloan Management Review*, *41*(4), 69–80.

Marchand, D. A., Kettinger, W. J., & Rollins, J. D. (2001). *Information orientation: The link to business performance*. New York: Oxford University Press.

Marks, E., & Bell, M. (2006). *Service oriented architecture: A planning and implementation guide for business and technology*. Hoboken: Wiley.

Nevejan, C. (2007). *Presence and the design of trust*. University of Amsterdam, Unpublished doctoral thesis.

Porter, M. E. (1996). What is strategy?. *Harvard Business Review*, *74*(6), 61–78.

Sabherwal, R., & Chan, Y. (2001). Alignment between business and IS strategies: A configurational approach. *Information Systems Research*, *12*(1), 11–33.

Sauer, C., & Burn, J. M. (1997). The pathology of strategic alignment. In: C. Sauer & P. Y. Yetton (Eds.), *Steps to the future — fresh thinking on the management of IT-based organizational transformation*. San Francisco: Jossey-Bass.

Shapiro, C., & Varian, H. R. (1998). *Information rules: A strategic guide to the network economy*. Boston, MA: Harvard Business School Press.

Simonsen, J. (1999). How do we take care of strategic alignment?. *Scandinavian Journal of Information Systems*, *11*(2), 51–72.

Smaczny, T. (2001). Is an alignment between business and IT the appropriate paradigm to manage IT in today's organisation?. *Management Decision*, *39*(10), 797–802.

Thackara, J. (2005). *In the bubble: Designing in a complex world*. Cambridge, MA: The MIT Press.

Tiernan, C., & Peppard, J. (2004). Information technology: Of value or a vulture?. *European Management Journal*, *22*(6), 609–623.

Ward, J., & Peppard, J. (1996). Reconciling the IT/business relationship: A troubled marriage in need of guidance. *Journal of Strategic Information Systems*, *5*, 37–65.

Weill, P., & Broadbent, M. (1998). *Leveraging the new infrastructure — how market leaders capitalize on information technology*. Cambridge, MA: Harvard Business School Press.

Wilson, T. D. (2002). The nonsense of "knowledge management". *Information Research*, *8*(1), available at: http://InformationR.net/ir/8-1/paper144.html

Wisse, P. (2007). *Ontology for interdependency: Steps to an ecology of information management*. Working Paper 2007–05, University of Amsterdam, PrimaVera.

SECTION I:

THE CIO BEFORE ICT

It is a commonplace to state — although this does not mean that it is popularly understood — that information management existed long before the computer; but this usually goes no further, and rarely, if ever, proves to be a starting point for analysis and insight.

The following chapters seek to examine the ways in which some key aspects of information management can be better understood if focus is turned to the period before the development of ICT and computer technology. In so doing the core characteristics of information management, the role of the CIO, and the impacts of ICT on organizational processes and sustainability are brought into focus against a wider and more profound historical context.

Alistair Black takes a wide view, focusing on the forces and technological background behind the emergence of a specifically labelled 'information' function in commercial organizations, coupled with the appearance of the role of 'information officer'.

The chapter by Rodney Brunt focuses on the way in which the gathering of 'intelligence' in the UK from the early 20th century led, by necessity, to several key developments crucial to information management. Many of these advances were only really implemented on a large scale during the world wars, often based on a fortuitous combination of exigency and serendipity.

Antony Bryant then places these two chapters in a wider context, underlining the importance of developing a historical understanding of the ways in which information management and associated roles and features appeared in the twentieth century.

Taken together this section not only contributes an important historical perspective on information management, but critically it also stresses the ways in which the initial impulse and organizational motivation for the IM function have changed. As Black states in his chapter — '[T]he identity of this early breed of information officer differed considerably from that of the late-twentieth century (and beyond) information officer whose role was very much defined by the management of digital infrastructure in the organization'. In some regards this can be seen as part of what Beniger has termed 'The Control Revolution', with authority and influence moving away from users and in favor of managers; but it can also be seen as an alteration in the balance from the demand-side of information in favor of the supply-side. Recognition of this should lead to an enhanced and more equitable concept of the IM function, and equally to the range of skills required by information specialists; thus, also raising the question whether or not these functions and skills should all be focused in one department, and under the *aegis* of the CIO.

Chapter 3

The 'Information Officer' in Britain Before the Age of the Computer

Alistair Black

ABSTRACT

The 'information function' as a core function of management has a history that breaches the confines of the computer age, stretching back into the late-nineteenth century when corporations and other large organisations first began to 'learn' effectively. Fashioned by, and contributing to, a manual and mechanised revolution in office technology and information management in the decades either side of 1900, a variety of specialised information occupations emerged to fulfil the information requirements of organisations. Such occupations included research work, the management of mechanisation and filing and registry work. In Britain, another information occupation appearing at the time was the 'information officer', whose identity was formed in the in-house libraries and information bureaux that began to appear in relatively large numbers during and after the First World War and whose function was highly distinct from that of the CIO of the late-twentieth century and beyond.

Introduction

In 1952 a leading British engineering professor advised that the first step any leader of a large concern should take was that of 'charging a senior executive with the responsibility for reviewing and reporting upon and maintaining the essential key information services required by the organisation at all levels' (Matthew, 1952, p. 202). This statement acknowledged the *information function* as a core function of management, but what was being suggested was not new. In fact, an awareness that organisations required their information to be managed, and that an individual or set of individuals should be charged with the responsibility for improving 'information flow' to create and transfer knowledge and assist organisational learning, had been prevalent for a number of decades.

Information Management: Setting the Scene
ISBN: 978-0-08-046326-1

From the late-nineteenth century onwards, beginning in the United States, corporations began to invest heavily in both mechanical information technology and sophisticated marketing and management techniques. As firms — and other organisations indeed, such as state bureaucracies — grew in size, the importance of the document and the 'office', and the rational management of both, also grew. In short, organisations became 'records-conscious' (Hudders, 1916; Robins & Webster, 1989, p. 43; Warren, 1920). This hastened an information management revolution on a scale of effect similar to that later ushered in by the computer-mediated information technology revolution. The first information management revolution was very much an office technology revolution which, like many changes in the running of organisations, was underwritten by a new science of management promulgated in management literature and manuals (Galloway, 1918; Kaiser, 1908, 1911; Leffingwell, 1917; Taylor, 1911). The decades either side of 1900 saw the introduction of a number of devices that soon became 'everyday' aspects of life in office administration, including the telephone, the typewriter, the vertical-filing cabinet, the card index, the addressing machine, the comptometer, the punch-card machine and the dictaphone (Beniger, 1986; Campbell-Kelly, 1992, 1998; Orbell, 1991; Yates, 1991).

These technological developments were overseen by a new breed of professional, salaried and hierarchically arranged managers who exercised, as Chandler (1977) put it, a 'visible hand' of rational control — in contrast to the classical image of enterprise as a spontaneous and adventurous 'go-getting' individualism that complemented the 'invisible' forces of the self-correcting free market. Historians like Chandler (1977, 1990) and Yates (1989, 1991) have shown that the most successful early corporations were those that continually learnt, first, about customers and suppliers, to ensure the coordination of inputs and outputs (throughput); second, about products and processes, to gain technological leadership and economies of scale; and third about the management of labour. Each required the gathering of 'intelligence', accompanied by its efficient storage and organisation for retrieval and future use. In essence, from the late-nineteenth century onwards corporations developed 'organisational capabilities' deeply dependant on information (Chandler, 1992).

Nowadays, we refer to the existence of such capabilities as 'organisational learning'. The term might be new, but the knowledge-management mechanisms that it entails — training programmes and manuals; written protocols; in-house magazines, bulletins and newsletters; reports and analyses; presentations; graphic representations; messages, letters and memoranda; minuted management meetings; databases (manual and automated); and what is fancifully referred to by Kulkarin and Freeze (2006, p. 606) as 'knowledge documents' of all kinds — have a long history (Black, Muddiman, & Plant, 2007, pp. 105–147). Each of these mechanisms, or techniques — and the machines, or technologies, that complemented them — gave rise to new groups of professionals with specialist information skills and discrete informational responsibilities.

This chapter focuses on the pre-computer history, in the context of Britain, of one such category of professional, the information officer. The identity of this early breed of information officer differed considerably from that of the late-twentieth century (and beyond) information officer whose role was very much defined by the management of digital infrastructure in the organisation. Having provided a brief history of the most important information functions resulting from the first information management revolution and of the early in-house library and information services that gave birth to, and nurtured, the information officer, an attempt is made to establish and explain the identity of the information officer by reference, first, to the various specialist functions that the job entailed and second, to the (at times) bitter war that was waged against traditional librarianship in an effort to carve out a 'particular' professional consciousness.

Information Functions and Occupations in the Early-Twentieth Century Organisation

The first information management revolution served as both a catalyst and a helpmate to the growth in organisations of various information functions and occupations, such as those in advertising, public relations, accountancy and financial planning, archiving and in-house journalism. For the purpose of this book, I restrict myself to a small selection of these functions and occupations: research work, the management of mechanisation and filing and registry work.

Research Work

Around the dawn of the twentieth century much greater emphasis began to be placed by enterprises on research and development. The *ad hoc* nature of technological innovation gave way to organised scientific research as the basis of production, a trend accelerated by the First World War that revealed the lamentable state of many aspects of British technology (Edgerton & Horrocks, 1994).

High-level applied research was supplemented by general business research on the *external* commercial environment. Such 'desk research' involved the development of expertise in statistical, forecasting and marketing work, as well as knowledge of the broader social and political environments in which commerce operated (e.g. Dobbs, 1933; Lyall, 1925; Nightingale & Bennie, 1927; Tattersall, 1927; Wallace, 1927).

Research in the form of the systematic surveillance of activity within the 'plant' was part and parcel of the rise of scientific management (which was reliant on information) and resulted in the evolution of early information management systems, as in the British coal industry (Boyns & Wale, 1996). On a visit to the United States in 1934, Miss Myra Curtis, Superintendent of Women Staff at the Post Office Savings Bank, found that in advanced American offices the *systems/methods branch* was invariably run 'by someone who had actually read the textbooks' and who was 'invested with a considerable degree of authority over the executive heads of the operating branches as to the use of mechanical devices and other time-saving methods' (American Office Management, 1934). Although scientific management did not penetrate British management theory and practice to the extent that it did in the

United States, significant aspects of it were to be found in British organisations in the first half of the twentieth century (Whitson, 1996).

The escalation of in-house research resulted in an increase in documentation and a commensurate need to control it. It also led to the establishment of in-house research laboratories and departments and associated technical libraries (more about these later). All of these functions required a new range of occupations that in today's parlance would be described as information or knowledge work, the management of mechanisation and filing and registry work.

The Management of Mechanisation

The massive expansion of office technology in the early-twentieth century meant that the management of 'information machinery' became a distinct and visible component of overall management strategy. The work of managing the entire stock of manual information technology may in places have been fulfilled by the methods/systems department in an organisation (alluded to above). Thus, Miss Curtis found on her visit to the United States that the 'Methods staff are in constant consultation with the salesman of the office machines companies, who perhaps do as much genuine constructive thinking as anyone about office problems' (American Office Management, 1934, p. 122). However, there is evidence that many large organisations chose to establish a *central mechanisation department*, directed by someone of fairly high managerial status.

This was certainly the case at the Bank of England. During the Second World War three essentials for the development of mechanisation were identified. The first was the appointment of a chief officer for mechanisation, who would supervise and coordinate mechanisation throughout the Bank. The second essential was the establishment of a Central Machine Office, under the leadership of the chief officer. The Office would be comprised of two elements: a Machine Section and a Training Typing and Duplication Section. The Machine Section would offer a central service to offices and departments by providing a repository for all permanent records relating to mechanisation (e.g. regarding rentals, maintenance work etc.), by serving as a medium of communication with all external companies, and by acting as a liaison between the various parts of the Bank. This section's overall aim was to reduce duplication of effort and processes. The second element of the Machine Office, the Training Typing and Duplication Section, would oversee training throughout the Bank not only for work on typewriters but also keyboarding work on accounting, adding and punched-card machines (although it should be noted that training was also given externally, at Hollerith (for punched-card) and Burroughs (for accounting) Machine Schools.[1] The third essential for the development of mechanisation was the continued existence of 'experts' in charge of mechanical aids in offices and departments — for despite the appointment of a chief officer and the establishment of a Central Machine Office, it was deemed necessary to retain

---

[1]Training on a Hollerith punched-card machine took approximately 2–4 weeks.

technological expertise 'at the coal face', as it were, and not simply concentrate it in a central resource.[2]

Filing and Registry Work

Intensified database assembly, encompassing new filing and indexing methods for documents, placed a premium on the operation of an organisation's registry. The central registry became a widely adopted method of document control in the early large-scale organisation. It was the registry's job to coordinate and control documents in the organisation (Jenkinson, 1937). The primary role of the registry was to register and distribute incoming letters and dispatch the outgoing.

By the 1920s the growing tendency was, where possible, to bring all files and indexes into one department, sometimes termed the 'registry', sometimes described as the 'filing department/room'. In 1920 it was advised by one expert on office methods that this department be placed in the charge of 'a file clerk who is trained for such work and who is also a competent executive'; information from a central document repository would be sent to various employees, as needed, 'by means of a messenger service, house phones, or by lending materials to departments in much the same fashion that patrons borrow books from the public library' (Warren, 1920, p. 22). The flow of huge amounts of information into MI5, as described by Brunt in this volume, resulted in the development of systematic storage and auxiliary indexes, to provide access to materials in a way that offered an alternative to the principal physical filing order. Supervising the work of the MI5 Registry and its hundreds of clerks (mostly women) was a task of considerable responsibility, one fulfilled in the Second World War by the chief clerk, Miss Paton-Smith, an ex-store detective dubbed the 'Registry Queen' (Black & Brunt, 2000, p. 192; West, 2005, p. 441).

The In-House Library and Information Bureau

The nursery for the growth of the information officer in Britain was the in-house company library — synonyms for which were constructed from various combinations of the prefixes 'information' and 'intelligence' with the suffixes 'bureau', 'department' and 'office' (Black, 2004). Nineteenth-century organisations were relatively slow to develop in-house library and information services. It was not until after 1914, and especially during the inter-war period, that company libraries began to appear in anything approaching significant numbers. It is difficult to gauge the

---

[2]Memorandum to Holland-Martin (2 May, 1940), and '[Memorandum on] Mechanization' (8 May, 1940), both in Bank of England Archives, ADM15/11.

precise level of early company library activity, but by 1927, of the 343 members of the Association of Special Libraries and Information Bureaux (ASLIB) — established in 1924 and now named the Association for Information Management — some 95 (around 25%) were industrial and commercial concerns. This total increased to 965 (around 35%) in 1963 (Burkett, 1965, p. 219). In the late 1950s, an ASLIB survey of information and library units found there to be 486 company libraries, although it must be stressed that the list was confined to those units led by someone described as a 'librarian' or 'information officer' (ASLIB, 1960, pp. 3–4). In 1953 Jason Farradane, who went on to found the Institute of Information Scientists, confidently observed that 'The majority of industrial concerns … remain ignorant of the full possibilities of an information service, or perhaps even of the need for information' (Farradane, 1953a, p. 327); and the following year estimated that just 2% of industrial firms maintained an information service (Farradane, 1954, p. 299). This said, by the early 1950s it was reckoned that between 1200 and 1500 British firms had established libraries or information departments, facilitating the observation that 'industrial libraries now exist in sufficient numbers to be accepted as integral parts of a *large* [my emphasis] concern' (Piggot, 1958, p. 75).

The several reasons for the post-1914 escalation in in-house company library provision can be summarised as follows:

1. *War, Economic Depression and Organised Science.* The growth of company libraries paralleled the rise of organised science, which was galvanised by the First World War. The war threw into sharp relief the relative scientific and technological inadequacies of British industry. A national crisis materialised at the start of the First World War when it was found that Britain was almost entirely dependant on imports from Germany of such goods as dynamos for motor vehicle engines and dyestuffs for fabrics, including military uniforms. The poor progress of British forces in the war led to accusations that over many decades science and technology had been neglected. The requirements of technological, total war, allied to the prospect of intense post-war international competition, enhanced the systematic and scientific approach to the development of technology. Thereafter, research in science and technology, and the library and information services required to support it, moved up the industrial agenda.
2. *American Influences.* The company library had originated in the late-nineteenth century in the United States, when corporations in both industry and commerce began to establish them in response to burgeoning markets and the increasing complexity of production and service provision. This initial experiment provided good evidence as to the efficacy of the in-house company library, and this experience, along with knowledge of best practice, were readily exported to Europe.
3. *The Inadequacy of Public Provision.* It might be argued that had *public* provision of technical and commercial information been more generous, then private enterprises may not have been forced to commence and develop their own information services. Distinct technical and commercial departments in public libraries did not

emerge until the First World War and its immediate aftermath: in cities like Glasgow (1916), Leeds (1918) and Manchester (1919). However, neither these libraries, nor those that grew extensively in size and reputation between the wars (e.g. Sheffield), offered an alternative to independent provision in large and even some medium-size firms.

4. *New Industries.* There was a high correlation between company library activity and the development of new sectors in the economy — i.e. industries of potentially high-productivity and high-yield where science, technology and research were at a premium. Such industries included: chemicals; synthetic dyestuffs; artificial silk (rayon); precision instruments; oil; aluminium; rubber; plastics; aircraft; motor vehicles; canned foodstuffs; electrical engineering, generation and supply; electrical and radio equipment and a wide variety of household, confectionery and consumer goods.

5. *Increased Merger Activity.* Company library activity was boosted by changes that occurred in the scale and ownership of enterprises. In response to intensifying competition, businesses between the wars developed a philosophy of rationalisation, which in practice meant increased concentration of ownership — the essential ingredient of what the British business historian Leslie Hannah (1976) called the 'rise of the corporate economy'. Larger firms meant information services like libraries could not only be afforded but became necessary in assisting the good flow of information through complex organisations.

6. *Technical Education.* A relatively inconspicuous, yet important, function of the company library was the provision of technical education, the need for which was emphasised by the war. As repositories of technical knowledge, company libraries offered the potential to support the technical education of employees at a variety of levels, whether in support of the discharge of their duties or as tools for those seeking promotion.

7. *Scientific Management.* Company libraries helped to underwrite the development of the scientific management regimes which Taylorist teachings and Fordist organisation had popularised. In mass-production enterprises (whether industrial or commercial), with a detailed division of labour and intense specialisation, good supervision and personnel management were critical. In-house library holdings reflected the new science of management, and included literature on production and personnel management, administration and supervision, as well as on what Ernest Savage termed 'collateral subjects', like industrial organisation, advertising, wage systems, the labour question and industrial psychology. If made widely accessible in the organisation, company libraries could be employed as an antidote to the monotony created by the mass-production and minute division of labour that characterised Fordism. It was argued that library use could help restore 'mental equilibrium' by combating acute specialisation.

8. *Information Management.* Information management, which mushroomed in the early-twentieth century, was a prime responsibility of many early company libraries. At the Manchester electrical engineering firm Metropolitan-Vickers, the Intelligence Section, established during the First World War, served as an

important junction in the exchange of information between the various companies in the global corporation of which the company was a part; a role reflected by the fact that the department started life as the 'Intelligence and *Interchange* [my emphasis] Section'.[3] The librarian was a conduit of information in the organisation, a crucial node in its system of knowledge, a person who over time gained knowledge of the organisation by fielding enquires from across it and who, by passing that knowledge on, helped build what in modern parlance is termed the 'learning organisation'. There is evidence that libraries acted as repositories of last resort for organisational protocols. In planning the new library for the Post Office in the mid-1930s, it was recommended that 'the Library should contain complete sets of Post Office rules and instructions, and that these should be kept up-to-date by the Library staff' (although the repository of official and historical documents remained the Records Room).[4] As 'switching centres', company libraries oversaw the distribution of knowledge in the form of surveys of the literature, tailored bibliographies, technical periodicals and bulletins of abstracts. Once circulated, libraries retained materials for later consultation, appropriately indexed and sometimes 'guillotined' into pamphlets (discrete journal articles) or subject files. At a less technical level, some libraries maintained a service by which company employees were notified of forthcoming lectures, conferences and symposia covering subjects in which they were interested (GEC Research Laboratories, 1957, p. 13). Company libraries were primarily concerned with managing externally generated — essentially published — information, but some were also charged with a responsibility for storing and organising internally generated information, as well as external unpublished material such as correspondence. In the 1940s it was reported that in the library of Mond Nickel Company Limited: 'Much unpublished information is available, and this is certainly being added to, for the department is shown all the correspondence and papers of the firm which can possibly contain anything useful' (Roberts, 1949, p. 33). In 1953 Brian Vickery (p. 5) observed that two types of literature — correspondence and reports — were creeping into special libraries, adding that 'Particularly in the field of technology, it is found that every communication received or issued by members of a group may be of value to the group as a whole, and so letters, telegrams and even telephone calls are being brought under the bibliographic control of the library'. When a central library was being planned in Imperial Chemical Industries (ICI) in 1928, it was advised that 'to enable the librarian to be in a position to supply complete information on a given subject, all departmental technical reports, memoranda etc., at present filed in the Central Filing Department, should in future be deposited in the Central Library, or as an alternative, that this particular

---

[3]'Research Department report' (1929) p. 32. Metropolitan-Vickers Archives, Manchester Museum of Science and Technology, 0531/19–24.

[4]'[Post Office] Headquarters Library, Report of the Committee' (August 1935), Royal Mail Archives, POST 72.

section of Mr. Barbour's department (i.e. central filing) should be housed adjacent to the Central Library'.[5] At Nobel Explosives in the early 1920s the librarian undertook a daily perusal of letters received the previous day in the Commercial Department. Letters containing useful technical information were selected and indexed, and the letters returned (Barbour, 1921, p. 169).

The Emergence of the Information Officer

It is evident, therefore, that from the outset information management, including records management, was an important function of many early-twentieth century in-house libraries. As this information management function became more prevalent, organisations began to increase their investment, both financially and semantically, in the 'information bureau' and the 'information officer' (although it is important to stress that the in-house library and librarian, named as such, by no means disappeared). In Europe, of course, the terms 'documentation' and 'documentalist' emerged to describe the new functions (they were also used sporadically in Britain) (Pearce, 1918). One such documentalist was Donker Duyvis, who was employed in the Dutch Patent Office and was also active locally and nationally in a number of organisations concerned with managerial efficiency and standardisation such as NIDER (Netherlands Institute for Documentation and Filing) which for a time offered a specialised information service to industry in the Netherlands (Netherlands Institute for Documentation and Filing, 1964).

In Britain the term 'information officer' (an earlier designation was 'intelligence officer') was more common. This professional group emerged largely from the in-house library and information bureaux that, as described above, began to appear in large corporations during and after the First World War. These early information professionals — a relatively high proportion of who were women (Black et al., 2007, pp. 219–234) — defined themselves less as organisers and disseminators of books than as managers, abstractors and communicators or publicists, of information that was packaged in a variety of formats and often hewn from whole documents. They also stressed the importance of subject knowledge; a pro-active approach to users; a new approach to classification and indexing; and new information technologies, such as the vertical file, punch-card machines and microfilm. The identity and purpose of the embryonic, company-based information professional in Britain was reflected in the work of ASLIB, and eventually, and more definitively, in the formation of the Institute of Information Scientists in 1958.

The information bureau and its information officer were natural outgrowths of the company library. In reality the term in-house library stood for a range of functions much wider in scope than the provision of a collection of books and periodicals. Company libraries were also 'information services'. Moreover, in places they were highly influential in shaping the kind of corporate information infrastructure

---

[5]'Report of the [ICI] Library Committee' (1928), ICI Archives, ICI/93/29Y (Box 198).

arrangements we nowadays refer to as 'information management'. The informational dimension of the company library was stated just after the First World War by the technical librarian of the confectionary firm Rowntree and Co., Vincent Garrett, who explained that 'for business purposes we tend to disassociate information from literature; we do not want books, we want information'.[6] He later reinforced this position when he reported that 'ninety-five percent of the inquiries handled in my library are not for specific books, but for *information* ... this type of library is not a Book Department but an Information or Intelligence Department' (Garrett, 1925, p. 39). This message was echoed three decades later by one of Garrett's successors as librarian: 'As a matter of fact I sometimes wonder whether the name "Library" as far as we are concerned is not a misnomer, for I should like to say that we are 40% Library and 60% Information Service.'[7]

The complexities of embryonic library and information provision in enterprises, and hence the problems of nomenclature which this gives rise to, is illustrated by the structure of the information service established by Metropolitan-Vickers, as part of its research department, in 1916. The blueprint for an Information and Intelligence Section identified four functions: Economic Survey (the production of market reports for other departments in the company and for some outside bodies); Westinghouse Liaison (the exchange of technical information with the firm's American parent company, Westinghouse); Pure Scientific Liaison (the exchange of information with individual experts and scientific bodies); Intelligence and Library Service (including a reference library, an abstracting service, a periodical circulation service and a service for translating foreign-language technical literature).[8] In reality all four functions of the section were inter-woven. The fact that the 'intelligence' and 'library' services were grouped together made sense, in a certain way. After all, when considering their value to production and organisational efficiency, to draw a line between internally and externally produced information, and between information (or intelligence) and books, is effectively a sterile exercise. However, as the century progressed, many began to believe that such distinctions were important and that a specific set of professional skills, different in their totality from traditional librarianship, should be brought to bear on organisations' (internal) information management requirements and on the acquiring and dissemination of recorded knowledge not simply in the form of books. Those who professed this strategy styled themselves 'information officer', and the units they worked in 'information bureau/service/office/department'.

---

[6]H.V. Garrett, 'Library bulletins and card index' (16 May, 1919), Rowntree-Mackintosh Archives, Borthwick Institute, University of York, R/D/TL/9.

[7]'Talk given at York Public Library on 20 September, 1951 to the Reference and Special Libraries Section (Yorkshire Group) of the Library Association', Rowntree-Mackintosh Archives, Borthwick Institute, University of York, R/DH/TL/9.

[8]'Report of the Research Department' (8 October, 1924), Metropolitan-Vickers Archives, Manchester Museum of Science and Technology, 0531/1.

Identity Formation Through Struggle: The Information Officer's Battle with Traditional Librarianship

Despite the synergies that existed between the library and librarian on the one hand and the information bureau and information officer on the other, after 1945 battle lines were drawn between these two professional areas — paralleling, incidentally, a similar tension between librarians and documentalists that existed in the United States at the time (Taube, 1953; Bowles, 1999). 'The conflict between librarians and documentalists has become bitter', wrote Piggot in 1958 (p. 80) in reviewing the industrial library field. 'There appears', he observed, 'to be an attitude of indifference and lack of cooperation with the actions taking place in documentation circles' (p. 78), as well as a 'lack of ability of the more conservative librarians to appreciate the requirements of the new situation' (p. 75). In the late 1940s and in the 1950s the ancestor of the documentalist, and the progenitor of the information scientist, came to be termed the 'information officer'. These years witnessed a running debate as to the definition and legitimacy of the 'information officer', and the nature and exclusivity of his or her professional practices.

The most outspoken advocate of the new domain of 'information work' was Jason Farradane, scientific information officer at the research laboratories of the sugar giant Tate and Lyle, cofounder of the Institute of Information Scientists in 1958 and the architect of Britain's first course in information work in 1961 (at the Northampton College of Advanced Technology, later City University, London). Farradane sought a strict separation between the librarian and the information officer. He was convinced 'that the interests of librarians and information officers diverge, and will continue to diverge more as the information officer profession develops ... the information officer lays little or no claim to the techniques of librarianship' (Farradane, 1953b, p. 411). He was supported in his fight to secure a discrete status for information work by a healthy number of professionals working in the information services and libraries of private enterprises and research establishments. 'When will a minority of librarians eventually realise', asked one of these supporters rhetorically, 'that something new and different has come up with the information officer' (Sontag, 1959, p. 568). Librarians, for their part, resisted the 'information officer' discourse by dismissing it as a fad, arguing, amongst other things that the term should be reserved to describe an organisation's press, or public relations, officer, its propagandist (during the Second World War, of course, 'information officers' had formed part of the government's propaganda machine) (Grant, 1999).

The causes of the conflict that existed in the 1940s and 1950s between the two warring factions can be clarified by distinguishing in detail the components of information work (the work of the information officer and later the information scientist) from those of librarianship. It was said that the information officer/scientist:

1. *Dealt with information extracted from whole documents*, the organisation of the latter being essentially the responsibility of the librarian.

2. *Sought to anticipate demand*, unlike the librarian who was more 'reactive', and therefore relatively passive, in this regard.
3. *Vigorously exploited new technological opportunities and was comfortable with a multiplicity of formats*; the librarian, by contrast, certainly stereotypically, was a technological laggard, concerned essentially with books.
4. *Was mostly anchored in 'practical', 'relevant' and 'productive' environments*, such as the industrial or commercial enterprise, unlike librarians who mostly displayed a predilection for the 'cultural'.
5. *Ideally displayed knowledge of the subject areas* — whether chemistry or banking, engineering or insurance — with which her/his information service was concerned; whereas the librarian dealt with general collections and therefore endeavoured to develop a broad and rounded familiarity recorded knowledge as opposed to a subject specialism.
6. *Claimed a higher professional status.* Information workers, many of whom began their careers as scientists, believed they could justifiably command the esteem commanded by the science profession.
7. *Emphasised customisation in classification and indexing*, and was less concerned with traditional bibliography.
8. *Demonstrated greater depth of analysis of materials*, and could be found involved in translation (or the provision of a translating service), editing, technical writing, abstracting, bulletin preparation, indexing and statistical work.

These distinctions were reflected in the continuing separation of the two professional associations representing the opposing camps: the Institute of Information Scientists (established, as noted above, in 1958) and the Library Association (which had been established as far back as 1877). In 2002, however, in response to a blurring of the boundaries of their separate domains, wrought not least by a shared reliance on digital ICTs, the two camps were re-united under a single professional body, the Chartered Institute of Library and Information Professionals (CILIP).

Conclusion

As accessible technologies of information management have developed and as flexible post-Fordist modes of production and service provision have emerged, specialisation in information occupations of all kinds has decreased and skills have converged to produce multi-tasking, 'portfolio' professionals. However, this analysis should not hide the fact that Fordism in the workplace, as in society generally, has by no means disappeared. Similarly, during the Fordist era not all information occupations were characterised by a strict division of labour and a culture of mono-skilling. It is true that in the early-twentieth century, in the wake of the rise of the corporation and mechanical information and office revolution, a number of discrete information occupations, many of professional, salaried status, emerged in organisations; but equally there is also evidence of hybrid professionalisation, not least in the form of the information officer of the pre-computer era who was able to turn his/her hand to a number of information task demanded by the modern organisation (the desire to be distinct from the librarian is not to be taken as an indication of acute specialisation). The identity of the early information officer in Britain differed markedly from its distant digital descendant, reminding us that information and its organisation can exist outside the technological world of the computer.

References

American office management. (1934, January 26). *The Municipal Journal and Public Works Engineer*, pp. 122–129.

ASLIB (Association of Special Libraries and Information Bureaux) (1960). *Survey of Information/Library Units in Industrial and Commercial Organizations*. London: ASLIB.

Barbour, W. (1921). The library at the Ardeer Factory of Nobel Explosives. *Library Association Record*, 23, 166–179.

Beniger, R. (1986). *The control revolution: Technological and economic origins of the information society*. Cambridge, MA: Harvard University Press.

Black, A. (2004). Technical libraries in British industrial and commercial enterprises before 1950. In: W. B. Rayward & M. E. Bowden (Eds.), *The history and heritage of scientific and technological information systems: Proceedings of the second conference* (pp. 281–290). Medford, NJ: Information Today, Inc.

Black, A., & Brunt, R. (2000). MI5, 1909–1945: An information management perspective. *Journal of Information Science*, 26(3), 185–197.

Black, A., Muddiman, D., & Plant, H. (2007). *The early information society: Information management in Britain before the computer*. Aldershot: Ashgate.

Bowles, M. D. (1999). The information wars: Two cultures and the conflict in information retrieval. In: M. E. Bowden, T. B. Hahn & R. V. Williams (Eds.), *Proceedings of the 1998 conference on the history and heritage of science information systems* (pp. 156–166). Medford, NJ: Information Today, Inc.

Boyns, T., & Wale, J. (1996). The development of management information systems in the British coal industry, c.1880–1947. *Business History*, 38(2), 55–80.

Burkett, J. (1965). Industrial libraries. In: J. Burkett (Ed.), *Special library and information services in the United Kingdom* (pp. 216–265). London: Library Association.

Campbell-Kelly, M. (1992). Large-scale data processing in the Prudential, 1850–1930. *Accounting Business and Financial History*, 2(2), 117–139.

Campbell-Kelly, M. (1998). Information in the business enterprise. In: E. Higgs (Ed.), *History and electronic artefacts*. Oxford: Clarendon Press.

Chandler, A. D. (1990). *Scale and scope: The dynamics of industrial capitalism*. Cambridge, MA: Belknap Press.

Chandler, A. D. (1992). Organizational capabilities and the economic history of the industrial enterprise. *Journal of Economic Perspectives*, 6(3), 79–100.

Chandler, A. D. (1977). *The visible hand: The managerial revolution in American business*. Cambridge, MA: Harvard University Press.

Dobbs, S. P. (1933). Market research. In: Association of Special Libraries and Information Bureaux, *Report of the Proceedings of the Tenth Conference* (pp. 111–119). London: ASLIB.

Edgerton, D. E. H., & Horrocks, S. M. (1994). British industrial research and development before 1945. *The Economic History Review*, 47, 427–446.

Farradane, J. (1953a). Information service in industry. *Research*, 6(8), 327–330.
Farradane, J. (1953b). [Letter to]. *Library Association Record, 55*, 411–412.
Farradane, J. (1954, June). The chemist and his work — XVI. The technical librarian and the information officer. *Journal of the Royal Institute of Chemistry, 78*, 299–304
Galloway, L. (1918). *Office management: Its principles and practice.* New York: Ronald Press.
Garrett, H. V. (1925). The technical library at Rowntree and Company's Cocoa Works. In: *Information Bureaux and Special Libraries, Report of the Proceedings of the First Conference, 1924* (pp. 38–41). London: Standing Committee Appointed by the Conference.
GEC Research Laboratories (1957). *Readers' guide to the library.* London: GEC Research Laboratories.
Grant, M. (1999). Towards a Central Office of Information: Continuity and change in British Government Policy, 1939–1951. *Journal of Contemporary History, 34*(1), 49–67.
Hannah, L. (1976). *The rise of the corporate economy.* London: Methuen.
Hudders, E. R. (1916). *Indexing and filing: A manual of standard practice.* New York: The Ronald Press Company.
Jenkinson, H. (1937). *A manual of archive administration.* London: Percy Lund, Humphries and Co.
Kaiser, J. (1908). *The card system at the office.* London: McCorquodale and Company.
Kaiser, J. (1911). *Systematic indexing.* London: John Gibson.
Kulkarin, U., & Freeze, R. (2006). Measuring knowledge management capabilities. In: D. G. Schwartz (Ed.), *Encyclopedia of knowledge management* (pp. 605–613). Hershey: Idea Group Reference.
Leffingwell, W. H. (1917). *Scientific office management.* New York: A.W. Shaw.
Lyall, H. G. (1925). Business research and market analysis. In: *Information Bureaux and Special Libraries, Report of the Proceedings of the First Conference, 1924* (pp. 53–59). London: Standing Committee Appointed by the Conference.
Matthew, T. U. (1952). The significance of information in the present-day industrial society. *Aslib Proceedings, 4*(4), 202. [single-page article].
Netherlands Institute for Documentation and Filing (1964). *F. Donker Duyvis: His life and work.* The Hague: Netherlands Institute for Documentation and Filing.
Nightingale, S. J., & Bennie, A. L. (1927). Statistical analyses in the engineering industry for use in the formation of a sales policy. In: *Association of Special Libraries and Information Bureaux, Report of the Proceedings of the Fourth Conference* (pp. 77–85). London: ASLIB.
Orbell, J. (1991). The development of office technology. In: A. Turton (Ed.), *Managing business archives* (pp. 60–83). Oxford: British Archives Council.
Pearce, J. G. (1918). The future of documentation. *Library Association Record, 20*, 162–166.
Piggot, W. D. (1958). Industrial libraries. In: P. H. Sewell (Ed.), *Five years' work in librarianship 1951–1955* (pp. 75–86). London: Library Association.
Roberts, A. D. (1949). Special libraries. In: J. H. P. Pafford (Ed.), *The year's work in librarianship. Vol. XIII: 1946* (pp. 16–63). London: Library Association.
Robins, K., & Webster, F. (1989). *The technical fix: Education, computers and industry.* Basingstoke: Macmillan.
Sontag, W. (1959, December 4). [Letter to] *Engineering*, p.568
Tattersall, F. W. (1927). Cotton statistics: their relation to marketing and market estimating. Association of Special Libraries and Information Bureaux, Report of the Proceedings of the Fourth Conference (pp. 85–89). London: ASLIB.
Taube, M. (1953). Implications for professional organization and training. *American Documentation, IV*(3), 122–125.

Taylor, F. W. (1911). *Principles of scientific management*. New York: Harper and Bros.

Vickery, B. (1953). Recent trends in special libraries. *Library World, 55*(637), 4–8.

Wallace, W. (1927). Business forecasting. Association of Special Libraries and Information Bureaux. In: *Report of the Proceedings of the Fourth Conference* (pp. 111–118). London: ASLIB.

Warren, I. (1920). Office records — their filing and indexing. *Journal of Electricity* [USA], *44*(1), 22–23.

West, N. (2005). *Historical dictionary of British intelligence*. Lanham, MD: Scarecrow Press.

Whitson, K. (1996). Scientific management and production management practice in Britain between the wars. *Historical Studies in Industrial Relations, 1*, 47–75.

Yates, J. (1989). *Control through communication: The rise of system in American management*. Baltimore, MD: Johns Hopkins University Press.

Yates, J. (1991). Investing in information: Supply and demand forces in the use of information in American firms, 1850-1920. In: P. Temin (Ed.), *Inside the business enterprise: Historical perspectives on the use of information* (pp. 117–154). Chicago, IL: Chicago University Press.

Chapter 4

The Information Officer as Intelligence Officer: Aspects of Information Management in British Military Intelligence 1909–1945

Rodney M. Brunt

ABSTRACT

The function and activities of the 'documentalists' of the British security services (MI5 and Secret Intelligence Service (SIS)) are explored in the wider context of the information officer in the knowledge organisation. In time for the Great War, MI5 created its Registry to ensure the efficient use of the information it gathered on suspect aliens. SIS in the World War II (WWII) saw similar information management activity that included those of the Government Code and Cypher School (GCCS) in Bletchley Park, the centre for the processing and exploitation of Ultra. The chapter describes briefly the activities of these 'information officers' and the means by which the intelligence could be put to efficient use to provide effective and efficient support to their customers.

a good indexer had the qualities of an intelligence officer in that the capacity to spot and remember detail and make connections was vital to the effectiveness of the work.[1]

Introduction

While military history can supply us with many illustrations of the role that intelligence might play in both strategic and operational decision making, it might be said, in British terms at least, that it was not until well into the 19th century that there

---

[1] National Archives (1948). HW3/119-120. *The History of Hut 3* (Vol. 1, p. 118).

Information Management: Setting the Scene
Copyright © 2007 by Elsevier Ltd.
All rights of reproduction in any form reserved.
ISBN: 978-0-08-046326-1

was a formalisation of this aspect of military planning and resources. The attitude of senior officers to the gathering and use of information about the enemy's where-abouts, strength and intentions ranged from its 'not being cricket' to a carelessness about seeking or even making available already recorded information, as illustrated, for example, by the unfortunate experience of Hamilton at Gallipoli (Barthorp, 1999). All was to change dramatically over a relatively brief half century under the pressure of modern technical warfare and momentous developments in telecommunications.

Some time after the conclusion of the Crimean War, the War Office established its Intelligence Department; but it was not until 1887 that the Directorate of Military Intelligence (DMI) emerged as a major organisation in the military establishment. (Herman, 1996, p. 17) Later the intelligence services, both internal and external, were to undergo massive expansion and with that expansion came the need for management, not only in organisational terms but also of the raw materials. Of course, intelligence means information; and what emerged from the period just preceding the Great War was the application of various information management techniques to control the vast amounts of that raw material generated as a result of the formalisation of the intelligence gathering process. Information management needs information managers and, while the term was to take some time in its coining, these managers were among the forerunners of the information officers of today.

This paper explores the functions and activities of the 'documentalists' of the British security services in the wider context of the information officer in the knowledge organisation. It advances the hypothesis that intelligence staff of all ranks and categories in the likes of MI5 and SIS[2] were engaged in the tasks now accepted as belonging to the corporate information officer: obtaining intelligence, organising it (for retrieval and displaying relationships), extracting the useful kernel and transmitting it to customers for direct action based on it.

The history of the establishment of the British intelligence services is now well documented (Andrew, 1985; West, 1981, 1986) and the exploits of the different sections and departments in counter espionage and information gathering and analysis has been extensively covered over the past 20 years or so. What have been less fully explored are the information management aspects of their operations which were concerned with the organisation and retrieval of the intelligence gathered from sources ranging from overheard conversation (HUMINT) to stolen documents (COMINT) to interception of wireless signals (SIGINT).

In keeping with their functions these organisations accumulated prodigious quantities of intelligence, information that could only be controlled and made useful by means of information-management techniques such as indexing. In their introduction to *Codebreakers*, Hinsley and Stripp (1993, pp. 11–12) observe that Ultra[3] shortened

---

[2]SIS has been selected as the term to identify the external security organisation sometimes known as MI6. Its scope included the operations of Government Code and Cypher School (GCCS) located at Bletchley Park.

[3]Ultra was the designation given to high-grade intelligence, specifically that gained by breaking messages encrypted by Enigma.

the World War II (WWII)by 2 years. It would perhaps be more accurate (and just) to say that it was the documentation of the intelligence, which was responsible for that shortening, for pure intelligence out of context and unrelated is valueless.

Three establishments: the Central Registry of MI5, the information section of the London Reception Centre (LRC) and the Government Code and Cypher School (GCCS) section of SIS provide useful exemplars and will be considered case-by-case in the text below and on which conclusions will be drawn.

If the hypothesis is to be accepted as proved, it must be clear that the work of the intelligence organisation fits in with that now accepted as the work of the information officer. In order to provide some background prior to considering the individual cases, the following aspects will be treated first: the nature of the information handled and recruitment and training of staff. The sections on the cases themselves will cover processes and procedures specific to each; and conclusions will be then drawn highlighting effectiveness in customer service.

Information Handled

The nature of the information to be handled has a bearing on the processes devised and implemented in each case. While it might at first be assumed that the data gathered for internal security (by MI5 and LRC) would be essentially personal, and there indeed was where the business started (given the concern for spies), it soon emerged that intelligence personnel would also have to contend with 'subject' data. There could be no exclusion of facts and details of the most minute and diverse kinds since anything could influence the progress of a case and provide evidence for conviction.

The reverse is true when we consider the SIS side of the picture. Where interception of SIGINT could rightly be regarded as being focused on non-personal data such as Order of Battle (OB)[4], supplies, movements and morale, it soon turned out that the details about a single individual could indicate something crucial about his or her unit, or the establishment of a new organisation.

These types of information throw up a number of different indexing problems and these are exacerbated by the nature of their acquisition and the fact of their very ordinariness.

One of the principles on which the work was based was the need to index the common, in addition to the uncommon, and was based on the assumption (and experience) that it was impossible to recognise the unusual without the reference marks provided by the ordinary. This reflects practise in the LRC information index of 'carding the sheep and the goats'. In one of the naval section indexes the commonplace abbreviation 'ggf' (*gegebenfalls*, i.e. 'if need be') was included, assumed to denote some piece of equipment until its true significance was appreciated.

Unlike the work of libraries, where author (as personal) information could be tied neatly to context and data linked to other bibliographic and biographical machinery,

---

[4]Order of Battle (OB) was the structure of military forces showing formations and strengths and could include non-combatant units.

the 'authorship' of intelligence can be obscure (purposefully or otherwise) and the subjects of the 'biographies' uncertain, even as to their existence, let alone the veracity of the claims about them.

Subjects (i.e. factual data) might be more easily handled in that information about a weapon or a formation relates to tangibles; but as the early experimentation with subject catalogues showed, it is difficult to establish universal headings or even generally acceptable methods to ensure efficiency and consistency in handling and retrieval (Brunt, 2006b, p. 580).

It fell therefore to the staff of these organisations to devise their own methods and develop them to meet changing circumstances as different and new types of information presented themselves. What else were they doing, therefore, but acting as information scientists and information officers?

Recruitment and Training

In WWI, while the intelligence officer was often a man invalided out from the front, there is evidence of the recruitment for the duration on service commissions from the knowledge industries such as librarianship, business and the universities. (Andrew, 1985; Jones, 1990, p. 115). Registry clerks were essentially socially well-placed women, many of whom were university trained. WW II intelligence officers were recruited from academic and civilian backgrounds and given nominal ranks, and included the likes of pilot officer Cullingham who never saw a cockpit and Commander Tandy who never stood on a bridge (Erskine, 1986). Many women, principally linguists and often graduates, were recruited to GCCS intelligence work, and included the respectable society types who had been 'finished' in Germany and Austria and so had fluent German.

Training was by apprenticeship to the most experienced and it was expected that trainees would become independent in 4–6 weeks, though it would take many more months for them to become fully fledged. This was probably not a lot different from contemporaneous library and information bureau training. There were very few opportunities for formal training (there was only one library school in the UK) and professional qualifications of the Library Association would have been gained by correspondence. Aslib (Association of Special Libraries and Information Bureaux) was formed in 1924 and it had a major influence on training *via* its conferences and publications (Muddiman, 2005). However, there seems to be little evidence of any interest in such training as preparation for work in the MI5 Registry or GCCS, probably because these organisations would have followed civil service procedures and depended on general in-service training.

While mathematicians and crossword puzzle enthusiasts were recruited for cryptology, and linguists were sought for translation and the watch,[5] none was

---

[5]This term was used to denote the groups of intelligence officers who undertook the initial translation and assessment of decrypted intercepts.

recruited expressly for his or her experience in documentation. Joyce Thomas, a part-time librarian while an undergraduate at the University of Durham, was recruited for her German and no interest was shown in her other strength. Cullingham, later to be the founder of the air index at GCCS was more likely to have been recruited for his fluency in German gained as Hamburg representative of Kelly's directories than for his expertise in indexing (Calvocoressi, 2001).

When a reorganisation of MI5's Registry commenced in July 1940, Horrocks, a specialist in business methods, was recruited from Roneo, but it appears indexers, librarians or documentalists were not. Similarly when de Grey grasped the need for indexers to handle the increasing amounts of Ultra, he found only two members of the unit familiar with card indexing. He observed that there was difficulty in trying to find people to keep the index current; however, it seemed not to occur to him that the resources offered by the civilian indexing community might have been tapped.

The indexers trained not only themselves but also the newly appointed intelligence officers (Howard, 1987), who while invariably of high academic standing were clueless about the German armed forces. The indexers were recognised as fulfilling valuable roles additional to the (presumed at the time) associated lowly clerical duties and were acknowledged to be crucial to the intelligence operation. Plainly their contribution was viewed as valuable as it led to what was regarded as advancement — air, military and naval indexers were promoted away from the index to posts more conventionally regarded as intelligence work (Howard, 1987; Smith, 1998, p. 115). Doreen Tabor, head of the GCCS Air Index, recounted that she constantly lost her indexers as they were moved to other work (Tabor, 2002).

Central Registry of MI5

The Central Registry of MI5 was set up soon after the bureau was first established in 1909. Part of its brief was to ensure '...that all Names, Places, and Subjects mentioned in the documents should be minutely indexed' to allow action to be 'based on a knowledge of all the available facts, a knowledge which is to be obtained by consulting all relevant documents'. Under Vernon Kell a highly efficient and well-organised machine had been created by the end of the Great War. It included files and associated indexes on some 250,000 individuals. While the Registry declined during the interwar years because of inadequate funding, the reorganisation of 1940 paved the way to its becoming by the end of the war a very much more efficient unit incorporating an index of over 1,250,000 entries.

The creation of the Registry involved first the making of files for every suspect, after which the personal file and subject file sections were responsible for the indexing of every paper, which came into the bureau from whatever source. Indexing machinery to facilitate 'look-up' 'had been evolved as the occasion arose'. 'When MI5 first started there were comparatively so few files that they were known individually to the staff, who found no inconvenience in the fact that there were two files under the name 'Smith' (no Christian name) one being described as Smith of Norwich and the other Smith of Amsterdam'. This soon proved unworkable as the amounts of intelligence expanded, and remedies sought which resulted in revised procedures. It is interesting to note the observation that what evolved 'was possibly more combersome [sic] than if a scheme had been formulated early in the war to embrace all the unforeseen contingencies which afterwards occurred'. A greater awareness of library and other indexing methods might have inspired that scheme.

As the accession rates grew to 2000 new files per month, procedures were tightened up and by 1916 some codification of practise had been established. A document published internally as 'office instructions'[6] was 'intended to give such information regarding the registration, filing and indexing as will enable new members of the staff ... to obtain a general idea of the mechanism at their disposal'. In 1918, the practise of indexing the various spellings of a name under its most common form was established. Thus the entry for 'SCHMIDT. Johann' would be a reference to 'SMITH', and 'Johann Schmidt' would be found in the 'SMITH' sequence.[7]

In WWII a similar and more specific manual was issued which had the appearance of the sort of codification found in libraries. Included in the file 'Arrangements of security service central indexes' including carding and amending procedures'[8] is a series of documents that relate to the preparation of index cards. They include instructions for the handling of personal names and other details for indexing information about corporate bodies such as firms, societies and ships. Other documents in the file refer specifically to the problems of handling Spanish names along with exhortations that indexers pay particular attention to their forms and filing conventions. There is, however, little by way of guidance on, for instance, the forms in which escape routes, fishing regulations, labour conditions, etc might be prescribed as terms for headings.

London Reception Centre Information Index

The LRC had been opened to handle large numbers of alien refugees flooding into Britain from occupied Europe. To facilitate confirmation of their bona fides, the LRC information section established its information index, which came to contain a great variety of relevant material about the countries from which they arrived along with details of methods and routes used by enemy agents or members of allied resistance movements. The index, eventually containing some 100,000 cards, was in two separate parts: the name index and the geographical index, which also covered entries by subject.

---

[6]National Archives (1916). KV1/56 Organisation and Administration: Annexures; Office Instructions.

[7]This resembles Berghöffer filing — devised for the Frankfurter Sammelkatalog, 1891, as modified for the Swiss Union Catalogue.

[8]National Archives (1940) KV4/152 *Arrangements of Security Service Central Indexes including carding and amending procedures.*

The name index was a single sequence of cards, each containing the full name and all relevant details regarding history and circumstances. The geographical index, a more complex index, was arranged by country with each country sub-arranged by addresses, towns and subjects. Every entry on each card referred to a source, in much the same way as in an abstracting publication. Officers in charge of investigations were responsible for marking their reports for 'carding', i.e. indexing. However, considerable discretion was left to the 'carders' themselves. Indexing policy was plainly driven by the use made of the information index. This was principally used by staff for checking names on arrivals lists and as part of report writing, with officers visiting with their notes to check details before writing up.

The LRC index would have suffered the same sorts of problems regarding names found in MI5 Registry and also adopted similar solutions. However, the great complexity of the geographical index opened it up to all sorts of additional dangers of misfiling and duplication. The address index was first sorted by towns in alphabetical order, then by further location devices such as telephone numbers, streets in alphabetical order and restaurants. Subject index material was assigned to broad areas such as 'organisations' and 'intelligence services'. Each of these categories covered several sub-categories, e.g. 'organisations' included 'resistance movements' and 'passwords'. They seemed not to be subject headings in the conventional indexing sense but guidance on what should be indexed. This of course opened up dangers of inconsistency and possible loss of vital information.

The LRC information section and particularly the information index was the only point at which information from MI5, SIS and numerous other sources was recorded and collated for the benefit of MI5. As a result other organisations also made use of it such as Special Operations Executive and Supreme Headquarters Allied Expeditionary Force (SHAEF).

Government Code and Cypher School Indexes

Soon after the establishment of the GCCS at Bletchley Park it became clear that arrangements would have to be put in place to exploit fully the intelligence it was obtaining from breaking Enigma.

Unlike intelligence gathered from more conventional sources such as observation, interrogation and captured documents, which might be said to have a degree of context into which the information might be placed, SIGINT arrived as disembodied strings of letters. Very often the decrypts, while having the appearance of being clear messages in a recognisable language, turned out to be constructed from jargon and contractions, and were highly specific to the knowledge and experience of the sender and intended recipient(s). Unless these non-conversational German messages could be clarified, their sharing with allied commanders in the field could range in effect from useless to dangerous.

To this end various recording and documentation facilities were established by the units, which were directly involved in the exploitation of decrypted signals. Of these, the principal units were air intelligence (3A), military intelligence (3 M) and general intelligence (3G) found in Hut 3 and naval intelligence located in Hut 4.[9] The documentation of the intelligence effectively took two forms: factual indexes which recorded details relating to specific topics (such as military equipment, locations, formations) and individuals; and reference indexes which could be used to translate, clarify, explain and conceptualise words, abbreviations, acronyms and arbitrary strings of characters, which emerged in the decrypts (Brunt, 2004).

In addition were to be found indexes maintained by specialist research or 'back room' parties such as those concerned with railways, field post offices, secret weapons and technological developments such as radar, directional beams and V-weapons. Traffic analysis[10] also involved much indexing, of call signs, for instance.

At GCCS, once each message had been translated and its contents used, it was passed to the indexers who identified the words and phrases to be indexed. All the details to be indexed were underlined in red and before the cards were written, the work was checked by the head of that index who would supplement or draw attention to unnecessary or inaccurate work. In Hut 3, for instance, the air index had five main sections: units, locations, personalities, equipment and general subjects; the military index had six. According to Calvocoressi (1981, p. 73) the list of interesting details was endless as might have been expected in a process, which was indexing, in effect, the entire universe of military knowledge and much else.

The major problems resulted from the great and unexpected successes in breaking Enigma. This produced overwhelming quantities of information and consequently increased the speed at which the analytical work had to be done. The air index grew from 4 inches of cards in a shoe box in early 1941 to a room full of trays and special racks which by the end of hostilities contained half a million cards, each card holding several 'entries' or abstracts of intercepted messages. As a result there could be scatter of related material until some message drew together different cards, which related to the same topic. For instance the city of Zagreb was treated in the military index for some time as being different from Agram (Thomas, 2002). The problem of the occurrence of the same character string in different contexts was also recognised and addressed, e.g. 'TAURUS' might be a cover name, a type of aircraft, a detachment and the term would appear in all the appropriate sequences.

In the air index, a continuity book was maintained which recorded, among other aspects of the work, decisions on indexing procedures. Its counterparts were to be found in the logbook of the military index and the diaries maintained in the naval section records parties. However, the sorts of authority control devices common in libraries (such as inverted files of references and subject indexes) were not established. These functions were, in effect, discharged by the very characteristics of the

---

[9]While these designations were based on their original locations, the sections housed in them retained the identities after they had been moved into other buildings, thus 'Hut 3' remained the label for air and military intelligence after relocation to 'Block D'; and 'Hut 4' remained that for naval intelligence even after its relocation to 'Block A'.

[10]Traffic analysis enabled intelligence to be obtained from the external details (as opposed to the contents) of the intercepts such as call signs, transmission frequencies and encryption keys.

organisations such as the closed systems, apprenticeship training and the ready sharing of problems.

We may now draw some conclusions from the foregoing case studies.

Solutions

Solutions to problems were the results of continuous reaction to those problems as they presented themselves — the remedies were found on the hoof and were reflective of the early days of library catalogue codification (Brunt, 2006b). The indexes were in constant flux, with segments being moved or hived off as exigencies demanded, e.g. the abbreviations sequence in the air index in 3A was relocated in the abbreviations index maintained by Jones in 3G (Brunt, 2006a).

These are all the functions of information officers, not only in the documentation processes but also in the development of procedures, experimentation and the working of vocabulary control (Thomas, 2002). The main difference from civilian practise lies in the lack of stability. Where conventional information officers could enjoy the luxury of the long-term view and little chance of catastrophic change, the pressures of work under war conditions meant that not only had changes to be appropriate and effective, they had to be taken at pace.

Customer Service

While the customers of MI5 and LRC were case officers engaged essentially in assembling information to support decision taking regarding spies and saboteurs, or the bona fides of refugees and others landing at ports, those in Bletchley Park represented a much wider range of clientele. GCCS staff discharged many responsibilities, ranging from the elucidation of messages of extreme urgency to the relatively long-term project aimed at assessing new secret weapons.

Customers in MI5 included the Registry clerks themselves who did the 'looking-up' for the intelligence officer to locate the set of files relevant to the case in hand, which might include material about other personalities and subjects referred to such as equipment or routes. The LRC information index was used by both the indexers on behalf of the officers and the officers themselves, possibly an indication that the index was easy to use. This contrasts with the observation that in WW I, intelligence officers tended to lack confidence in such use and this enhanced the role of the clerks.

In GCCS, the wide variety of indexes was available to, and in constant and rigorous use, by different groups of staff: the indexers themselves, the translators and emenders of the decodes and the 'advisers' who were responsible for creating and dispatching what would have been the essence of each enemy signal to the appropriate command. The work of researchers (often referred to as 'back room') who were working on specific projects concerned with more elaborate and in-depth analysis was facilitated by consultation of the indexes.

The relationship between the documentation staff and their intelligence officer customers was different in many ways from that which existed in civilian information bureaux and libraries, principally in the fact that the customers were not external to the information system. Close relationships generated by war, *esprit de corps* and sharing the same harsh conditions and emotional and other stresses, meant that there was a much more intimate relationship between provider and customer. In the military index 'each indexer marked and indexed at her own discretion ...' and '... a large amount of discretion on the part of each indexer was inevitable and encouraged', '... a good indexer had the qualities of an intelligence officer in that the capacity to spot and remember detail and make connections was vital to the effectiveness of the work'.

Effectiveness

There is no doubting the effectiveness of all these information retrieval machines in meeting the needs of their customers. Fulsome is the testimony to their efficiency in supplying the required intelligence in a timely fashion to case officers, intelligence analysts and research parties in both MI5 and SIS.

The historical record produced by MI5 after the Great War recounts in considerable detail the ways in which the women of the Registry supported their intelligence officers and lists the recipients of letters of commendation and honours bestowed in recognition of work well done.

Sir Dick White (the only person to have directed (at different times) both MI5 and SIS) wrote in highly complimentary terms about the performance of the information index in facilitating the work of the LRC (Curry, 1999, p. 227). Not only was it effective in supporting the work specifically relating to the interception of spies posing as refugees the information index but it was also of use to other intelligence organisations prior to Operation Overlord and became a key element in the War Room Registry established after the landings.

Many are the positive comments on the value of the indexes in Bletchley Park in the historical memoranda and other contemporary sources. Perhaps the strongest, though, are the understated observations of senior intelligence officers (Bennett, 1989; Calvocoressi, 1981; Lewin, 1978), which testify to the importance of the documentation system in the prosecution of the war. The strongest of all, perhaps, is the deafening silence in the major studies of intelligence in WWII which, in failing fully to acknowledge their role effectively indicates their value in just being there when needed — had they been less so there might well have been produced more (and adverse) comment.

Final Observations

With the advantages of hindsight and the perspective of library and information science, it is easy to see that the workers in the military intelligence units discharged the functions of information officers. It was true at every level — commissioned intelligence officers, MI5 Registry clerks and intelligence officers' secretaries, Bletchley Park intelligence staff. All were involved in the accumulation of information, its organisation for later retrieval and the extraction and assembling of discrete pieces of information from diverse sources to facilitate the development of the fuller story.

What emerges, though, is a picture of uninformed groping towards appropriate and efficient information management systems, which often entailed reaction to rather than control of information management problems as they cropped up. Thus we find the lack in the MI5 Central Registry of a systematic approach felt to be necessary if the information system was to function efficiently (Black & Brunt, 2000, *passim*); and the fluid nature of the air index and naval section index, where parts of the indexes could be hived off to others.

Nonetheless, what systems did emerge proved crucially effective in their different contexts. While drawing on contemporaneous civilian indexing practise might have prepared both MI5 and SIS for that particular aspect of their work, it has been argued elsewhere (Brunt, 2005) that the peculiar circumstances and contexts meant that only the home made and flexible methods they developed could have met the challenges they had to face.

The evidence presented here justifies the hypothesis that to a great extent the intelligence officer, of whatever grade or status, discharged the functions of information officers or information scientists. Black and Hoare (2006) have written about 'hidden libraries' and this term might well be applied to the organisations, which managed the intelligence. If this be accepted then how else might their staff be described than as special librarians; or as the Institute of Information Scientists would prefer 'information scientists', and as members of Aslib would have it, information officers?

A Note on Sources

The principal sources for this work are found in the HW and KV series in the National Archives, Kew, London. Crown copyright material is reproduced with the permission of the Controller of HMSO and the Queen's Printer for Scotland.

References

Andrew, C. M. (1985). *Secret service: The making of the British intelligence community*. London: Heinemann.
Barthorp, M. (1999). Guardsman & intelligencer: Lord Edward Gleichen at http://www.vms.org.uk/features/archive1-06.html [visited 3 November 2006]; abridged in *Soldiers of the queen: Journal of the Victorian Military Society*, number 97 (June 1999).
Bennett, R. (1989). *Ultra and Mediterranean strategy 1941–1945*. London: Hamish Hamilton.

Black, A., & Brunt, R. M. (2000). MI5 1909–1945: An information management perspective. *Journal of Information Science, 26,* 185–197.

Black, A., & Hoare, P. (2006). Introduction: Sources and methodologies for the history of libraries in the modern era. In: P. Hoare & A. Black (Eds.), *Cambridge history of libraries in Britain and Ireland. Vol. 3: 1850–2000* (pp. 1–6). Cambridge: Cambridge University Press.

Brunt, R. M. (2004). Indexes at Government Code & Cypher School, Bletchley Park 1 940–1945. In: M. E. Bowden & W. B. Rayward (Eds.), *The history and heritage of scientific and technological information systems* (pp. 291–299). Medford, NJ: Information Today http://www.chemheritage.org/pubs/asist2002/24-brunt.pdf.

Brunt, R. M. (2005). Some aspects of indexing in British intelligence 1939–45. In: R. V. Williams & B. Lipetz (Eds.), *Covert and overt: Recollecting and connecting intelligence service and information science* (pp. 81–106). Medford, NJ: Information Today.

Brunt, R. M. (2006a). Special documentation systems at the Government Code and Cypher School, Bletchley Park, during the 2nd World War. *Intelligence & National Security, 21,* 129–148.

Brunt, R. M. (2006b). Organising knowledge: Catalogues, indexing and classification as a reflection of changing needs. In: P. Hoare & A. Black (Eds.), *Cambridge history of libraries in Britain and Ireland: 1850–2000* (Vol. 3, pp. 568–583). Cambridge: Cambridge University Press.

Calvocoressi, P. (1981). *Top secret Ultra.* London: Sphere Books.

Calvocoressi, P. (2001). Interview.

Curry, J. C. (1999). *The security service 1908–1945: The official history.* Kew, London: Public Record Office.

Erskine, R. (1986). From the archives: GC and CS mobilizes men of the professor type. *Cryptologia, 10*(1), 50–59.

Herman, M. (1996). *Intelligence power in peace and war.* Cambridge: Cambridge University Press.

Hinsley, F. H., & Stripp, A. (Eds.) (1993). *Codebreakers: The inside story of Bletchley Park.* Oxford: Oxford University Press.

Howard, J. (1987). *Interview 9819/6.* Imperial War Museum Sound Recordings Department.

Jones, R. V. (1990). *Reflections on intelligence.* London: Mandarin.

Lewin, R. (1978). *Ultra goes to war: The secret story.* London: Hutchinson.

Muddiman, D. (2005). A new history of ASLIB, 1924–1950. *Journal of Documentation, 61,* 402–428.

Smith, M. (1998). *Station X: The codebreakers of Bletchley Park.* London: Channel 4 Books.

Tabor, D. (2002). Personal Communication.

Thomas, J. (2002). Interview.

West, N. (1981). *MI5: British security service operations 1909–1945.* London: Bodley Head.

West, N. (1986). *GCHQ: The secret wireless war, 1900–1986.* London: Weidenfeld and Nicolson.

Chapter 5

Information and the CIO

Antony Bryant

ABSTRACT

As the chapters by Black and Brunt make clear, the role of the information officer or its equivalent emerged and developed at least from the late 19th century; both in the commercial world and in government, particularly what we would now term 'the intelligence services'. Moreover, many of the key activities and responsibilities have a far longer history, in many respects dating all the way back to the establishment of the libraries of the ancient world. The core around which all these activities and responsibilities revolve is that of 'information management', and the person charged with overall command and control of this domain came to be termed the 'Chief Information Officer' (CIO) in the last years of the 20th century. The terms 'CIO' and 'information management' are of recent coinage; but their focus and core characteristics have a far longer, more complex, and ambivalent status as will be demonstrated in this chapter.

The Tangled Roots of the 'Information Age'

Black and Brunt rightly draw our attention to key developments which led to the identification and specific allocation of information management roles and responsibilities, and Black in particular has been at the forefront of those arguing that if there is an 'information age' or 'information society', then its roots lie in the 19th rather than the 20th century. (Black, Muddiman, & Plant, 2007; Black, 2001; Weller & Bawden, 2005, 2006).

Yet the 20th century certainly marks the beginning of an information era in some senses. Previously seen largely in peripheral terms, information — and its conjoined concept 'communication' — took on a far more central and influential role as the century progressed. By the 1940s and 1950s Barnard (1938/1972) was stressing the communicational aspects of organizations, Simon (1947) and March and Simon (1958) was focusing on the ways in which information and decision making were related, and the first computer-based information systems were being introduced

Information Management: Setting the Scene
Copyright © 2007 by Elsevier Ltd.
All rights of reproduction in any form reserved.
ISBN: 978-0-08-046326-1

into commercial organizations (the first being LEO in the UK — see Ferry, 2003). Recognition of the role of information in social systems, including the market, organizational development, and institutions in general was developing — albeit only slowly. Thus the 2001 Nobel Prize for economics was awarded to Akerlof, Spence, and Stiglitz for their work on asymmetric information and the role of information in markets; work largely completed and published in the 1960s and 1970s (see the announcement of the prize — Nobel Prize, 2001). Influential models of the 1970s, such as Porter's value chain, were revised and amended by the early 1990s (e.g., Rayport & Sviokla, 1994, 1995) to take account of the many intangible but highly influential factors often ignored up until then, particularly those centring on information, communication, and social interaction.

Information was thus taking centre stage by 1990, particularly in connection with information and communications technology (ICT); dramatically altering the ways in which people conceived of markets, transaction costs, business models, and organizational design. Moreover, companies were changing their top-level management structure so that IS specialists were included at board level, usually with a title such as 'IS Director'; but by the late 1990s the post of CIO was becoming fairly common, although what it actually entailed differed markedly from one organization to the next, and sometimes within one organization from one incumbent to the next.

On the other hand, many of the wilder claims made by information and ICT publicists — the consultants of spin — gradually turned out to be no more than vainglorious wishful thinking, with little or no foundation in organizational or social reality. The information age was not going to usher in a new era of riches for all; the misty-eyed optimism of the dotcom boom of the 1990s was soon exposed by the harsh economic realities of the dotcom bust. The info-utopians included Daniel Bell, Chris Evans, Alvin Toffler, and Peter Drucker (see Bell, 1976; Drucker, 1994; Evans, 1979; Toffler, 1970; Webster, 2004) — i.e., sociologists, IT specialists, futurologists, and management gurus. Many of these excessive claims were and continue to be anchored in a failure to understand the complexities of the socio-economic context of the late 20th and early 21st centuries, founded upon a misconception about the nature of information and communication. Black and Brunt offer a historical context against which to develop a consideration of information management and the role of the CIO, to which a clearer conceptual framework needs to be added.

The main purpose of this chapter is to address some of the key misconceptions about information, since these relate directly to the topic of the role of the CIO, thereby complementing the other two chapters in this section. (Those interested in the wider issues can start by consulting Bryant, 2006.) The information management literature has not been silent on these matters, but in many regards the ramifications of several key critiques have not been taken on board, either in the curriculum or in practice.

Information MISconceptions

As early as 1967 Russell Ackoff was pointing out what he saw as five crucial misconceptions about Management Information Systems (MIS), themselves heralded as the key to organizational survival and success at the time. The misconceptions identified by Ackoff (1967) were:

- Managers do not lack information, they struggle with excess.
- Managers ask for more information than they need, and designers supply more than is requested.
- Decision making does not necessarily improve with more information.
- Performance is not necessarily enhanced by better communication.
- Managers must understand more about information systems.

These mostly emanate from a more-is-better view of information, with information seen as a resource much like any other material input to organizational operation and output.

Another aspect of the misconception of information was presented in a paper by Feldman and March (1981) published in 1981. Here they pointed out that any idea that information served simply as a formal and potentially optimizable input to rational decision making was grossly mistaken. In organizational settings information is not simply gathered with a particular aim in mind, and even if it was the original intention, it is often not used for that purpose. Thus information gathered in response to specific requirements is often not even considered for the purpose for which it was requested. Information used to justify a decision is often collected and used after the decision has been made. Regardless of the information available, more is always requested; while there will be simultaneous disregarding of the information already to hand. In contrast to this Feldman and March pointed out that there is a key distinction between what they termed 'actual human behaviour and apparently optimal information behaviour' (p. 171). Whereas the latter is anchored in an engineering model, the former must contend with social beings acting in organizational and social contexts. Thus Feldman and March were at pains to point out that from this latter perspective, information behaviour is far less oriented towards rational decision making, and far more concerned with coping with uncertainty and social interaction. As a consequence they stressed a range of reasons for organizational investment in information, including surveillance, learning and environmental scanning, and what they term symbolizing a 'commitment to rational choice'; hence the distinction they offer between information is 'signal' and 'symbol'.

Writing in the early 1980s, Feldman and March were not arguing for new information strategies as such; their focus was on actual behaviours, and the ways in which strategies, rules, and procedures actually embody the full richness of organizational use of information, even if the formally stated objectives only reflect a limited and somewhat misconceived view of such activities. In effect they were outlining an anthropological orientation towards understanding and guiding information activities in organizations, setting it in contrast to mechanistic engineering-type models. This became even more critical in the last decades of the 20th century as these activities became more critical to organizational development and survival.

Ackoff, writing from the systems perspective, and Feldman and March, writing perhaps unwittingly from something akin to an anthropological one, were laying the foundation for a far more profound understanding of information systems. Yet the predominant view at this time largely ignored this, favouring a computer-centred orientation. Ackoff stressed the need for managers to understand more about information systems, but this was unlikely to happen if the specialists, IS professionals, themselves were often equally lacking in insight.

In many regards this was not too surprising given the rapid developments in computer and communications technology during this period. ICT for a time did indeed appear to be the solution to all problems; but now we know better or at least we know that we are in a far more complex context not amenable to simple ICT-based 'solutions'. Yet in many organizations the role of the CIO still seems wedded to this misconceived view. Thus the role of the CIO is seen in techno-centric terms as a resource manager or engineer, ensuring efficient and effective information and ICT use in a context of rational decision making and technical communication. In part this is because work emanating from Ackoff, Feldman and March, and others has not been taken into account — all too often being effaced by the largely unfounded claims being made for the latest ICT advances in products and services. This is not easily remedied, but the re-opening of the historical development of organizational use of information as demonstrated by Black and Brunt, together with a revised conception of information itself may help in this endeavour.

Feldman and March hint at some aspects of this when they introduce the distinction between 'actual behaviour' and 'engineering models', and also in their choice of the terms 'signal' and 'symbol', similarly indicated by Ackoff in his implicit critique of information as a resource. Both arguments can be seen as exposing the limitations of an engineering model of information and communication; a model that retains significant influence in university curricula, business models, organizational design, management practices, and the IS profession. The model encompasses, and probably emanates from, two key assumptions, both crucially incorrect:

- Information is something refined from data, essentially a raw material;
- Communication is accomplished through the movement of information, in a fluid-like manner, from (active) sender to (passive) receiver.

If both of these assumptions were valid then the role of the CIO would be akin to a combination of a fluid mechanic and a specialist in hydraulics, transposed to a context of computers and communications technology. But neither one is correct, and so in order to establish the basis for understanding the role of the CIO — before or after the advent of the computer — each must be displaced or remedied.

Data and Information

The first assumption, that information is somehow the result of refining data, is found in many if not most standard texts on topics such as databases, data management, information systems, software engineering, and the like. (A number of examples are listed in Bryant, 2006, pp. 54–55.) It has been termed the 'chemical engineering metaphor', raw data being turned into refined information in a manner similar to that which results in petroleum being produced from crude oil. Most likely it arises from the attribution of computer-like processes to humans; something at least as common as the converse and just as erroneous (think of *artificial* intelligence). The examples in the literature are as likely to locate the processing within computers as they are to associate the processing within humans; but it is the latter that is the more pernicious and in need of rectification for our present purposes. The fault can be termed *praxeomorphism*, the ascription of technological features and facilities to human beings; as opposed to anthropomorphism, the incorrect attribution of human characteristics to the non-human — both animate and inanimate.

Computers do indeed process data in the sense that the machines perform various operations, but the processes and the processors are themselves devoid of meaning. Humans cannot do this. People cannot engage directly with anything to do with data, as soon as they pay any attention to anything we are in the realm of meaning. Scanning a book into a computer is a data process; someone trying to read it — and make sense of it — immediately is in the realm of information because it inevitably involves meaning. If there is any sense in which humans engage with data then it is the sense in which we all constantly buy books, download documents, collect papers; failing to read any of them. In this sense they are data, since we have failed to attend to them. If later we pick up and open the book, or read the paper, then we are immediately and ineluctably in the realm of meaning. But to characterize this as a process of *transformation* is both incorrect and highly misleading. Nothing has been transformed — the book or paper is the same as it was previously. Human beings are intrinsically and inherently information-oriented; silicon-based ones are data-oriented, the efforts of the *artificial* intelligence brigade notwithstanding.

As a consequence the role of the CIO should involve negotiating the ways in which humans use and manage information in a context in which ICT has come to play a significant role — in some ways clarifying the earlier forms of information management as outlined by Black and Brunt, and in other regards doing this very differently as a consequence of these technological advances, as will be explained in the later sections of this chapter.

Information and Communication

This misconception of the nature of data and its putative relationship with information is to some extent sustained and developed in the second aspect centring on information and communication. The basis for this pervasive misconception can be found in the pioneering work of Shannon and his colleagues in the early decades of the 20th century. Shannon's work in Bell Laboratories starting in the 1940s resulted in what is now recognized as the mathematical theory of communication, and also provided the basis of information theory (see Shannon, 1948; Shannon & Weaver, 1959).

The diagrammatic form at the heart of this work is shown in Figure 5.1, and might appear to be non-controversial. The labelling of the boxes is perfectly acceptable, but the arrows are more problematic, specifically those labelled 'Message' and 'Received Message'. While there is no doubt that signals are passed between transmitter and receiver, through a medium of some kind — the channel — such assurance is

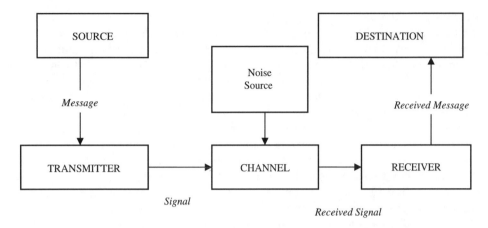

Figure 5.1: Shannon's model of communication.

misplaced for the preceding and succeeding operations. The underlying assumption for the model as a whole is that communication operates as a form of hydraulics, with information flowing from sender to receiver through channels or conduits: The sender despatching the message which eventually arrives at its designated destination. An everyday example — at least before the advent or email — would be posting a letter. The letter is put in the envelope, posted, collected, sorted, transported, and finally delivered to the designated address: A model of communication, but one that entirely ignores the actual writing of the letter and the reading of it at the other end; also disregarding any of the context, motivations, and assumptions underlying these actions. As such it exemplifies what Michael Reddy has termed 'the conduit metaphor' for communication, a trope particularly prevalent in the English language. Reddy argues that this metaphor evokes images of waterways, channels, ducts, pipes, streams etc. Reddy characterizes what he terms the four categories that constitute the critical features of the conduit metaphor

> (1) language functions like a conduit, *transferring* thoughts bodily from one person to another; (2) in writing and speaking, people *insert* their thoughts or feelings in the words; (3) words accomplish the transfer *by containing* the thoughts or feelings and conveying them to others; and (4) in listening or reading, people *extract* the thoughts and feelings once again from the words (Reddy, 1993, p. 170).

He illustrates this in many ways, e.g., with regard to the question — 'What do speakers of English say when communication fails or goes astray?' (1993, p. 166) His examples include the following:

– Try to *get* your *thoughts across* better
– None of Mary's *feelings came through to* me with any clarity
– You still haven't *given me* any *idea* of what you mean

From these and other detailed examples the imagery is stark and clear, information is something to be despatched, transported, delivered, and received; understanding, interpretation, and the like are barely perceptible if at all. The conduit model (a metaphor is a model) is misleading; partial at best, and crucially misconceived in general. Simultaneously it is highly influential, largely at the level of implicit ideas and assumptions operating at the metaphorical level.

Reddy's 'conduit' operates in a fashion similar to Shannon's 'channel'; yet if Reddy's argument is valid, then Shannon's model must be flawed. In fact Shannon came to regret the way in which he had presented his model. He was adamant from the outset that his model precluded meaning, being solely focused on the ways in which signals were transmitted and then used as the basis for selection of which possible series of symbols matched the set of symbols that had actually been received. As such the argument that the model is an adequate one for characterizing delivery, but not for any semantic, social or human aspects of communication, is correct. Indeed Shannon tried to revise his model, seeking to replace the term 'information' with 'entropy'; but he failed to do so as the latter term was so difficult for people to understand — his exact phrase was that the concept of entropy 'is too difficult to *communicate*' (stress added). Unfortunately he did not consider the possibility that the misunderstanding engendered by his model itself might prove to be so pernicious and difficult to eradicate.

The situation is that people's understanding of information and communication rests on a doubly misconceived foundation:

- Information is seen as processed data, with people performing the processing in a fashion similar to that done by computers;
- Communication is seen as a form of transfer, with the receiver in a completely passive role.

These misconceptions have been exacerbated with the advent of ICT. In some regards they predate these technologies, but in others they have developed in concert with them. The conduit-type imagery in English existed well before the 20th century, although discussion of *communication* has altered significantly with the advent of the telephone, TV, and ICT. Everyday use of the term *data*, however, is far more closely bound up with the development of the computer. The danger is that on such bases the role of information management in general and the CIO in particular come to be understood, and put into practice; also having influence far beyond this domain. That this is indeed happening is attested to by many of the current texts on information management, websites, and journals devoted to the role of the CIO, and many other examples of 'best practice' and 'core competencies' around ideas such as 'knowledge transfer', 'e-learning', 'learning outcomes', and 'information architectures'. This is not to disparage some aspects of these, but it is to underline their limitations and anchoring in the two key misconceptions outlined above.

The Role of the CIO: Mechanist or Cultivator?

There are various ways in which this situation can begin to be rectified. The work of Maes (1999) in recent years has demonstrated the extent to which information management has to be distinguished from IT management, and this forms the background for many of the contributions to this volume. Reddy's endeavours to highlight the ubiquity and deficiencies of the conduit metaphor, point to the crucial ambiguities in the ways in which Shannon's model has been generalized for all forms and aspects of communication. Ideas such as 'alignment', 'transfer', 'processing', and so on are attractive because they suggest problems and issues that are amenable to relatively simple, mechanistic solutions. Unfortunately the really existing problems arising from information management, the development of ICT, and the like, are more complex, and require more insightful approaches.

In the light of this the role of the CIO is to ensure that an organization's information system is one centred on meaning and sharing; along the lines of Maes' model. Black and Brunt's historical work helps us to understand this in a broader context, as well as to appreciate the changes wrought by general social developments as well as those specifically related to ICT. Consideration of this broader historical scenario allows us to understand what is core to the management of information, and what is not; in much the same way as Brooks distinguished between the 'essential' and the 'accidental' in software development. In many cases technological advances often occur at such a pace, and across such a wide range of application that an appreciation of these distinctions is only possible at a later stage. Writing in the 1970s Raymond Williams (1974) argued that it was only then, some 40 years or more after its first appearance, that people could begin to grasp the true impact and potential of television; an observation largely premised on the assumption that the technology would not develop much further. In the case of ICT, the emergence of the technology only occurred comparatively recently, but it has continued to develop and gone through several transformations since its appearance.

In much the same fashion, information management needs to be re-evaluated in the light of the impact of ICT: With the technology understood to have had a transformative effect which alters some of the earlier ideas about information management and the role of the CIO or its equivalent, but also having the consequence of enhancing our understanding of the core continuities between information management before and after the emergence of ICT as it exists in the first decade of the 21st century.

This duality was hinted at by Beer (1981), writing in the 1970s as computer technology was starting to become a key factor in organizational contexts. His target was the technology of mainframe computers, but his ideas have an immediate relevance to all forms of ICT. His ideas are best summarized in a set of questions that he posed concerning the ways in which computer technology was being used and introduced in organizations:

> The question which asks how to use the computer in the enterprise, is, in short, the wrong question. A better formulation is to ask how the enterprise should be

run given that computers exist. The best version of all is the question asking, *what, given computers, the enterprise now is.* (stress in original)

If this is applied to information management and the role of the CIO, then it should lead to our asking 'what, given the existence of ICT in its current forms, the practice of information management and the role of the CIO now is?'

Are We All Information Managers Now?

What Black and Brunt demonstrate is that to some extent people have always been practising information management whether they realized this or not; much as Monsieur Jourdain in Moliere's *Le Bourgeois Gentilhomme* had been speaking prose all his life. The examples described by Black and Brunt show what happens as the scope, range, and variety of available and potentially relevant information increases beyond the capacity of a single individual — 'a head-full' — or that of a small group of closely interacting individuals. In particular they illustrate the various mechanisms used to manage and control information by a mix of new management tasks, emerging specialisms and skills, control and containment of the information, and various ways in which the information about the information could be processed and structured: Hence the work on indexing, cataloguing, establishing of company data repositories, information officers and so on, sometimes coupled with technologies such as Hollerith cards, index cards, protocols, and indexes.

All of this was underway well before computers were anything more than an experimental technology aimed specifically at mathematical calculations. As Black and his colleagues have argued (Black et al., 2007) the information age if it exists in any form at all must be seen as originating from at least the late 19th century. This must be combined with recognition that the impact of computers and ICT in the 20th century was at least as much to do with demands from (pull) the social context as the potential offered by the technology itself (push). This view has been developed and endorsed by writers such as Beniger (1989), Berman (1989), and Ellul (1980), among many others. It has been perhaps most eloquently summarized by Weizenbaum (1984) who argued that the 'remaking of the world in the image of the computer started long before there were any electronic computers' (1984, p. ix). Berman makes a similar point:

> If the growth of capitalism based on hierarchy, controlled sequence and rapid iteration remade the world in the image of the computer, then the seemingly uncontrollable growth of corporate and state bureaucracy was the crisis that was averted by the computer's appearance (1989, p. 23).

Thus the tendencies highlighted by Black and Brunt were part of a wider trend of explosive information growth that accompanied the development of large-scale industrial economies. It was no coincidence that apart from being the person who built the first computer, Charles Babbage was a factory owner, specifically interested in the ways in which labour could be sub-divided and manufacturing operations dismantled and then integrated to ensure a more efficient rate of production. In extending Adam Smith's work he developed what is still referred to as the 'Babbage Principle'

> the master manufacturer, by dividing the work to be executed into different processes, each requiring different degrees of skill or force, can purchase exactly that precise quantity of both which is necessary for each process; whereas, if the whole work were executed by one workman, that person must possess sufficient skill to perform the most difficult, and sufficient strength to execute the most laborious, of the operations into which the art is divided (Babbage, 1832, pp. 175–176 — quoted by Berman, 1989, p. 12)

The early information technology referred to by Black and Brunt was brought in to the service of organizational and manufacturing exigencies; but in so doing, the way was opened up for transformations and changes well beyond the imagination and control of Babbage and others of like mind. The initial ideas about harnessing ICT — even in the form of punched-cards, indexes, and the like — were probably anchored in Beer's first question. This is borne out by the points made by Black and Brunt. Brunt offers examples from the intelligence context, such as MI5, which include the creation of a Central Registry, the development of indexes, and the appearance of characters who might be regarded as embryonic CIOs. Black also offers examples of people who might now be regarded as CIOs, or certainly as 'information managers', as well as highlighting the ways in which large, bureaucratic organizations such as the Bank of England had to restructure their information services in a far more overt and mechanized fashion in the early part of the 20th century.

What both exemplify are the ways in which the technology initially takes on the terms and characteristics of the surroundings. Organizations have long been seen in terms of either organisms or mechanisms — sometimes both simultaneously. What is not always so obvious is the way in which early computer technology was seen in terms of organizational hierarchies and divisions. For instance, Brunt makes extensive mention of the Central Registry as the core of the emerging information function — acting as a control and monitoring mechanism as well as a record keeping one. Black makes similar allusions to the central mechanization department. In many regards the CPU took on precisely this role in computer architecture, and the most common use of the term 'registry' now refers to the database at the heart of the Windows operating system: Similarly the transformation in the meaning of terms such as 'file', 'desktop', 'editor', and 'printer'. What the chapters and sources offered by Black and Brunt also indicate is that the early use of information technology was largely at the level of Beer's first question — i.e., 'how can we use this technology as part of our existing practices?' Yet what rapidly happens is that, if people do not pose Beer's second and third questions for themselves, then the context soon forces a confrontation with just such challenges. Brunt points to the ways in which the use of some information management type technologies in the intelligence community led to them mimicking, and eventually learning from and enhancing, the practices of librarians and professional indexers. Black shows even more clearly the ways in which the emergence of information officers or their like led to new domains of responsibility, associated demarcation disputes, claims for professional status and recognition, and a host of other unintended consequences of organizational adoption of technologies and mechanization in general. Whether they wished to or not, organizations had to face the question — 'Given this technology; what is the nature of our enterprise?'

In *The Adventure of the Sussex Vampire*, Sherlock Holmes receives a letter from a correspondent asking him to investigate a case that seems to involve a vampire roaming the countryside in Southern England. Holmes is sceptical, but his attention is sufficiently engaged for him to ask Dr Watson to 'Make a long arm ... and see what V has to say' — i.e., Watson should stretch across to the shelf holding the set of reference books, presumably with a volume for each letter of the alphabet. (Conan Doyle, 1924) Reading this story in the early 21st century, there are several remarkable aspects that would not have been noteworthy at the time it was written. Why does someone as intelligent and incisive as the great Sherlock Holmes need to use a reference book to find out (more) about vampires? In other stories we are told that he is an expert on different forms of newsprint, cigar and cigarette ash, and even the more esoteric forms of malingering. Why then does he feel the need to look at a reference book to find out about vampires? Furthermore, how can we understand his confidence that simply reaching for the volume 'V' will produce a satisfactory conclusion to his quest? We are clearly led to assume that an introduction to the sum of all things requiring to be known is contained in a collection of 26 volumes; and that Holmes has the complete set ready to hand. Had there been no entry for 'vampire' then this might have been sufficient reason for Holmes to deduce that the matter was outside his purview. On the other hand it may simply have intrigued him all the more.

Clearly we have moved well beyond the information management context evoked by this scene, but the contexts described by Black and Brunt begin from similar circumstances. Brunt refers to the impromptu manner in which names were recorded, exceptions were dealt with, and indexes multiplied: All stemming from an initial system hardly any more complex or extensive than Sherlock Holmes' bookshelves. The backdrop to Brunt's chapter is war and conflict; the information function develops during WWI, falls into abeyance and neglect thereafter, but is revived during WWII. Black lists this as part of one of the eight factors he identifies behind the expansion in the provision of information services in post-1914 UK.

What emerges in the 20th century is a set of specific responsibilities and roles for the information officer, information manager, CIO, and so on. At first these seek to incorporate the technology as it is developed within existing organizational practice and procedures. But as the technology develops, people become specialists and develop expertise in the technology; seeing new potentials and developing new practices and protocols. In these ensuing developments some skills are discarded and others developed and encouraged. All of these issues are at least as much at the behest of social and political pressures as they are of technical ones.

Consideration of the historical bases of the information function in organizations helps us outline some of the core features of information management. In particular it forces our attention on the way in which the early stages of information management centred on the organization of information — or of records — to facilitate access and retrieval. The protocols, the indexes, and so on that feature in Black's and Brunt's chapters were devices developed to enhance information management as the volume of information expanded beyond a simple head-full. Indeed it was not simply the gross amount of information that expanded beyond human grasp, but what we now might term meta-information, or information-about-information. Brunt's (2004) work on the developments at Bletchley Park demonstrates the ways in which classifying, cataloguing, and indexing of information are key characteristics of any information function. In a world increasingly dominated by Google and Wikipedia it might seem retrograde to look back on these indexing and cataloguing skills, and lament their demise. Yet it is becoming apparent that without some more powerful forms of information classification and retrieval the 'information age' is in danger of becoming a 'data age' — an era marked more by storage and growth of repositories than in actual intelligent use of information itself: A challenge for the CIO and information managers in general.

References

Ackoff, R. L. (1967). Management misinformation systems. *Management Science, 14*(4), 147–158.

Babbage, C. (1832). *On the economy of machinery and manufacture*. London: Charles Knight.

Barnard, C. (1938/1972), *The functions of the executive* (30th anniversary ed.). Cambridge, MA: Harvard University Press.

Beer, S. (1981). *The brain of the firm: Managerial cybernetics of organization*. London: Allen Lane.

Bell, D. (1976). *The coming of post-industrial society*. New York: Basic Books.

Beniger, J. (1989). *The control revolution: Technological and economic origins of the information society*. Cambridege, MA: Harvard University Press.

Berman, B. (1989). The computer metaphor: Bureaucratizing the mind. *Science as Culture*, 7–42.

Black, A. (2001). The Victorian information society: Surveillance, bureaucracy and public librarianship in nineteenth-century Britain. *The Information Society, 17*(1), 63–80 January–March.

Black, A., Muddiman, D., & Plant, H. (2007). *The early information society: Information management in Britain before the computer*. Aldershot, UK: Ashgate.

Brunt, R. (2004). Indexes at the Government Code and Cypher School, Bletchley Park, 1940–1945. *Journal of the American Society for Information Science and Technology*, 291–299; available at http://www.chemheritage.org/events/asist2002/24-brunt.pdf

Bryant, A. (2006). *Thinking informatically: A new understanding of information, communication, and technology*. Lampeter, UK: Edwin Mellen.

Conan Doyle, A. (1924). *The Adventure of the Sussex Vampire*, available at http://sherlock-holmes.classic-literature.co.uk/the-adventure-of-the-sussex-vampire (originally published in The Casebook of Sherlock Holmes, 1924).

Drucker, P. (1994). *Post-capitalist society*. New York: Harper Business.

Ellul, J. (1980). *The technological system*. New York: Continuum.

Evans, C. (1979). *The mighty micro*. London: Gollancz.

Feldman, M. S., & March, J. G. (1981). Information in organizations as signal and symbol. *Administrative Science Quarterly, 26*, 171–186.

Ferry, G. (2003). *A computer called LEO: Lyons tea shops and the world's first office computer*. London: Fourth Estate.

Maes, R. (1999). Reconsidering information management through a generic framework. *Prima-Vera* Working Paper 99-15; available at http://primavera.feb.uva.nl/PDFdocs/99-15.pdf.

March, J. G., & Simon, H. (1958). *Organizations*. New York: Wiley.

Nobel Prize. (2001). Available at http://nobelprize.org/nobel_prizes/economics/laureates/2001/press.html

Rayport, J. F., & Sviokla, J. J. (1994, November–December). Managing in the marketspace. *Harvard Business Review*, 141–150.

Rayport, J. F., & Sviokla, J. J. (1995, November–December). Exploiting the virtual value chain. *Harvard Business Review*, 75–85.

Reddy, M. (1993). The conduit metaphor: A case of frame conflict in our language about language. In: A. Ortony (Ed.), *Metaphor and thought*. Cambridge, UK: Cambridge.

Shannon, C. (1948). The mathematical theory of communication. *Bell Systems Technical Journal*, 27; available at http://cm.bell-labs.com/cm/ms/what/shannonday/shannon1948.pdf

Shannon, C., & Weaver, W. (1959). *The mathematical theory of communication*. Urbana, IL: University of Illinois Press.

Simon, H. (1947). Administrative behavior: A study of decision-making processes in administrative organizations (4th ed. in 1997). New York: The Free Press.

Toffler, A. (1970). *Future shock*. New York: Random House.

Webster, F. (Ed.) (2004). *The information society reader*. London: Routledge.

Weizenbaum, J. (1984). *Computer power and human reason*. London: Penguin.

Weller, T., & Bawden, D. (2005). The social and technological origins of the information society: an analysis of the crisis of control in England 1830–1900. *Journal of Documentation, 61*(6), 777–802.

Weller, T., & Bawden, D. (2006). Individual perceptions: A new chapter on Victorian information history. *Library History, 22*(2), 137–156.

Williams, R. (1974). *Television: Technology and cultural form*. London: Fontana.

SECTION II:

RISING ABOVE OBJECTIVISM AND SUBJECTIVISM

Following Maes (2007, in this volume), it can be said that information management is still (or once again?) searching for its identity and the theoretical foundations upon which that identity might be built. He suggests an integrative approach to information management, the aim of which would be to deliver 'value to people' and not 'people to systems' (*ibid.*: 24). Nevertheless, the question remains which theoretical bases could be effectively applied to ground such a comprehensive approach. Should information management's identity be built upon 'technology', 'information', 'management' or any combination of these notions? Or does an integrative approach mean that we seek to base information management on a number of sciences such as economics, technology, philosophy, sociology and psychology? In short, what is information management? What could or should it be?

This section addresses these questions by making a distinction between objectivism and subjectivism. We explore these opposing philosophical traditions to help indicate what it is that needs to be combined for an approach to information management to be rightfully called integrative, and why such an integrative approach is needed. In objectivism, information and knowledge are seen as disembodied objects that can be managed as such, which is the dominant view in disciplines such as economics, technology, accountancy and financial management. Subjectivist views on information and knowledge, on the other hand, can be found in disciplines like sociology and psychology. Here, information and knowledge are related to situated processes of sense making and the construction of meaning. In subjectivism, knowledge evolves from human interpretation and interaction; in objectivist economics, human contact is stripped down to what is considered its core — the transaction of objects. Objectivism and subjectivism oppose each other in many regards and, hence, differ substantially in their theoretical and practical implications. What perspective is taken decides which aspects of reality get highlighted and which remain hidden.

Hence, combining objectivism and subjectivism is a hard task. As a legacy of Descartes' object–subject split, the divide between mind and body, both traditions act as dueling rivals that hardly inform each other. Like two football teams from competing cities fighting a constant battle, they tend to downplay each other's existence. In the information management literature also, the one can be seen to deny or even ridicule the other. Living with the two traditions entails switching from *dualism* to *duality*. Seeing objectivism and subjectivism in duality implies recognizing that both world views cannot exist without the other, just as dueling football teams require each other to create interesting champion leagues. Neither one is good or bad; more of one does not mean less of the other. Integrative information management means seeing objectivism and subjectivism as inseparable and mutually constitutive strands of thought. Hence, information managers face the difficult task of better understanding of how these traditions interact to improve their added organizational value.

In the first two chapters of this section, Ard Huizing unpackages objectivism and subjectivism, respectively, in relation to information management. He uses micro-economics to deepen our understanding of objectivism and practice-based social theory to do the same for subjectivism. In both chapters, the question is posed whether or not a sound and solid basis for information management has been found. In both cases, the answer is negative which leads to the inescapable assertion that both objectivism and subjectivism are needed for an integrative approach to information management — neither one can replace the other. Subsequently, the idea of foregrounding and backgrounding borrowed from psychology is presented to help information managers rise above the deep divide between both philosophical perspectives. This idea illustrates that when either objectivism or subjectivism is foregrounded in real-life actions, one should not lose sight of the other perspective. Foregrounds cannot exist without backgrounds; the one is better off when informed by the other.

In his chapter, Chun Wei Choo draws our attention to joint decision making in organizational groups, such as management or project teams. While group discussions are an important means to, for instance, discuss organizational goals and choose a course of action, they can also suffer from subjective information behaviors impairing the group's decision-making capacity. After Choo has examined a number of psychological processes negatively affecting the sharing and processing of information in groups, he illustrates how information management can help reduce such subjectivity in organizations and improve intersubjective information use in organizational teams.

Chapter 6

Objectivist by Default: Why Information Management Needs a New Foundation

Ard Huizing

ABSTRACT

In this chapter, I illustrate how closely information management is rooted in the philosophical tradition of objectivism. I then address my second goal, which is to probe the question of whether or not objectivism provides a sound and solid foundation for information management. With these goals in mind, I first explain what objectivism is, for which I extend this philosophical tradition with microeconomics, one of its most influential elaborations. I subsequently illustrate how deeply information management and the adjacent field of knowledge management have been affected by objectivist thinking. Objectivism has determined the domain, rationale, definition and goal that are commonly ascribed to information and knowledge management as well as the definitions of their core concepts information, knowledge, communication and learning. Moreover, information and knowledge management show a deep appreciation for the market form of organizing, as suggested by microeconomics. Being an influential theory means that the underlying theoretical assumptions get internalized into people's belief systems, which can then become an established ideology. As a result, these assumptions help frame what the organizational challenges are and how to manage them. Summarizing this chapter, Table 6.1 includes the objectivist and related economic assumptions upon which information management has been built. Finally, I return to the foundation question. With objectivist economics, information management has chosen a theoretical basis that has ironically proven to be incapable of dealing with the very core of its existence: information. *Stigler's (1961) observation still applies: "[Information] occupies a slum dwelling in the town of economics" (in Babe, 1994, p. 49). Objectivism and economics are and will remain helpful in information management, but need to be complemented by subjectivist theories that seek their contribution in the problems objectivism and economics cannot solve.*

What is Objectivism?

Objectivism is by far the dominant worldview in Western culture. I use objectivism as an umbrella term for all of those schools of thought and theories that are based upon the idea that for knowledge development we should view the world as consisting of distinct objects that can and should be separated from their originators and users. Building on a long tradition of rationalist and empiricist theory construction, this idea is deeply entrenched in sciences such as economics, computer science, mathematics and sociology as well as in business disciplines like accountancy and financial management. It also governs large parts of information management and the adjacent fields of knowledge and learning, both in theory and in practice. Information management is objectivist by default.

In a general sense, objectivism is associated with "scientific truth, rationality, precision, fairness and impartiality" (Lakoff & Johnson, 1980, p. 189). Objectivists claim that human behavior is determined by forces in the external world. People, however, cannot control these external forces and find them difficult to comprehend. They should therefore be supported with knowledge to help them master their environment, which would lead to successful performance. Consequently, for developing knowledge relevant to practice, we should be focused on the external aspects of how we understand our worlds.

The world external to individual human beings is thought to be made up of distinct, real objects. These objects are supposed to have *inherent* properties, implying that objects are not affected by the way we think of them or how we use them. A rose is a rose is a rose, regardless of how someone perceives it, if at all. Objects live on their own, immune to our subjective thoughts, feelings and emotions. They have fixed meanings that can be known by investigating their inherent properties. Roses have thorns, distinctive smells and other fixed properties that together define our interactions with and understandings of this flower category. Once these properties are fully understood, true and lasting knowledge has been gained.

Building theory upon the inherent properties of information and knowledge is an approach favored in the relevant literatures (Shapiro & Varian, 1999; Boisot, 1998, respectively). Commonly the reasoning is that traditional theories have been developed for the industrial age that aim to support organizations in managing physical goods. Information and knowledge, however, have properties characteristically deviating from those of physical goods. Typical examples of such idiosyncratic properties implicating management and organization are, for instance, that information can easily be copied perfectly at minimal costs or that knowledge can appreciate with use. Understanding these inherent and objective properties and structuring them into a framework of abstracted cause and effect relationships create theory that guides organizations in the information or knowledge society. The related implication for information management is that its identity could be built upon such distinct expert knowledge. It is what could set information management apart as a value-adding business function.

Hence, we can better understand our external environment by exploring and abstracting the inherent properties of the objects in it and using the knowledge thus gained to determine our relationships to the objects. In objectivism, knowledge consists of discrete and abstracted granules of understanding representing objective realities and learning is a step-by-step process directed toward the constant refinement of these factual representations. Clearly delineating objects' inherent properties and understanding how these properties relate to each other is considered to be the gateway to knowledge and to mastery over the environment for those who have that knowledge.

Moreover, since knowledge in objectivism is factual, objective and fixed, it is transferable to others by means of communication. Through communication, the fixed meanings of objects are transferred from an active sender to a passive receiver, a view on communication that is known as the conduit metaphor (see Bryant, 2007, Chapter 5 in this book). In this view, the main source of communication failure is human subjectivity. Communication failures might occur when the sender has used inaccurate language or when the receiver was unaware of the exact meaning of the language used and subsequently misinterpreted the message.

In objectivism, subjectivity is also to be suspected for other reasons. Because successful performance in the external environment is fully dependent upon it, knowledge creation cannot be left to individual people, prone as they are to human error instigated by personal and cultural biases, prejudices and other subjective limitations. The only real knowledge is considered to be objective, rational knowledge, for which we need science's drive toward precision and timeless truths. Science allows us to abstract experiential knowledge from practice in such a way that ultimately correct, general and definitive accounts of reality can be given that are objectively, universally and unconditionally true. People can be objective, but only if they use clear and precise language consisting of words with fixed meanings, which match the reality that is being described. Science provides us with such language. Moreover, scientific methodologies allow us to present the resulting models of rational behavior as prescriptive theories that tell us how to be successful in the external environment. This positivist view on science, methodology and knowledge is also prevalent in the information and knowledge literatures.

Finally, objectivity is preferred over subjectivity, because it helps to rise above personal judgments, illusions and errors, and in that way, advances fairness and impartiality in human relationships. A management development program with promotion criteria clear to all those involved is a typical example of such intentions.

Table 6.1 includes the points just made about objectivism. It also summarizes the remainder of this chapter with the intention to depict the deeper structure of objectivism and objectivist information management.

The Transactional Edifice of Microeconomics

As a philosophical tradition, objectivism directly affects our views on information management, and also indirectly through more mature, paradigmatically advanced sciences from which well-developed ideas and theories are imported. In the relatively young field of information management, many references are made to neoclassical

Table 6.1: Pinpointing objectivism.

Objectivism's transactional edifice

Definitions
1. Information and knowledge are granules of understanding representing objective realities.
2. Learning is a step-by-step process directed toward the constant refinement of objective representations.
3. Communication is the transfer of granules of understanding from a sender to a receiver.

Information (and knowledge) management
1. The domain of information (knowledge) management is the information (knowledge) supply side, culminating in the moment of truth.
2. The rationale of information (knowledge) management is promoting unfettered information (knowledge) exchange.
3. The goal of information (knowledge) management is getting the right information (knowledge) in the right form to the right person at the right time.
4. Information (knowledge) management is the gathering, refining, storing, preserving and dissemination of information (knowledge).

Organizing principles
1. Shape information and knowledge exchange as a market and create effective mechanisms to fully exploit the market's self-organizing capacity.
2. Maximize participation, discourage erection of entry barriers and promote competition among participants.
3. Commoditize information and knowledge to render economic power.

Core assumptions in objectivism
1. Human behavior is determined by forces in the external world.
2. People cannot control these external forces and find them difficult to comprehend.
3. People should therefore be provided with truthful knowledge to help them master their environment.
4. Mastery over the environment leads to successful performance.
5. For developing relevant knowledge, we should focus on these external aspects of understanding.
6. Understanding is dependent on truth.
7. The environment consists of distinct objects that exist independently of human cognition and use.
8. People understand the environment when they have knowledge of these objects.
9. Such knowledge is developed by studying objects' inherent properties.
10. These inherent properties can be objectively known through codification and abstraction.
11. Objects' inherent properties are fixed and objective; meanings are therefore also fixed and objective.
12. The only real and truthful knowledge is disembodied, abstracted and objective.

Table 6.1: *Continued*

Objectivism's transactional edifice

---

13. Only positivist science produces real, truthful knowledge and reliable, prescriptive theory.
14. Objectivity promotes fairness and impartiality in social matters.

Additional assumptions in microeconomics

1. Successful performance is defined by its economic value.
2. Efficient exchange maximizes economic value.
3. Hence, efficient exchange at the moment of truth should be the focal point of attention.
4. Transactions stand on their own, implying that context, time and people's identities, values and beliefs are irrelevant for theory and practice.
5. People are economically rational and maximize their personal welfare.
6. Competition among large numbers of nonhierarchical participants enhances market efficiency.
7. Maximizing economic value requires commoditization of information and knowledge.
8. Commoditization enables measurement of performance and management control.
9. ICT is a neutral medium.

---

microeconomics, which is a highly influential application of this philosophical tradition. Deconstructing these references can show us what objectivist information management is and what it is not.

The influence of neoclassical economics can be read from a number of metaphors pervasive in information management: information exchange, information transfer, information use and information management itself, among others, while similar metaphors are also common in knowledge management. The core idea imitated is that we should take the transaction of objects as the focal point of attention in building relevant theory. A transaction or exchange is understood as "a voluntary agreement involving the offer of any sort of present, continuing or future utility in exchange for utilities of any sort offered in return" (Weber in Woolsey Biggart & Delbridge, 2004, p. 31).

In microeconomics, objects are scarce and should therefore be used as efficiently as possible, whether they are "dollars, a bowl of whipped cream, available time or even a reputation for honesty and skill" (Stigler, 1988, p. 193). However, most objects can be used in many ways and for different purposes, and can render a plethora of products and services. That possibility presents us with a pivotal organization and management challenge: how can scarce and thus valuable objects be optimally distributed over the alternative ways in which they can be deployed?

The straightforward answer of neoclassical economics is: by using the market form of organization. As expressed in the neoclassical model of the perfect market, transacting objects on markets is the best way of securing optimal distribution, meaning that objects find their most efficient and profitable use through exchange. The relationship established between *efficient distribution* of objects and *market exchange* and then to *economic-value realization* epitomizes the transactional edifice of neoclassical economics.

Despite a number of fundamental problems in economics' transactional edifice, which I will address later in this chapter, the model of the perfect market remains remarkably yet understandably influential. In business literature and practice, the moment of transacting is insightfully called *the moment of truth*, implying that it is at this particular instance in time that organizations realize their economic value. All organizational effort, so to speak, is geared toward this value-realizing moment when products and services are transferred *quid pro quo* to customers and clients. It is through efficient exchange that organizations maximize their value added and hence, their economic growth. Part of this larger picture is the exchange of information and knowledge, which is gaining significance with the development of a postindustrial economy. Information and knowledge are increasingly being considered the principal strategic resources for organizations and societies, and the ability to create and apply them, the core competences for building and sustaining competitive advantage or economic rent. Hence the need to adequately theorize information and knowledge.

The Logic Behind Objectification

The prospect of value realization and economic growth through efficient exchange explains not only the generally strong appeal of transactional thinking to decision makers in both private and public sectors, but also the logic behind objectification, or codification, as it is called in the knowledge management literature.

Firstly, objectification is needed because exchange entails the conveyance of property rights, which requires legal ownership of that which is being transferred, and legal ownership in turn requires clearly defined objects. As reflected in the adage, "possession is nine-tenths of the law" (Boisot, 1998, p. 87), the only route open for organizations to claim ownership of information and knowledge in a meaningful way is to turn them into such distinct objects, disembodied from their producers and consumers.

Secondly, the objectification and transactionalization of information and knowledge is justified by the potential of capturing informational economies of scale. Once objectified into unaffiliated documents, files or software, information and knowledge can be replicated and reused endlessly at minimal additional costs. As a result of this inherent property, the average cost per information or knowledge exchange will be lower for high-frequency transactions; that is, the value of information and knowledge increases as more people use it. Moreover, we often talk about information and knowledge *sharing* instead of exchange, indicating that information and knowledge are retained upon transaction. Unlike physical objects, their consumption does not eliminate them. The economic consequence of these inherent properties is that information and knowledge are more likely to be optimally distributed than physical goods, ideally becoming available to everybody who can put them to productive use.

Knowledge management's dictum *if we only knew what we know* perfectly reflects this ideal of entirely efficient markets.

Thirdly, viewing information and knowledge as distinct and exchangeable objects gives us a clear sense of what it is that needs to be organized, managed and evaluated. Objects can be gathered, stored, refined and distributed — all activities that can be managed and quantitatively measured. Quantification is an absolute requirement for economic modeling and analysis. The consequence of this prevalent view is that the subjectivists' perspective of information and knowledge residing in human minds and relationships that cannot be disembodied into distinct objects is ignored in economics. What cannot be quantified is consistently assumed away.

Conceptual Implications: Information Management's Domain, Rationale, Definition and Goal

The objectivist-economic considerations mentioned above have helped frame the domain, rationale, definition and goal commonly ascribed to information management. Following economics creates a *natural* distinction between the *information supply side* and the *information demand side*, mediated by the moment of truth. It also contributes to a distinct preference for the information supply side, for a number of reasons.

As described in the previous section, the business need to maximize economic value urges the objectification and transactionalization of information and knowledge. The logic behind objectification furthermore drives attention toward exploiting what we have or know rather than toward exploring what we do not have or understand. In objectivist information management, therefore, the focus is on resolving supply-side issues, such as objectifying available information and knowledge, storing the resulting information and knowledge objects independently from subjectivity of producers and consumers, and improving their availability and accessibility to enhance information and knowledge distribution. Generally, there is little concern for what people actually do with information and for how creative and dynamic learning processes may result in innovation and the creation of new knowledge. The objectivist default is: information use is not our business! Information management might help fix the objective meanings of relevant words by such means as thesauri, taxonomies and data committees, but beyond that, the information demand side is viewed as the concern of others or is seen as relatively unproblematic. This perspective on information management is reinforced by the conduit metaphor of communication and by economists assuming prices to be the quantitative expressions of the utility buyers and sellers subjectively attach to products and services.

Moreover, the introduction of information and communication technology mediating human interaction has also been a contributing factor to information management specializing on the supply side. In economics, ICT is seen as a neutral medium that transports information objects from the supply to the demand side. It helps in objectifying practice, for instance by reducing the cost of information replication and reuse, and in transactionalizing information objects by paving electronic roads between information suppliers and users. By its very nature, ICT aids in enhancing the availability and accessibility of information and knowledge and contributes little toward making sense of the messages conveyed. Moreover, the complexity of technology as such and of applying it successfully into organizational contexts has contributed to a technology-driven approach to information management. As a next logical step in the ever-increasing division of labor that is so important for economic growth, ICT has become its own domain of expertise.

Consequently, economic reasoning stimulates information management to choose the supply and exchange of information as its *domain* of expertise and the promotion of this exchange by helping to remove any barrier that prevents information from flowing as freely as possible as its *rationale*. In theory and practice, therefore, information management is generally *described* in terms of acquiring, refining, storing, preserving and disseminating informational representations of practice and its *goal* is described as getting the right representations in the right form to the right person at the right time (Gurbaxani & Whang, 1991). These attributes of information management can be clearly recognized in ICT or IS-driven approaches to information management. What happens with the information after it has been disseminated is occasionally included in the definition of information management (Wilson, 1997), but often this aspect is ignored or minimized. Acquiring, refining, storing and preserving information are information-management processes which relate to the objectification of reality, and disseminating information relates to market mechanisms optimizing the distribution of the resulting information objects.

The observations made regarding information management in the previous paragraph also apply to knowledge management. Knowledge management is often defined in the same terms as information management, and is attributed a similar domain of expertise, rationale and goal (Davenport & Prusak, 1998). The same erosion of notions can be discerned in practice, when a bookstore is suddenly called a *knowledge shop* or a database with frequently asked questions an *interactive knowledge center*. Precisely because of this identical emphasis on the objectification and economic value of knowledge, knowledge management cannot be anything else than information management and vice versa. How could a knowledge object be different from an information object or, for that matter, a data object? In objectivism, *data*, *information* and *knowledge* can and are used interchangeably.

Organizational Implications: What the Market Metaphor Highlights and Hides

Apart from the conceptual implications for information management's domain, rationale, definition and goal, building information management's identity upon economics' transactional edifice has considerable implications for organization theory and management practice. Transactions need to be organized, one way or another. The objectivist view that information and knowledge can be separated from its generators and users into transferable objects determines how transactions can be best organized, managed and evaluated.

Neoclassical orthodoxy favors the market form of social organization, which can be applied to organizations' external transactions with, for instance, suppliers or customers as well as to their internal transactions. The assumptions upon which the neoclassical model of the perfect market rests reflect the organizing principles involved and, in that way, also those assumptions and principles that are hidden. I will apply these assumptions and principles to information and knowledge management under three headings: (1) create effective market mechanisms, (2) maximize participation and (3) commoditize information and knowledge.

The promise of economics is: the more closely information and knowledge management adhere to the neoclassical assumptions and the organizing principles implied, the more perfect the established information and knowledge markets will be, and the more efficiently information and knowledge will be distributed. This appealing promise, however, obscures other aspects of reality that have been effectively wished away in economics' drive toward theoretical rigor. Once captured by economics' attractiveness, these other aspects of reality run the risk of getting ignored or downplayed, in theory as well as in practice. It is precisely at this point that the theory of the perfect market can become a market ideology. As will be illustrated in the next chapter of this book, the very same aspects of reality hidden in objectivism and economics are the ones emphasized in subjectivism.

Create Effective Market Mechanisms

The marvel of markets (Hayek, 1945) is that they are self-organizing, once effective market mechanisms are in place. In theory, these market mechanisms ensure that every bit of information or knowledge necessary for decision making will be available at the right moment, which in turn allows people to be seen as fully rational agents regardless of their computational and cognitive limitations. The assumptions in neoclassical orthodoxy have been designed in such a way that prices contain all information and knowledge for transactions to take place efficiently. All that people need to know to efficiently transact is the price of the object at hand. The price is the market's information system; the *invisible hand* will take care of the rest. The perfect information and communication assumption furthermore entails that any relevant change on the market is instantly reflected in a price change, which is immediately communicated to and processed by all market parties.

In the field of information and knowledge, however, prices are often absent, which turns the intrinsic and extrinsic motivations of people to share their information and knowledge with others into a core organization issue. If prices are unknown, why would anybody consider sharing information or knowledge? Extending the neoclassical assumption that rational people always maximize their self-interests and personal welfare, this issue can be solved by assuming that rational people will readily objectify and exchange their information and knowledge through market mechanisms other than price if they expect to be proportionately rewarded with tangible or intangible returns such as pay, promotions and bonuses or reputation, respect and prestige. Google and the many social networking sites available such as LinkedIn exemplify how deeply the market metaphor can inform the shaping of information and knowledge exchange.

The transactional edifice of neoclassical economics is built upon other assumptions as well. Economics' methodological individualism (Babe, 1994) suggests that both people and transactions can be seen as anonymous and independent atoms, which add up to nothing more than the sum of their parts. People pursue their own individual goals, driven by self-interest, each to themselves. Their identities are unimportant and their relationships need not become personal, because each transaction stands on its own for which, if needed, alternative exchange partners are readily found in our competitive markets. Moreover, anonymous exchange relationships do not require values and beliefs to be shared. Exchange partners, so to speak, do not have to be friends for transactions to be successfully accomplished.

The organizing messages implied in these neoclassical assumptions are that people's self-interested drive to maximize their individual welfare should be explicitly addressed when establishing an information or knowledge market. Create effective market mechanisms, observe how self-organizing information providers and users find each other, and adjust the mechanisms, if and when that seems appropriate. Information or knowledge management in this sense is manipulating people's behavior by carefully addressing their self-interests.

Hence, neoclassical orthodoxy provides a static equilibrium model characterized by supply and demand forces that ignores any influence of context, time and immaterial values such as imagination, creativity or trust on people, relationships and transactions. The focus is entirely on the objects being discretely transacted, here and now, which is *the* aspect of reality the market metaphor exposes and emphasizes. What it hides are the relationships between people engaged in exchange, their history and future, their affiliations with the objects exchanged, the interaction of which the exchange of objects is just a part, the context in which transactions take place and the dynamics of the organizational processes involved. Economics is a science of nouns, not of verbs. It deals with static objects rather than with dynamic subjects, with information, not in-forming; with knowledge, not with knowing or learning.

Maximize Participation

Another assumption of neoclassical economics is that for markets to be efficient, they should consist of large numbers of transacting actors, none of whom has sufficient economic or political power to exert influence over the other. Ideally, there are no entry barriers either, so that all who wish can actually join. Large numbers of providers and users are furthermore needed to promote competition among as many information and knowledge sources as possible. The more people participate in competition, the more information and knowledge are generated and used, the more efficient information and knowledge will be distributed, and the higher the likelihood that they will be put to their most productive uses.

The implications for management and organization are straightforward: for information or knowledge management actions taken or technologies implemented, we should maximize the availability, accessibility and use of information and knowledge by attracting as many participants as possible and by avoiding creation of any entry barriers.

This is the economists' way of presenting markets as nonhierarchical and power-less institutions, where everybody can and should find whatever one is looking for. Praising intranets or virtual communities, for instance, for their capacity to cross vertical and horizontal organizational boundaries clearly hinges on this element of the market metaphor, as does the alleged social nature of wikis and other social software tools. Moreover, all these instruments express the belief that group con-sensus on the basis of free exchange discloses a more *objective* and thus more *accurate* analysis of reality than any individual ever could. *Crowds* are assumed to be un-conditionally wiser than any single expert could wish to hope for. What this sup-posed nonhierarchical *wisdom of crowds* conceals is that all kinds of monopolies and power structures are at work in all information and knowledge ecologies. It also hides the fact that the participation of more people or availability of more infor-mation may not necessarily translate into higher-quality decisions or superior knowledge creation (see also Choo, 2007, Chapter 8 in this book). More is not always better.

Commoditize Information and Knowledge

Finally, neoclassical economics tells us that, sooner or later, everything of economic value will be commoditized. Commodities are standardized, homogeneous goods, meaning that each copy is physically identical to the other. Such standardization permits counting and measurement, which is needed to set equilibrium prices for the relevant commodities. It also allows quantitative evaluation of performance and value realized, which adds to economics' theoretical and practical attractiveness. Commoditization furthermore entails that the identities of the exchange parties and their relationships can be considered irrelevant for economic analysis, because if goods are homogeneous, it does not matter who the buyer or seller is. Under these conditions, the price is the only factor remaining in deciding with whom to trade. Moreover, these conditions allow parties to transactions to be treated as mere pro-ducers or consumers — as anonymous atoms who do not interact with each other in any other way than by exchanging standardized objects. Finally, commoditization enables organizations to be maximally streamlined, with optimized business proc-esses supported by ICT enhancing organizational efficiency.

Commoditization renders economic power, which also applies to information and knowledge. Ceasing informational economies of scale is possible only to the extent that information and knowledge are turned into standardized objects. Think for instance of best practices stored in a database or seeing information and knowledge as reusable intellectual capital (Stewart, 1998). Objectivists focus on extracting in-formation and knowledge from people through standardization and centralization processes to transform them into disembodied, decontextualized commodities. Such standardization and centralization turns information and knowledge into economic values that can be hierarchically controlled 'from above' and measured in quantitative terms. Commoditization enables that, for example, information management's contribution to organizations can be evaluated in terms of its storing and processing capacity. Interestingly, contributions to the information supply side are easier to quantify than those to the demand side, which adds to information management's inclination to specialize on the supply side as its sole domain of expertise.

Economics' strong emphasis on value realization and measurement giving a clear sense of what and how to organize for the moment of truth makes it relatively easy to sell to management and other decision makers (Bonifacio, Camussone, & Zini, 2004). That clear-cut virtue, however, comes at a price. The market metaphor hides the inability of economics to talk about informational content instead of the hardware through which that information is distributed (Babe, 1994). This inability is caused by the impossibility of quantifying the economic value of informational content, which obstructs economic modeling and is, thus, excluded from the economist's mind. That is, it is true that information is increasingly commoditized into tradable objects such as books, software, mp3-files, or screens full of bits. However, their price is based on the technology to store, distribute and transmit these objects rather than on the informational value for their users. *Ceteris paribus*, a book that results in a major breakthrough in one's intellectual development has the same price as the one that was bought but never read. Moreover, the same book can be highly valuable for one reader, but worthless for another. Put differently, information's value is fully dependent upon the meanings people attach to that information and to the contexts they live in. That makes information subjective rather than objective and heterogeneous instead of homogeneous, implying that there is no fixed relationship between economic value and informational content. When a one-to-one relationship between value and informational content is missing, it is impossible to set equilibrium prices. And without equilibrium prices, the entire neoclassical edifice collapses.

Economics' Strongest and Weakest Quality

In summary, highlighting economic value to be successful in competitive environments is arguably both the strongest and the weakest quality of economics and the market metaphor. It determines their attractiveness for organizations and societies as well as their most fundamental shortcoming. The attractiveness of economics comes from its consistent view of the world resulting in nonconflictive expectations and clear *how to* implications for organizational practice. Missing a measuring standard, however, the main shortcoming of economics is that the effects of information upon people's perceptions, values, cognitive schemas or relationships are beyond its reach. Informational content defies valuation, quantification and commoditization, as opposed to the information objects carrying this content. The easy response of information management would be to concentrate on the information or knowledge supply side where this shortcoming is least felt, and ignore the demand side. As noted previously, that is exactly what often happens in and with information management, in theory and in practice. Framing it this way, however, robs information management of half of its potential identity.

The Future of Objectivism

The objectivist-economic view on information, knowledge and communication can be traced back to the times when modern bureaucracies — nation states and corporations — were erected. Faced with more complex entities to govern and control, the politicians, administrators and managers of the day increasingly needed *statistics* (Capurro & Hjorland, 2003), abstracted information visualized in the form of objectified reports, graphs, charts and models. As a result, the premodern notion of information as *in-formation* giving form or shape to the human mind was gradually being replaced by information as *structured data* (Boland, 1987) representing intangible realities too large to be directly experienced by people's senses. Information became an objective object, separated from human experiences and minds. Arguably the most profound implication of bureaucratization is that decisions of *life and death* (Douglas, 1986) are made on the basis of such disembodied information. Nowadays enabled by ICT, our lives are increasingly subjected to objectification — as civilians, patients, customers, employees and so on — on which basis institutional decisions are taken for us. In *this* sense, ICT helps to connect, but also to disconnect.

In current times, the objectification of information and knowledge is gaining even more significance, mainly due to marketization, globalization and digitization to which it is recursively related. Exemplary in this regard is the inclusion of all kinds of knowledge products into the framework of the World Trade Organization through the General Agreement on Trade in Services. Induced by the logic of objectification, the idea behind this legally binding agreement is that knowledge is a *commodity like any other product*, which should be traded freely around the world while protecting the intellectual property rights of their owners. Ideas and knowledge are increasingly seen as if they are tradable objects, the effects of which are spread globally by modern communication.

Another consequence of the economic transformations mentioned is that human interaction and communication become more transaction-based. "The culture of the new capitalism is attuned to singular events, one-off transactions, interventions" (Sennett, 2007, p. 178). The growing importance of bonuses for specific accomplishments in the remuneration policy for top managers perfectly reflects this trend. The same policy applies to their most important advisors such as merchant bankers assisting in mergers and takeovers and to lower echelons of managers. Consequently, the view that organizations are long-term cooperations between capital, labor and management is increasingly being substituted by a short-term perspective stressing shareholder value.

Another example of the shift toward a more transaction-based culture is the emergence of *network sociality* (Wittel, 2001). Due to the new economic conditions, working practices are increasingly typified by a high degree of specialization, rapid knowledge development, short-term projects, relentless changes caused by sequences of mergers and acquisitions and decreasing job security resulting from disappearing lifetime employment. In such situations where flexibility is needed (Beck, 1992), people organize themselves in ever-broader, ICT-mediated networks that are characterized by fleeting forms of cooperation, weak social ties and the exchange of ephemeral information to keep abreast of new developments. Network sociality stands for the commoditization of social relationships that arises from viewing *the other* predominantly as a social capital tool to enhance one's own personal market value.

So, the future of objectivism looks bright. Despite its shortcomings, it remains helpful in explaining and guiding real-world phenomena. The many concerns of global economic developments expressed in academic literature, popular press and daily newspapers, however, put the future of objectivism in a controversial perspective. Objectivity can promote fairness and impartiality in human relationships, because it makes us less dependent on the whims of subjectivity. The chapter by Choo (2007) in this book illustrates how information management can help reduce such subjectivity in organizations.

Objectivist approaches, however, can also be unfair, inhuman and dangerous (Lakoff & Johnson, 1980). Core to the current economic transformations is that ever larger parts of our private and organizational lives get objectified, stored in databases, and managed as such. Think of search engines commoditizing our search profiles or of customer relationship management systems. Objectivist practices can become unfair, inhuman and dangerous when such objectifications are taken as objective, nonnegotiable truths rather than what they truly are — incomplete and sometimes inaccurate representations of reality. Objectivism is focused on the *external* world in order to better understand how to operate successfully in the environment, an aspiration also commendable for information management. Emphasizing impersonal relations of cause and effect, however, this philosophical tradition neglects the *internal* aspects of how people understand and subsequently shape their lives. In that sense, objectivism and information management that is solely based upon this world view can result in losing touch with reality.

Discussion and Conclusions: A Sound Foundation?

So far I have illustrated how deeply information management has been influenced by objectivism and economics, in theory and practice. Both will keep on exerting their influence, also because university curricula throughout the world sustain the objectivist images of information and knowledge. Nevertheless, the question begs to be posed: Does objectivism provide a sound and solid basis for information management? The answer to this question depends upon which of the four economic images of information and knowledge we are observing: (1) as free goods, (2) as other tangible, physical goods, (3) as idiosyncratic products and (4) as idiosyncratic resources or assets.

Information and Knowledge as Free Goods and as Tangible Products

In neoclassical economics, information and knowledge are viewed as *free goods* or as any other *tangible product*. The model of the perfect market has been constructed for the industrial age with the primary intention to theorize the transaction of tangible, physical products. There was no need to model information and knowledge as objects of exchange in their own right, simply because information products as we know them today hardly existed. Instead, economists saw information and knowledge as means merely supportive of the exchange of physical goods. Being *only* supportive of exchange, information and knowledge could be assumed to be free goods, which miraculously given, are unconstrained and nonproblematic resources that can be justifiably excluded from economic analysis. Treating information and knowledge alternatively as any other physical product served the same purpose. By denying information and knowledge, a distinctive character and role in economic processes, the price could be assumed to contain all the information economic agents need to know to efficiently coordinate their transactions. In this way, information and knowledge could be discarded without the model of the perfect market losing any of its explanatory power.

These two neoclassical views on information and knowledge lead to a paradoxical situation for information management — by having itself influenced so much by neoclassical economics, its identity is based upon a well-established theory that either denies its economic contribution or sees information management as *business as usual* not requiring any special attention. When information and knowledge are perceived as free goods, the harsh verdict is that information management cannot add any economic value. Free goods are economically insignificant. And when information and knowledge are regarded as equal to physical products, organizations can do without a specialized information management function. In both cases, the economic value of information, ICT and information management is hard to substantiate and verify, which could explain why so many organizations pursue the trend of outsourcing. Furthermore, should one be tempted to do so, the view on information-as-free-good cannot be easily put aside as irrelevant for information management. As many organizations experience, when present on the internet for instance, information seekers are often not prepared to pay for their information or information services. Information-as-free-good explains the sometimes frantic search for alternative business models.

These economic judgments of information management can be contradicted by questioning their underlying assumptions. If all information needed for decision making would be included in the price, nobody would be willing to invest in the gathering, production and communication of information. A simple observation in the real world, however, is that people, organizations and societies do spend time, energy and money on these informational activities. Moreover, other than in the industrial age, many digital information products such as mp3-files, for example, exist that are sold on markets. Finally, information and knowledge are increasingly seen as the main sources of wealth creation and competitive edge for individuals, organizations and societies.

Consequently, economists have created two new images of information and knowledge that better resemble the real world: information and knowledge as idiosyncratic products and as idiosyncratic resources or assets.

Information and Knowledge as Idiosyncratic Products and Idiosyncratic Resources or Assets

Both views of information and knowledge entail focusing intellectually on the inherent and idiosyncratic properties of information and knowledge that make them behave differently in an economic sense. Deep expert knowledge of those inherent properties and their implications for practice could provide a sound basis for information management's identity.

However, these relatively new views on information and knowledge also present information management with idiosyncratic problems. As to the view of information-as-idiosyncratic-product, so-called *information economists* (Shapiro & Varian, 1999) have not succeeded yet in quantifying the informational content of these products. Instead, pricing such products is based upon the technology to store, distribute and convey information objects. A more appropriate name for this branch of economics would therefore be *information technology economics*. Nevertheless, information economics deserves to be included in information management's curriculum. It deals with a part of the digital world that is not captured by other academic disciplines.

In the last economic view, information and knowledge are seen as idiosyncratic resources or assets capable of generating wealth in their own right. Building upon, among others, the knowledge-based view of the firm (Boisot, 1998), the practical implications of the economic differences with physical assets are considered to be so profound that knowledge-intensive organizations need a new theoretical perspective. This assertion is confirmed by Maes (2007, Chapter 2 in this book) who states that the core of information management is shifting from information systems and technology to the management of information as a business resource. With information and knowledge as the heart of business, the potential value added of information management would become instantly clear.

Nonetheless, the resource view on information and knowledge is not without its own intellectual challenges. Calling information and knowledge a resource or asset symbolically transforms these entities into objects, which biases our understandings of what information and knowledge are and what we can do with them. Due to limited space, I cannot address other recent developments in economics, such as defining information as uncertainty reduction, but that does not change the bottom line: economic reasoning is *always* imbued by the logic of objectification. As a result of this engraved drive to objectify, three core problems arise that relate to objectivism in general and, thus, to all four economic views on information and knowledge.

Three Core Problems

The first core problem of objectivist economics is that dynamic *processes* are beyond the analytical reach of economics because they do not demand an exclusive focus on the exchange of static objects and they are not required to conform to rigorous quantification requirements. To fit economics' modeling capabilities, information and knowledge *simply* have to be reduced to that which can be codified and commoditized, complex human communication and interaction to discrete, one-off transactions, and learning to the passive consumption of factual representations. As a result, economics is helpful in clarifying that knowledge needs to be codified in tradable objects to extract and protect its economic value. It is, however, not helpful in gaining understanding of how people and organizations use and create information and knowledge to shape their everyday life (Kakihara & Sørensen, 2002). Moreover, economics contributes to an artificial and confusing divide between information supply and demand, stressing the first and largely ignoring the latter. Could this divide help explain that so many of us seem to believe that once information has been delivered, it has also been consumed?

Secondly, the emphasis in objectivism on discovering universal truths precludes *context* as a factor important to economics. Once again, information poses insurmountable problems. Economic, not sociological, reasoning is as follows (Babe, 1994). When all suppliers charge the same price for the same good, the price is less informative for buyers than when it is sold at different prices. Hence, the value or meaning of information, here the price, is context-dependent, much to the dismay of mainstream economists.

Thirdly, truth and meanings are relative not only to context, but also to people's mental frameworks or conceptual systems of how the world works. For both reasons, human beings cannot act differently than to impute their own meanings to information. Hence, it is also possible that different people attach divergent *interpretations* to the same information or that the same person interprets the same information differently when faced with a different context. Economists cannot deal with such divergent sense making behavior. Information is supposed to help bring supply and demand together in an equilibrium price. For information to have such equilibrating effects, however, all economic agents have to interpret it in the same direction (Boisot, 1998). *Without* this crucial assumption, information would become an unpredictable phenomenon that cannot be analyzed or even observed *a priori*, which would cause the neoclassical edifice to fall apart. *With* this assumption, however, economists exclude a major source of learning and innovation. Once again, relevance is sacrificed for rigor.

Conclusions

In summary, no matter how much progress has been made ever since, Stigler's (1961) remark still applies: "[Information] occupies a slum dwelling in the town of economics" (in Babe, 1994, p. 49). One conclusion is that the so-called information or knowledge economy still misses one of its critical cornerstones — an economic theory of information, knowledge and learning. Another — ironic — conclusion is that information management with its choice for objectivism and microeconomics as its foundation has precisely selected a philosophy and theory that are incapable of justifying and grounding the very heart of its existence: information. This conclusion also means that an integrative approach to information management should entail more or something different than "the management of information as a business resource" (Maes, 2007). In the next chapter, I will look for inspiration in subjectivist theories that seek their contribution in the problems objectivism and economics cannot solve.

References

Babe, R. E. (1994). The place of information in economics. In: R. E. Babe (Ed.), *Information and communication in economics* (pp. 41–67). Boston: Kluwer Academic Publishers.

Beck, U. (1992). *Risk society*. London: Sage Publications.

Boisot, M. H. (1998). *Knowledge assets: Securing competitive advantage in the information economy*. Oxford: Oxford University Press.

Boland, R. J. (1987). The in-formation of information systems. In: R. J. Boland & R. A. Hirschheim (Eds.), *Critical issues in information systems research*, Wiley, pp. 363–379.

Bonifacio, M., Camussone, P., & Zini, C. (2004). Managing the KM trade-off: Knowledge centralization versus distribution. *Journal of Universal Computer Science, 10*(3), 162–175.

Bryant, A. (2007). Information and the CIO, this book.

Capurro, R., & Hjorland, B. (2003). The concept of information. In: B. Cronin (Ed.), *Annual Review of Information Science and Technology* (Vol. 37, pp. 343–411). Medford, New Jersey: American Society for Information Science and Technology and Information Today.

Choo, C. W. (2007). *Social use of information in organizational groups*, this book.

Davenport, T. H., & Prusak, L. (1998). *Working knowledge*. Boston: Harvard Business School Press.

Douglas, M. (1986). *How institutions think*. London: Routledge.

Gurbaxani, V., & Whang, S. (1991). The impact of information systems on organizations and markets. *Communications of the ACM, 34*(1), 59–73.

Hayek, F. A. (1945). The use of knowledge in society. *American Economic Review, 35*(4), 519–530.

Kakihara, M., & Sørensen, C. (2002). Exploring knowledge emergence: From chaos to organizational knowledge. *Journal of Global Information Technology Management, 5*(33), 48–66.

Lakoff, G., & Johnson, M. (1980). *Metaphors we live by*. Chicago: The University of Chicago Press.

Maes, R. (2007). *An integrative perspective on information management*, this book.

Sennett, R. (2007). *The culture of the new capitalism*. New Haven: Yale University Press.

Shapiro, C., & Varian, H. R. (1999). *Information rules — a strategic guide to the network economy*. Boston: Harvard Business School Press.

Stewart, T. A. (1998). *Intellectual capital: The new wealth of organizations*. London: Nicholas Brealey.

Stigler, G. J. (1961). The economics of information. *Journal of Political Economics, 69*, 213–225.

Stigler, G. J. (1988). *Memoirs of an unregulated economist*. New York: Basic Books.

Wilson, T. D. (1997). *Information management: International encyclopaedia of information and library science*. London: Routledge.

Wittel, A. (2001). Toward a network sociality. *Theory, Culture & Society, 18*, 51–76.

Woolsey Biggart, N., & Delbridge, R. (2004). Systems of exchange. *The Academy of Management Review, 29*(1), 28–49.

Chapter 7

The Value of a Rose: Rising Above Objectivism and Subjectivism

Ard Huizing

ABSTRACT

After my conclusion in the previous chapter that objectivism does not provide a firm theoretical foundation for information management, the question probed in this chapter is whether or not subjectivism can offer a convincing alternative basis. Ultimately, the answer is negative because subjectivists rarely specifically pay attention to what is the bottom line for private and, increasingly, public organizations: the realization of economic value. Hence, there is no other way than to combine objectivism and subjectivism into a comprehensive, integrative approach to information management. However, as illustrated in this chapter, the differences between both philosophical strands of thought are fundamental. In recent years, advocates of subjectivism and practice-based social theory as one of its main applications have taken a giant leap forward in transcending the split between the object and the subject by suggesting that we should focus our attention on social practices and object-centered sociality. Following their suggestion, I demonstrate what subjectivist, practice-based information management could be, which includes a new definition for our discipline. However, due to the neglect of economics in subjectivism, the divide between objectivism and subjectivism still exists. At the end of the chapter, therefore, I present the concept of 'figure' and 'ground' from Gestalt psychology as a metaphorical aid for all of us to rise above this unproductive divide.

A Story

The noble game of cricket is played across the globe. Originated in the United Kingdom, British expatriates exported their cricket knowledge, partly implicit and partly codified in manuals and regulations, to countries such as India and Pakistan. As we now have the world championships of cricket, the knowledge transfer must

Information Management: Setting the Scene
Copyright © 2007 by Elsevier Ltd.
ISBN: 978-0-08-046326-1

have been successful. However, the new knowledge was respected in all countries — but Papua. Trobiand Papuas do play cricket, but have enacted the game in a unique way to make it their own. They have, for instance, abolished the dangerous habit of games needing winners and losers. With a history of headhunting and cannibalism, new conflicts arising over something as silly as a game need to be avoided. Defensive batting is not appreciated as that would slow down the play and to make the game even more entertaining, each score is celebrated with a ritual dance. And one of the locals, dressed as a Western tourist and armed with wooden field glasses, is the mascot of both teams, presumably to mock the British inventor.

The point of this Papua story is that people interpret information to make sense of their worlds and adapt it to local circumstances. Codification can be helpful in 'transferring' knowledge, but people still impute their meanings on information. Searching for universal laws, objectivism cannot deal with human sense making, the possibility of interpretation differences among people, and context as the interpretative lens through which experiences are read. Subjectivism is built upon these notions.

Introduction

Subjectivism is the philosophical tradition that has emerged in the twentieth century out of dissatisfaction with objectivism generally playing such a pervasive role in scientific theory. I use subjectivism as an umbrella term for all of those schools of thought and theories that depart from the idea that for knowledge development, we should focus on human beings and see them as acting on the world through sense making, and in that way modifying the context they live in. It is not my ambition to give a complete overview of subjectivist theories; that is a task too daunting. With the intention to present a number of basic subjectivist understandings and relate these to information management, I will instead follow the same approach as in the previous chapter. As I used the neoclassical model of the perfect market to demonstrate the close relationship between objectivism and information management, I will now discuss so-called practice-based approaches to organizational phenomena as they have been developed in contemporary sociology and anthropology to illustrate what subjectivist information management could comprise. I consider neoclassical micro-economics and practice-based social theory to be representative applications of objectivism and subjectivism, respectively, shedding insightful light on both thought worlds.

Developed in hermeneutics, phenomenology, interpretative sociology and critical theory, subjectivism has particularly gained significance in sciences such as sociology, anthropology, psychology and semiotics. Subjectivism can also be found in the management and organization literatures, for instance, in cognitive theories of organizations or social theories of organizational learning (Bonifacio, Camussone, & Zini, 2004). This is not to say that subjectivism has become the dominant strand of thought in many sciences. Rather, it is often taken as a respected alternative to objectivist thinking, which is also the case in the information and knowledge management literatures that, as discussed in the previous chapter, are governed by objectivism. There is, however, a growing awareness that information and knowledge are social phenomena rather than economic objects.

No matter how obvious this may sound, the philosophical differences between objectivism and subjectivism have profound implications for every item mentioned in Table 7.1 that summarizes this chapter in the same way as the table in the previous chapter. Both tables are provided to assist readers in recognizing objectivism and subjectivism, in their own organizations and within themselves. As can be seen from both tables, the differences between both philosophical traditions are fundamental. Comparing it with objectivism, subjectivism entails redefining the core concepts of information management, a new set of underlying assumptions, a reformulation of its domain, rationale, goal and definition and a different perspective on management and organization. Subjectivism is a different world view, indeed.

What is Subjectivism?

As a philosophical tradition opposing objectivism, subjectivism stands for "supplying an alternative account in which human experience and understanding instead of objective truth" occupies central stage (Lakoff & Johnson, 1980, p. x). In objectivism, human behavior is the result of forces acting out in the external world that people cannot control and find difficult to comprehend. The motivating concern of objectivism is therefore to provide people with law-like, rational knowledge that will help them function successfully in the external world. Whereas objectivism is directed toward the external aspects of understanding, its internal aspects are the primary domain of subjectivism.

What motivates subjectivism is the awareness that understanding, truth and meaning are relative to the cultural and physical context people live in as well as to their mental frameworks of how the world functions (Putnam, 1983). When contexts and people's mental conceptions seriously conflict with each other, there can be no objective, universally valid understandings, truths and meanings. On the other hand, understanding, truth and meaning are not strictly personal either. When meaning would be entirely private, each individual understanding could be called a truth. In this case of extreme subjectivity, human sense making would be totally unconstrained. The imaginative sky would be the limit.

The above-mentioned story of the Trobiand Papuas illustrates that the objectivist and extreme subjectivist views are both inadequate, at least for those aspects of reality that are related to human agency, such as information management. The meaning the Papuas have given to cricket is neither objective nor personal, but *intersubjective*. They have jointly made sense of the foreign game, which is now common knowledge. In their context, in their social practice, this common knowledge is true. The locality of this truth prevents them from participating in the world championships, but presumably they could not care less. Intersubjectivity is relevant to every form of organization, as it enables collective action in organizational

Table 7.1: Pinpointing subjectivism.

Subjectivism's constructing interaction

Definitions
1. Information is a difference that makes a difference *to* a hearer or reader.
2. Knowledge is a set of distinctive evaluations.
3. Learning is constructing new truths, understandings and meanings to guide action that results from actively participating in social practices.
4. Communication is a symbolic process of producing, maintaining, repairing and transforming reality.

Information (and knowledge) management
1. The *domain* of information (knowledge) management is sociality-centered-around-informational-objects
2. The *rationale* of information (knowledge) management is the need to understand why people gather around informational objects.
3. The *goal* of information (knowledge) management is (better) supporting processes of communication, interaction, knowing and learning.
4. Information (knowledge) management is the theory and practice of shaping informational object-centered sociality while directing people's interaction toward organizational or societal goals.

Organizing principles
1. Organize for what people engaged in social practices actually do.
2. Support actual internal and external information behavior.
3. Support the actual ways in which people organize themselves.
4. Support multiple realities.

Core assumptions in subjectivism
1. Human behavior determines and is determined by the external world; people are part of the world.
2. Understanding, truth and meaning are relative to people's context and their mental frameworks.
3. Understanding, truth and meaning come from interaction with the environment and with other people.
4. Understanding, truth and meaning are intersubjective.
5. Meaning is always meaning to someone.
6. Intersubjectivity is relevant to every form of organization, as it enables collective action.
7. Truth and true knowledge are dependent on understanding.
8. Understanding is dependent on what people find meaningful and significant.
9. What people find meaningful and significant is reliant on their imagination, intuitions, emotions, values, beliefs, experiences and ambitions, and their objective knowledge.
10. These aspects of understanding guide us in our private and organizational lives; we rely on them.
11. For developing relevant knowledge, we should focus on the internal and external aspects of understanding.

Table 7.1: *Continued*

Subjectivism's constructing interaction

12. People construct their relationships with objects, not the objects themselves.
13. Knowledge is developed by studying objects' interactional and inherent properties.
14. People are imaginatively and economically rational.

Additional assumptions in practice-based social theory
 1. Objects constrain and enable human behavior; human agency constrains and enables objects.
 2. Objects are contextualized tools for meaning, understanding and learning.
 3. Intersubjective meanings determine why, how and to what degree objects are used.
 4. Organizations are sets of varying social practices.
 5. Social practices transcend the divide between objectivism and subjectivism.
 6. Social practices consist of individuals embedded in those practices.
 7. For developing knowledge, we should focus on what people actually do in social practices.
 8. Focusing on social practices means seeing multiple realities.
 9. Science should give up the claim to universal truth; alternative research methodologies are needed.
10. ICT is not a neutral medium.

units — a department, a management team, a network of professionals — on the basis of locally shared experiences and understandings (Weick, 1995).

The Papua example furthermore illustrates that truth and true knowledge are always dependent on how people experientially understand their worlds, which is dependent on what people find meaningful and significant to their lives. In turn, what people find important is not solely reliant on their rational objectivist knowledge, but also on their imagination, intuitions, emotions, values, beliefs, experiences and ambitions. As any Papua could explain, we are not only objectively rational, as economists would have it, but also 'imaginatively rational' (Lakoff & Johnson, 1980). Sometimes we want something and 'go for it'. We imagine a dream and spend irresponsible amounts of time, energy and money pursuing it. And sometimes we do not share information with others simply because we do not like them, even if that impairs our reputation.

This imaginative rationality is elaborated in subjectivist literature by, for instance, relating ICT to hospitality (Ciborra, 2004), learning to identity (Wenger, 1998), information to power (Introna, 1997) and technological objects to sociality (Knorr-Cetina, 1997). In objectivism, these all too human aspects are silenced. In the objectivist search for economic rationality and disembodied truths, human beings are separated from the objects in their environment. The fundamental concern of subjectivism is to restore 'the balance' between the world of objects and subjects. We are part of the environment and as such, we change it and are changed by it.

Hence, in subjectivism, understanding, truth and meaning come from ongoing interaction with the physical environment and with other people. When developing knowledge relevant to practice, we should not focus so much on the inherent properties of objects, but rather on their *interactional* features (Lakoff & Johnson, 1980). Interactional properties are the intersubjective meanings given to objects that arise out people making sense of their world in situated processes of human communication and negotiation, reflecting what they believe is important to their private and organizational lives.

Returning to the example of roses (see the previous chapter), objectivist knowledge represents a rose by its inherent properties, the characteristics of a rose that are independent of any human observer, such as thorns. However, nobody gives roses to a loved one because they have thorns, but because they are mutually understood as tokens of love. When both giver and receiver attach that symbolic meaning to roses, the message comes across. Objectivists are right when they claim that objects exist in an objective reality independent of human will and thought. However, we do not construct objects themselves — a rose is still a rose — but our interactions with them (Tsoukas, 2005). Understanding, truth and meaning are therefore neither fixed nor entirely residing in objects, waiting to be 'conveyed' and 'extracted', but are dynamically and socially negotiated and constructed. Being a symbol of love is not an inherent property of roses, but an interactional property that has emerged from people's imagination. We learn to understand such meanings by engagingly interacting with the world. We learn by doing.

Constructing Interactions in Social Theory

Sociology is another science that has been plagued by objectivism dueling with subjectivism, both fighting over what should be taken as the basic domain of study: the object *or* the subject, structure *or* agency, social system *or* human conduct, the larger entity *or* the individual inhabiting that entity, whether that is the group, the organization or a technological infrastructure. In objectivist sociological theories such as functionalism and structuralism, the larger entity determines human behavior, whereas subjectivity, action and meaning are accorded primacy in, for example, subjectivist interpretative sociology. Both sides lived in parallel empires, seeing the other as the enemy.

In the last two decades, transcending objectivism and subjectivism into *duality* has been a pivotal theme in sociology (Bourdieu, 1977; Giddens, 1984), which has resulted in new social theories such as activity theory (Engeström, 1999) and actor-network theory (Latour, 2005). A duality is "a single conceptual unit that is formed by two inseparable and mutually constitutive elements whose inherent tension and complementarity give the concept richness and dynamism" (Wenger, 1998, p. 66). As a result, the larger entity — the organization or an information system, for example — is not seen anymore as merely putting constraints upon individual freedom and creativity, but also as providing harmony and coherence giving sense to potentially fragmented and dissenting human agency. Every organization or information system constrains *and* enables the behavior of its members and is, simultaneously, continually recreated and reshaped in and through the actions of its members. In short, the object and the subject co-constitute each other; they make each other possible.

Given that object and subject are mutually constitutive, we need to better understand how they interact with each other. How does an intranet (object) interact with its users (subjects)? How does a virtual world such as Second Life engage its millions of users to participate? Subjectivists suggest viewing objects as contextualized tools for meaning, understanding and learning. They try to unravel what it is that people find meaningful and significant when they are constructing their social practices around objects. Objects become 'affiliated objects' (Suchman, 2005), when they, for instance, help people build cohesiveness as a group and help create, sustain and value identity; when they stir people's imagination, creativity and, thus, enthusiasm; when they allow people to intersubjectively learn and develop situated knowledge by telling each other stories about their experiences; when they enable people to enact a part of the world, much in the same way as the Papuas have appropriated the cricket game.

All these affiliating processes turning 'cold', lifeless objects into social objects are captured in the notion of *sociality*: why do people shape their lives as they do and how is that shaping influenced by what they find meaningful and significant? Why do I share information with others and what precludes me from doing so? Knorr-Cetina (1997) has coined the term 'object-centered sociality' to indicate that people's lives increasingly occur around objects such as websites, games and social networking tools. The notion of sociality is helpful in explaining why they choose to do so and why some objects are more attractive than others.

Put differently, subjectivists do not perceive ICT and technology in general as neutral media that simply transfer objects from producers to consumers, as objectivists contend. On the one hand, technology is seen as providing and sometimes imposing a context that implicitly structures social practices by encoding how content should be interpreted, such as in ERP systems. On the other hand, technology adoption always entails negotiation among the various groups involved — managers, designers, users — in which process they all inscribe the technology with their own meanings, and 'finish the design' (Bijker, Hughes, & Pinch, 1987). Once again, the co-constitutive nature of objects (in this case technology) and subjects (all stakeholders in negotiation) is emphasized.

Subjectivist information management means understanding social practices and object-centered sociality. Creating an information management identity upon such understandings requires more than knowing objects' inherent properties, as objectivists tell us. Apart from, for instance, knowing what the inherent possibilities and impossibilities of technologies are — what technologies in and of themselves can and cannot do — information managers should be aware of their interactional features to learn how the intersubjective meanings people attach to objects determine why, how and to what degree these objects are actually used.

In contemporary sociology and practice-based social theory, focusing on *social practices* is seen as the way to rise above the traditional divide between objectivism and subjectivism. Social practices are structured spaces where individuals intersubjectively interact with the larger social enablers and constraints (Giddens, 1984). Each organization or department consists of many such practices. For example, my work at the university relates to research, teaching and administrative practices. All practitioners involved in such organizational practices intersubjectively create their own truths, understandings and meanings in relation to the entire organization as the constitutive structure. In its turn, the organizational perspective on reality is determined in negotiation among these practices in co-constitution with the larger environment.

Conceptual Implications: Communication, Information, Knowledge and Learning

After this brief introduction of subjectivism as a philosophical tradition and of practice-based social theory as an increasingly influential application of this tradition, the question rises what the implications of subjectivism are for information management. What is or could be subjectivist information management?

In the upcoming sections, I will first present subjectivist definitions for information management's core concepts communication, information, knowledge and learning. Illustrating the fundamental differences with objectivism, I will then draw some implications for (information) management and organization before continuing with subjectivist interpretations of the domain, rationale, goal and definition of information management.

Reflecting the ambition to theorize on dynamic individual and social processes, subjectivists prefer verbs, not nouns. They favor words such as understanding, sense making, informing, knowing and learning. In this way, they simultaneously differentiate themselves from objectivists and their static concepts as well as avoid the often mechanistic discussions about the nature and content of data, information and knowledge and their sequencing. There are however attempts to define these notions in such a way that both objectivist and subjectivist perspectives are accommodated (Bates, 2005). Likewise, the notions of 'information management' and 'knowledge management' are seldom used because subjectivists frequently protest against the implied views on information and knowledge-as-objects, and against the suggested implication that information and, in particular, knowledge can or should be managed. To be sure, the notions of information and knowledge management originated from objectivist minds. Moreover, thousands of years of philosophical debate have not resulted in clear, undisputed definitions of knowledge. On the contrary, epistemology or the science of 'how people come to know' is and has always been a respected branch of philosophy. With all of these deliberations in mind, I will nevertheless present definitions of information management's core concepts, not to hint at any definitive conclusions, but rather to illustrate what subjectivist information management is or could be.

Communication

In objectivism, communication consists of singular information exchanges between people maintaining anonymous relationships. Human interaction and communication are stripped down to what is considered its essence — the transaction of disembodied objects. In this 'informational' approach to communication, discrete objects are transferred from an active sender to a passive receiver, the conduit metaphor that is relevant *only* when the meaning of the words exchanged is fixed and not amenable to any human interpretation and sense making.

Subjectivists underline that truths, understandings and meanings are anything but fixed in real life, and are instead dependent on situated processes of human interaction and negotiation. People's mental frameworks, their unarticulated common knowledge and their context determine what is considered to be true, how they understand their contexts and which meanings are constructed, all co-constitutively related to the larger world.

As soon as words and language become intrinsically part of human sense making, implying that interpretation differences among people do occur, a broader and less linear perspective on communication and interaction is required. Subjectivism embraces the possibility of divergent sense-making behavior, seeing such divergences as inescapable facts of life. A subjectivist definition of communication and interaction that takes this possibility explicitly into account is: "a symbolic process whereby reality is produced, maintained, repaired and transformed" (Carey, 1989, p. 23). Communication and interaction are about generating intersubjective meanings, mutual understandings and non-anonymous, socially binding relationships. Meanings are not just exchanged, but intersubjectively constructed in interaction with the world, as the Trobiand Papuas have constructed the game of cricket. In their enactment of the British game, they have adapted it to what they believe is important to their lives, in their spatial–temporal context, expressing and reinforcing their group identity.

This broader view on communication negates the objectivist-economic inclination to artificially divide communication processes into information supply and demand. Moreover, it would be a fallacy to see the information supply side as the natural realm of objectivism and the information demand or use side as subjectivism's dominion. In meaningful communication, people constantly switch between asking and responding, making and giving sense, verbally and non-verbally. In this regard, mediating human communication by ICT or any other artifact *dis*connects us, feeding the impression that information supply and demand can be divided into divorced domains, and managed separately. Neither object nor subject can be isolated from reality, however, and both are interactionally bound to incessant, dynamic processes that call reality into being.

Furthermore, the subjectivist view on communication and interaction brings back into focus all those interactional properties that people attach to objects, which are unscrupulously assumed away in objectivism for purposes of economic rationality and quantification. As the earlier example suggests, the popularity of the virtual world Second Life cannot be explained solely by its inherent, technological features.

Arguably, its attractiveness is predominantly explained by having succeeded in turning technological objects into social, affiliative ones. People choose Second Life to become part of their lives for varied reasons and in that process, they constitute the technology and at the same time they are constituted by it.

Information

The emphasis by subjectivists on situated sense making and interpretation in relation to larger entities also affects their views on information. Information is typically defined as 'a difference that makes a difference' (Bateson, 1972), which always implies a difference *to* a hearer or reader. Many signals — data — reach us every day and those that pass our perceptual filters have to be interpreted to make sense to us. What surprises us in this sense-making process, in smaller or larger ways, is called information; it is the constructed 'difference' that in-forms us. Next, subjectivists emphasize that these same signals or data can be interpreted in multiple ways. People differ in their goals and ambitions, they have different mental frameworks of perception, sense making and evaluation, and they live in varying cultural, social and institutional contexts. Would Papuas also see roses as symbols of love? For all these reasons, divergent understandings might result from the same data. Even the same person might arrive at other meanings in other times or contexts.

This definition of information differentiates subjectivism from objectivism once again. Aiming at universal, objective truths, objectivists have excluded divergent sense-making behavior from their repertoire. Consequently, they cannot meaningfully distinguish between data, information and knowledge. From a supply-side perspective, a newspaper can be called a data, information or knowledge system. Knowledgeable journalists have crafted their articles, so why could not we say a newspaper is a knowledge system? From a demand-side view, such naming does not make any 'difference' and, hence, is not informative. The newspaper is still a newspaper and whether or not it 'makes a difference' can be left only to the discretion of the reader. Hence, it is impossible to predefine what the right information for the right person is and at what time and in which format that should be delivered, as is assumed in the objectivist definition of information management. We can provide people with 'structured data' (Boland, 1987); what they do with it can only be partly suggested by others. For the same reason, what information economists call information — everything that can be digitized (Shapiro & Varian, 1999) — subjectivists would describe as data.

Another difference between objectivism and subjectivism relates to the economic theory of uncertainty. In more recent developments in economics, information — data really — is defined as reduction in uncertainty (Babe, 1994). Here, information is attributed the role of increasing rationality in human decision making. If all information would be available, there would be no uncertainty anymore. However, people are usually not capable of processing all information required for rational decision making and are therefore boundedly rational at best (Simon, 1976). Furthermore, people are inclined to use information opportunistically (Williamson, 1975); they appropriate information in ways that suit their social practices (Putnam,

1983); they always ask for more information, and then not use it (Feldman & March, 1981); for justification purposes, they gather information after the decision has been made (Weick, 1995); the medium can affect the form and content of a message (Trevino, Daft, & Lengel, 1990); yes, even how people are dressed can be important to how they use information (Fiske, 1991). Information is a much more complex phenomenon than economists can handle.

Irrespective of an adequate subjectivist definition of information being available, it can finally be said that data are hardly problematized in the social sciences. There is an unsurpassed body of literature on the sociology of knowledge (Berger & Luckmann, 1966) that is not even remotely matched by a similar interest in data or information. As in economics, data are apparently assumed to be there, mysteriously pouring down from heaven. Therefore, not only should the gathering, acquiring, refining, storing, preserving and dissemination of data be considered part of information management's job (which is usually the case; see the previous chapter), but we should also be paying attention to the generation of data.

Knowledge and Learning

In objectivism, knowledge consists of representations abstracted from practice that are cognitively stored in human minds, while learning is perceived as absorbing objective information. The experiential knowledge manifest in social practices emerging from social interaction and negotiation, however, is fundamentally unlike the representational knowledge that we have of the world's objects. Saying that truth, understanding and meaning are intersubjectively constructed implies that knowledge not only resides in individual minds, but also in people's relationships. There is a reality beyond individuality, intersubjectively constructed.

Consequently, knowledge cannot be solely defined in terms of its individual, cognitive dimension. Economists' methodological individualism needs to be extended with a social, interactional dimension, a need subjectivists underline by using the word *knowing* instead of knowledge (Choo, 2006). In academic jargon, a pluralist epistemology is required which recognizes that individual knowledge is inextricably related to the social practices that are created and sustained in communities, networks and organizations. Individual knowledge obtains its significance only by knowing the habits, norms, values and dynamics of the context in which it is situated.

A typical definition of knowledge or knowing that fits these requirements is a 'set of distinctive evaluations', which is "a toolkit of distinctions the [...] actors have ready-to-hand to facilitate and shape their rational and agentic practice as they construct and reconstruct their context" (Spender & Scherer, 2007, p. 24). As a prerequisite for action, knowing enables us to distinguish good from bad, tasteful from distasteful, and all those other distinctions that inform our sense and decision making. It interactionally emerges from learning. A matching definition of learning is the construction of new truths, understandings and meanings to guide action (Berger & Luckmann, 1966) that results from actively participating in social practices (Wenger, 1998). Communication, interaction, knowing and learning 'in action' are the dynamic processes that generate and are generated by the social practices in which they occur.

These views of knowing and learning question the popular divide between tacit and explicit knowledge (Nonaka & Takeuchi, 1995). Once again, the artificial split between the supply and demand sides of information and knowledge generates confusion. Calling data in a database, groupware system or intranet explicit knowledge more than suggests that the tacit and explicit dimensions of knowledge can be isolated from and 'converted' into each other. Objectivists assume that knowledge can be fully captured in objects and that these objects have meaning in themselves. These assumptions can only lead to disappointments as to what can be realistically expected from technologies. Technologies do not construct meaning; they distribute data that patiently await human sense making, no more, no less. As intended by Polanyi (1966), the inventor of these notions, tacit and explicit knowledge mutually constitute each other. They can be conceptually distinguished, but never separated, neither in theory nor in practice.

In short, information and knowledge are human and social phenomena in subjectivism that cannot be separated from 'producers' and 'consumers'. Nonetheless, economists do have a point when they say that codification and objectification are needed for deriving economic value from information and knowledge. Information and knowledge are sometimes best seen as objects to be traded on markets. I will return to this point later in this chapter.

Organizational Implications: Practice-Based Organizing and Managing

The subjectivist definitions discussed above lead to very different answers about how communication, information, knowledge and learning could or should be organized and managed. Although subjectivists are much less specific and united in this regard, I see four main organizing principles at work.

First, compared with objectivism, subjectivism moves our attention away from the larger entity to the organization's social practices and the 'individuals-embedded-in-practice' (Tsoukas, 2005). Academics call this move the ontological shift. In objectivism, people are separated from the world because the environment is considered to consist of distinct objects that exist independently from human agency. As a result, objectivists prefer to talk about *the* organization, *the* business processes or *the* information architecture, and tend to underestimate the active role people play in making these objects work. In subjectivism, people *are* part of the world, immersed as they are in mutually constitutive social practices. Objects and subjects dynamically interact and make each other possible. What is an information system without its designers, managers and users? Transcending the divide between objects and subjects, the individual-engaged-in-practice should therefore be our focal point of attention. Information management can help support the communication and interaction processes through which these individuals generate their social practices and, in that way, their organizations and societies.

The second implication of subjectivism for theory and practice is methodological. On the basis of what knowledge do we ground our interventions in organizational practice? The deceivingly simple message of practice-based social theory is that we have to build our organizing knowledge on what people actually do when they realize social practices, rather than on theories abstracted from practice, such as the perfect market model discussed in the previous chapter. The bright mirror held in front of us is that without in-depth knowledge of social practices, we are unable to effectively manage such practices or to construct useful theory. Subjectivists invite information managers to have a look in the same bright mirror and focus on people's actual information behavior.

For studying actual information behavior, we need different methodologies from the ones which are applied in objectivist model-theoretic approaches or in top-down organizational policies and strategies that are based on such approaches. Ethnographic and participant observer methodologies are prime candidates because they allow us to gain rich understandings of 'organization as it happens' (Schatzki, 2006) and use the knowledge thus gained to better support social practices. Virtual ethnography is a recent development in research methodology that extends the traditional notion of context as being physical and local with the idea of connectivity between distributed people and systems (Hine, 2000).

The third implication of subjectivism for managing and organizing is that focusing on actual information behavior in social practices opens the door to the many other forms of interaction that people increasingly use to shape their information behavior, within or exceeding the boundaries of the organization they work for. Market-like exchange is not denied in subjectivism, but complemented with such other forms of organizing as 'intensional networks' (Nardi, Whittaker, & Schwarz, 2002), 'actor-networks' (Latour, 1996), 'networks of strong and weak ties' (Granovetter, 1973) and 'knots' (Engeström, Engeström, & Vähääho, 1999), to mention a few of the headings mentioned in literature. Examples are people flocking around the many social networking tools available such as del.icio.us. The implication for information management is that new balances have to be found between internal and external information systems in search of enhanced support for the organization's members. When it comes to their communication, interaction, knowing and learning behavior, the boundaries of organizations increasingly become artificial.

The last implication of practice-based social theory relates to the sharpest distinction between objectivism and subjectivism: do we see and pursue only one 'objective truth' or do we recognize and organize for multiple realities? For information management: do we only offer 'one size fits all' solutions or are we (also) much more fine-grained in our support of varying social practices? What do we do, so to speak, with the Papuas in our organization (and are we not all Papuas at times)? Organizing for 'one truth' goes hand in hand with, for example, the aspiration to apply ICT for standardizing and controlling business processes. The prime motivation is management control. However, as soon as we begin talking about constructing information to make sense, learn and make decisions (Choo, 2006), such standardization and control of meaning and understanding starts chafing. Subjectivists aim to support rather than control multiple realities, appreciating that we all need to construct intersubjective truths in negotiation with the larger structures we live and work in. And that is what subjectivist information management is all about — support.

Conceptual Implications: Information Management's Domain, Rationale, Goal and Definition

Summarizing this chapter so far, the following shifts in perspective differentiate objectivism from subjectivism:

– from transaction to interaction;
– from inherent properties to interactional properties;
– from information objects to information as a difference;
– from information exchange to communication;
– from knowledge to knowing;
– from learning as absorption to learning as construction;
– from the larger entity to social practices;
– from model-theoretic approaches to practice-based approaches;
– from the market to all forms of organizing;
– from one objective truth to multiple realities;
– from control to support.

All of these perspective shifts amount to a need to reformulate information management's domain, rationale, goal and definition. The *domain* of subjectivist, practice-based information management, I propose, is sociality-centered-around-informational-objects, whether the objects are databases, documents, intranets, websites, virtual games, archives, libraries, information infrastructures or any other informational object. Its identity is built upon knowledge of the inherent properties of objects — what these objects can and cannot do in and of themselves — and their interactional properties — the meanings people attach to these objects.

The *rationale* of subjectivist information management is that we need to understand what it is that people — managers, employees, designers, customers and so on — find meaningful and significant that makes them gather around such objects. Such illuminations are needed for information managers to aspire to the *goal* of (better) supporting processes of communication, interaction, knowing and learning through which people co-constitutively create their social practices around informational objects by providing them with facilitating technological and non-technological objects and assistance. In the next chapter, Choo (2007) demonstrates how information management can help organizational groups increase their intersubjective use of information in decision-making processes, making these processes less dependent on individual subjectivity.

Finally, as management always entails exerting directed influence toward chosen goals, information management can be *defined* as the theory and practice of shaping informational object-centered sociality while directing people's interactions toward organizational or societal goals. How this function of information management can be best organized — in separate departments or otherwise — is clearly highly relevant to practice, but cannot be dealt with in this chapter.

So, subjectivist information management goes beyond the rational, objectivist management of information objects, regardless of whether they are called commodities, resources or assets. It signifies processes of communication, interaction, knowing and learning, which relate to people constructing intersubjective truths, understandings and meanings, which in turn relate to what people find crucial to their organizational and private lives.

This definition of information management is so all-embracing that a word of modesty as to the manageability of these human social processes should be added. As systems of interpretation specifying what people should and should not do, organizations are 'organizers of information' (Douglas, 1986) that guide human sense making, whether that guidance is intentional or not (Moran & Ghoshal, 1999). Organizations are 'formative contexts' (Ciborra & Lanzara, 1994) that not only make sense, but also give sense (Weick, 1995). Nevertheless, human sense making flags constraints to management and organization. In a quest for identity (Wenger, 1998) and economy (Boisot, 1998), people participate in all kinds of social practices, both formal and informal, and create meanings for themselves, mediated or unmediated by their employer. Moreover, on any topic, many different meanings are dynamically produced worldwide and compete for acceptance. For both reasons, organizations can only *indirectly* affect the generation of meanings by facilitating processes of communication, interaction, knowing and learning and by providing a formative context in which the potential value of these processes can be realized. In this sense, information management cannot *manage* meaning; it can only help people construct intersubjective truth, understanding and meaning in relation to organizational goals, whether they are, for example, employees or customers visiting the organization's website.

Lastly, if subjectivist information management is defined as I have outlined, what then is subjectivist knowledge management? As with the case of objectivism, I do not see much difference between information management and knowledge management, but for a different reason. Mainstream economists cannot usefully distinguish between information and knowledge because sooner or later they will turn these rich concepts into disembodied objects in search of economic value. Subjectivists do distinguish information from knowledge in a meaningful way, but see information as but one means in the generation of knowledge and sociality. This distinction, however, does not make any difference for the nature and content of information or knowledge management. From a pragmatic point of view, information or knowledge managers are engaged in precisely the same line of work.

Discussion and Conclusion: Rising Above the Divide

In the previous chapter, I posed the question whether or not objectivism and economics provide an adequate foundation upon which information management could build its identity. My answer was negative, because objectivists are unable to satisfactorily incorporate realistic conceptions of communication, information, knowledge and learning into their rigorous models of the world. In this section, I first ask the same question with regard to subjectivism: have we found a convincing alternative foundation for information management? I then present the overall conclusion relating to information management and the divide between objectivism and subjectivism.

Likened to objectivism, subjectivism offers additional and often superior insights to information managers. It illustrates how human beings understand reality, including all of their limitations in this regard, and gives in-depth insights in the organizational dynamics involved. Moreover, it does not reduce objects to themselves, but sees them as contextualized tools for meaning, understanding and learning. To return to the title of this chapter: the rose is the object, its economic value is the price, but getting it from that one special person can be priceless. The *real* value of a rose is in people's interaction, neither in the rose itself nor in its price. It is in the symbolic meaning people imaginatively attach to objects. Economics cannot capture the gap between the symbolic and economic value of objects, although 'closing the gap' is precisely the dedication of one-to-one marketing, for example. Subjectivism includes this 'higher truth' (Lakoff & Johnson, 1980). Insight into this 'higher truth', in people's imaginative rationality can help information managers improve the use and design of informational objects.

However, subjectivism is not without its disadvantages. It lacks a single coherent framework and well-established paradigm such as, for instance, the model of the perfect market in microeconomics that could support organizations in organizing their information and knowledge. Instead, there are many heterogeneous and disconnected approaches, which are difficult to turn into reliable, actionable knowledge. Furthermore, subjectivist theories are often accused of a lack of theoretical rigor, are descriptive rather than prescriptive, are poor on practical implications, and are therefore more difficult to 'sell' to managers or politicians (Bonifacio et al., 2004).

Most importantly, however, subjectivists rarely specifically focus their attention on what is the bottom line for private and, increasingly, public organizations: the realization of economic value. As a result, they downplay that information and knowledge have to be codified and objectified to result in economic value. My conclusion is therefore that subjectivism also does not offer a sufficient basis for information managers, because economics is part and parcel of their organizational life. Even though subjectivism has recently taken a giant leap forward in transcending the Cartesian split between object and subject by emphasizing social practices and object-centered sociality, the inglorious divide still exists. How can we rise above it?

Regarded superficially, objectivism and subjectivism exist in opposition. They look like dueling rivals. Objectivism is geared toward the external aspects of human understanding and aims at supporting people with objective knowledge to operate successfully in the external world. Subjectivism is directed more toward the internal aspects of understanding and aspires to illuminate the irreducible complexity of the social processes involved. As a result, both perspectives miss the motivating concern of the other. Yet, both relate to how humans come to understand (Lakoff &

Figure 7.1: An ambiguous picture.

Johnson, 1980), so we would benefit if we could combine the two strands of thought, one way or the other.

Given that information management is governed by objectivism (see Chapter 6), I hold that for information management to increase the economic value it adds to the organizations in which it is embedded, it should paradoxically incorporate that line of thinking that largely ignores economics: subjectivism. For information management to become a discipline dealing with the capacity to combine and compromise objectivism and subjectivism, the dualism between these two philosophical traditions needs to be re-conceptualized into a duality, expressing that both traditions require, enable and enrich each other.

Figure 7.1 demonstrates what it means to see objectivism and subjectivism as a duality. What do you see first? A white vase on a black background or two faces on a white background?

This example illustrates the concept of 'figure' and 'ground', as it has been developed in Gestalt psychology (King, 2005). This concept implies that we are all inclined to foreground a dominant shape (figure) and relegate our other concerns to the background (the ground) when confronted with ambiguity.

I use this concept of foregrounding and backgrounding as a metaphor underlining that we all tend to favor one interpretation over the other. Some of us prefer objectivism and others subjectivism, and use this preference as the interpretative lens through which the world is selectively enacted. The figure–ground concept also accentuates, however, that the world is not objectively 'out there', but constructed while making sense of ambiguous situations. Finally, this concept indicates that the whole is more than the sum of its parts. Irrespective of what our preferences are, foregrounds cannot exist without backgrounds, and *vice versa*. They are mutually constitutive and should therefore never be separated.

Seeing objectivism and subjectivism in duality entails knowing that the value of both can be enhanced by combining them. It implies that the information manager knows when to foreground the one while holding the other in the background. In management meetings, for instance, objectivism might be foregrounded, whereas observing actual information behavior in social practices might be an occasion to foreground subjectivism. Whatever the occasion, however, integrative information management implies that the one should always inform the other.

Acknowledgments

I am greatly indebted to Wim Bouman, René Jansen and others in our extending nexus of practice around objectivism and subjectivism for their priceless support and friendship. Another thanks goes to Mary Cavanagh for bringing to my attention the figure–ground concept of Gestalt psychology and for all the other help she has so kindly offered me, also priceless.

References

Babe, R. E. (1994). The place of information in economics. In: R. E. Babe (Ed.), *Information and communication in economics* (pp. 41–67). Boston, MA: Kluwer Academic Publishers.

Bates, M. J. (2005). Information and knowledge: An evolutionary framework for information science. *Information Research*, 10(4); Paper 239 available at http://InformationR.net/ir/10-4/paper239.html

Bateson, G. (1972). *Steps to an ecology of mind: Collected essays in anthropology, psychiatry, evolution, and epistemology.* Chicago: University Of Chicago Press.

Berger, P. L., & Luckmann, T. (1966). *The social construction of reality: A treatise in the sociology of knowledge.* New York: Anchor Books.

Bijker, W. E., Hughes, T. P., & Pinch, T. (Eds.) (1987). *The social construction of technological systems: New directions in the sociology and history of technology.* Cambridge, MA: MIT Press.

Boisot, M. H. (1998). *Knowledge assets — securing competitive advantage in the information age.* Oxford: Oxford University Press.

Boland, R. J. (1987). The in-formation of information systems. In: R. J. Boland & R. A. Hirschheim (Eds.), *Critical issues in information systems research* (pp. 363–379). Chichester: John Wiley & Sons.

Bonifacio, M., Camussone, P., & Zini, C. (2004). Managing the KM trade-off: Knowledge centralization versus distribution. *Journal of Universal Computer Science*, 10(3), 162–175.

Bourdieu, P. (1977). *Outline of a theory of practice.* Cambridge: Cambridge University Press.

Carey, J. W. (1989). *Communication as culture: Essays on media and society.* Winchester, MA: Unwin Hyman.

Ciborra, C. U. (2004). *The labyrinths of information: Challenging the wisdom of systems.* Oxford: Oxford University Press.

Ciborra, C. U., & Lanzara, G. F. (1994). Formative contexts and information technology: Understanding the dynamics of innovation in organizations. *Accounting, Management and Information Technologies, 4*(2), 61–86.

Choo, C. W. (2006). *The knowing organization: How organizations use information to construct meaning, create knowledge, and make decisions.* Oxford: Oxford University Press.

Choo, C. W. (2007). Social use of information in organizational groups, this book.

Douglas, M. (1986). *How institutions think.* London: Routledge.

Engeström, Y. (1999). Activity theory and individual and social transformation. In: Y. Engeström, R. Miettinen & R. L. Punamaki (Eds.), *Perspectives on activity theory* (pp. 19–38). Cambridge: Cambridge University Press.

Engeström, Y., Engeström, R., & Vähääho, T. (1999). When the center doesn't hold: The importance of knotworking. In: S. Chaiklin, M. Hedegaard & U. Jensen (Eds.), *Activity theory and social practice: Cultural-historical approaches.* Aarhus, Denmark: Aarhus University Press.

Feldman, M. S., & March, J. G. (1981). Information in organizations as signal and symbol. *Administrative Science Quarterly, 26,* 171–186.

Fiske, J. (1991). *Introduction to communication studies* (2nd ed.). London: Routledge.

Giddens, A. (1984). *The constitution of society.* Cambridge: Polity Press.

Granovetter, M. (1973). The strength of weak ties. *American Journal of Sociology, 78,* 1360–1380.

Hine, C. (2000). *Virtual ethnography.* London: Sage Publications.

Introna, L. D. (1997). *Management, information and power.* London: Macmillan Press.

King, D. B. (2005). *Max Wertheimer & Gestalt theory.* New Brunswick, NJ: Transaction Publisher.

Knorr-Cetina, K. (1997). Sociality with objects: Social relations in postsocial knowledge societies. *Theory, Culture and Society, 14,* 1–30.

Lakoff, G., & Johnson, M. (1980). *Metaphors we live by.* Chicago, IL: University of Chicago Press.

Latour, B. (1996). *Aramis, or the love of technology.* Cambridge, MA: Harvard University Press.

Latour, B. (2005). *Reassembling the social: An introduction to actor-network theory.* Oxford: Oxford University Press.

Moran, P., & Ghoshal, S. (1999). Markets, firms, and the process of economic development. *Academy of Management Review, 24*(3), 390–412.

Nardi, B. A., Whittaker, S., & Schwarz, H. (2002). Networkers and their activity in intensional networks. *Computer Supported Cooperative Work, 11*(1/2), 205–242.

Nonaka, I., & Takeuchi, H. (1995). *The knowledge-creating company.* New York: Oxford University Press.

Polanyi, M. (1966). *The Tacit dimension.* London, UK: Routledge & Kegan Paul.

Putnam, L. L. (1983). The interpretative perspective: An alternative to functionalism. In: L. L. Putnam & M. E. Pacanowsky (Eds.), *Communication and organizations: An interpretative approach* (pp. 31–54). Beverly Hills, CA: Sage Publications.

Schatzki, T. R. (2006). On organizations as they happen. *Organization Studies, 27*(12), 1863–1873.

Shapiro, C., & Varian, H. R. (1999). *Information rules — a strategic guide to the network economy.* Boston, MA: Harvard Business School Press.

Simon, H. A. (1976). *Administrative behavior* (3rd ed.). New York: Free Press.

Spender, J. C., & Scherer, A. G. (2007). The philosophical foundations of knowledge management: Editor's introduction. *Organization, 14*(1), 5–28.

Suchman, L. (2005). Affiliative objects. *Organization, 12*(3), 379–399.

Trevino, L. K., Daft, R. L., & Lengel, R. H. (1990). Understanding managers' media choices: A symbolic interactionist perspective. In: J. Fulk & C. Steinfield (Eds.), *Organizations and communication technology*. Newbury Park, CA: Sage Publications.

Tsoukas, H. (2005). *Complex knowledge*. Oxford: Oxford University Press.

Weick, K. E. (1995). *Sensemaking in organizations*. Thousand Oaks, CA: Sage Publications.

Wenger, E. (1998). *Communities of practice — learning, meaning, and identity*. Cambridge: Cambridge University Press.

Williamson, O. E. (1975). *Markets and hierarchies: Analysis and antitrust implications*. New York: Free Press.

Chapter 8

Social Use of Information in Organizational Groups

Chun Wei Choo

ABSTRACT

Although group discussion is a vital part of organizational decision making, it is fraught with difficulties. Groups tend to focus their discussion on information that is common to most members at the expense of unique information known to few members. Groups often emphasize their initial point of view during discussion, leading the group to make more extreme decisions than what individual members would do on their own. Groups that are cohesive may strive for consensus to such a degree that they neglect information which threatens group unity. This chapter discusses information behaviors that affect a group's decision-making capacity, highlighting implications for information management.

Social Use of Information in Organizational Groups

We start from the premise that the goal of information management is to improve the use of information in organizations. We note that group discussions — whether in management teams or project groups — are an important means to clarify objectives, combine information and expertise, and select and commit to a course of action. Important as they are, group deliberations are fraught with difficulties. Groups tend to concentrate their discussion on information that is common to the group at the expense of unique but relevant information known to a single member. In the process of deliberation, groups often accentuate their initially dominant point of view, leading the group to make more extreme decisions than what individual members would do on their own. Highly cohesive groups may strive for unanimity and agreement to such an extent that they dismiss information that threatens group unity. This paper discusses these and other tendencies that can compromise a group's capacity to share and process information. We also highlight some suggestions, drawn from research, on how these difficulties might be mitigated.

Information Sharing and Use in Small Groups

Studies in social psychology and small group research over the past 40 years have uncovered how information is made to serve many social functions during group discussion and decision making. While this *social* use of information is a natural aspect of group interaction, there are a number of resultant tendencies that can impede the effective use of information. In this section, we look at how information is channeled and construed by group members for social ends:

- Information as hidden profile
- Information as cognitive influence
- Information as social credit
- Information as social comparison
- Information as concurrence seeking

Information as Hidden Profile

Organizations assume that task-oriented groups would perform better than individuals working alone because group members can share and combine their information and knowledge to arrive at more optimal decisions. Unfortunately research has determined otherwise. In a study that has influenced small group research for many years, Stasser and Titus (1985) found that groups tend to discuss and incorporate into their decisions information that is known to all members (shared) at the expense of information that is known to a single member (unshared). Thus, although we might expect group discussion to surface and use the relevant information possessed by all group members so as to arrive at a well-informed decision, this may not in fact happen (Stasser & Titus, 2003).

Research on group information sampling analyzed the performance of groups engaged in *hidden profile* tasks. A hidden profile exists when group members individually possess only part of the information required to reach an optimal decision or solve a problem confronting the group, so that the group needs to pool this information to make the optimal decision or to solve the problem. The profile, or complete problem representation, is initially hidden and emerges only after all decision-relevant information is incorporated into the group's information set.

In their study, Stasser and Titus (1985) simulated a political caucus by having group members read and discuss candidate descriptions that contained partial information biased against the most favorable candidate. Even though groups could have produced unbiased profiles of the candidates through discussion, they decided on the candidate initially preferred by many members rather than the most favorable candidate. By comparing members' recall of candidate attributes before and after discussion, the authors saw that discussion tended to perpetuate, not to correct, members' biased views of the candidates. Stasser and Titus (1985) proposed two explanations. First, group members' recall would be imperfect, especially when there is much information that can be sampled and when the meeting is lively. Second, members may feel that their main responsibility is to defend the alternative that seems best so they assume the role of advocates who introduce information selectively for discussion.

This research has implications for organizations that form groups to make important decisions based on the expectation that *'many heads are better than one'*. If information that is critical for making the optimal group decision is unshared (i.e., uniquely held by single members), then groups' inability to recall and discuss unshared information may result in suboptimal decisions. When group members cannot effectively pool their unique information, the quality of their decision making may be no better than that of individuals.

A related phenomenon is the *common knowledge effect* observed by Gigone and Hastie (1993) in their study of groups: "The influence of a particular item of information is directly and positively related to the number of group members who have knowledge of that item before the group discussion and judgment" (p. 960). They found that groups did not adjust their judgments to reflect unshared information that was pooled during group discussion. Instead, information during discussion served mainly as justification by members for their judgments, rather than as input into the judgment of the groups. Thus, "placing individuals in groups did not result in better judgments than would have been obtained by simply averaging together the judgments of the same individuals" (p. 973).

The difficulties of hidden profiles and the common knowledge effect may be exacerbated in, for example, IT project teams that are tasked with implementing interdepartmental or interorganizational information systems. Insofar as these teams are composed of members from disparate functional areas with knowledge unique to their domains, the sharing and integration of hidden but relevant information becomes a major challenge.

Information as Cognitive Influence
Kameda, Ohtsubo, and Takezawa (1997) analyzed decision-making groups as socio-cognitive networks, in which group members share not only social links, but also cognitive links in terms of shared information and arguments. A group member is then described as *cognitively central* when that person's knowledge is predominantly shared with other members (i.e., has many information links to others). On the other hand, a *cognitively peripheral* member knows mostly unique items (i.e., has few information links to others). Kameda et al. (1997) showed that cognitively central members were more influential and participated more during group discussions. They reasoned that cognitively central members can provide social validation for other members' knowledge most frequently in the group, and that, concurrently, their knowledge is confirmed by other members, leading to the perception of the cognitively central members' well-balanced knowledge or expertise in the focal task domain. In this way, social validation becomes a key to information use in a group; unshared information that cannot be validated socially is then underutilized in groups (p. 298).

Kameda et al. (1997) calculated a centrality score for each member based on the number of arguments that the member shared with others. More than 110 students at Hokkaido University were given a group decision task — to make a parole decision for two juvenile prisoners. Information about positive and negative traits of each prisoner was distributed and controlled. Participants then met in groups, each consisting of two majority members who endorsed one prisoner and one minority member who endorsed the other. The results showed that "members exerted stronger, more definite social influence on the final consensus when they were cognitively central than when they were peripheral in a group. ... cognitively central members acquire pivotal power in a group and can exert not-negligible influences on group consensus ... central members took a more active part in group discussion and were more resistant to other members' persuasion that were cognitively peripheral members" (pp. 304–306).

Cognitive centrality may be related to the idea that sharing unique information can carry some social risk. Conversely, communicating common information may be a method for a member to gain status in the group. By building a reputation as someone who is knowledgeable, a group member creates a socially secure place in the group. Indeed, Kameda et al. (1997) suggested that cognitively central people acquire a reputation as credible sources and, once this reputation is established, they risk less when they do communicate unique information.

Many decision-making committees are characterized by an uneven distribution of cognitive influence among members. For example, in a management committee that is deciding about IT deployment, we might see a majority of cognitively central business managers who share much common knowledge, and a minority of IT managers who are cognitively peripheral with their specialized knowledge. In such situations, group decisions may be subject to the effects of the imbalance of influence and information noted above.

Information as Social Credit
When groups discuss much information that is common to the group, members evaluate each other as more competent, knowledgeable, and credible than when they discuss much unshared information. Wittenbaum, Hubbell, and Zuckerman (1999) referred to this as a *mutual enhancement* effect: "Shared information validates members' knowledge and eases the interaction by helping members relate to one another. Those who communicate shared information receive positive evaluations from other members for doing so. Moreover, recipients of shared information feel better about their own task knowledge when another member mentions their information. Members who are positively reinforced (verbally or nonverbally) for communicating shared information may continue to do so because they enjoy the validation and encouragement from others. It may be this interactive validation process that fuels a group's tendency to repeat previously mentioned shared information. That is, members may prefer to mention and repeat the kind of information that other members encourage and view as important" (p. 977).

Wittenbaum et al. (1999) asked participants to review resumés of two job candidates and then list ten pieces of information about them that they would share with a partner. In return, each participant received a list containing mostly shared information or mostly unshared information from an imaginary partner. Participants who communicated much shared information were perceived (by their partners and by themselves) as being more knowledgeable, task competent, and credible. Wittenbaum et al. (1999) suggested that "when group members communicate much shared information, all members may experience a collective high — judging themselves and other members as quite capable" (p. 974). Focusing on common information leads to mutual enhancement: introducing and receiving common information establishes one's competency and credibility. Significantly, this mutual enhancement was not due to the perceived opinion similarity or liking between participants and partners: it was due to "the validating role of the information rather than validation of opinions or liking" (p. 974). The effect may be more pronounced in new groups when unacquainted members discuss common information in order to put each other at ease, and to establish credibility and expertise.

In summary, mutual enhancement may be an important reason why groups focus discussion on shared information. If a member mentions shared information, others will positively value the communicator and themselves. Members who communicate shared information are positively reinforced for doing so, and members who communicate unshared information are negatively reinforced. The warm reception to communicated shared information may encourage members to repeat or communicate more shared information of a similar nature. Wittenbaum and Park (2001) observed that "not only are groups inefficient in accessing their unshared information, but if members do communicate unshared information, they may be undervalued for doing so" (p. 71). The net result is that group members may bias their discussions toward information that all members know.

If we return to the management committee that is deciding about the use of IT, we might imagine a scenario where managers share, repeat, and embellish the idea that *IT doesn't matter*, based perhaps on a reading of the popular article and book with that title. Influenced by this mutual enhancement of their common knowledge, the committee might be predisposed to underestimate the strategic significance of IT. Avison, Gregor, and Wilson (2006) analyzed three major IT failures in Australia (in a utility company, university, and telecommunications startup) and concluded that it was shared managerial indifference about IT that contributed to the complacency and poor governance which scuttled the IT projects.

Research Study at the Center for Creative Leadership
The effects of common knowledge, cognitive influence, and mutual enhancement were discovered in laboratory experiments. Recently, a study of senior executives at the Center for Creative Leadership (CCL) in Colorado found evidence of the group tendencies we have discussed so far (Abele, Stasser, & Vaughan-Parsons, 2005). CCL offers top-level executives a course on leadership and decision-making styles. As part of the course, executives participated in a group decision exercise where they evaluated candidates for the presidency of a company's product division. Participants in 25 small groups were given information about the company and the candidates. They then met with their groups in a small room with video recording and observation facilities. They discussed the candidates, ranked them, and recorded strengths and weaknesses for each candidate as a group.

Results showed that individuals were more likely to mention an item when more group members knew it prior to discussion. Thus, the executive teams were more likely to refer to information that was widely shared and unlikely to refer to information that was sparsely sampled before discussion. Moreover, common information was more likely to be repeated once it was mentioned than was unique and partially shared information. Whether information was repeated during group discussion depended most directly on how many members had accessed the information before discussion. The study also found that members' cognitive centrality enhanced influence, so that members who shared more information links with others were more likely to get the group to adopt a solution that was close to their initial individual solution.

The researchers concluded that group discussions amplify common information and do not effectively pool unique information: whatever is commonly known before group discussion is intensified in the content of discussion, and the choice supported by what is commonly known will likely be the group's choice.

Abele et al. (2005) also noted that executives seemed to have selected information in a way that created common information that was socially valued. Executives subscribed implicitly to the belief that a certain set of information was important for making a hiring decision. There was a socially shared perspective that some types of information were more important or relevant for that decision. These *information norms* not only predicted whether an item was mentioned but also how many group members were likely to look it up. The normative use of information defined the socially accepted way of solving the task.

Information as Social Comparison
In addition to studies on how groups use their shared and unshared information, another body of research discovered that group discussion tends to enhance the initially dominant point of view — there is an accentuation of the initial average response of the group. A number of studies have observed that the average post-discussion response will tend to be more extreme in the same direction as the average of the pregroup responses (Myers & Lamm, 1976; Myers, 1982). Myers and others suggest that a fundamental social process combining informational influence and social comparison can explain this *group polarization.*

Informational influence happens when persuasive discussion arguments predominantly favor the initially preferred alternative, thereby enhancing it. Using *persuasive arguments theory*, Hinsz and Davis (1984) reasoned that group-induced shifts occur because certain persuasive arguments are not known initially by all members. During discussion these unshared arguments are introduced to those who have been unaware of them, and these novel arguments then persuade them to change their opinions on the issue. The persuasiveness of an argument depends on its validity (do members feel it is correct and accurate) and novelty (do members feel it is new and interesting). Myers (1982) also noted that spoken arguments tend to favor the socially preferred choice more predominantly than do privately processed arguments. Responding to other people in conversation elicits a more one-sided line of thought than does private contemplation of an issue (p. 143).

Social comparison arises because people are motivated to perceive and present themselves favorably, so that exposure to others' positions may stimulate them to adjust their responses in order to maintain a desirable image. During discussion, group members continually compare their opinions with others and adjust their opinions in the direction valued by others. An important mechanism that induces polarization is one-upmanship (Isenberg, 1986), where group members become aware of shared positions during discussion, and try to surpass each other by moving their positions in the socially desirable direction.

Persuasive arguments and social comparison can work together to induce group polarization in this way: persuasive arguments introduced or generated during group discussion cause members to move toward the collective position; this then gives rise to social comparison that causes people to move beyond the original collective position.

A behavior linked to polarization is *risky shift*, when group discussion leads members to prefer more risky decisions than they would if acting alone (Stoner, 1968). One explanation of this shift, again based on social comparison, is that during discussion we compare our decision with the decision of others. At the outset we may think of ourselves as being fairly risk taking, perhaps because this is considered a valued trait in Western societies. If, during group discussion, we realize that we are not particularly risk seeking compared to others, we then increase the level of risk of our decision when asked to remake the decision. The reverse cautious shift can occur in situations where caution rather than risk is the socially valued trait. When management teams are evaluating innovative but risky IT projects, it is possible to see how an unwarranted shift toward excessive risk avoidance or risk taking can bias the decision making.

Information as Consensus Seeking

Groupthink occurs when people working in highly cohesive groups strive for concurrence to such an extent that it undermines their ability to seek and use information, and to consider alternative explanations (Janis, 1982). This can result in complacency, shared misperceptions about self and others, and a failure to consider alternative interpretations of the available information. Groupthink was discovered by Irving Janis, who analyzed a number of major failures in US foreign policy decision making (Bay of Pigs invasion; escalation of Vietnam War; Watergate cover-up). In each case, decisions were made by a cohesive group of people who were smart, experienced, motivated, and respected for their expertise. Despite these qualities, the decisions they made led to disastrous outcomes. Janis (1982) attributed the errors to a tendency of members of cohesive groups to neglect, censor, or rationalize information in order to maintain group solidarity. He used the term *groupthink* to refer to "a mode of thinking that people engage in when they are deeply involved in a cohesive in-group, when the members' strivings for unanimity override their motivation to realistically appraise alternative courses of action" (p. 9).

There are three symptoms of groupthink. First, group members share a feeling of invulnerability, which leads to optimism and a willingness to take risks. Second, group members are close-minded, collectively rationalizing or discounting aberrant information, and maintaining stereotyped views of threats or rivals. Third, group members press toward uniformity, sustaining a shared impression of unanimity through self-censorship as well as direct pressure against dissenting views. As a result of these perceptions of invulnerability and solidarity, the group's seeking and use of information is compromised, and decision making becomes defective.

Specifically, members fail to survey alternatives and objectives adequately; do not examine risks of preferred choice or reappraise alternatives that were initially rejected; search for information poorly; process information in a biased, selective way; and do not make contingency plans (Janis, 1982). Groupthink is more likely when decision makers are members of a cohesive group, when organization structure insulates the group or lacks norms to require methodical procedures, and when the decision situation is highly stressful due to external and internal threats. Threats can cause the group to close ranks and rely on each other for social and emotional support, thereby heightening the desire to seek concurrence and consensus.

Recently, groupthink was identified as a major cause of the faulty intelligence assessment on *weapons of mass destruction* in Iraq. The US Senate Select Committee on Intelligence Report concluded that intelligence community personnel "demonstrated several aspects of groupthink: examining few alternatives, selective gathering of information, pressure to conform with the group or withhold criticism, and collective rationalization" (US Senate Select Committee on Intelligence, 2004, p. 18). Groupthink can be prevented. The same team of President Kennedy and his advisors that launched the disastrous Bay of Pigs invasion (a textbook example of groupthink) subsequently handled the 1962 Cuban Missile Crisis effectively, creating a model of crisis management.

Summary

In the Table 8.1 below, we summarize the various social roles that information can play during group deliberation, and how they can impede the pooling and collective use of information.

Table 8.1: The social roles of information.

Social roles of information	Research concepts	Group tendencies
Information as hidden profile	Hidden profiles, common knowledge effect	Groups discuss shared more than unshared information
Information as cognitive influence	Cognitively central and peripheral members	Cognitively central members are more influential
Information as social credit	Mutual enhancement, social validation	Group members socially validate each other's knowledge
Information as social comparison	Group polarization, shifts in decision choices	Groups accentuate their initially dominant point of view
Information as concurrence seeking	Groupthink, close-minded decision making	Groups discount information that threatens group cohesion

Under certain decision-making conditions, such as when discussion time is short, when deliberation is dominated by a few individuals, and when members engage in one-upmanship, these group information tendencies could reinforce each other, eroding the quality of the decision process even further.

Information Practices for Group Deliberation

Our discussion of the social dynamics of group information use can help us understand why effective decision making by organizational groups is so hard. What might be done to militate against some of these difficulties? Again we turn to research — from the information systems and social psychology disciplines — that has produced prescriptive implications. These implications fall into six areas: information access, use of group support systems (GSS), group diversity, expert roles, deliberation process and information norms.

Information Access

Studies have found that providing access to information during discussion can enhance group information processing. For example, Hollingshead (1996) observed that members who kept their information sheets during discussion mentioned more information than those who relied on memory. Wittenbaum, Hollingshead, and Botero (2004) reported that access to information during discussion did improve hidden profile solution when group members had information sheets that identified which pieces were shared and which were unshared. Furthermore, it may be helpful to provide group members with access to a database where accuracy of information can be checked, thereby reducing the social risk of introducing new information that other members might find to be inaccurate. Parks and Cowlin (1996) noticed that unique information was more likely to be mentioned in groups when databases of information were available during decision-making and could be used to confirm information. Mentioning and repeating unique information became less risky because there was an objective way of verifying the information.

Group Support Systems

A growing number of studies in the information systems field examine the effects of using computer-based GSS on the hidden profile problem and group polarization. Dennis (1996) studied groups working on a *hidden profile* task in which each participant received different information that they needed to combine to determine the optimal decision. Verbally interacting groups exchanged only a small portion of the available information and made poor decisions as a result. Groups interacting using a GSS exchanged about 50% more information, providing sufficient information to enable these groups to arrive at the optimal decision. Unfortunately, GSS groups did not actually process this information accurately — only one GSS group chose the optimal decision.

Lam and Schaubroeck (2000) compared a GSS with face-to-face group discussion on characteristics of information exchange and decision quality. Participants given conflicting information tended to share more of their unique data and argued more critically when using the GSS than when meeting face-to-face. However, when information was consistent among members, there were no such differences. The GSS groups also significantly outperformed the face-to-face groups in agreeing on the superior hidden profile option, especially when there was no prediscussion consensus.

El-Shinnawy and Vinze (1998) compared *group polarization* effects in over 30 groups of MBA and other students who met face-to-face and *via* a GSS to make decisions on two business problems (Intel's reaction to the Pentium chip problem, and its overall business strategy). When group members used a GSS, group polarization occurred to a significantly lesser degree than in face-to-face situations. In the GSS setting, members did not feel that they were being pressurized socially or being persuaded by dominant members, resulting in lower group polarization.

Somewhat differently, Sia, Tan, and Wei (2002) found that using a GSS was associated with *stronger* group polarization. They reasoned that in the GSS setting, anonymity or the removal of visual cues lowered social presence, encouraging group members to contribute more novel arguments and to display one-upmanship behavior, thereby increasing group polarization. When the identity of individuals was made known, group polarization was reduced in both settings.

The use of GSS continues to grow and evolve. As the technology becomes more flexible and as people become more sophisticated users, some of the negative effects seen in earlier studies may become less important. For now, we note the capacity of GSS to facilitate information access and retrieval, and to reduce social pressures and the social risk of sharing information.

Group Diversity

The relationship between group diversity and group performance is complex. Jehn, Northcraft, and Neale (1999) conducted a field study of 92 workgroups in one of the top three firms in the household goods moving industry. They analyzed the influence on workgroup performance of three types of diversity: demographic diversity (sex, age), value diversity (goals, beliefs), and *information diversity*, which refers to members' differences in knowledge and perspectives. Information diversity was found to be more likely to lead to improved performance when tasks were nonroutine: "For a team to be effective, members should have high information diversity and low value diversity. For a team to be efficient, members should have low value diversity. For a team to have high morale …, it should be composed of participants with low value diversity" (Jehn et al., 1999, p. 758). If people in a group do not like each other and spend their time in personal conflict, the group as a whole will perform badly. But when the underlying tasks are complex and call for a degree of creativity, dissenting views and a measure of conflict about how to perform those tasks lead to better outcomes. Among the various types of diversity, information diversity appears to be the most important variable.

Expert Roles

Stasser and Birchmeier (2003) suggested that one way to enhance the consideration of uncommon or unique information is to assign *expert roles* to group members. Research has generally found that groups are more likely to discuss unshared information and correctly solve a hidden profile when members are known experts. In laboratory groups, assigned expertise has increased the mentioning and repetition of unique information. Also, unshared information was better remembered by members after discussion in groups composed of experts rather than nonexperts. Assigning expert roles to group members can thus enhance the consideration of uncommon or unique information (Stasser & Birchmeier, 2003). Moreover, based on their study at the CCL, Abele et al. (2005) suggested that expert roles, and especially differentiated expert roles, may reduce the undesirable effects of cognitive centrality. If expert roles are emphasized during a discussion, and if experts are expected to contribute information that others do not have, then in terms of cognitive influence, experts are necessarily cognitively peripheral (because of their unique information). In such a setting cognitive centrality may not be an asset for promoting an individual's own position.

Deliberation Process
The quality of a group's deliberation is a function of the procedures that the group adopts to seek, evaluate, and process information. Davis (1992) argued that procedural routines shape how a group defines its task, how discussion is scheduled, how preferences are made known, and how a rule for arriving at a decision is selected and used. Hollingshead (1996) discovered that when face-to-face groups were asked to *rank order* the decision alternatives (three companies as potential investments), group members mentioned more information and solved a hidden profile problem better than groups who were asked to simply select one best alternative. With regard to avoiding groupthink, Janis (1982) and others have identified measures by analyzing the practices of effective decision groups. To reduce conformity tendencies, the group should create an environment that encourages the frank exchange of dissimilar views. The leader should be impartial and avoid stating preferences at the outset. To counter close mindedness, the group should actively seek information from outside experts, including those who can challenge the group's core views. The group could divide into multiple subgroups that work on the same problem with different assumptions. A member could play the role of a devil's advocate who looks out for missing information, doubtful assumptions, and flawed reasoning.

Information Norms
The cultural norms and values of the group can have a powerful effect on members' information behaviors. In one of the few studies to focus directly on group norms in decision making, Postmes, Spears, and Cihangir (2001) found that when groups have a norm of critical evaluation, they are more likely to solve correctly a hidden profile and to value positively unshared information compared to groups with a consensus norm. The content of group norms is an important factor influencing the quality of group decision processes and may also be related to the group's proneness for groupthink. In a series of case studies at a law firm, an engineering company, and a public health agency, Choo et al. (2006) found that strongly held information values related to sharing, proactiveness, integrity, and transparency accounted significantly for the variance in information use outcomes in the study organizations.

Table 8.2: Major impediments and prescriptive possibilities.

Social roles of information	Group tendencies	Prescriptive possibilities
Information as hidden profile	Groups discuss shared more than unshared information	• Provide information access before and during discussion	• Increase awareness of group information biases
Information as cognitive influence	Cognitively central members are more influential	• Assign or recognize expert roles	
Information as social credit	Group members socially validate each other's knowledge	• Increase group information diversity	• Create a rigorous but open information culture
Information as social comparison	Groups accentuate their initially dominant point of view	• Raise cognitive vigilance during deliberation	
Information as concurrence seeking	Groups discount information that threatens group cohesion	• Establish norms of critical evaluation, open sharing	• Introduce the use of group support systems

Implications for Information Management

Groups and group discussion remain an important means for organizations to identify goals, consult with interested parties, and gain commitment to a course of action. Group deliberation can also combine the information and expertise of members, but as this paper has tried to show, this information sharing is not automatic and is often problematic. We summarize the major impediments as well as prescriptive suggestions that research has identified in the Table 8.2 above.

The practical implications for information management might include the following:

- increase information and knowledge sharing before the start of group decision process, thus enlarging the pool of common information;
- make information more accessible (*easier to retrieve*) and more assessable (*easier to evaluate*) during group deliberation;
- differentiate expert roles based on group members' specialization and experience, so as to encourage the introduction and use of unique information;
- consider the distribution of information and influence among group members, identifying members who are cognitively central and peripheral;
- engender a safe and open information culture that promotes information sharing and use.

Acknowledgments

The author is grateful to Erik de Vries for reviewing the chapter, and offering helpful comments and suggestions. I also thank Ard Huizing for his generosity in sharing ideas and insights, and for his stimulating cognitive influence.

References

Abele, S., Stasser, G., & Vaughan-Parsons, S. (2005). *Information sharing and cognitive centrality*. Rotterdam, NL: Erasmus Research Institute of Management (ERIM), No. ERS-2005-037-ORG.

Avison, D., Gregor, S., & Wilson, D. (2006). Managerial IT unconsciousness. *Communications of the ACM, 49*(7), 89–93.

Choo, C. W., Furness, C., Paquette, S., van den Berg, H., Detlor, B., Bergeron, P. et al., (2006). Working with information: Information management and culture in a professional services organization. *Journal of Information Science, 32*(6), 491–510.

Davis, J. H. (1992). Some compelling intuitions about group consensus decisions, theoretical and empirical research, and interpersonal aggregation phenomena: Selected examples, 1950–1990. *Organizational Behavior and Human Decision Processes, 52*(1), 3–38.

Dennis, A. R. (1996). Information exchange and use in group decision making: You can lead a group to information, but you can't make it think. *MIS Quarterly, 20*(4), 433–457.

El-Shinnawy, M., & Vinze, A. S. (1998). Polarization and persuasive argumentation: A study of decision making in group settings. *MIS Quarterly*, *22*(2), 165–198.

Gigone, D., & Hastie, R. (1993). The common knowledge effect: Information sharing and group judgment. *Journal of Personality and Social Psychology*, *65*(5), 959–974.

Hinsz, V. B., & Davis, J. H. (1984). Persuasive arguments theory, group polarization, and choice shifts. *Personality and Social Psychology Bulletin*, *10*, 260–268.

Hollingshead, A. B. (1996). The rank order effect in group decision making. *Organizational Behavior & Human Decision Processes*, *68*(3), 181–193.

Isenberg, D. J. (1986). Group polarization: A critical review and meta-analysis. *Journal of Personality and Social Psychology*, *50*, 1141–1151.

Janis, I. (1982). *Groupthink: Psychological studies of policy decision*. Boston, MA: Houghton Mifflin.

Jehn, K. A., Northcraft, G. B., & Neale, M. A. (1999). Why differences make a difference: A field study of diversity, conflict, and performance in workgroups. *Administrative Science Quarterly*, *44*(4), 741–763.

Kameda, T., Ohtsubo, Y., & Takezawa, M. (1997). Centrality in sociocognitive networks and social influence: An illustration in a group decision-making context. *Journal of Personality and Social Psychology*, *73*(2), 296–309.

Lam, S. S. K., & Schaubroeck, J. (2000). Improving group decisions by better pooling information: A comparative advantage of group decision support systems. *Journal of Applied Psychology*, *85*(4), 565–573.

Myers, D. G. (1982). Polarizing effects of social interaction. In: H. Brandstätter, J. H. Davis & G. Stocker-Kreichgauer (Eds.), *Group Decision Making* (pp. 125–161). London, UK: Academic Press.

Myers, D. G., & Lamm, H. (1976). The group polarization phenomenon. *Psychological Bulletin*, *83*, 602–627.

Parks, C. D., & Cowlin, R. A. (1996). Acceptance of uncommon information into group discussion when that information is or is not demonstrable. *Organization Behaviour and Human Decision Processes*, *66*(3), 307–315.

Postmes, T., Spears, R., & Cihangir, S. (2001). Quality of decision making and group norms. *Journal of Personality and Social Psychology*, *80*(6), 918–930.

Sia, C. L., Tan, B. C. Y., & Wei, K. K. (2002). Group polarization and computer-mediated communication: Effects of communication cues, social presence, and anonymity. *Information Systems Research*, *13*(1), 70–90.

Stasser, G., & Birchmeier, Z. (2003). Group creativity and collective choice. In: P. Paulus & B. Nijstad (Eds.), *Group Creativity* (pp. 85–109). New York: Oxford University Press.

Stasser, G., & Titus, W. (1985). Pooling of unshared information in group decision making: Biased information sampling during discussion. *Journal of Personality and Social Psychology*, *48*, 1467–1478.

Stasser, G., & Titus, W. (2003). Hidden profiles: A brief history. *Psychological Inquiry*, *14*(3 and 4), 304–313.

Stoner, J. A. F. (1968). Risky and cautious shifts in group decisions: The influence of widely held values. *Journal of Experimental Social Psychology*, *4*, 442–459.

US Senate Select Committee on Intelligence (2004). *Report on the US Intelligence Community's Prewar Intelligence Assessments on Iraq*. Washington, DC: US Government Printing Office.

Wittenbaum, G., Hubbell, A., & Zuckerman, C. (1999). Mutual enhancement: Toward an understanding of collective preference for shared information. *Journal of Personality and Social Psychology, 77*, 967–978.

Wittenbaum, G. M., Hollingshead, A. B., & Botero, I. C. (2004). From cooperative to motivated information sharing in groups: Moving beyond the hidden profile paradigm. *Communication Monographs, 71*(3), 286–310.

Wittenbaum, G. M., & Park, E. S. (2001). The collective preference for shared information. *Current Directions in Psychological Science, 10*(2), 70–73.

SECTION III:

ICT, STRATEGY AND IDENTITY

In this section we explore the interrelation between information technology, strategy and identity. On the surface the relation between these phenomena are not evident. In this section we will, however, show and argue that there is in fact a very intimate, complex and subtle connection between them. This will be done through two short and evocative essays and two longer chapters. To start our journey let us take identity as being the necessary conditions (attributes, relations, etc.) for us to take something (see it, interact with it, identify it, etc.) as that which it is or supposed to be. Given such a definition what is the relationship between these phenomena?

In the first chapter of this section Introna explores this relationship by considering the way we relate to technology. He suggests that in this relationship we and our technologies co-constitute each other. By this he means that we condition each other's identities. Thus, in making (and using) our technologies they also simultaneously make (and use) us. This argument has important implications for how we understand the transformative role of information technology in organisations but also ultimately the sort of humans (society) we are becoming. In the second chapter Ilharco provides a stimulating discussion of strategy. He suggests that the essence of strategy is to take a stand on ones' identity — to be authentic. Strategising is not simply the making of choices about the future but rather more fundamentally, choosing to choose authenticity. As such authenticity is a prior way of being in the organisation which grounds and gives meaning to all strategising practices.

This theme is taken up again by Introna in the third chapter of the section. In this chapter Introna critiques the popular conception of strategy as alignment. Drawing on autopoietic theory he suggests that strategy is not a matter of structure (as such) but rather a matter of identity. He provides an outline of an autopoietic theory of strategy that sees strategy as ongoing process of strategising in which identity (stability and continuity) is maintained in the face of environmentally induced structural drift (change and innovation) at the same time. He suggests that it is the ongoing simultaneity of stability and change that is the challenge for strategising practices.

In the final chapter of the section Brigham and Introna provide a discussion of the implementation of a vehicle mounted data system in the fire service in the UK. They show that the implementation of a system that was merely supposed to replace a seemingly inefficient paper system was the start of a relationship in which the very nature of the work of the fire crew as well as the understanding of how to manage fire services were fundamentally reframed. They argue that the ongoing emergence, expansion and contraction of patterns of strategic, organisational and technological activities challenge the view that information technology has reified impacts which can be aligned with strategic intentions (as the alignment school suggests). The implication of this is that the concept of strategy as a pluralistic practice has to be accompanied with a thoroughgoing sense of the dynamic interplay between the making, remaking and unmaking of technology mediated activities and organisation as an integral part of strategising practices.

The underlying theme of this section is that strategy, technology and identity are not separate phenomena (as the dominant Cartesian views suggest). Rather that they are intimately connected and mutually constitutive of each other. As such, managers do not have the agency to simply 'align' things up. Strategising and organising are much more complex than that — as experienced managers know well.

Chapter 9

Thoughts on Becoming (or Being) Technological

Lucas D. Introna

ABSTRACT

In this short chapter, I will discuss our relationship with technology more generally, and information technology more specifically. I will suggest that our relationship is more intimate than we might want to acknowledge. I will suggest that our technology makes us as much as we make it. We and our technology are intertwined to such a degree that we can (never could) separate the technical from the social. I will suggest that we have always been cyborgs. I will also suggest that it is fundamental for managers to understand this if they are to appreciate the implications of technology for organising.

Becoming or Being Cyborgs

A cyborg is a cybernetic organism, a hybrid of machine and organism... (Donna Harraway)

The human body has its limits. When it comes to nails the hands are just not good enough, we need a hammer. With the hammer in our hand we can extend the human body, and more importantly, the range of actions that the body is capable of. The development of human capacity to act (to do things) is directly linked to the development of our tools. However, as our tools dramatically extend our domain of action they do not leave us unchanged. We tend to think of our tools as passive things just lying there for us to take up as and when we need them (or not). This is a rather simplistic view of our relationship with our tools. This view of tools does not appreciate the complexity and subtlety of our technologically mediated existence.

As we take up the hammer the hammer and we are transformed quite fundamentally. The hammer is not 'a hammer' if it is not in my hand — hammering

Information Management: Setting the Scene
Copyright © 2007 by Elsevier Ltd.
All rights of reproduction in any form reserved.
ISBN: 978-0-08-046326-1

requires a hand or rather a body as well as a target, something requiring hammering. In my hand the hammer becomes a possibility to exert a force, to knock down a brick wall, for example. Furthermore, with the hammer in my hand the brick wall becomes, for me holding the hammer, soft and penetrable rather than impenetrable. I now embody the possibility of knocking down a wall. I am a person that can go through brick walls; but more than that, a whole range of actions previously impossible suddenly seems possible. In this simple example we see that the hammer transformed me and I it. But we have moved too quickly.

There was something more fundamental that we have not talked about. Even recognising the object lying on the table as 'a hammer' presumes familiarity with practices of hammering. If we can imagine a world where the practices of using large weights to increase the force that one can exert is not present at all then one can ask: why would one even take the object lying on the table as 'a hammer'? Maybe the example of a hammer is a bit too difficult to imagine since hammering is such a pervasive and intuitive action (we might ask why?). Imagine rather a pen in a culture where the practice of writing does not exist. Why would the person encountering a pen take it to be a 'pen'? Thus, we take up tools as relevant 'tools' within a range of cultural practices that *already reveal it as such or such a possibility to act*. But even more than this, I do not take up tools for their own sake. Rather, I take up tools to do something as part of being somebody in particular. As a consultant I take up a mobile phone as a 'mobile phone' to contact my clients, or be contactable for my clients, because that is what it means to be a consultant. In taking up the tools within the cultural practices as part of being somebody we not only transform the tools and ourselves, but also transform (enact) the cultural practices that render possible (and meaningful) the world (of management consulting, for example) where we are what we are (as consultants) and our tools are what they are (as mobile phones). As we and our tools interpenetrate each other we become each other's possibility to be what we are. Is it possible to be a consultant without my mobile phone in a world of global mobile communication systems?

What has happened here in our discussion? We have shifted from a view where we saw tools as simple extension of our capabilities to a view where we and our tools constitute each other's possibility to be the who or what that we are. We have become (or rather have always been) cyborgs. Our tools are now the conditions for being the sort of entities we have become (as consultants and managers, etc.). Our CCTV cameras augment our eyes. PDAs help us remember. Mobile phones enable us to communicate wherever we are. As we delegate actions to technology to extend our being we are becoming more and more cyborgian — human/machine hybrids — by the day (Harraway, 1991). Our looking is now *also* a non-human looking, as is our memory, our communication, and so forth. Indeed one can question whether we can be who we are, as politicians, business people, teachers, writers, policemen, etc., without our extended machine capability. Our way of being, our very existence, has become entangled with a technological world in which it has become difficult to say where we end and where our machines begin. The technical has become (always been) social and the social has become (always been) technical. If this is the case, as I hope I have shown through some simple examples, then this has profound consequences for us. Technical decisions are also social decisions. Choosing our technologies is simultaneously choosing the sort of humans (or organisations) we want to be or become. Let us explore this theme some more and try to discern what it might mean for us (also see Brigham & Introna, 2007, Chapter 12 of this book).

Consciousness, Awareness and Forgetting in the Digital World

There is a fine line that divides consciousness and awareness. We might think that one implies the other or that there might be supervenience between consciousness and awareness. The problem of the consciousness is also related to another problem, that of the unconscious. There is a whole dimension of ourselves that is impossible to perceive directly even though we may be able to become aware of it through a cultural historical perspective, as reflected in our art, our writing and our ways of doing. And maybe this is good? Is full awareness really what we want or need? Do we really want to be aware of everything? We might want to argue that everybody would be better of, that it would be better for our society, if we were all always fully aware. But have we considered what it might mean for us?

As our lives are increasingly being 'recorded' in the digital world we are more and more confronted with our digital selves, and hence with our past. Celebrities find pictures of themselves on the web in situations they thought they had left behind and would want to forget — instead they remain in the perpetual 'now' of our collective digital awareness. Through this digital awareness our lives are also becoming increasingly transparent and available to others, and even to ourselves. We get categorised and sent mail because our buying habits are being recorded and analysed. One could say that we are forever recorded in the awareness of the digital mind when we are online. Our activities are increasing visible through logs, websites, blogs, etc. Digital cameras and digital video capture us and these digital images may start to circulate in the digital awareness in ways that we no longer control. Our past may return to our present whether we want it or not. We may no longer control our memory. As our lives become increasingly mediated by the virtual digital world a mountain of 'aware material' is building up. As this happens, forgetting, being no longer aware of this or that matter or event, becomes more and more difficult to do.

Forgetting is important to our human way of being. It is an essential part of our survival that we can forget bad experiences and not stay crippled by them. We all make mistakes that we *need* to forget if we are to 'move on'. In the digital world forgetting is becoming more and more difficult to do. Our collective digital awareness no longer allows things to simply slip away into our unconscious being. Our mind, individually and collectively, is increasingly a publicly available digital mind that remembers what we might want to, or need to, forget. As we become increasingly digitally mediated we may lose our possibility to forget. What sort of humans (or organisations) will we be or become? Do we want such a future?

Two Kinds of Memory and Two Kinds of Times

Our nervous system is a mobile memory so is our PDA. However, there is an important difference between our memory and that of the PDA. The best way to understand this is with regard to time. For the PDA time is a linear stream of events, with specific beginnings and specific ends. It is a matter of quantity. Time, to be machine time, must be quantified (when will the meeting be and how long will it take?). The PDA's time — machine time — is also chronological; it ends when it breaks. For the machine there is no connection between an hour ago and later on today except in the terms of chronology. Our human temporality is very different. Our 'here and now' is full of the past and already full of the future. We find ourselves in the 'now' already with some level of awareness of where we have just been and already with some expectation of where we are heading. Our past, present and future blends into each other in such a way that we cannot say where the one ends and the other begins — it is not linear or chronological. Our time is different because we conceive it as a quality; it is our feeling of being or non-being in our situation. Our memory has times and moments all mixed together. Our memory is an improbable collection of images; it does not simply record our activities, it lets us grow.

But what happens if our lives are becoming increasingly defined by machine memory and machine time? When people make appointments with us in our digital diary, enter our memory, without our mediation (as happens in groupware systems)? What happens when we are being conceived of as available (or not) in machine time but we actually live our busy lives in human memory and human time? Will machine time and memory transform our human time and human memory? What if we become so imbedded in machines that human time and human memory slip away?

Virtuality and Community

As our lives become digitised it enters the domain of the virtual. Virtuality allows for mimesis. With mimesis we can mime — 'as if' it was happening. Once you appear in the database, as a record, I can ask you questions, query you (virtually) without your involvement. I can change your status by simply updating your record, without your involvement. I can interact with you, get to know you, without your involvement. Many people know me through my website and my virtual wondering in the digital space called the Internet. I have two lives (maybe more) — an embodied situated life and a digital virtual life. Sometimes these 'parallel' lives support and confirm each other; sometimes they disturb and contradict each other. As we become increasingly virtual (a virtual community and a virtual society) we need to reflect on what it means. Clearly it is not helpful to suggest that the virtual is 'superficial and trivial' and the situated embodied co-presence (often referred to as the 'real') is 'thick and significant'. For some their virtual lives are very significant because they share significant concerns (an illness) with their virtual partners; for others it may just be a form of escape, like a messenger chat with a stranger. Nevertheless, as we embrace the digital world we cannot avoid becoming virtualised.

But what is the relationship between the actual and the virtual. I cannot kill you but I can delete you from the database — or can I? As our life possibilities become enmeshed in the virtual world how should we treat these virtual strangers? Can we talk about them as mere representations when people's identity becomes intimately tied to their virtual lives? When my 'I' becomes co-constituted through the virtual, the virtual becomes like the actual, equally real. We are becoming virtual/actual hybrids. As technology becomes our constitutive condition we need to rethink many of our categories — self/other, real/virtual, human/machine and so forth. We can no longer treat the machine as the alien. The alien and we are now one.

The Technological Mood and the Post-Human Way of Being

Martin Heidegger, the philosopher, famously claimed that 'the essence of technology is nothing technological' (Heidegger, 1977). Technology is not merely an artefact or our relationship with this or that artefact; rather, the artefact — and our relationship with it — is already an outcome of a particular 'technological' way of seeing and conducting ourselves in and towards the world. We live in the age of the techno-logical mood. In this technological mood problems show up as immediately *requiring* technical solutions. This technological mood frames the way we see, and make sense of the world. As the already technologically oriented human beings that we have become, we will tend to conceive of communication as a problem requiring a tech-nological solution, hence the proliferation of communication devices. Of course we now communicate more (through our e-mail, mobile phones, blackberrys, etc.) but what is the nature of this communication? Technologically mediated communication reframes what communication is. Is communication becoming equivalent to being able to make a connection? Furthermore, once in place technology allows the world to 'show up' in particular ways. You are a different person to me with a mobile phone than without one. With a mobile phone you become revealed, or show up, as 'contactable', 'within reach' as it were. As we incorporate our technical devices in our everyday world we become more and more immersed in our technological mood. It seems more and more obvious that this is the way the world is and should be. As technology reframes the way we understand our activities *and ourselves* we become increasingly framed and set-up as technological beings. Indeed we could say that technology has become the *a priori* horizon of meaning that conditions the way the world shows up for us. Can we escape this technological mood? Do we want to? Have we not already become (or have always been) post-human?

Cyborgs and (Cyborg)Organisation

Organisation is increasingly tied to information technology. We can organise globally because technology has extended our reach. We can fragment our organisation in as many parts as we need and locate them wherever we need because we can always tie them together through global systems of transportation and communication.

However, if my speculations above are correct we are not just building a more efficient system of production and consumption, we are also simultaneously building a different society — a different way of being human. Who is deciding our future? As we embrace technology, do we know what we are becoming? If human values and culture is the 'glue' that makes organisations work, what will happen to organisations as these values become displaced (or transformed) into human/machine values and culture? Maybe there are longer term implications to our technologically mediated organisations which we have yet to grasp? But even more mundane is: if we implement a new ERP system we are not just making things for efficient or effective; we are changing the way of being in the organisation; we are choosing a very different type of organisation — not just technically but also socially in a very fundamental way. Do we understand this intimate connection? I would suggest mostly not.

References

Brigham, M., & Introna, L. D. (2007). Strategy as hospitality, bricolage and enframing. *Information Management: Setting the Scene, 1*, 159–172.

Harraway, D. (1991). *Simians, cyborgs and women: The reinvention of nature.* New York: Routledge.

Heidegger, M. (1977). *The question concerning technology and other essays.* New York: Harper Torchbooks.

Chapter 10

Strategy without Theory

Fernando Ilharco

ABSTRACT

This chapter argues that strategy is not just about making choices with regard to the future that might have long-term implications. It suggests that strategy is more fundamental than that. It suggests that strategy is not a theory or a plan but rather about an authentic way of being. It is not about strategic choices but rather about taking a stand, about choosing to choose in the first instance. Although subtle, this distinction has profound implications for how strategy is practised, as this essay will suggest.

Introduction

There are many theories of strategy; yet it is difficult to know what strategy is as such. Strategy is a notion most often used in the domain of management and government policy. Each of these areas takes strategy as something that belongs fairly obviously to itself. Nonetheless, in each of these areas there is also a lack of agreement as to what strategy essentially is.

Having said this we need to note that a theory of strategy is obviously not strategy itself. A theory of strategy is a "theory" of strategy. That is, it is a way in which strategy, the phenomenon in question, is articulated. Likewise, other theories of strategy are other ways of strategy being articulated. For us the issue is this: what is the key, or essential, criterion that enables us to recognise something as strategy or not? In other words, what is the essence of strategy? This short essay takes this question as its problem to be understood.

Phenomenology, the method of investigation that inspired this essay, was designed to give access to the essence of phenomena (e.g., Heidegger, 1962, 1977; Husserl, 1964, 1970; Moran, 2000; Spiegelberg, 1994). As such, it holds the promise of clarifying what phenomena are. Although phenomenology traditionally has been used for researching highly philosophical subjects, such as what is knowledge, the subject, being, man, a person and so on, Heidegger (1977), in 1955, used it to investigate

Information Management: Setting the Scene
ISBN: 978-0-08-046326-1

technology. Since then, particularly from the 1980s onwards, phenomenology has been used, most of the cases together with other approaches, to research information technology, decision making, managing, entrepreneurship, innovation, group work, the Internet, screens, etc.

From a phenomenological standpoint, the various articulations of the *appearances* of strategy are fairly obvious. For example, Porter's (1980) theory of strategic positioning is an articulation of the appearance of strategy just as is von Clausewitz's (1976) theory of war. Yet its essence, the necessary and grounding basis for the phenomenon of strategy to be what it is, seems to be less intuitive and clarified in these articulations.

Reading these texts one might ask: what is the common and decisive ground (or foundation) that unites all the appearances of strategy as strategy? What enables us to recognise a text, a theory, a discourse, or an action "as strategic"? What is essential in strategy? In order to answer this question we analyse some key organisational texts phenomenologically. These texts are taken as articulations of the *appearances* of strategy that can be taken as a starting point in order to reach towards the essential grounds of strategy in organisational terms.

Strategy as it Appears

There are many theories on computers' usage, impact, and so forth, just as there are many theories, studies, and approaches on strategy. Yet, one knows what a computer is and one really does not know what strategy, in itself, is. To start to clarify this state of affairs we will briefly look at what is fundamental in some of the relevant theories about strategy in the organisational field: the design school, the positioning school, and the resource-based approach. As we will see they are all concerned with the notion of fit, coupling, and relationship of a specific entity with its environment.

In the management field, strategy is overwhelmingly related to the long-term profitability and survival of the firm. For Ansoff and Sullivan (1993) strategic success relies on the optimisation of the firm's *profit potential*, in the form of new products, markets, and technologies and competitive strategies. This optimisation process is achieved when the strategic behaviour of the firm is aligned with the environment.

The concept of strategy remained within the military context until the Industrial Revolution, when it began to enter large business enterprises. Chandler (1977) considered the modern business enterprise an institutional response to increasing consumer demand and the rapid pace of technological development. The first experiences of separating the task of setting the companys' objectives (which would be the work of strategists) from actions effectively taken to reach those objectives (which would be, at least in theory, the criterion for setting a structure) were carried out early in the 20th century in the USA, particularly by the firms Dupont Nemours and General Motors (Godet, 1993).

The positive economic and technological environment along with the relative political stability of the post-World War II era, led to the first sound proposals of management strategy, namely those of Selznick (1957), Chandler (1962), Ansoff (1965), and Andrews (1971). All of them set the ground for the very influential strand of strategic management identified as the design school. Ansoff's (1965) proposal was more focused on formalised planning than the proposals of the others referred to above, who emphasised the analysis and working of a company's key strengths and weaknesses, and environment opportunities and threats (the widely used SWOT technique), for achieving an optimum fit between the firm and its environment. Chandler (1962) established the notions of business strategy and organisational structure — until we know strategy, we cannot begin to specify the appropriate structure. The separation of thought and action, grounded on Descartes' subject–object method, lies at the roots of this claimed need for structure to follow strategy, and last but not the least to understand organisation by conceiving and separating strategy and structure. In this light, formulation and implementation are, and should be, clearly separated. That is also Ansoff's (1965) position on the subject. The strategic planning models are based on three areas of concern: the setting of the premises (fundamental organisational, social and economic purpose, values of top management, and SWOT analysis); the planning itself (mission, long-range objectives, policies and plans, as well as medium- and short-range horizontal policies and programs, and vertical plans and procedures); and the implementation and evaluation (monitoring, feedback, and adjusting); just as in the original design school models, these planning techniques would deliver unique strategies.

In 1980 a new proposal on strategy appeared in the field of management: a school whose main aim was to position the company in its specific competitive environment. The underlying philosophy of this school is "the selection of optimal strategy of literal position in the context of military battle" (Mintzberg, Ahlstrand, & Lampel, 1998, p. 85). This school owes much to von Clausewitz's (1976) *On War*. Porter (1980) argues that there are a limited number of strategies that each given company might follow. Just like the design and planning models, in Porter's theory "the essential notion of strategy is captured in the distinction between ends and means" (Porter, 1980, p. xvi). "Essentially, developing a competitive strategy is developing a broad formula for how a business is going to compete, what its goals should be, and what policies will be needed to carry out those goals" (Mintzberg et al., 1998, p. 35). Porter's proposal is the carrying out of an analysis of the industry and choosing one of the four potentially successful generic strategies to outperform other firms in that industry: overall differentiation, overall cost leadership, focus differentiation, and focus low cost. At stake is the firm's choice. Trying to compete in all segments, not choosing what kind of trade-off, either low cost or differentiation, the firm is going to be engaged with, is a recipe for poor performance; not choosing, consciously and decisively, the company will end up by being "stuck in the middle" (Porter, 1980) — the bad place to be in Porter's terms.[1]

---

[1]Other positioning proposals had considerable success in the business community, namely the Growth-Share Matrix, which addresses the allocation of resources to the different businesses of the firm depending on the current market share and the growth potential of the business (Henderson, 1979), the "experience curve", which suggests that as the cumulative production doubles its overall cost declines by a constant percentage, the PIMS (Profit Impact of Market Strategies) model, which identifies a high number of variables and estimates expected returns, profits, market share and so forth (Schoeffler, 1980).

More recently, strategy researchers have been drawing on game theory — following the article of Brandenburger and Nalebuff (1995). Game theory tries to analyse how rational, self-interested, actors are likely to behave in very well-defined situations (Von Neumann & Morgenstern, 1980). In all of these proposals the central strategic issue is one of choosing a position — geographical or in any other relative competitive aspect, such as volume, quality, prices, technologies, and so forth.

Both the design and positioning schools are focused on the external environment and what firms' strategies should be. In contrast to these perspectives a different proposal on strategic management, either focused on learning, power, cultural, or psychological issues, has been advancing for some decades now. This understanding of strategic management, identified as the resource-based approach, focuses on the firms' internal capabilities and resources and attempts to address how strategies actually happen.

Two particular works dating back almost 50 years — Lindblom (1959) and Penrose (1959) — can be said to be at the origin of the resource-based approach to strategy. Lindblom's paper questioned the premises of "rational" management. He argued that policy is not an orderly and controlled process but a messy one in which executives try to cope in many ways with the complexity of a world well beyond their control. So Penrose not only pointed out the firm's resources as the basis for its growth, but also identified knowledge as the one resource that can make the difference between companies. For Penrose the "input" of production is never the resources themselves, but the way in which they are used according to the firm's experience and knowledge. Wernerfelt (1984) developed Penrose's insights in the field of strategic management, claiming that a firm's strategy is the balance between exploring existing resources and developing new ones. This approach is interested in: physical capital (IT hardware and software, plant and equipment, geographic location, access to raw materials, etc.); human capital (experience, training, judgement, intelligence, relationships, etc.); and organisational capital (formal systems and structures, informal relations, practices and comportment).

According to this approach strategy is about leveraging resources, developing core competencies, and stretching the company in order to shape and capture future markets. "Creating stretch, a misfit between resources and aspirations, is the single most important task senior management faces" (Hamel & Prahalad, 1993, p. 78). This means that strategy as stretch is more than a pattern in a stream of incremental decisions. It is a clear view by the top management of the goal ahead, as well as an open path to follow and discover through leadership in the field. (Hamel & Prahalad, 1989, p. 84).

Authenticity and the Essence of Strategy

From the management theories on strategy we see that strategy addresses the question of fit, coupling, and relationship of an entity with its environment, so that the entity in question might survive and thrive in the future. For the design school it is clear that until an organisation has not specified its strategy it cannot begin to specify the appropriate way in which it will compete. The positioning school owes much to Clausewitz. The underlying philosophy of this school is the selection of an optimal position, much like the context of a military battle. Essentially, developing a strategy is developing a formula for how a business is going to compete? Where? On what basis? What are its goals? This is very much the business translation of Clausewitz idea: "When, where, and with what forces an engagement is to be fought?" Strategy is positioning the organisation in terms of the geographical area of its activity, of the industry where it competes, of the segments in which it is present, of the trade-offs low cost/differentiation and industry wide/niches — the clearer the positioning, the clearer the strategy. At stake are organisational choices. This is true but not only this.

At stake is something more fundamental to which all these choices (which are very important) already refer and which they all take as necessary — *the necessity of the organisation to choose to choose, to take a stand*. Thus, strategy essentially refers to, or has its necessary being in, the organisational readiness and with steadfastness to choose to choose. If this is so why or how would an organisation not choose to choose? Do not all organisations always make strategic choices? Are there not always decisions made about products, markets, etc.? This is true, choices are made and these choices may have strategic implications but this does not necessary mean that the organisation has a strategy. We would rather suggest that not choosing to choose is not about whether choices are made or not, or even the potential implication of these choices. *It is about the fundamental basis of such choices.* When an organisation simply follows where the markets are taking it, where the competition is going, where its technology is suggesting it should go, and so forth, then it is making choices but it is not choosing to choose. It is simply *following* (the market, the trends, the competitors, etc.) — that is, what "they" are doing. Choosing to choose is to take a stand, to care to be (or become) something specific — in short it is to be *authentic* (Heidegger, 1962). This is what is most fundamental about strategy, its essence.

Managers can *choose to choose* (act strategically) because they *care.* Their identities as managers are intimately connected to the identity of the organisation in which they are what they are for a great part of their lives. Left to themselves they can choose to choose or not to choose (Heidegger, 1962, pp. 312–314). From the outside choosing to choose may indeed have no apparent consequences in the sort of "objective" actions they are performing when they think about the future and make plans. However, if managers take a stand — choose to choose — then these actions (planning, thinking, deciding) are authentically appropriated by them. The world opens up more clearly, and the possibilities they face show up as intensely meaningful. They can make a difference because things and actions truly and instinctively matter to them — *they are resolute* (Heidegger, 1962, p. 343). When things matter, they notice them, they attend to them, they are involved, and thus action unfolds in a world where they are responsible for themselves and their organisations. Only by being authentic can they have the possibility of fully grasping what they intend to make of themselves (and their organisations) in their common future. This projection (or projectedness) into the future (that strategy presumes) becomes intensely meaningful precisely because they have chosen and as such things matter intensely to them. This enables the manager to make decisive choices and to take vital actions. However, this resoluteness needs to be reinforced again and again because of humans' tendency to fall into "the they" (Heidegger, 1962). Only by continuing to be authentic can strategy, as an authentic intention, plan, or pattern, come to be a fulfilment of the possibilities the manager and the organisation aims at for their future. Strategy thus relies on a recurrent experiencing of identity *in* authenticity. Theories of strategy only make sense once this essential insight is understood and enacted.

Concluding Remarks

Grounding strategy in authenticity means that its effectiveness is ultimately not dependant on plans, theories, consultants, or frameworks, but on the degree in which the organisation resolutely chooses to choose. Being authentic, we care for what we are and for what we are doing. By being authentic an organisation makes strategy part of its ongoing way of being, and as such, by continuing to be authentic, it becomes an organisation driven not only by "strategic" decisions, but also by strategy itself.

References

Andrews, K. R. (1971). *The concept of corporate strategy.* Homewood, IL: Irwin.

Ansoff, H. I. (1965). *Corporate strategy.* New York: McGraw Hill.

Ansoff, H. I., & Sullivan, P. A. (1993). Optimizing profitability in turbulent environments: A formula for strategic success. *Long Range Planning, 26*(5), 11–23.

Brandenburger, A. M., & Nalebuff, B. J. (1995, July–August) The right game: Use game theory to shape strategy. *Harvard Business Review,* 57–81.

Chandler, A. D. Jr. (1962). *Strategy and structrure: Chapters in the history of the industrial enterprise.* Cambridge, MA: MIT Press.

Chandler, A. D. Jr. (1977). *The visible hand: The managerial revolution in American business.* Cambridge, MA: Harvard University Press.

Godet, M. (1993). *Manual de prospectiva estratégica: Da antecipação à acção.* Lisbon: Publicações Dom Quixote.

Hamel, G., & Prahalad, C. K. (1989, May–June). Strategic intent. *Harvard Business Review,* 63–76.

Hamel, G., & Prahalad, C. K. (1993, March–April). Strategy as stretch and leverage. *Harvard Business Review,* 75–84.

Heidegger, M. (1962). In: J. Macquarrie & E. Robinson (Trans.), *Being and time.* Oxford, UK: Blackwell.

Heidegger, M. (1977). *The question concerning technology and other essays.* New York: Harper Torchbooks.

Henderson, B. D. (1979). *Henderson on corporate strategy.* Cambridge, MA: Abt Book.

Husserl, E. (1964). *The idea of phenomenology.* The Hague: Martinus Nijhoff.

Husserl, E. (1970). In: D. Carr (Trans.), *The crisis of European sciences and transcendental phenomenology: An introduction to phenomenological philosophy.* Evanston, IL: Northwestern University Press.

Lindblom, C. E. (1959). The science of muddling through. *Public Administration Review*, *19*(2), 79–88.

Mintzberg, H., Ahlstrand, B., & Lampel, J. (1998). *Strategy safari*. Hertfordshire: Prentice Hall.

Moran, D. (2000). *An introduction to phenomenology*. New York: Routledge.

Penrose, E. (1959). *The theory of the growth of the firm*. New York: Wiley.

Porter, M. (1980). *Competitive strategy*. Boston, MA: Free Press.

Schoeffler, S. (1980). *Nine basic findings on business strategy*. Working paper. The Strategic Planning Institute: Cambridge, MA.

Selznick, P. (1957). *Leadership and administration: A sociological interpretation*. Evanston, IL: Row Peterson.

Spiegelberg, H. (1994). *The phenomenological movement — a historical introduction* (3rd rev. and enlarged edn.). Dordrecht: Kluwer Academic Publishers.

von Clausewitz, C. (1976). In: M. Howard, P. Paret (Eds. & Trans.), *On war*. Princeton, NJ: Princeton University Press.

Von Neumann, J., & Morgenstern, O. (1980). *Theory of games and economic behavior*. Princeton, NJ, USA: Princeton University Press.

Wernerfelt, B. (1984). A resource-based view of the firm. *Strategic Management Journal*, *5*, 171–180.

Chapter 11

Strategy-as-Identity: An Autopoietic Contribution to the IS/IT Strategy Debate

Lucas D. Introna

ABSTRACT

Organizational IS/IT strategy, as a possible source of organizational failure and success, has been widely discussed in both academic and business circles. Several different models for the process of IS/IT strategy formation and implementation have been presented — mostly linking it to the organizational corporate strategy through the notion of alignment. This chapter discusses different perspectives on organizational IS/IT strategy and provides a critique of the dominant alignment model popular in the management literature. The work of Ciborra, Mintzberg and the strategy-as-practice approach is discussed to show that an alternative view, to the alignment model, is emerging in the literature. The chapter brings together these insights in a strategy-as-identity approach based on the theory of autopoiesis. The implications of this approach for IS/IT strategy are briefly discussed.

Introduction[1]

If there were one concept in management that managers might single out as the most important, elusive and possibly the most controversial, it would be strategy. The idea of strategy has gained increasing attention since the inception of modern industrial management (e.g. in Taylorism) and has come to dominate the management literature in the last two decades. This is in spite of the fact that reflections on military and war strategy were already recorded in the 19th century by Clausewitz and even previously by Sun Tzu in the 4th century B.C. In the last decade the idea of strategy has been defined and redefined in a large and eclectic body of literature. Its

---

[1]This chapter is partly based on an earlier paper coauthored with Clarissa Drysdale-Anderson for the European Conference on Information Systems in 2000.

implications have been scrutinized under the most diverse perspectives and its concepts applied widely (Angell & Smithson, 1991; Aspesi & Vardhan, 1999; Beinhocker, 1999; Handel, 1986; Johnson, Melin, & Whittington, 2003; Johnson & Scholes, 1984; Markides, 1999; Mintzberg, 1994; Mintzberg & Lampel, 1999; Mintzberg et al., 1985, 1998; Porter, 1980; Whittington, 1993, 2003, 2006).

Most managers might suggest that strategy represents some sort of plan or set of intentions, elaborated mostly by senior managers, in order to obtain results according to their expectations. The work of Henry Mintzberg (1987) has become one of the strong and lasting voices in the debate. He claims that strategy may require more than one definition. He suggests that strategy should be seen as a plan, a pattern, a position, a perspective and a ploy. Thus, for him strategy is a *plan*, a direction or a path, a "looking ahead" attitude (*intended strategy*). Strategy is a *pattern*, a perceived trend based on past behavior (*realized strategy* when derived from deliberate plans or *emergent strategy* when derived unintentionally). Strategy is a *position* because it involves choice of advantageous locations or postures. Strategy is a *perspective*, a view of the organization. Finally, strategy can also be seen as a *ploy*, a maneuver to deceive the competitor. Indeed, Mintzberg makes a strong case for strategy as a multifaceted phenomenon. He argues that strategy sets direction, focuses efforts, defines the organization and provides consistency. The pioneering work of Mintzberg together with the recent theoretical developments in management studies more generally — the so-called *practice turn* — has also led to the emergence of the *strategy-as-practice* approach to strategy (Whittington, 2003, 2006; Johnson et al., 2003; Jarzabkowski, 2003, 2004). This approach suggests that strategy is what managers do, strategy as it happens, or strategy as a process rather than as content.

Together with the business strategy debate emerged another debate: the relationship between business strategy and IS/IT strategy. In this debate the alignment school became dominant in the 1990s (Baets, 1996; Berry & Taggart, 1998; Brockway & Hurley, 1998; Chan, 2002; Currie, 1995; Currie & Bryson, 1995; Galliers & Baker, 1994; Henderson & Venkatraman, 1990, 1992; Hu & Huang, 2006; Jones et al., 1995; Karake, 1997; Kearns & Sabherwal, 2007; Luftman, 2003; Luftman & Brier, 1999; Moody, 2003; Ormerod, 1998; Reich & Benbasat, 2000; Sabherwal & Chan, 2001; Smits et al., 1997; Venkatraman, 1991). This school of thought proposed that IS/IT infrastructure would only be effective if aligned with business strategy. They proceeded to propose models, methods, and analysis to demonstrate this. In 1994, Claudio Ciborra started to critique this work. He suggested that this work was based on metaphors that assume that strategy somehow existed outside of the situated practices of organizational action. He proposed an alternative perspective in which he showed that strategy formulation and implementation could not be separated from action in the way that the alignment school proposed or assumed. He showed how bricolage and improvisation played a major role in the shaping and crafting of *strategy in action*. These ideas also resonated well with the work that Mintzberg was beginning to produce in the area of business strategy and the work that later became known as the *strategy-as-practice* approach.

It is logically and empirically clear that the IS/IT infrastructure should not become divorced from the business intention and focus. In this insight the alignment school was correct. However, they were predisposed to a Cartesian worldview that made them elaborate this insight in a completely inappropriate manner. It is also true that Ciborra's very original analysis of improvisation and bricolage requires a more systemic framework in order to provide a coherent description of the strategic processes in organizations. A complete elaboration of such a framework is beyond the scope of this chapter. However, this chapter will propose *autopoietic theory* as an appropriate frame for such elaboration. In doing this the chapter will be structured as follows: First, we will provide a brief discussion of autopoiesis theory; second, we will discuss strategy in general and IS/IT strategy as alignment in particular; third, we will provide a brief exposition of strategic-as-identity by applying autopoietic insights to the phenomenon of strategy; fourth, we will suggest how this framework can provide useful and interesting insights for our understanding for strategy more generally and for the relationship between business strategy and IS/IT strategy more specifically.

A Brief Introduction of Autopoiesis

The word autopoiesis comes from the Greek (*auto = self, poiesis = production*). An autopoietic system is therefore a self-producing, self-organizing system. Because it refers only to itself, it is also called self-referential (Jantsch, 1980). A living cell, for example, produces and is produced by itself. It generates its own components and processes, which are therefore what generate it, in a circular, ongoing process as shown in Figure 11.1 below. All living systems, according to Varela and Maturana (1987), are autonomous autopoietic entities. There are several concepts within autopoiesis theory, which are central to understanding the theory and its possible applications in organization studies. We will consider them before moving to strategy itself.

Structure and Organization/Identity

Varela and Maturana (1987) give a very particular meaning to these two concepts. *Organization* refers to the *necessary* relations between components of a unity that constitute this unity to be that unity we claim it to be. For example, the organization of a table is the relations a table must have for us as observers to designate it as a

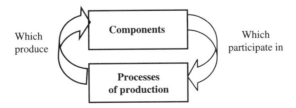

Figure 11.1: Circular processes of production (Adapted from Mingers, 1995, p. 12).

table and not as something else such as a chair, or a door. In other words, it is the necessary relations that, if not present, would transform the thing into something other than that claimed. It would therefore be accurate to say that the *organization* of a system is its identity and the frame within which it must be addressed as a whole (Whitaker, 1995). In the rest of the chapter we will use the term *identity* rather than *organization* to avoid confusion. The notion of identity is often implicit rather than explicit. We may not necessarily be able to list the particular relations required for a thing to be what observers would claim it to be. Nevertheless, in as much as we know the thing (a table) we do know when it is, or no longer functions as, a table[2]. *Structure* comes from the Latin and means, *to build*. It refers to the *actual* components and the *actual* relations between them. It constitutes a particular example of a type or of entity. A structure does not determine the identity of the unity as such. "A unity may change structure without loss of identity, so long as its organization/ identity is maintained" (Whitaker, 1995). We have many diverse empirical examples of table that differ in structure but which we still designate as *tables*. Nevertheless, although the identity is more than the structural relations it is *never separate from them*. Structure realizes or actualizes identity but does not determine it. Whatever something *is*, it is it in, and only in, its ongoing actual structural relations. In the example of table that we use the relationships are fixed. However, in social systems relationships are enacted on an ongoing basis in a process called *structuration* by Giddens (1984).

Structure-Determined Systems

The behavior of a system is limited by its own constitution. The actual changes that a system may undergo depend on its structure in a particular instant, moment or event. The environment can only trigger changes, which are actually determined internally. I can only respond to you if you speak in a language I can understand. I can only see the color of the light if I have sight. The structure therefore limits, and makes possible the system's range of potential transformations as well as the set of possible perturbations from the environment that could trigger changes of state in that system. This is a very important point. Changes in a system are neither entirely autonomous nor entirely free from constraint. They are constrained/enabled by the dispositions of their structure and dependent on the way in which these dispositions open/close them to perturbations from the environment.

Identity (Organizational) Closure

Identity closed systems are systems that do not have inputs or outputs as such, "all possible states of activity must always lead or generate further activity within itself" (Mingers, 1995, p. 32). Autopoietic systems are *identity closed* since the result of their

---

[2]There is a strong connection between Maturana and Varela's notion of organization (identity) and the phenomenological notion of essence as found in the work of Husserl (1970) and Heidegger (1962).

transformations or activity is identity itself — it is both medium and outcome. In an autopoietic system every operation serves only to maintain identity (also referred to as *internal coherence*) and nothing besides. It is important to explain that identity closed systems are not isolated systems that have no interactions with the environment. Instead, they are *interactively open* to their environment through their structure. In terms of the input/output-type description the system is seen as taking inputs from the environment and transforming it into outputs *via* the transfer or transformation function. This is the description of classical systems theory and the one most commonly used. However, in the closure type description of autopoiesis, systems are characterized not by their inputs and transformations but by, and only by, their identity or internal coherence that arise out of their interconnectedness. Their relation with their environment is such that "specific environmental inputs are bracketed as unspecific perturbations or simply noise. An input becomes a perturbation when it is *no* longer necessary to specify the systems' organization (identity), i.e. it has become noise" (Varela & Maturana, 1987, p. 26, my emphasis). Thus, the environment can cause changes in the system but can never determine these changes since every change is dealt with *only* in terms of the system's internal coherence, identity or organization.

A relatively simple example of such identity closure is a normal everyday conversation. Every participant tries to make a point, for sure, but only in regard to that which has already been said (by both participants). Every statement is added to keep the dialogue coherent (and alive) and not merely to transform a point (input) into a next point (outputs). Every statement is reflected upon by the discussants and steers the selection of the next statement (or point) in such a way that is impossible to know exactly what the next statement in the conversation will be (or what will be said at any point in the conversation). The criterion for selection is always only the ongoing internal coherence of the conversation. If another participant enters from the environment then these statements are treated as perturbations that might be incorporated but not at the expense of the internal coherence of the existing dialogue. Thus, the ongoing identity (internal coherence) of the conversation is both medium and outcome — i.e. it is identity closed.

Structural Coupling

Structural Coupling happens "whenever there is a history of recurrent interactions leading to the structural congruence between two (or more) systems" (Varela & Maturana, 1987). It is a similar concept to that of adaptation, but in this case the environment cannot dictate the adaptive changes that may happen — in the way suggested by classical Darwinism. Changes can occur and maintain identity, or not occur, and lead the system to disintegration (Mingers, 1995). It is the congruence in structure (of system and environment) that makes the recurrent interactions persist and not the adaptation of the system to a fixed environment. The environment is both medium and outcome for and of the interaction. Structural coupling is always mutual; both organism and environment undergo transformations in and through their *ongoing* interactions. Thus, structurally coupled systems are systems that have structurally converged — through recurrent and ongoing interaction — to the point that they *respond* to each other while maintaining their identity. To make this discussion more clear let us do a small *thought experiment*. Let us assume that you are a person who is completely immobile in a bed in a room with a door. You have never been outside the room and nobody has ever entered the room. Can you recognize the door as a place/opportunity for entry or exit? The answer to this question is very difficult to imagine since we have a whole history of interactions with doors. However, if we have never interacted with a door because our structure does not allow such an interaction, we will simply not recognize the door *as a door*. The door is merely part of the wall. Let us assume that one day somebody enters through the door. Suddenly the wall gets *broken down* into spaces that are fixed and a space that can open. This perturbation changes your structure. You now, every so often, glance at the wall that has become an opening, expecting somebody to enter there. One can imagine how over time you may try to improvise ways to fix your position in such a way as to see the door more clearly, of getting closer to the door, even attempting to exit through it. These attempts to change your structure to be open to the possibilities presented by the door, if maintained, would lead to structural convergence between you and the possibilities presented by the perturbations of the door (who enters, when, to do what, and so forth). However, if nobody ever comes through the door again, you will eventually stop glancing at it and it will return to being *wall* again.

Ontogenic Structural Drift

The history of interactions that occurs within the lifetime of a system is usually referred to as the systems' ontogeny. Maturana uses the term ontogenic drift to denote the structural changes, which occur within this lifetime — while identity is kept intact. Drift can be thought of as the result of ongoing openness (to the environment) and simultaneous closure (of identity), without which the system could not survive over time. Autopoietic systems are deeply historical. They are what they are, not because they choose to be such or such a type of being, but because of their ongoing becoming that results from their ontogenic drift. They are autonomous in maintaining their identity but not autonomous agents in being able to determine the path of their drift. In terms of our conversation example above we can say that the discussants are autonomous in selecting the next statement but could not determine the development of the conversation without risking losing the coherency of the dialogue (and with it the other discussant).

Let us summarize these points. Autopoietic systems are identity closed — they exist to maintain, and only to maintain their identity. In as much as they are always already in an environment they are structurally coupled with that environment while conserving identity — if not, they would cease to exist. Structural coupling is the convergence of structure within the constraints of identity. Structural coupling results from a convergence in which systems continue to disturb one another to increase their structural *openness* to each other while conserving identity. The way in which the structure of systems emerges, in this openness or coupling to each other, is referred to as structural drift. Neither the system, nor the environment, determines this drift. It is the outcome of the emerging structural coupling within the constraint of identity. Thus, autopoiesis refers to systems "that maintain their defining organization (identity) throughout a history of environmental perturbation and structural change and regenerate their components in the course of operations" (Varela & Maturana, 1987 in Coleman, 1999).

It is important to note that the use of autopoietic theory — developed in the natural sciences — in interpreting social systems in not entirely uncontroversial (Introna, 2003). Nevertheless, Luhmann (1986, 1990, 1993, 1995) has shown in his voluminous work that autopoiesis can, in fact, provide rich insight into social systems (also see Seidl, 2005). We will not pursue the debate here. Before using these autopoietic concepts to rethink strategy and in particular the business strategy and the IS/IT strategy relationship we will consider the current thinking in this area.

IS/IT Strategy and (Mis)alignment

IS/IT have gained in importance in the last twenty years by becoming the major modality of change in organizations. Academics and consultants have produced an enormous amount of literature on the benefits and drawbacks that IS/IT brings to firms, and the importance of linking IS/IT to corporate strategy. The substantial investments together with the complexity of modern organizations have created an urgent need for some clarity in this dispute domain (Carr, 2003).

In most modern organizations, IT has shifted from a traditional position of support of business activities to a more strategic role (Venkatraman, 1991). Information and IT are seen by most managers as assets that can improve the organization effectiveness and efficiency when managed appropriately (Karake, 1997). More and more IS/IT is seen as the main modality for organizational transformation and success. Hence, companies have been urged to either incorporate an IS/IT component into the overall corporate strategy or create a separate IS/IT strategy, which is aligned with it. In the first case, IS/IT play a major role in the business strategy formation. The second brings about the concept of alignment between corporate and IS/IT strategies, assuming that they are conceived separately in some way and then integrated. This has been the most discussed and widely accepted idea. It has been described in different forms from both an empirical and a theoretical basis. In these discussions the same essential idea is proposed and defended (Baets, 1996; Berry & Taggart, 1998; Brockway & Hurley, 1998; Chan, 2002; Currie, 1995; Currie & Bryson, 1995; Galliers & Baker, 1994; Henderson & Venkatraman, 1990, 1992; Hu & Huang, 2006; Jones et al., 1995; Karake, 1997; Kearns & Sabherwal, 2007; Luftman, 2003; Luftman & Brier, 1999; Moody, 2003; Ormerod, 1998; Porter, 1985; Reich & Benbasat, 2000; Sabherwal & Chan, 2001; Smits et al., 1997; Venkatraman, 1991). This notion of alignment is not necessarily new and it can be traced back to "early days" as depicted in Thompson's (1967) statement: "Survival rests on the co-alignment of technology as task environment with a viable domain, and of organizational design and structure appropriate to that domain" (quoted in Henderson & Venkatraman, 1990).

Walton (1989) also claims that strategic alignment is more than IT plans that are linked to the overall business strategy. Following this argument, most authors describe IS/IT strategic alignment as a process that includes *business strategy, business organization, IS infrastructure* and *IT strategy.* Assuming that managers have enough information and knowledge about each of the four domains, they can use such a model to focus attention in the company (Baets, 1996). Figure 11.2 depicts the IS strategic alignment model made popular by Venkatraman (1991). Henderson & Venkatraman (1992), introduces the notion of *fit* (vertical alignment of the external and internal environments of the organization) and *linkage* (horizontal alignment of the business and the IT domain of the firm) to account for the different forms of alignment. The *business fit* is the attempt to align strategy formation and implementation. The *IT fit* is analogous to it and supports the idea that an IT strategy should be aligned to the IT infrastructure that defines the architectures and processes in the IT domain.

The fact that IS/IT has become a major mode of organizational transformation seems evident. However, the way in which these models of alignment, such as the one depicted in Figure 11.2, are employed in practice remains unclear and controversial. Currie and Bryson (1995) did a survey in 1994 on IT strategy and found out that, although, 75% of 180 participant companies in the UK and Ireland stated that they had an IT strategy that was aligned to the overall organizational strategy, very few were able to give information on the alignment process itself. We would suggest that the reason they could not explain it is because these models (and concepts) do not in fact reflect reality. They are deeply rooted in a Cartesian worldview. They make all sorts of assumptions about the phenomena being confronted. For example they assume that strategy is an object that can be aligned. Thus, when we align business strategy and IS/IT strategy, as suggested above, what do we *in fact align*? Do we

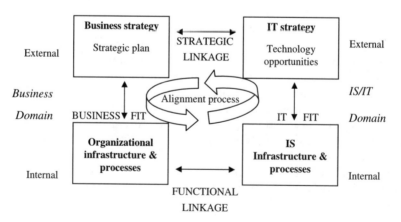

Figure 11.2: IS strategic alignment model (Adapted from Venkatraman, 1991 and Baets, 1996).

make the strategic plans (documents) agree — i.e. say the same things? Do we make the formulation and language of the objectives (or even intentions) in these two documents agree? But we know that strategy is more than the plan. Do we make the thinking of the business managers agree with the thinking of the IS/IT managers? Even if we can do it, we know that strategy is more than thinking (or intentions). We can go on with this list — plans, thinking, intentions, infrastructure, processes, practices, and so forth. However, every time we add one more *component* we have to admit that strategy is not really *in* that component. Moreover, strategy is not even *in* the way all of these connect together (or couple). Strategy is not on the *outside*, it is *inside*. What do we mean by this?

Up to now we have only talked about the relation between business strategy and IS/IT strategy. What about all the other relationships shown in Figure 11.2? The problem is that there is no external point, place or perspective where one could *stand* or be to perceive all of these things together, like objects on a table — so that one might say they are *aligned*.[3] This alignment thinking, as seen in Figure 11.2, conceptualizes these phenomena *as separate* and then raises the problem of how we align them. What if they were never separate in the first place? The problem is that we, as organizational actors (that is humans and technology), are always and already only in the inside (in the midst of it as it were). We are in strategy (already finding ourselves practicing it) and strategy is already in us (already imposed on us by emerging conditions). There simply is no *outside* perspective that will allow us to somehow *align* things. We can formulate this problem in autopoietic language by stating that: *strategy is not a matter of structure; it is a matter of identity*. We will develop this idea further below.

In contrast to the *alignment school* Ciborra (1994a, 1994b, 1996, 1997, 1998) has defended a more emergent approach to the concept of strategy based on the notions of tinkering, bricolage and improvisation — in the strategy-as-practice tradition. He argues that when we look at what practitioners actually do we find that improvisation is in fact a very common process. He suggests that improvisation acknowledges the already embedded and situated nature of individuals (and individual action) in organizations. He criticizes the ability of top management executives to control and realize strategies. Like Mintzberg he suggests that *crafting* strategy is a continuous and adaptive process of learning where *thinking* and *action* happens simultaneously, reversing the traditional sequence of formation first followed by implementation (Introna, 1997). In this line of argument, strategy may not precede action but instead it can emerge retrospectively once action has taken place — as Whittington (1993) suggests, the craftswoman "is intimately involved with her materials: she shapes her clay by personal touch, imperfections inspire her to artistic improvisation, hands and mind work together in a process of constant adaptation" (p. 25). Ciborra suggests that understanding the process of improvisation should help

---

[3]This is the Cartesian assumption that we (the mind or consciousness) are separate from the body (the extended world). What we find, however, is that the mind is already the world and the world is already in the mind. They are each other's possibility for being.

us not to be seduced by the tidy world of models, frameworks and formalized structures and the external rational view they assume. We should rather look at the world of "ordinary, sense-making and experience" (Ciborra, 1996) in the daily organizational activities. Drawing on the insights of Ciborra and the strategy-as-practice approach let us look at how autopoietic theory can help us to formulate an approach we will call *strategy-as-identity*.

Autopoiesis and Strategy-as-Identity

In this section, we want to introduce some outlines of an approach we will call strategy-as-identity using the insights provided by autopoietic theory whilst keeping in mind the work of Ciborra, Mintzberg and the strategy-as-practice research. When referring to *strategy* in our discussion we have in mind, not some content or object that is produced (like a plan), but rather *strategizing* as an ongoing process (of doing) that happens in all parts of the organization and not just in privileged places such as senior management meetings.

To start off, it is worth first posing the question of what strategizing is for, what is it supposed to do? We would suggest, and most authors would agree with this, that the purpose of strategizing is for an organization (or entity more generally) to survive in a complex and dynamic environment. Fundamentally strategizing is about long term survival. Given this formulation one might ask *what is it that is to survive?* Most certainly it is not structure — or rather structuration (Giddens, 1984) — since the organization is structurally open and coupled with its environment. This means that the ongoing structuration will be subject to structural drift. Rather, for an autopoietic system to survive it must maintain its *identity*. Thus, the question of identity is central to strategizing. However, one must immediately point out that identity does not exist *separately* from structuration (Varela & Maturana, 1987). For a chair to be identified *as a chair* certain necessary structural relationships need to remain present. Nevertheless, the structural relationships of a chair can be changed without it losing its identity as a chair. Identity is *always* immanent in structure/structuration but not reducible to it. Furthermore, structuration — in as much as it wants to retain structural coupling with its environment (which is a condition of its survival) — can only change in response to the perturbations provided by its environment. This means that in strategizing the question of *who or what we are, or want to be* (identity) can never be thought of separately from the question of *what are we becoming* (structuration) or from the question *what we are allowed/constrained to become* (structural coupling), which is again inseparable for the question *who or what we are, or want to be* (identity), and so forth, as depicted in Figure 11.3.

If identity is central to strategizing then it is vital that the emergence and maintenance of identity be understood. In the autopoietic social system (or entity) the emerging identity is the result of the ontogenic structural drift. This means that strategizing is not the making of a choice as such (of alternative possible futures as often suggested in the strategy literature). *It is rather the maintenance of an emerging identity in and through structural drift.* It is the historical becoming as the outcome of

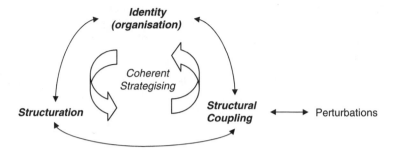

Figure 11.3: The autopoietic relationships of strategy-as-identity.

structurally mediated interactions with the environment. Again, it is important to note that the interaction here is always structurally mediated (recall our thought experiment of the door discussed above). Identity emerges as a result of structurally mediated perturbations within the constraints of identity — i.e. identity is medium and outcome of structural drift. Indeed, we will claim that identity (re)formation that does not flow from ontogenic structural drift will expose the system to the risk of structural decoupling, which if persists could destroy the system.

To summarize: strategizing has two important counterpoints and a structuration process. The first counterpoint is the need to be exposed to ongoing structurally mediated perturbations from the environment. This generates the need and basis for ongoing change. The second counterpoint is the maintenance of identity in the face of the need to change. Thus, strategy is about stability (identity) and change (structural drift) *at the same time*. The structuration process that holds or brings these two counterpoints together in a coherent way is improvisation as correctly identified by Ciborra (1999, 2000).

Improvisation is not simply incidental activities *added on* by incompetent organizational actors that ought to be targeted so as to bring the system *back under control*. They are essential practices of skillful coping by actors that have a subtle understanding of the simultaneity of change (structural drift) and stability (identity). How does this skillful coping happen? Ciborra (1999, 2001) argues that improvisation happens as part of our *Befindlichkeit* (a term he takes from Heidegger). *Befindlichkeit* "combines the idea of situatedness and of feeling and faring, of where and how one finds itself" (Ciborra, 2001, p. 6). It reflects a certain mood in which we find ourselves. Mood is understood as a certain attunement with the situation — such as the *sensing of the mood of the meeting*. Importantly, the *mood of the meeting* is not something we choose, it is rather something we already find ourselves in when we become aware of it. Ciborra suggests that the disclosure of the world, in mood, can overwhelm us and shift to a mood of panic or we can respond to it with resoluteness (see Heidegger, 1962, p. 296). Most improvisation, bricolage, and tinkering happens, however, as an integral part of *simply getting the job done.* Nevertheless, they are all based on a certain *attunement* (Dreyfus, 1992). Thus, improvisation by its very nature always starts with an attunement to the *already there* structure — it admits the always already situated and boundedness of action but also simultaneously the possibilities to be. Improvisation, in the moment of enactment fuses together situatedness and possibilities in what Ciborra (1999) calls the *Augenblick* (the moment of vision):

> During the 'moment of vision' of improvisation, recollection and anticipation reach far beyond the immediate interval defined by retention [memory] and protention [anticipation]. They go both below the 'iceberg' reaching deep-seated because of motives of action, and above, attaining an open projection into the future (p. 91).

Thus, improvisation is never simply an *ad hoc* and haphazard process, as often characterized. It is indeed the most fundamental basis of all autopoietic action. We see improvisation most clearly in the way language functions in everyday life. When confronted with a thing or a situation we are unfamiliar with, or somehow unique, we do not immediately invent new words to describe it. Rather, we search for what *we have* and try to improvise a description in which the words retain their known meaning but are used in such a way as to indicate something more than what is merely there. If we were to use a completely new set of words no one would understand (structural decoupling). If we use only the usual descriptions, the uniqueness confronting us will not be indicated. Through improvisation, the rigidity of language is made plastic. We describe *and* create. In improvisation, language is both medium and outcome. Strategizing (through improvisation) emerges and is crafted at the same time. The strategizing process cannot simply choose a new identity. In strategizing identity is not simply selected; it rather emerges as the ongoing coherence (between change and stability) crafted through improvisation in response to environmental perturbations. The task of management is not to *make* strategy but rather to improvise (interpret, reinterpret, articulate and rearticulate) the emerging identity — to shape and be shaped by it.

IS/IT Strategy-as-Identity in Practice

Let us now consider the vertical split in the alignment model (as depicted in Figure 11.2). This split refers to the relationship between business strategy/processes and IS/IT strategy/processes — the issue of *linkage*. Our argument is that such a *split* is not there in the manner suggested by these models. Of course it might be that the IS/IT practitioners conceive the identity of the organization differently to the business practitioners. This will mean that their improvisation may be conditioned in a different way. This could lead to a fragmentation of the structural drift, which could endanger the organization in the long run. Thus, the most important strategic question for IS/IT practitioners as well as business practitioners in the organization is to (re)articulate a cohesive, coherent and situated identity as an ongoing strategizing practice. Are there examples of such practices?

Ciborra discusses an example of this strategy-as-identity approach in Olivetti (Ciborra, 1994a). According to him identity has been an important requirement to its successful ongoing strategizing process, which has been very pragmatic and under-pinned by uncertainties, in spite of the rational appearance of top management's actions. He argues that Olivetti's global technology strategy does not consist of selecting the best alternatives in the market, but instead it involves constantly confronting the question: "what business are we in". By doing this, it tries to recognize and interpret its product and market identity as well as its boundaries (i.e. what sort of structural drift will make it become something other than what it is). The result has been an organization structure and strategy that emerges implicitly through ongoing improvised tinkering rather than being clearly specified beforehand. Ciborra (1998) also defends the impossibility of enforced top-down alignment by analyzing the pharmaceutical company *Hoffmann La Roche* and their use of Internet/ Intranet as their backbone of strategic marketing. He describes the transition from the corporate network *MedNet*, aimed at increasing the globalization and integration levels through standardization to an Internet/Intranet platform. The first system, which started in the second half of the 1980s, was finally discontinued in the mid 1990s, after being considered a total failure due to its low levels of adoption. The second alternative furnished an emerging context grounded on decentralization, autonomy and loose coupling where organizational unit were expected to improvise (Ciborra, 1998). However, what made this emergent alternative work is a well established and understood identity.

This chapter set out to challenge much of the contemporary work on IS/IT strategy. It asks that managers take a fundamentally different view of strategy as an ongoing process of strategizing. The process that drives this strategizing is ongoing improvisation in which identity (stability and continuity) is maintained in the face of environmentally induced structural drift (change and innovation) *at the same time*. It is the ongoing simultaneity of stability and change that is the challenge for strategizing practices. It is hoped that this chapter will start this *cosmological shift* in the world of practicing managers, even if the full implications of this approach cannot be articulated here (for a further critique of the alignment school, see Brigham and Introna (2007) in this volume).

References

Angell, I., & Smithson, S. (1991). *Information systems management: Opportunities and risks.* London: Macmillan.
Aspesi, C., & Vardhan, D. (1999). Brilliant strategy, but can you execute it? *McKinsey Quarterly, 5*(1), 88–99.
Baets, W. (1996). Some empirical evidence on IS strategy alignment in banking. *Information & Management, 30*, 155–177.
Beinhocker, E. (1999). Robust adaptive strategies. *Sloan Management Review, 40*(3).
Berry, M., & Taggart, J. (1998). Combining technology and corporate strategy in small high tech firms. *Research Policy, 26*, 883–895.
Brockway, D., & Hurley, M. (1998). Achieving IT success. *Information Management & Computer Security, 6/5*, 199–204.

Carr, N. (2003). IT doesn't matter. *Harvard Business Review, 81*(5), 41–49.

Chan, Y. E. (2002). Why haven't we mastered alignment? The importance of the informal organization structure. *MIS Quarterly Executive, 1*(2), 97–112.

Ciborra, C. (1994a). A platform for surprises: The organization of global technology strategy at Olivetti. In: R. Baskerville, S. Smithson, O. Ngwenyama & J. I. DeGross (Eds.), *Transforming organizations with informations technology (A-49)*. North-Holland IFIP: Elsevier Science.

Ciborra, C. (1994b). *Strategic information systems*. New York: Wiley.

Ciborra, C. (1996). Improvisation and information technology in organizations. *Proceedings of the ICIS (1996)*.

Ciborra, C. (1997). Crisis and foundations: An enquiry into the nature and limits of models and methods in the discipline. *Proceedings of the 5th ECIS*, Vol. 3.

Ciborra, C. (1998). From tool to gestell — Agendas for managing the information infrastructure. *Information Technology & People, 11*(4), 305–327.

Ciborra, C. (1999). Notes on improvisation and time in organizations. *Accounting, Management & Information Technology, 9*, 77–94.

Ciborra, C. (2000). *From control to drift: The dynamics of corporate information infrastructure*. Oxford: Oxford University Press.

Ciborra, C. U. (2001). *In the mood for knowledge: A new study of improvisation*. Working Paper 94, Working Paper Series, London School of Economics and Political Science, London [WWW document] http://is2.lse.ac.uk/wp/pdf/WP94.PDF (Accessed 1 December 2005).

Coleman, H. (1999). What enables self-organizing behaviour in businesses. *Emergence Journal, 1*(1), 33.

Currie, W. (1995). *Management strategy for IT*. London: Pitman Publishing.

Currie, W., & Bryson, C. (1995). IT strategy: Formal rational orthodoxy or contingent adhocracy? *Omega-International Journal Management Science, 23*(6), 677–689.

Dreyfus, H. (1992). *What computers still can't do: A critique of artificial reason*. Cambridge, MA: MIT Press.

Galliers, R., & Baker, B. (1994). *Strategic information management*. Oxford: Butterworth-Heinemann.

Giddens, A. (1984). *The constitution of society*. Berkeley: University of California Press.

Handel, M. (1986). Clausewitz in the age of technology. In: M. Handel (Ed.), *Clausewitz and modern technology* (pp. 51–94). London: Frank Cass.

Heidegger, M. (1962). In: J. Macquarrie & E. Robinson (trans.), *Being and time*. New York: Harper and Row.

Henderson, J., & Venkatraman N. (1990). Strategic alignment: A model for organizational transformation via information technology, Center for Information Systems Research WP No. 217, *Sloan* WP No.3223-90.

Henderson, J., & Venkatraman, N. (1992). Making Sense of IT: Strategic Alignment and Organizational Context, *Center for Information Systems Research* WP No. 247, *Sloan* WP No. 3475-92BPS.

Hu, Q., & Huang, C. D. (2006). Using the balanced scorecard to achieve sustained IT-business strategic alignment: A case study. *Communications of the AIS, 17*, 181–204.

Husserl, E. (1970). *The crisis of European sciences and transcendental phenomenology: An introduction to phenomenological philosophy*. Evanston, IL: Northwestern University Press.

Introna, L. (1997). *Management, information and power*. London: Macmillan Press.

Introna, L. D. (2003). Complexity theory and organisational intervention? Dealing with (in)commensurability. In: E. Mittleton-Kelly (Ed.), *Complex systems and evolutionary perspectives on organisations* (pp. 205–220). Oxford: Elsevier.

Jantsch, E. (1980). *The self-organizing universe.* Oxford: Pergamon Press.

Jarzabkowski, P. (2003). Strategic practices: An activity theory perspective on continuity and change. *Journal of Management Studies, 40*(1), 23–55.

Jarzabkowski, P. (2004). Strategy as practice: Recursiveness, adaptation and practices-in-use. *Organization Studies, 25*(4), 529–560.

Johnson, G., Melin, L., & Whittington, R. (2003). Micro strategy and strategizing: Towards an activity-based view?. *Journal of Management Studies, 40*(1), 3–22.

Johnson, G., & Scholes, K. (1984). *Exploring corporate strategy.* London: Prentice Hall.

Jones, M. C., Taylor, G., & Spencer, B. (1995). The CEO/CIO relationship revisited: An empirical assessment of satisfaction with IS. *Information & Management, 29*, 123–130.

Karake, Z. (1997). Managing information resources and environmental turbulence. *Information Management & Computer Security, 5/3*, 93–99.

Kearns, G. S., & Sabherwal, R. (2007). Strategic alignment between business and information technology: A knowledge-based view of behaviors, outcome, and consequences. *Journal of Management Information Systems, 23*(3), 129–162.

Luftman, J. N. (2003). Assessing IT/business alignment. *Information Systems Management, 20*(4), 9–15.

Luftman, J. N., & Brier, T. (1999). Achieving and sustaining business — IT alignment. *California Management Review, 42*(1), 109–122.

Luhmann, N. (1986). The autopoiesis of social systems. In: F. Geyer (Ed.), *Sociocybernetics paradoxes.* London: SAGE Publications.

Luhmann, N. (1990). *Essays on self-reference.* New York: Columbia University Press.

Luhmann, N. (1993). Ecological communication: Coping with the unknown. *Systems Practice, 6*(5), 527–540.

Luhmann, N. (1995). *Social systems.* California: Stanford University Press.

Markides, C. (1999). A dynamic view of strategy. *Sloan Management Review, 40*(3).

Mingers, J. (1995). *Self-producing systems.* New York: Plenum Press.

Mintzberg, H. (1987). The strategy concept 1: Five Ps for strategy. *California Management Review, 30*, 11–24.

Mintzberg, H. (1994). *The rise and fall of strategic planning.* New York: The Free Press.

Mintzberg, H. et al., (1985). Of strategies, deliberate and emergent. *Strategic Management Journal, 6*, 257–272.

Mintzberg, H., Ahlstrand, B., & Lampel, J. (1998). *Strategy safari.* London: Prentice Hall.

Mintzberg, H., & Lampel, J. (1999). Reflecting on the strategy process. *Sloan Management Review, 40*(3).

Moody, K. W. (2003). New meaning to IT alignment. *Information Systems Management, 20*(4), 30–35 New York.

Ormerod, R. (1998). Putting soft OR methods to work: Information systems strategy development in Palabora. *Omega-International Journal Management Science, 26*(1), 75–98.

Porter, M. (1980). *Competitive strategy.* New York: The Free Press.

Porter, M. (1985). *Competitive advantage: Creating and sustaining superior performance.* New York: Free Press.

Reich, B. H., & Benbasat, I. (2000). Factors that influence the social dimension of alignment between business and IT objectives. *MIS Quarterly, 24*(1), 81–113.

Sabherwal, R., & Chan, Y. E. (2001). Alignment between business and IS strategies: A configurational approach. *Information Systems Research*, *12*(1), 11–33.

Seidl, D. (2005). *Organisational identity and self-transformation. An autopoietic perspective.* Ashgate: Aldershot.

Smits, M. et al., (1997). Assessment of information strategies in insurance companies in the Netherlands. *Journal of Strategic Information Systems*, *6*, 129–148.

Thompson, J. (1967). *Organizations in action: Social sciences bases of administrative theory.* New York: McGraw-Hill.

Varela, F., & Maturana, H. (1987). *The tree of knowledge.* Boston: Shambhala.

Venkatraman, N. (1991). IT-induced business reconfiguration. In: M. Scott-Morton (Ed.), *The Corporation of the 1990s: IT & Organizational Transformation.*

Walton, R. (1989). *Up and running: Integrating information technology and the organization.* Boston: Harvard Press.

Whitaker, R. (1995). Self-organization, autopoiesis and enterprises. http://www.acm.org/siggroup/ois/auto/Main.html

Whittington, R. (1993). *What is strategy — and does it matter?.* London: Routledge.

Whittington, R. (2003). The work of strategizing and organizing: For a practice perspective. *Strategic Organization*, *1*(1), 119–127.

Whittington, R. (2006). Completing the practice turn in strategy research. *Organization Studies*, *27*(5), 613–634.

Chapter 12

Strategy as Hospitality, Bricolage and Enframing: Lessons from the Identities and Trajectories of Information Technologies

Martin Brigham and Lucas D. Introna

ABSTRACT

The purpose of this chapter is to contribute to the debate and practice of technologically mediated changes in organised contexts. The chapter develops an approach to understand the relations between technologies, organising and strategising based upon the concepts of hospitality, bricolage and enframing. With the support of case material from a longitudinal study of a mobile incident management system at a UK fire service, we set out how the largely ignored concepts of hospitality, bricolage and enframing provide a basis to reorient management practice away from dominant preoccupations with internal and external alignment, top-down planning and a coherence view of the firm and its activities. Strategic changes are better understood as iterative, ambiguous and paradoxical hospitable/hostile relations between hosts and guests. The chapter concludes with practical and ethical implications for the reflective practice of managing.

Introduction[1]

Management theory and practice since the 1990s has emphasised the importance of aligning information technologies with the strategic direction and goals of the organisation. Alignment begets, it is argued, integration, coherence and complementary capabilities from which the organisation can develop a distinctive and coherent

---

[1]For an extended version of the argument in this chapter see Brigham and Introna (2006).

strategic focus that will provide sustainable competitive advantage (e.g. Porter, 1985).

For the purposes of this chapter we suggest that the concept of strategic alignment, and the implications associated with it, is premised upon two problematic assumptions. The first is that it is possible and desirable to align (in some sense) the internal and external activities of an organisation to its IT infrastructure. Recent research in the strategy literature, particularly research that has emphasised strategy as a practice, has begun to challenge this view. Jarzabkowski (2005), for example, describes organised contexts as irreducibly pluralistic and how this has implications for firms because it means that they often enact multiple and conflicting strategic objectives (see also Whittington, 2003). For Jarzabkowski, the *normal science* of strategising is characterised by divergent and fragmented rationalities and goals. Strategies compete with one another rather than cohere unproblematically around singular organisational goals. The implications for organising are significant because if the practice of strategy is pluralistic, the identity work undertaken as part of strategising activities becomes a central feature of managers' activity (see Ciborra, 1994; Introna, Chapters 9 and 11).

The second problematic assumption related to the concept of strategic alignment is that it presupposes that IT can be deployed to leverage organisational transformation in a way that is largely controllable and can be *a priori* measured and determined — i.e. introducing IT is associated with the ability to manage impacts in a determinable manner. This is based on a view of technological infrastructures as material devices that are *objective*, i.e. separate from us that we can simply use to do, or not to do, whatever we want. According to this realist *tool* paradigm, we need to understand and manage the *impact* that IT has on organisations, or social practices more generally, as it is taken up and used in everyday situations (see Introna, 2007 for a critique of this tool view of technology). To manage this *impact* it is proposed that we study many different examples and then inductively build general models that are supposed to inform us how to best manage IT. Such approaches are underpinned by a view that we can design and use these tools without the tools immediately and simultaneously (re)making what counts as human activity and *using* us (Arnold, 2003; Brigham & Introna, 2006).

This chapter suggests that concepts from modern European philosophers, such as Martin Heidegger, Jacques Derrida and Emmanuel Levinas, can make significant contributions to the emerging problematisation of management as strategic alignment. The European phenomenological tradition is, we suggest, particularly well attuned to issues related to the problematic of identity and how capacities to act are mutually constitutive (i.e. the social and the technical are mutually and simultaneously co-constitutive). In order to set out our approach we begin by describing briefly the concepts of *hospitality, bricolage and enframing*. Next we present case material from the implementation of a mobile incident management system at a UK fire brigade in order to exemplify the value of our concepts. We conclude by discussing the implications of taking seriously management practice as hospitality, bricolage and enframing.

Three Concepts to Rethink the Practice of Strategy

Hospitality

Hospitality is derived from the Latin *hospes* meaning stranger or hostile stranger. It is, according to Derrida (1997, p. 110), the "welcoming of the other; the invitation to the stranger" that is made possible by the asymmetrical capacities of a host and a guest (see also Dikeç, 2002). Here we can note that the etymology of hospitality contains within itself the possibility of hostility from either host or guest such that either may need to reconsider their practices, rituals and customs — the guest well may bring their own world with them. In terms of IT, Ciborra (1998, p. 196) suggests that hospitality "describes the phenomenon of dealing with new technology as an ambiguous stranger". But how does this hosting relationship manifest itself in relation to IT? Ciborra (2004, p. 114) explains that "technology, as a guest, presents itself to the host endowed with affordances.... But that is just the beginning of an open-ended process: the guest also possesses its own dynamics and will begin to align the host according to certain needs and constraints". In this sense, information technology is not just a passive possibility for doing something, which just sits there until being used (or not). Rather, its mere presence in the situation already brings with it new ways or possibilities for doing things, new ways of talking about doing and new ways of thinking about doing — some of it expected, some of it not at all (see Introna in Chapter 9 for a discussion of co-constitutive nature of the socio-technical relationship).

Bricolage

Improvisation and working around things in novel ways are important features of accommodating a guest — an integral and ongoing part of organising. It is an essential practice of hospitality. For our purposes we can suggest that bricolage is not an incidental activity *added on* by users once IT implementation has been complete (see Robey, Ross, & Boudreau, 2002). In organised contexts bricolage occurs as an integral part of *simply getting the job done*. But as Ciborra (1999, 2001) notes, improvisation happens, importantly, as part of our *Befindlichkeit* or situated and prevailing mood. So, for instance, the *mood of the meeting* is not something we choose, it is rather something we already find ourselves in when we become aware of it. Skilled actors, or improvisers, are in tune with the disclosure of the prevailing mood, grasps *in the moment*, the world as a totality with all its (im)possibilities to enact necessary improvisation.

Enframing

Heidegger (1962) argues that we as human beings (and managers in particular) are always and already immersed in a whole nexus of concern, a situated mood, in which

certain activities are considered possible while others are not. IT — and our relationship with it — is, in these terms, an outcome of a particular *technological* way of
seeing and form of conduct that apprehends the world as something to be ordered
and shaped in line with our projects, intentions and desires. This *technological enframing* or *Gestell* (as he calls it) means that problems to be solved show up as
requiring technical solutions: "Enframing means the gathering together of that
setting-upon that sets upon man, i.e. challenges him forth to reveal the real, in the
mode of ordering, as standing-reserve" (Heidegger, 1977, p. 20). Ciborra and
Hanseth (1998, pp. 321–322) suggest that IT exemplifies enframing as positing a
world available for our ordering. IT infrastructures act as "formative contexts, [that]
shape not only the work routines, but also the ways people look at practices, consider
them *natural* and give them their overarching character of necessity.... Imagining,
world views and reform initiatives, or new designs are moulded by the subtle and
hidden influence of infrastructures". With this new vocabulary to think about the
relation between strategy, organising and technologies, we now turn to the empirical
case material we will draw upon to illustrate the concepts of hospitality, bricolage
and enframing within the context of organising and strategising.

Formative Contexts and Legacies: UK Fire Services

Fire services respond to emergency fire calls and have a statutory duty to attend fire-
related incidents and undertake fire safety work.[2] The UK Fire Service is publicly
funded, but brigades are directly accountable to local fire authorities, which receive
funding, policy guidance and instructions from the central/national government. A
recent major policy review (Bain, Lyons, & Young, 2002) concluded that fire services
were characterised by a *weak managerialism* and *lack of strategic leadership* by senior
officers and central government. This review recommended *top to bottom* modernisation comprising of a strategic shift from incident management to fire prevention,
devolved conditions and working practices, the allocation of resources based upon
changing levels of risk throughout the day, regionalised fire provision and greater
collaboration between emergency services.

Policy statements and reviews of the public sector, such as the White Paper on
Modernising Government bring to the foreground *joined up* working and collaboration through IT as a key driver of efficiency and public sector modernisation
(Cabinet Office, 1999). The role of IT, by contrast, has been remarkable by its
insignificance in national reports and reviews of the fire service throughout the last
two decades. The 1990s and early 2000s context of uncertainties about government
funding for IT projects across the fire service, meant that IT initiatives were focused

---

[2]The research described here is an ethnographically inspired long-term case study of a mobile data infrastructure known as the vehicle mounted data system (VMDS). See Brigham and Introna (2006) for a
detailed description of the research methodology. Research was conducted *via* interviews, observation of
fire crews, attending meetings and collecting archival material from the late 1990s and continued perio-
dically to date.

on individual brigades with little emphasis upon standardisation or collaboration between brigades or interoperability between emergency services.

Hereford and Worcester Fire Brigade was the focus of the case study research. The brigade is a comparatively small, non-metropolitan brigade, not known for being a leader of fire service reform (Cox, 1994). The brigade has over 700 firefighters, plus over 100 control room and non-uniformed staff. Stations have designated *turn out* areas that set out the geographical boundary of station responsibility, but fire crews move outside these boundaries for major or concurrent incidents. The brigade is responsible for a large geographical area of mostly semi-rural countryside but also busy motorways.

Hospitality and the Vehicle Mounted Data System

Hospitality does not usually begin with hostility. Guests are to be welcomed by the hosts and the guest must present itself as something worth inviting in. Even, perhaps, something needing to be invited. The brigade installed a mobile incident management system — called the vehicle mounted data system or VMDS — on 36 of its fire appliances in March 1996. It represented a major strategic endeavour for the brigade and was the first such system to be implemented into the UK fire service. VMDS screens provide access to risk information on buildings; tactical plans for large-scale risks; standard incident officer procedures; chemical information and ordnance survey maps (Goodwin, 1997). The VMDS integrates a wide range of operational information that was previously held on paper, based at stations, communicated by radio or kept by watches (working groups of firefighters) into a standardised and real-time IT infrastructure. In addition to providing real-time access through the VMDS the project also moved the management of information from stations to a newly formed operational intelligence unit.

When it came to the inviting the VMDS guest into the brigade nothing was as compelling as the death of colleagues. In September 1993 two of the brigade's firefighters died at a major fire incident at a large factory. After the incident, and an investigation into the deaths of two firefighters, two Health and Safety Improvement Notices were served on the brigade in May 1994 — one for breathing apparatus procedures and the other for *inadequate provision of information*. The latter Notice led to the implementation of the VMDS.

At the time of the factory fire, the brigade's practice, common to brigades across the UK, was to hold a series of paper-based risk cards in A4 folders that were kept in fire appliances. The Improvement Notice served on the brigade set out a two-fold failure of these practices. The first failure was not to have taken advantage of the benefits of IT: fire services lagged behind other emergency services that had introduced IT. The second, and related, information failure was that paper-based records did not afford quick access to information to all fire crews.

In response to the Improvement Notice, the brigade's operational intelligence unit concluded that there were considerable constraints with the existing paper-based system and recommended the replacement of paper with electronic records. Problems with the A4 folders included the spatial dislocation of folders, physical storage and the temporal problems of accessing risk information before arriving at an incident, especially for crews attending incidents outside of their turn out boundaries (Hereford & Worcester Fire Brigade, 1997).

Framing the implementation of the VMDS as necessary for the effective management of information constituted the technology as a tool to improve record keeping and to provide access to information as and when it was required. There were few voices of dissent from the association of the VMDS as a useful device for front-line fire service work. Thus, the perceived failure of the previous paper-based folders and maps was an important precondition for constituting the VMDS as a necessary and welcome guest. But what did the guest bring with it?

Hostility, Forgetting and Remembering

Constituting the VMDS as the solution for the inadequacy and failure of the paper-based system meant that it became possible to forget the potential hostility of the VMDS — to forget its limits and that guests might have their own preoccupations and demands. Recalling the deaths of two other firefighters in the mid-1970s provides a reminder of how the framing of *information failure* depended on practices through which information was maintained, shared and consulted before the introduction of the VMDS. It reminds us, in other words, of how certain practices of remembering and informing engender simultaneously also a forgetting. Such forgetting becomes decisive if it sets up the limits within which choices about future information practices are considered.

Firefighters were sometimes reluctant to talk about the death of colleagues, particularly with reference to the adequacy (or not) of information management practices in such cases. One reason for this was that there were few practices apart from formalised records that sustained collective remembering (see Orr, 1996). Nonetheless one officer, with over 25 years service, recounted the death of two firefighters in the mid-1970s. He emphasised the situated realities of fire incidents that cannot be known completely in advance and that demand improvisation, but also that information failure is marked out by absences.

> that fellow that died in the incident, went [with two others] off on Monday morning to go and have a look at it [the incident] ... they went along and said there's definitely a need here to get risk visits on it so luckily we did have a fair bit of knowledge about the building before we went in ... we also found out they had disconnected the sprinkler system.... No matter what information — sometimes you could provide people with every scrap of information that is available on a particular risk tragedies will still occur ...

This account of an incident over 25 years ago evokes a failure of information management practices in two very important (and seemingly forgotten) senses: (a) the impossibility of complete and *a priori* knowledge of the future irrespective of the level of information available beforehand, and (b) the marginal presence, in the collective memory, of accounts of this significant incident. Narratives from long-serving fire-fighters, the exchanging of *war stories* between fire crews, for example, were largely absent from organisational records, which often comprised of formalised, single sentence bullet points. Adopting the VMDS presupposed an evaluative comparison *with existing paper-based practices* because this is the technological mood through which pre-VMDS practices (or pre-IT practice more generally) are most often evaluated. However, that which made these paper-based practices work (or not) was the tacit improvising practices not included in such evaluation (mere traces in the collective memories of the fire crews).

Even if fire crews remembered the limits of such a technological framing of frontline information, we were surprised that crews were so welcoming of the VMDS — senior officers could not understand this either. Would not highly unionised fire crews anticipate the standardisation of their work practices and task rationalisation based on the potential capabilities (or affordances) embodied with the VMDS? Maybe this welcoming attitude was to do with crews' assumed understanding of brigade autonomy and boundaries? However, the brigade's autonomy and boundaries, which it seems they presumed, were premised on the notion of locally and collectively held, often tacit, knowledge of the fire crews of the brigade. If the VMDS will transform local knowledge into explicit publicly available *common* knowledge (held in the database of the system) would this not challenge brigade autonomy and boundaries?

The implementation of the VMDS was framed, from the start, to coincide and consolidate existing organisational boundaries, particularly in terms of access, control and manageability of information vis-à-vis other brigades (see Bowker & Star, 1999). It was aligned with the existing brigade structure. The VMDS provided information to all fire crews, but access and control of information remains centred within the brigade and is compatible with the established brigade boundary for incident responsibility. Even the formation of a new Operational Intelligence Unit did not significantly undermine the social organisation of watches. Fire crews are expected to submit to new forms of surveillance, but risk assessments are still undertaken by fire crews and managed within the brigade. We would suggest that standardisation of access, control and manageability is most usefully conceptualised not only as a technical matter, but it also presupposes particular organisational practices that are inscribed into a technological infrastructure — at this time, however, we should note that standardisation was not necessarily associated with the challenging of watch practices or with inter-operability of IT between brigades.

Bricolage: Temporal and Spatial (Dis)connections

Welcoming a guest, into our house so to speak, also means adjusting to its modes of doing things. This might mean developing improvised *work-arounds* in order to live with this ambiguous stranger. Because the system was a high-profile initiative, the brigade was often involved in demonstrating the VMDS to other fire services, particularly at national fire services exhibitions and conferences. These highly choreographed formal demonstrations contrasted with the situated and collective character (see Suchman, 1987) of fire crews' work.

Interaction with the VMDS on the move gave rise to a number of spatial and temporal effects that crews described as compromising their readiness on the way to incidents. Before the VMDS was implemented, each fire crew had a formal and informal division of labour on the way to incidents. The VMDS made this collective structure of interaction much more difficult if not impossible. Bolted to the dashboard, only one member of the crew could access information on the move. Temporal pressures on the officer accessing the VMDS intensified because of the compression of interaction within fire appliances around the VMDS. Accessing information in addition to everything else that had to be done on the way to an incident was by no means a simple additional task. For many crews the spatial and temporal effects meant that VMDS would not be accessed until incident was reached and a more informal division of labour could be enacted.

The operational intelligence unit (created to standardise and facilitate the development of the database of the VMDS) undertook the task of transferring the A4 paper risk records to the VMDS. Stations sent their paper records to the unit for transferring onto the VMDS. It was quickly noticed by fire crews that a significant proportion of records had not been transferred onto the VMDS. Nor would they be transferred as part of the standardisation and rationalisation of the number of records available in the VMDS. Although stations were told to throw out their *spare* paper records and maps a number of stations were reluctant to do this and many crews kept copies of records and maps. Fire crews held these *in reserve* in their fire appliances as *back-ups* (see Faia-Correia et al., 1999). Not only had an attempt to remove paper records not occurred, but crews also consulted concealed *out of date* records in conjunction with the VMDS screens as they attempted to maintain the collective practice characteristic of pre-VMDS fire appliance collaboration.

Rationalising the number of risk records meant that although fire crews had *universal access* to records for the entirety of the brigade's area of responsibility, and the overall number of risk records fire crews could access increased, the number of risk records available for a particular station's turn-out boundary was often reduced. The problems of arbitrary, unsystematic and often out-of-date station-based records were replaced with absent records. For fire crews, the small number of records for a particular station was not, however, related to a lack of computer memory, but rather associated with the brigade's difficultly of recruiting a CAD/CAM specialists and a lack of financial resources at the operational intelligence unit.

The situated use of the VMDS (and informal demonstrations) problematised the supposed spatial reach and real-time temporality with which the VMDS was associated. The actual crew usage also brought to the foreground how the supposed *joined up* access to information on the move created spaces and times of disconnection (rather than connection). These situated activities (Brown & Duguid, 1991) illustrate how the ongoing ambiguities associated with IT infrastructures have to be resolved. But why did the crews accept this situation, i.e. create the improvised workaround to make it work? Acceptance of the VMDS by fire crews is possible because *full functionality* is deferred to the future: the identity of the VMDS is not yet complete. In this way fire crews can remain committed to the VMDS even while they continued to use *out-of-date* paper records and maps. The ambiguities associated with use of the VMDS, and the consequent enrolment of other actors by fire crews, brought to the fore two important points. First, whilst paper back-ups underpin the functionality of the VMDS, fire crews simultaneously demonstrate how their work is important. Second, within their particular structural location, backing-up the VMDS with paper records and maps is what fire crews can do to maintain the workability of this leading-edge IT infrastructure. This is indeed a requirement of hosting it.

The Enframing that (Re)constitutes the VMDS

Some five years after the VMDS was first implemented, the brigade set out the cost of the *second generation* VMDS, allocating a budget for 2003–2004 of £250,000 (Hereford & Worcester Fire Brigade, 2002). The remit of the VMDS also became translated into the brigade's strategic response to national e-government initiatives for local authorities. The investment in the electronic provision of local authority services through central e-government initiatives also indexes a shift away from a brigade approach to IT implementation. In November 2001, the Chief Fire Officers' Association submitted a bid to central government for a national e-government project (Chief and Assistant Chief Fire Officers Association, 2001; see also Department for Transport, Local Government & the Regions, 2002). The subsequent national project, termed *e-fire*, was "made up of five streams of work to develop products designed to help the Fire Service meet the government's 2005 e-government target" (London Fire and Emergency Planning Authority, 2005, p. 2). Significantly, one of the streams, *risk knowledge management and data sharing* draws upon brigades' VMDS initiatives. Information provision has been reworked from brigade level to *joined up* inter-brigade and inter-agency collaboration at a national level. In January 2005, the Office of the Deputy Prime Minister (ODPM) announced that the data-sharing stream of e-fire would be dropped due to the timetable of other e-government initiatives (London Fire and Emergency Planning Authority, 2005). Nonetheless, such initiatives demonstrate a pervasive technological mood of inter-operability and standardisation between brigades.

In 2003, the government's White Paper *Our Fire and Rescue Service* (ODPM, 2003) was published. This set out the government's commitment to modernisation of fire services based upon many of the recommendations made by Bain et al. (2002). For example, one of the central provisions of the 2004 *Fire and Rescue Services Act* is a shift toward regional fire services plus central government power to merge fire and rescue authorities *where authorities fail to work together through voluntary regional management arrangements* (ODPM, 2004, p. 2). As part of this move to regionalise fire service provision, and in the interest of public safety and *national resilience*, the legislation also provides powers for the central government to direct authorities on *the procurement of equipment in order to ensure a standardised approach*. In 2005, the ODPM also announced that a new nationwide digital radio system, to include both voice and data communication (including data held on mobile data systems), would be implemented by 2009. This national system will enable interoperability between fire services and other emergency services. From this we can suggest that as the boundaries between current and future practices is renegotiated, and mobile data system are constructed out of local, regional and national practices, these outcomes will not be determined by IT. Rather it will be the prevailing mood that requires technological solutions, which will shape strategising activities and constitute the fire service's conception of its future realities.

Implications for Strategy, Organising and Technologies

Our discussion has emphasised how the guest — the VMDS — can be understood as becoming increasingly a stranger to fire crews and the brigade. This is particularly apparent when the VMDS is considered over an extended period of time. Our description of the VMDS has suggested *that the guest can also become the host*. We have shown that the welcome guest (the VMDS), which started as a tool to help fire crews by replacing paper records with electronic ones (and in so doing prevent unnecessary deaths) emerges as more subtle and complex:

- It makes information available but it also simultaneously delegitimates informal tacit information that cannot be framed in its terms. Information is always incomplete and it is the tacit knowledge of the fire crew that is fundamental to making sense of risk information and how they relate to the situation *on the ground*.
- It transforms work practices in the fire appliance, but not in the way expected. Fire crew have to create a number of improvised work-arounds to make the VMDS work.
- Most profoundly the VMDS reframes (and enframes) the nature of work of the fire crews and the fire service. Through the standardisation and interoperability made possible by the VMDS, the understanding of what it means to manage fire services is fundamentally reconstituted. The guest, with all its hostility, becomes the host.

These insights have significant implications for fire service provision, but how might they contribute to rethinking the practices of strategy, organising and technologies generally?

The VMDS was implemented to rectify a perceived problem of a lack of information at the right place at the right time. It simultaneously reaffirmed access to information at the brigade level, top-down implementation, the existing crew structure and was mostly considered to be distinct from central government reforms and senior officer interests. Our case suggests that the implementation of IT infrastructures is often appraised by users against *existing* preoccupations and information management practices. Thus, the horizon of concern that configures reflections on IT is often, in the first instance, toward *alignment to institutionalised legacy practices*.

The VMDS was, then, assimilated into an existing formative context (Ciborra & Hanseth, 1998). But this is only one side of the effects associated with the VMDS. What counts as fire service work — what *business* the brigade are in — and actors' identities (fire crews and officers, the VMDS and the brigade more generally) cannot, we suggest, be taken as fixed *a priori* or unchanging over time. This is, then, a claim about the ongoing constitution of the identity of the VMDS and how interconnected practices associated with strategising and organising alter and remake the basis or *ground* on which demarcations are made and activities taken up as important ignored as irrelevant.

We have suggested that the ongoing emergence, expansion and contraction of patterns of strategic, organisational and technological activities challenge the view *that IT has reified impacts which can be aligned with strategic intentions*. The implication of this is that the concept of strategy as a pluralistic practice has to be accompanied with a thoroughgoing sense of the dynamic interplay between the making, remaking and unmaking of activities. When strategising is posited as a competing and fragmented practice we must simultaneously foreground the *identity work* that comprises the constitution of activities as contrasting, incoherent or aligned — i.e. the *mood* upon which strategic debate and deliberation occurs. From this we can suggest that strategising is equally about learning, changing and developing frames of understanding and practice as much as controlling and executing particular courses of action.

Our case material has demonstrated how the boundaries between organisational practices, technologies and strategies have been renegotiated on a terrain defined by a prevailing technological mood. With the implementation of the VMDS and the formation of the operational intelligence unit, the management of information, and the criteria for relevant information, is altered in significant ways. Electronic records are similar to paper records, but the introduction of brigade-wide information management practices presages what is denoted by hierarchy, standardised information and the boundaries of the brigade. What is conceived as *hierarchy* becomes connected to the bureaucratic practices set up by the operational intelligence unit whilst *standardisation* becomes associated with the management of information. Once this is grasped, we can begin to evaluate how the VMDS might expand and/or contract connections to local and national e-government initiatives, regional management and access to mobile data.

What might we make of our contention that the VMDS is implicated in remaking the *business of firefighting*? Our contention is that, in conjunction, the concepts of hospitality, improvisation and enframing, open up new horizons of intelligibility for reflective practitioners. Derrida (2000) suggests that hospitality is premised on an ongoing and irreducible double bind: to welcome a stranger requires the host to have the power to host, but unless the host surrenders their own power, there cannot be hospitality because the guest is subservient to the host's wishes. The possibility of hospitality arises, counter-intuitively perhaps, when host and guest begin to problematise their understanding of one another. It is only by going beyond hospitality, as it is conventionally conceived, that the guest would experience hospitality. We would claim that the real work of strategising is not alignment (and the coherence it assumes) but rather problematisation in which the identity of guest and host (the social and the technical) are continually questioned, interpreted and rendered problematic.

For Derrida (1999, 2000) and Levinas (1991, 1996) this double bind of hospitality invokes ethical dilemmas in relation to others — how to treat the guest in our midst (see also Jones, Parker, & ten Bos, 2005)? If by hospitality we mean welcoming that which is familiar, in a frame of calculative reciprocity and exchange, then forms of hospitality may be justifiable, but they may not be ethical. Fire crews, for instance, may consider their willing adoption of the VMDS an act of hospitality, but for Derrida and Levinas it would only be when the VMDS shifts from its taken for granted functionality and surprises the brigade, its officers and crews, that hospitality becomes an issue to be responded to — here, ethics is about the recurrence of decision making in the context of uncertainties, ambiguities and paradoxes. If an ethics of hospitality becomes possible when host and guest do not know how to treat each other, strategy as a practice of ethical hospitality is similarly invoked only when managing goes beyond the concepts of alignment and impact to an encounter with surprises and dilemmas that begin to confound taken for granted assumptions of identities and effects.

Not knowing what course of action to take or the basis for making a decision, paradoxically, opens up the possibility of strategising and organising as an ethical practice. When we are disturbed by others — people, events, policies or technologies — we encounter occasions for new ways of thinking and doing. Of course this does not mean that anything goes or that any decision is possible or desirable. Nor should we be taken as simply arguing against the importance of dominant ways of approaches to managing. We are, as we have suggested, always embedded in a nexus of concerns and practices. Rather we are indexing new ways of seeing, thinking and doing beyond what is possible when existing ways of speaking and acting are reevaluated.

We have suggested that information technologies can never be fully assimilated or domesticated. Acknowledging the irreducible and ongoing tensions associated with organisational practices and the problematic of strategizing — what business are we in? — becomes therefore a central feature of practitioners' responsibilities. Such work is also of course never finally accomplished. The concepts of hospitality, bricolage and enframing help us to foreground these responsibilities of managing and they open up new ways of thinking about strategising and organising as ethical practices. Our concern in this chapter has been to outline a different place to begin the activity of managing — one that we think provides for different forms of thought and practice. Reflective practitioners are, we suggest, those who notice, construct and engage, rather than disavow, the dilemmas constituted by activities associated with strategising, organising and technologies.

Acknowledgements

The empirical research was supported financially by the UK Economic and Social Research Council (ESRC number: R00429534042). Hereford and Worcester Fire Brigade provided generous access to research mobile information.

References

Arnold, M. (2003). On the phenomenology of technology: The "Janus-faces" of mobile phones. *Information and Organization, 13*, 231–256.

Bain, G., Lyons, M., & Young, A. (2002). *The future of the fire service: Reducing risk, saving lives. The independent review of the fire service.* London: ODPM.

Bowker, G. C., & Star, S. L. (1999). *Sorting things out: Classification and its consequences.* Cambridge, MA: MIT Press.

Brigham, M., & Introna, L. D. (2006). Hospitality, improvisation and Gestell: A phenomenology of mobile information. *Journal of Information Technology, 21*, 140–153.

Brown, J. S., & Duguid, P. (1991). Organizational learning and communities of practice: Toward a unified view of working, learning and innovation. *Organization Science, 2*, 40–57.

Cabinet Office. (1999). *Modernising Government White Paper.* Command Paper No: 4310, March, London: HMSO.

Chief and Assistant Chief Fire Officers Association [CACFOA]. (2001 November). *e-Fire: The fire service and e-government: Guidance for electronic service delivery.* Tamworth: CACFOA.

Ciborra, C. U. (1994). A platform for surprises: The organization of global technology strategy at Olivetti. In: R. Baskerville, S. Smithson, O. K. Ngwenyama & J. I. DeGross (Eds.), *Transforming organizations with information technology* (pp. 97–111). North Holland, IFIP: Elsevier Science.

Ciborra, C. U. (1998). Crisis and foundations: An inquiry into the nature and limits of models and methods in the information systems discipline. *Journal of Strategic Information Systems, 7*, 5–16.

Ciborra, C. U. (1999). Notes on improvisation and time in organizations. *Accounting, Management and Technologies, 9*(2), 77–94.

Ciborra, C.U. (2001). In the mood for knowledge: A new study of improvisation, Working Paper 94, *Working Paper Series, London School of Economics and Political Science*, London [WWW document] http://is2.lse.ac.uk/wp/pdf/WP94.PDF (Accessed 1 December 2005).

Ciborra, C. U. (2004). *The labyrinths of information: Challenging the wisdom of systems.* Oxford: Oxford University Press.

Ciborra, C. U., & Hanseth, O. (1998). From tool to *Gestell*: Agendas for managing information infrastructure. *Information Technology and People, 11*(4), 305–327.

Cox, J. (1994). How Wiltshire set about selecting new command and control "kit," *Fire*, July 23–27.

Department for Transport, Local Government and the Regions. (2002). *e-Gov@Local: Towards a national strategy for local e-government. A consultation paper*, London: Department for Transport, Local Government and the Regions.

Derrida, J. (1997). Community without community: Hospitality. In: J. D. Caputo (Ed.), *Deconstruction in a nutshell: A conversation with Jacques Derrida* (pp. 106–112). New York: Fordham University Press.

Derrida, J. (1999). *Adieu to Emmanuel Levinas* (P.-A. Brault & M. Nass, Trans.). Stanford, CA: Stanford University Press.

Derrida, J. (2000). *Of hospitality* (R. Bowlby, Trans.). Stanford, CA: Stanford University Press.

Dikeç, M. (2002). Pera, peras, poros: Longings for spaces of hospitality. *Theory, Culture and Society, 19*(1/2), 227–247.

Faia-Correia, M., Patriotta, G., Brigham, M., & Corbett, J. M. (1999). Making sense of telebanking information systems: The role of organizational back ups. *Journal of Strategic Information Systems, 8*(2), 143–156.

Goodwin, P. (1997). Vehicle mounted data system: Building on success, *Fire Engineers Journal,* September, 39–40.

Heidegger, M. (1962). *Being and time* (J. Macquarrie & E. Robinson, Trans.). New York: Harper and Row.

Heidegger, M. (1977). *The question concerning technology and other essays* (W. Lovitt, Trans.). New York: Harper and Row.

Hereford and Worcester Fire Brigade (1997). Vehicle mounted data system. *The Grapevine: The Official Journal of Hereford and Worcester Fire Brigade*, September, 8–9.

Hereford and Worcester Fire Brigade (2002). Budget working party agenda, *Hereford and Worcester Combined Fire Authority*, October, 1–26.

Introna, L. D. (2007). Making sense of ICT, new media and ethics. In: R. Mansell, C. Avgerou, D. Quah & R. Silverstone (Eds.), *Oxford handbook of information and communication technologies* (pp. 314–333). Oxford: Oxford University Press.

Jarzabkowski, P. (2005). *Strategy as practice: An activity based approach.* London: Sage.

Jones, C., Parker, M., & ten Bos, R. (2005). *For business ethics.* London: Routledge.

Levinas, E. (1991). *Otherwise than being or beyond essence* (A. Lingis, Trans.) Dordrecht: Kluwer.

Levinas, E. (1996). *Collected philosophical papers: Emmanual Levinas* (A. Lingis, Ed. & Trans.), Bloomington: Indiana University Press.

London Fire and Emergency Planning Authority [LFEPA]. (2005). *Progress report on the national fire service e-government project ("e-fire") and implementing e-government*, LFEPA Authority Meeting Minutes, Document No. FEP 657, 13 January.

ODPM (2003). *Our fire and rescue service.* Command Paper No: 5808, June, London: ODPM.

ODPM (2004). *Draft national procurement strategy for the fire and rescue service: A consultation document.* London: ODPM.

Orr, J. E. (1996). *Talking about machines: An ethnography of a modern job.* Ithaca, NY: ILR Press.

Porter, M. (1985). *Competitive advantage: Creating and sustaining superior performance.* New York: Free Press.

Robey, D., Ross, J. W., & Boudreau, M. C. (2002). Learning to implement enterprise systems: An exploratory study of the dialectics of change. *Journal of Management Information Systems, 19*(1), 17–46.

Suchman, L. A. (1987). *Plans and situated actions: The problem of human-machine communication.* Cambridge: Cambridge University Press.

Whittington, R. (2003). The work of strategising and organising: For a practice perspective. *Strategic Organisation, 1*(1), 56–65.

SECTION IV:

ICT (OUT)SOURCING

ICT sourcing has been an enduring theme in Information Management for the past 15 years. It is a reality for today's Chief Information Officers (CIOs), and a very confusing issue for many ICT workers, becoming unsure about their future in a global ICT market. In this chapter the main challenges as well as opportunities of various sourcing options are explored in a systematic way.

In the chapter of Hirschheim and George, three subsequent waves of ICT outsourcing are positioned, together with perspectives on the long-term evolution of ICT outsourcing. An overwhelming amount of quantitative reference material is provided, with a clear indication of the trends in ICT outsourcing. Willcocks et al. discuss the evolution of outsourcing capabilities in outsourcing markets during the past 15 years. It is shown how some characteristics of the outsourcing business changed dramatically during this period. A fairly complete methodological view is given on the supplier side of ICT outsourcing. In the chapter of Cumps et al. the Information Management impact on the demand side of outsourcing is discussed in two major outsourcing scenarios. The outsourcing process and structure elements are explicitly presented in the context of the integrative framework for information management of Maes, with an emphasis on the resource-based view of the firm. Finally, Dedene and Heene elaborate some operational issues in offshore outsourcing, including two case studies. Part of this chapter is devoted to practical guidelines that should lead to higher quality offshore projects.

The four chapters contain extensive references to the broad literature on ICT sourcing. Reading these chapters will unlock methodological views on dealing with sourcing from a CIO's point of view. The chapters all contain critical reflections on the long-term evolution of the ICT global sourcing market. It is clear that the long-term evolution of global ICT sourcing has a tremendous impact on governance and educational structures on this planet for the coming decade.

Chapter 13

Three Waves of Information Technology Outsourcing

Rudy Hirschheim and Beena George

ABSTRACT

Outsourcing, and in particular, offshore outsourcing has been the focus of much current debate in the U.S. recently. Opponents decry the job loss and other potential devastating effects on the economic structure of the country, while supporters contend that it contributes to the competitiveness of the organization and the growth of the economy. This chapter provides an overview of outsourcing and offshore outsourcing; it traces the evolution of outsourcing and discusses the role of information technology (IT) in outsourcing. While the commoditization of IT enabled the first wave of outsourcing, IT played an enabling role in the second wave. In the current and third wave of outsourcing, IT provides sophisticated tools to assist in the governance of outsourcing arrangements.

Introduction

Outsourcing as a means of meeting organizational information technology (IT) needs is now a commonly accepted and growing practice, and one that is continually evolving (Dibbern, Goles, Hirschheim, & Jayatilaka, 2004). From its beginnings as a cost-reduction tool, many now feel outsourcing has evolved into a vital component of a firm's overall business strategy (Linder, 2004). It has grown from the domain of IT embodying decisions such as where and how to source IT to a much wider set of business functions: logistics, payroll, human resources, legal, and so forth. To be sure, the generic notion of *outsourcing* — making arrangements with an external entity for the provision of goods or services to supplement or replace internal efforts — has been around for centuries. But IT outsourcing is fundamentally different. IT is pervasive throughout the organization. It is not a homogenous function, but rather is interrelated with practically all organizational activities. It is strategic. And up until the late eighties, strategic functions were thought to be incapable of being

Information Management: Setting the Scene
Copyright © 2007 by Elsevier Ltd.
All rights of reproduction in any form reserved.
ISBN: 978-0-08-046326-1

outsourced. Kodak changed all of that as will be described later in the chapter. But one thing is clear, whilst we may not know with certainty how the outsourcing industry will evolve, recent statistics show the IT service market growing at a rate of 19.6% per annum through 2004 and an overall market of $792 billion — of which IT outsourcing makes up 67%. This clearly indicates that outsourcing is no passing fad. It also helps to explain the significant interest in the subject.

This chapter offers a brief overview of the evolution of IT outsourcing and its role in the growth of outsourcing of other business functions. We believe that studying IT outsourcing helps one to understand how and why outsourcing is evolving to include other business functions as well as why offshore outsourcing is becoming so prominent. Examining the role of IT in outsourcing, the next section of the chapter identifies three waves in the evolution of outsourcing, with the role of IT differing in each. The three sections that follow discuss the evolution of outsourcing through the three different phases. The chapter concludes with some thoughts about where outsourcing might be headed and its likely implications.

The Role of IT in Outsourcing

Although much has been written on the pros and cons of outsourcing and offshoring, considerably less has been written about the underlying and enabling role of IT in these business practices. While *economics*, in particular, improving the profits of a company through cost savings, has clearly been the primary driver for outsourcing and offshoring, it is important to recognize the roles IT has played in making this a possibility.

When organizations first adopted IT, they had to develop capabilities in the areas of software development and IT management to be able to use the technology. However, these state of affairs changed with advances in technology and the accompanying increased capabilities of IT. The standardization in IT that was required for its widespread acceptance led to replicable processes for the creation of technology (Markus, 1996). *The first wave* of outsourcing is a result of this changing nature of IT — the commoditization of IT (Markus, 1996). These standardized and replicable processes did not have to be done in-house. In fact, it made economic sense to shift these to vendor organizations where the economies of scale and the efficiencies that could be achieved would ensure the availability of the same technology, but at a lower price. Thus, the commoditization of IT led to the first wave of outsourcing.

In *the second wave* of outsourcing, IT plays an enabling, albeit some would say, a sinister role. It revolves around the way IT has led to the commoditization of work (Hirschheim & Klein, 2003). The new terms "IT-enabled services" (Kern, Lacity, & Willcocks, 2002) and "utility computing" (Westerman & Ross, 2003) are suggestive of an important side effect of technology that has been one of the key characteristics of *modernization* since the beginning of the first industrial revolution — the expropriation of individual skills into explicit methods and techniques that are then coded in specific turn-key technology "solutions". From a systems perspective, the same phenomenon has been labeled as "black-boxing". The operators of these turn-key solutions no longer have to master the detailed craftsmanship to perform the work that the turn-key solution automates, because the original complexity has been hidden behind the levers and buttons of an interface. As a result, the operator of a programmable lathe needs fewer skills than the old blacksmith, or the factory-trained laborer in a semiautomated shoe factory has a fraction of the skills of the old shoemaker. Modern IT has facilitated extending this market logic of commoditization to white collar work — clerical work initially (e.g., payroll computations) but growing now to encompass business processes in general (business process outsourcing (BPO)). Hence, IT has served both as a medium and catalyst of turning subjective skills and know-how into a market commodity that can be contracted out to the lowest bidder. It is important to add that whilst commoditization is not wholly dependent on IT (the causes of commoditization are deeply rooted in the progress ideal of the enlightenment and liberalist ethics of market economics), IT does fundamentally extend the reach and speed with which it spreads throughout the economic system.

IT also plays a secondary enabling role in this second wave of outsourcing. The growth of offshoring would have been impossible were it not for the advances in and availability of high speed/high bandwidth, reliable global networks. Businesses have come to rely on such global networks as they offer myriad new strategic options for structuring IT and business operations. These technologically sophisticated networks have opened the door for outsourcing and offshoring. With these global networks, organizations have typically started with smaller projects as a *proof of concept* (e.g., that outsourcing IT to a third party offshore provider could be done). Such projects allowed organizations to feel comfortable with the viability of this option but also to develop the detailed know-how and skills to broaden its use. Today, most U.S. industry is poised to take full advantage of offshore outsourcing, moving many IT and other knowledge worker jobs from the U.S. to countries such as India and China.

With the increased acceptance of outsourcing, not only have the number of outsourcing deals increased, but also the complexity and importance of the nature of work outsourced. This has led to much-required attention to governance of outsourcing arrangements without which the expected outcomes from these deals would not be fully realized. With sophisticated outsourcing relationship management tools, IT now provides for efficient governance of outsourced operations. In *this third wave* of outsourcing, we see IT transforming the management of outsourcing. While outsourcing managers have relied on IT in the past, the current tools provide hitherto unreachable levels of real-time feedback that could reduce the risk of failure and facilitate the achievement of expected business benefits.

In the following section, a brief history of the first wave of outsourcing as it relates to IT is presented. The Second Wave: Offshore Outsourcing, Business Process Outsourcing specifically focuses on offshore IT outsourcing and begins with a description of the various models used to implement offshore outsourcing. A brief history of offshore outsourcing is presented next. This is followed by a discussion about the drivers and benefits as well as the challenges of offshore outsourcing. The Third Wave: IT and Outsourcing Governance briefly presents the events in the third wave of outsourcing, where an increasing attention to outsourcing governance presents another role for IT.

The First Wave: Outsourcing of IT

Although companies outsource IT for many reasons, industry watchers generally attribute the growth of the IT outsourcing market to two primary phenomena (Lacity, Hirschheim, & Willcocks, 1994). First, interest in IT outsourcing is largely a consequence of a shift in business strategy. Many companies have recently abandoned their diversification strategies — once pursued to mediate risk — to focus on core competencies. Senior executives have come to believe that the most important sustainable competitive advantage is strategic focus by concentrating on what an organization does better than anyone else while outsourcing the rest. As a result of this focus strategy, IT came under scrutiny. Senior executives frequently view the entire IT function as a noncore activity, and believe that IT vendors possess economies of scale and technical expertise to provide IT services more efficiently than internal IT departments. This transfer to external vendors was, of course, made possible by the commodity nature of IT — as explained in the previous section. Second, the growth in outsourcing may also be thought as a function of the unclear value delivered by IT. In many companies, senior executives view IT as an overhead — an essential cost but one to be minimized nevertheless. Thus, if through outsourcing IT can be done less expensively, it is adopted (Hirschheim & Lacity, 2000).

Initially, IT outsourcing consisted of an external vendor providing a single basic function to the customer, exemplified by facilities management arrangements where the vendor assumed operational control over the customer's technology assets, typically a data center. Outsourcing of information systems (IS) began to evolve in 1963 when Ross Perot and his company Electronic Data Systems (EDS) signed an agreement with Blue Cross of Pennsylvania for the handling of its data processing services. This was the first time a large business had turned over its entire data processing department to a third party. Such an arrangement was different from other 'facilities management' contracts that EDS had entered into because in the Blue Cross case, EDS took over the responsibility for Blue Cross's IT people. This deal extended the previous use of third parties to supplement a company's IS (e.g., the use of contract programmers, timesharing, the purchasing of packaged software, the management of the data processing facilities, systems integration, and service bureaus). Following on from the Blue Cross deal; EDS's client base grew during the 1970s to include such noteworthy customers as Frito-Lay and General Motors. However, the real interest in outsourcing occurred during the mid-eighties when EDS signed contracts with Continental Airlines, First City Bank, and Enron. These deals signaled an acceptance of outsourcing, which heretofore did not exist.

By the end of the 1980s, IBM entered the outsourcing arena. It formed its ISSC division that would compete directly against EDS. It was an immediate success. ISSC signed its first deal with Kodak in 1989. This deal, for all intents and purposes, signaled the arrival of the IS outsourcing mega deal. It also legitimized outsourcing. Prior to the *Kodak deal*, IT outsourcing deals had been entered into, but little interest seemed to be generated by such deals. Kodak's $1 billion outsourcing deal led to the widespread interest in outsourcing. Some have referred to this as "the Kodak effect" (Caldwell, 1995). No longer was it possible to say "IT is strategic and hence cannot be turned over to a third party". If Kodak could do it, any organization could do it. Indeed this became the mantra for IT outsourcing. Following on from the success of the Kodak deal, other well-known companies quickly followed suit — General Dynamics, Delta Airlines, Continental Bank, Xerox, McDonnell Douglas, Chevron, Dupont, JP Morgan, and Bell South. Nor is the trend strictly a U.S. phenomenon. Deals by Lufthansa in Germany; Inland Revenue, Rolls Royce, BP, and British Aerospace in Britain; KF Group in Sweden; Canada Post in Canada; the South Australia government, Telstra, Lend Lease, and the Commonwealth Bank of Australia in Australia; Swiss Bank in Switzerland; and Bank di' Roma in Italy signal the rise of outsourcing globally.

Outsourcing has evolved from the one vendor — one client arrangement where the vendor provides ostensibly all IT services to its client, to complex arrangements involving multiple vendors and multiple clients (Gallivan & Oh, 1999). Outsourcing now embraces significant partnerships and alliances — EDS likes to refer to them as "co-sourcing deals" — where client and vendor share risk and reward. The deals have moved beyond simple cost-savings to include value-based outsourcing, equity-based outsourcing, e-Business outsourcing, and BPO.

One of the attractions, and indeed a primary reason, that vendors enter into outsourcing arrangements is that it provides them with a relatively long-term revenue stream. This is in contrast to IT consulting engagements, with their attendant uncertainties and fluctuations. Long-term outsourcing arrangements help stabilize vendor business volume and revenue, making planning more predictable, and increase shareholder's comfort levels.

More recently, the industry has seen the growth of several new areas of IT outsourcing (Dibbern et al., 2004). One is web and e-Business outsourcing where vendors are contracted to provide web-based applications to enable a firm to move into the e-Business era. A second growth area surrounds the emergence of the application services provider (ASP) industry. ASPs buy, install, and manage enterprise applications at remote data centers and host them for customers *via* a broadband connection, usually over the Internet (Kern et al., 2002; Susarla, Barua, & Whinston, 2003). A third growth area is in backsourcing, where companies who initially outsourced their IT decide to bring it back in-house. This might occur through early contract termination or simply pulling the function back internally after the contract runs out (Hirschheim, 1998; Overby, 2003a). A fourth growth area — which many think will be the next major wave of outsourcing — is in offshore outsourcing or *offshoring* (Carmel & Tjia, 2005; Davis, Ein-Dor, King, & Torkzadeh, 2006; Morstead & Blount, 2003; Robinson & Kalakota, 2004). This trend is unmistakable and is explored in more depth next in the chapter.

The Second Wave: Offshore Outsourcing, Business Process Outsourcing

Today, firms of all sizes are rushing overseas to have their IT work performed by offshore vendors (Krishna, Sahay, & Walsham, 2004; Sahay, Nicholson, & Krishna, 2003). Some argue this change is nothing more than the natural progression of first moving blue-collar work overseas followed by white-collar work (Friedman, 2005; Sheshabalaya, 2004). IT jobs are the most visible to those in the IT field, but the same is happening (or will happen) to other business functions/processes in professional areas such as accounting, law, tax, and medicine. Some U.S. hospitals, for example, are already outsourcing X-ray diagnosis to medical personnel in India (Indiatimes, 2006).

An outsourcing arrangement is considered *offshore outsourcing* when the responsibility for management and delivery of IT services is delegated to a vendor who is located in a different country from that of the client (Sabherwal, 1999). Two possible scenarios exist here: near-shore outsourcing and offshore outsourcing;[1] the key difference between the two is the geographical distance between the client and the vendor. For U.S. clients, near-shore refers to Mexico or Canada and offshore refers to more remote countries such as India, China, Russia, Malaysia, Hungary, Hong Kong, Singapore, the Philippines, Ireland, Israel, and Eastern Europe (Apte, 1990; Carmel & Tjia, 2005; Jones, 2004; Lacity & Willcocks, 2001; Rottman & Lacity, 2004). Since these two scenarios are essentially the same in all aspects except the distance from client location to vendor location, most authors combine these alternatives when referring to offshore outsourcing. In this chapter also, the term "offshore outsourcing" will be used to refer to both scenarios and include any situation where a client contracts with a vendor in another country for the provision of part or all of the IT services.

While offshore outsourcing made up only 1.4% of total outsourcing contracts in 2003, the value of offshore outsourcing contracts rose 890% from the previous year to $1.66 billion in 2004 (EBusiness Strategies, 2004). Over 50% of Fortune 500 companies have offshore outsourcing as part of their sourcing strategy (EBusiness Strategies, 2004). IT outsourcing dominates offshore outsourcing; the numbers cited for offshore outsourcing of IT services range from 28% (Offshore IT Outsourcing, 2004) to 50% (http://www.neoIT.com) of all offshore outsourcing. Among the various IT services, applications development, maintenance, and support are most likely to be outsourced to offshore locations (http://www.neoIT.com).

A related development has been the outsourcing of IT-enabled services and BPO. Many offshore IT vendors have produced offshoots to manage BPO deals. Examples are Wipro's Spectramind and Infosys' Progeon. The BPO market is making giant strides; it is estimated that the offshore BPO market will grow at a rate of 79% annually to reach a size of $24.2 billion, while the offshore IT outsourcing market is expected to grow at a rate of 43% to $56 billion by 2008 (EBusiness Strategies, 2004). Outsourcing vendors are setting their goals higher up in the value chain to the realm of knowledge process outsourcing (KPO). It is projected that the global KPO market will grow to $16 billion by 2010, with about 75% of it in the hands of Indian vendors (Times of India, 2005).

In the following subsection, different business models for offshore outsourcing of IT are presented. This is followed by a short historical perspective of the offshore

---

[1]The term *global outsourcing* is sometimes used to refer to nearshore and offshore outsourcing together.

outsourcing industry in India and an examination of the business drivers of offshore outsourcing of IT. This section on offshore outsourcing concludes with a discussion of the challenges of offshore outsourcing.

Offshore Outsourcing Arrangements

Offshore outsourcing comes in a variety of flavors to match the client's desire for ownership and control; these are conventional offshore outsourcing arrangements, joint ventures (JV), build-operate-transfer (BOT) arrangements, and captive center arrangements.

- In *conventional offshore outsourcing*, a client enters into a contract with an offshore vendor through either the establishment of a direct relationship with the offshore vendor or through a partner organization established to channel work to the off-shore vendor (Khan, Currie, Weerakkody, & Desai, 2002; Kumar & Willcocks, 1996; Morstead & Blount, 2003; http://www.NeoIT.com). The client pays a deter-mined fee for services provided by the vendor. The offshore vendor usually main-tains a small marketing and personnel base in the client's country (Kumar & Willcocks, 1996). An offshore development center (ODC) is a special case of this arrangement, where the client requests the vendor to devote specific resources (both physical and human) to service its account (http://www.NeoIT.com). Examples of organizations using a conventional offshore outsourcing strategy are DoCoMo with Wipro; Johnson Controls with Infosys; Exult with Hexaware; and Nortel with Wipro, TCS, InfoSys and Sasken. A poll at the neoIT.com website conducted in May 2003 showed that clients are quite comfortable with this arrangement and have no qualms in handing over the work to offshore firms.
- A *JV* is an arrangement where a domestic client and an offshore vendor form a third entity with the goal of creating a synergistic solution (Khan et al., 2002; Kumar & Willcocks, 1996; Morstead & Blount, 2003; Rajkumar & Dawley, 1998; Sobol & Apte, 1995). Examples of offshore JVs are TRW and Satyam, MasterCard and Mascon, Cendant and IGTS, and Carreker and Master.
- A *BOT* is an arrangement where a domestic client contracts with an offshore vendor to set up an offshore center (Morstead & Blount, 2003; www.NeoIT.com, 2004). The vendor is responsible for the acquisition of facilities and personnel, and for running the center on predefined terms for a defined period. When the center and the services are properly established, the management and the ownership of the center established are transferred to the client if the client decides to buy the center at that point. Organizations that have entered into BOT arrangements in-clude P&O Lloyd, Peoplesoft, and AIG.
- A *captive center* is a subsidiary established by a domestic organization in a foreign country (Anthes, 1993; Khan et al., 2002; Kumar & Willcocks, 1996; Morstead & Blount, 2003; http://www.NeoIT.com). Examples of organizations using captive centers are GE, Intel, British Airways, Conseco, Citibank, Motorola, and Mattel.

While the client usually has a low to medium level of control on the operation and delivery services in conventional offshore outsourcing, the client retains full ownership and control of the assets, personnel, management, and operations of a captive center. In JV and BOT arrangements, the client is able to take advantage of the vendor's knowledge of the local market, while retaining a certain amount of control. In addition, such shared ownership can reduce the risk of offshore outsourcing.

Conventional offshore outsourcing is implemented using a mix of on-site (at the client's location), on-shore (vendor's office and/or development centers in the client's country), and offshore resources (Kumar & Willcocks, 1996). Pure offshore models call for all the work being done offshore and the finished product being delivered to the client site; often an account manager from the vendor side will be located at the client site. In a second business model, the vendor maintains an office in the client's location, which functions as the primary interface between the client and the vendor. In yet another variation of the mix, some of the vendor employees working on the project may be positioned at the client's site or different vendor employees may be rotated through the client's site. The pure offshore model offers the largest cost savings, by way of labor arbitrage (Kumar & Willcocks, 1996; McFarlan, 1995). In fact, some of the earlier offshore outsourcing arrangements were based on this model, as can be observed from the discussion in the next section.

Evolution of Offshore Outsourcing

While the Kodak deal is considered the turning point in the history of domestic IT outsourcing, no similar watershed event occurred in offshore IT outsourcing; it was more a case of 'water seeping under the door'. Offshore outsourcing is not a new phenomenon; U.S. organizations have been outsourcing to vendors in other countries for more than two decades. Outsourcing consultant, Jag Dalal, shared the story of such an offshore arrangement from the early eighties, with one of the researchers (Dalal, 2004a). While working as director of Management Information Systems at Data General[2] (a manufacturer of information systems storage systems and open systems servers) in the early eighties, Dalal entered into an agreement with an Indian firm called Data Conversion Inc.[3] (now known as Patni Computer Systems) for software development. Since the communications infrastructure available today was not in place at that time, requirements and other information were sent to India "in a pouch" on the Air India flight. The development work was done in India and code was sent back on next day's return flight, and comments and corrections were then sent to India by the same method. The exchanges continued in this manner for each project, until completion.

The origins of offshore outsourcing (in India) can be traced back to the seventies. In the mid-seventies, Tata Consultancy Services (TCS), the IT arm of the industrious Tata Group entered into an agreement with Burroughs[4] and developed applications

[2]Data General was acquired by EMC in 1999.
[3]Data Conversion Inc. was the distributor for Data General in India at that time.
[4]Now part of Unisys.

for them. TCS also got a contract from Institutional Group & Information Co. (IGIC)[5] to maintain and upgrade their information systems in the U.S. Meanwhile, a policy decision by the Indian government limiting foreign investment forced IBM (who had been in India since 1952) to pull out of the country. This sudden exit forced the Indian IT industry to be creative in their software development so that they could extract the most from the aging systems that remained and the limited computer systems that could be put together internally (Rapoport, 1996). The void created by IBM's exit also provided opportunities for firms like Infosys and Patni Computer Systems to enter the IT market. Economic liberalization in the early nineties changed the landscape yet again, and foreign firms that had left and new ones arrived in India to find "a home-grown expertise in elegant, economical software writing" (Rapoport, 1996) and the "India brand" was born.

The current wave of offshore outsourcing got its impetus from the Y2K phenomenon (Reingold, 2004). Faced with a lack of professionals to complete the Y2K remediation work, U.S. organizations looked to foreign shores for professionals capable of doing this work. Many foreign software organizations, which were biding their time to get into foreign and more lucrative markets, saw this as their opportunity to get the proverbial "foot in the door". Simultaneously, the telecommunications infrastructure developed to a level where it was practical and cheaper to do work remotely.

From there, there was no looking back and today offshore outsourcing is a well-accepted practice in business. There are many strong contenders in the offshore IT outsourcing industry from China, Ireland, Philippines, Vietnam, and other countries. In fact, offshore resources have been so well recognized that many U.S. and European IT firms have opened their own centers in India, China, Philippines, and other locations. The offshore outsourcing industry has also evolved in this process with mergers and acquisitions across and within national borders. Foreign firms are trying to firm up their foothold in the U.S. market by acquiring U.S. firms, while U.S. firms are trying to gain access to resources available elsewhere by entering into agreement with local firms in those locations (Currie, 2000).

All this activity has pushed offshore outsourcing into the limelight recently — unfortunately, not always in a positive vein. The dot-com bust and the resulting loss of jobs intensified the concerns about loss of domestic jobs to foreigners and fueled public sentiment against outsourcing, particularly in the 2004 election year. A number of reports in the popular media about 'outsourcing' — with arguments both 'for' and 'against' the practice — kept the issue in the public eye. However, if media attention can be considered indicative of public interest, it appears that the uproar has calmed down quite a bit. For instance in 2005, the New York Times carried close to 50 articles mentioning 'outsourcing' in February of that year, but by June, the number had come down to about 20. Similarly, the Wall Street Journal had more than 60 articles related to outsourcing in February 2005, but only 35 in June. Some are able to see a silver lining on this dark cloud; an Indian vendor firm representative

---

[5]A data center in the banking sector in northeast U.S., in the 1970s.

commented that this attention has served to increase the global awareness of the capabilities of IT firms all over the world.

Business Drivers of Offshore Outsourcing

While IT plays an enabling role, it is a complex set of business factors that drive the move toward offshore outsourcing. As in all outsourcing, a major factor is the continued pressure to cut costs associated with IT while maintaining and improving processes. Thus, the availability of less expensive but qualified resources in other countries makes offshore outsourcing quite an attractive option to these client organizations (Apte, 1990; Kumar & Willcocks, 1996; Kumar & Palvia, 2004; McFarlan, 1995; Nicholson & Sahay, 2001; Rajkumar & Dawley, 1998). Since labor costs in offshore countries are typically much lower, organizations considering offshore outsourcing can potentially save a significant amount of money through offshore outsourcing. In fact, some firms that have outsourced projects offshore claim to have saved 50–70% over the cost of outsourcing similar projects to domestic vendors.

Client organizations have also turned to offshore outsourcing because of the lack of IT resources to perform certain IT tasks. Faced with the unavailability of trained professionals, organizations look to foreign shores to gain access to knowledgeable IT personnel and valuable IT assets (Apte et al., 1997; Morstead & Blount, 2003; Terdiman, 2002). Many offshore vendors, especially those from India, have well-trained IT personnel with the requisite technical knowledge and skills that meet clients' needs. These vendors have also recognized the need to train their employees in the latest technologies and have established world-class facilities to do so (Khan et al., 2002).

In addition, offshore vendors have obtained certifications to prove their ability to execute and deliver quality work. These certifications assure the client organizations that the vendor is following quality practices in the management of the project. Initially, vendors aimed to align their practices with the ISO 9000[6] series of standards. Today, the CMM[7] certification has become the industry standard used in assessing a vendor's capability in the offshore outsourcing market. Clients are more likely to choose vendors with a level 3 or higher rating (Qu & Brocklehurst, 2003). Many vendor organizations, particularly those from India, have achieved the highest level of CMM certification, CMM5. Mohnot (2003) reports that of the 80 organizations achieving CMM5 by the end of 2003, 60 were Indian firms. Now, these vendor organizations are taking the next step and aligning their business practices with the People CMM[8] framework; they are also using the Six Sigma[9] methodology to reduce variation and assure quality in operations (NASSCOM, 2004). In addition,

[6]ISO 9000 series of standards was developed by the International Standard Organizations. ISO 9001 relates to software development and identifies the requirements for a quality system.

[7]CMM is a standard certification for software development process developed by the Software Engineering Institute at Carnegie Mellon.

[8]People CMM is a process targeted at developing, motivating, and managing an organization's work force and has five levels similar to the Capability Maturity Model for software (CMM).

[9]Six Sigma is a disciplined data-driven methodology for eliminating defects (www.isicsigma.com).

many vendor firms ensure they meet global security standards and obtain information security certifications such as ISO 17779[10] as well. To the client organization, the certification is a form of guarantee that offshore vendors have the ability to provide comprehensive IT solutions with good documentation methodology (Carmel & Agarwal, 2001, 2002; Ramanujan & Lou, 1997). The certifications also serve to enhance the reputation of the vendor firm by creating the perception that offshore vendors have the ability to provide higher quality services (Elmuti & Kathawala, 2000; Goolsby, 2002; Morstead & Blount, 2003; Pruitt, 2004; Ramarapu, Parzinger, & Lado, 1997; Terdiman, 2002). This assurance of quality at low costs is a major driving factor in the move toward offshore outsourcing.

Business organizations today are driven by the pressures of globalization, where it has become necessary to provide services constantly to customers around the world (Apte et al., 1997). With offshore outsourcing, the time differences between the client and the vendor allow them to have 24 × 7, *round-the-clock* services. Additionally, the longer work day and efficient distribution of work between the client location and vendor location helps to increase IT productivity (Carmel & Agarwal, 2001, 2002; Goolsby, 2002; Herbsleb & Moitra, 2001; Karamouzis, 2002; Rajkumar & Dawley, 1998; Terdiman, 2002). Finally, as in domestic outsourcing, the bandwagon effect (Lacity & Hirschheim, 1993) comes to play in offshore outsourcing as well. The sheer fact that these offshore choices are available and that other organizations are taking advantage of those options prompt other organizations to consider offshore outsourcing (Carmel & Tjia, 2005; Gopal, Mukhopadhyay, & Krishnan, 2002; Overby, 2003b; Qu & Brocklehurst, 2003).

Challenges of Offshore Outsourcing

Offshore outsourcing is not without its challenges; in a Gartner survey of 219 clients conducted in 2003, more than half failed to realize the expected value from offshore outsourcing (cited in "Shifting Work Offshore? Outsourcer Beware", *BusinessWeek Online*, Jan 12, 2004). A similar number was found in research conducted by Ventoro; only 45% of the 5231 client executives polled by Ventoro considered their offshore engagement to be a success (Ventoro Institute (2006)[11]). The geographical separation and cultural differences have posed a challenge for clients and offshore vendors in the management of outsourcing arrangements. Additionally, the recent political uproar and public disfavor toward offshore outsourcing has forced many organizations to reconsider their decisions or keep such moves beneath the public radar. Nevertheless, despite the challenges posed by offshore outsourcing — often divided into cultural factors, geographical distance, infrastructure and security issues, and morale and public opinion issues — it is clear that such challenges, whilst difficult, can be overcome.

---

[10]ISO 17779 is an information systems security standard that provides "a comprehensive set of controls comprising best practices in information security" (www.iso-17799.com).
[11]Ventoro is an outsourcing research and consulting firm based in Portland, Oregon.

The Third Wave: IT and Outsourcing Governance

The success of an outsourcing arrangement is critically dependent upon establishing and following an effective governance process, a process for managing the outsourcing arrangement. Unfortunately, this is a premise that many client and vendor organizations are just waking up to. The root cause of a large percentage of outsourcing failures can be traced to the lack of effective governance. Often organizations realize the need for a governance program only after they run into trouble in the outsourcing arrangement (Dalal, 2004b). Outsourcing governance encompasses a complex set of issues including performance measurement and management, staffing and talent management, and relationship building and development. Outsourcing consultants and researchers estimate that around 8% of the contract value will be spent on governance.

In today's multisourced environment, organizations managing multiple vendors and outsourced processes face additional challenges as these relationships become increasingly complex. Client and vendor managers need to analyze and manage huge amounts of information to satisfy the clauses of the contract and service level agreements. Typically, these tasks were completed using spreadsheets and e-mail or homegrown applications. However, as outsourcing projects have increased in complexity and magnitude, there is a need for tools that can manage a range of functions including performance monitoring and measurement, tracking of changes, and reporting — making governance operational. These tools need to pull data automatically from multiple sources within the organizations and thus must be capable of integration with existing applications and infrastructure in the organization.

Various technology solutions exist in this area — business intelligence tools, business process management tools, enterprise resource planning modules that offer performance analytics and reporting, and service level management tools. Vendors of the last set of tools have been pitching them directly to the outsourcing market. Examples of service level management tools include Digital Fuel's ServiceFlow®, Oblicore's Guranatee®, Enlighta's Govern®, and Janeeva's Assurance®, among many. These tools can bring real-time visibility and insight into the performance, quality, responsiveness, and compliance of services delivered by the service providers, as well as by in-house services organizations. The vendors of these new software tools promise considerable savings on costs associated with governance and higher probability of achieving expected outcomes through the management of compliance, performance, and relationship risks. Thus, in this third wave of outsourcing, IT could transform the management of outsourcing and ensure the realization of organizations' expectations from outsourcing.

Conclusion

Given the benefits and the continuing commoditization of IT, outsourcing and particularly, offshore outsourcing of IT products and services has become a feasible option for organizations to achieve their IT sourcing objectives. By most estimates, offshore outsourcing is expected to grow dramatically; for instance, Meta Group predicts that offshore outsourcing will grow by at least 20% annually (EBusiness Strategies, 2004). Practitioners and industry observers alike anticipate that offshore outsourcing will soon evolve to a maturation state where all stakeholders would be comfortable with the offshoring model. Once in that comfort zone, offshore outsourcing of IT and IT-enabled services will become an integral part of conducting business. In fact, many industry observers feel that we have reached the "tipping point" in offshore outsourcing of IT.

The bottom line is that outsourcing and offshore outsourcing are business practices that are here to stay. Despite what some opponents think or hope, it is not a passing fad. Organizations as well as their employees will have to prepare themselves for this change. Organizations can aid their employees in this preparation by communicating with them on a timely basis and providing opportunities for training and retooling. Meanwhile, organizations have to rethink their sourcing strategy. This examination will help them in selecting the best vendor(s) for their needs, developing a contract that supports their goals and creating a relationship management process that keeps the outsourcing project responsive to their current and changing requirements. Software tools that can assist them in this endeavor are available today; these tools will also continue to evolve.

Although outsourcing creates many challenges and uncertainties for both clients and vendors, it is a trend which is not only here to stay, but will continue to grow. Moreover, it is clear that as Hirschheim, Leobbecke, Newman, and Valor (2005) state, U.S. universities must step up to the challenge and prepare their IT graduates for working in this new global economy. The future won't be easy, but nobody said it would.

Acknowledgements

We are indebted to Heinz Klein for his thoughts on the subject of commoditization.

References

Anthes, G. (1993). In depth; not made in the USA. *Computerworld.*

Apte, U. (1990). Global outsourcing of information systems and processing services. *Information Society, 7*(4), 287–303.

Apte, U. M., Sobol, M. G., Hanaoka, S., Shimada, T., Saarinen, T., Salmela, T., & Vepsalainen, A. P. J. (1997). IS outsourcing practices in the USA, Japan and Finland: A comparative study. *Journal of Information Technology, 12*(4), 289–304.

Caldwell, B. (1995). Outsourcing megadeals — More than 60 huge contracts signed since 1989 prove they work. *InformationWeek, 552*(November 6).

Carmel, E., & Agarwal, R. (2001). Tactical approaches for alleviating distance in global software development. *IEEE Software, March/April,* 22–29.

Carmel, E., & Agarwal, R. (2002). The maturation of offshore sourcing of information technology work. *MIS Quarterly Executive, 1*(2), 65–78.

Carmel, E., & Tjia, P. (2005). *Offshoring information technology: Sourcing and outsourcing to a global workforce.* Cambridge: Cambridge University Press.

Currie, W. (2000). The supply-side of IT outsourcing: The trend towards mergers, acquisitions and joint ventures. *International Journal of Physical Distribution & Logistics Management*, *30*(3/4), 238–254.

Dalal, J. (2004a). Offshore outsourcing. E-mail to Beena George, 11 August, 2004.

Dalal, J. (April, 2004b). Governance — The secret sauce of outsourcing success. *Offshore Business Sourcing*, 5–11.

Davis, G., Ein-Dor, P., King, W., & Torkzadeh, R. (2006). IT Offshoring: History, prospects and challenges. *Journal of the Association for Information Systems*, *7*(11), 770–795.

Dibbern, J., Goles, T., Hirschheim, R., & Jayatilaka, B. (2004). Information systems outsourcing: A survey and analysis of the literature. *Database*, *35*(4), 6–102.

EBusiness Strategies (2004). Offshoring statistics — Dollar size, job loss, and market potential. www.ebstrategy.com/Outsourcing/trends (Aug 10, 2004).

Elmuti, D., & Kathawala, Y. (2000). The effects of global outsourcing strategies on participants' attitudes and organizational effectiveness. *International Journal of Manpower*, *21*(2), 112–128.

Friedman, T. (2005). *The world is flat: A brief history of the twenty-first century*. New York: Farrar, Straus & Giroux.

Gallivan, M. J., & Oh, W. (1999). Analyzing IT outsourcing relationships as alliances among multiple clients and vendors. *Proceedings of the 32nd Annual International Conference on System Sciences*, Hawaii.

Goolsby, K. (2002). *Offshore is not offhand*. Everest Group.

Gopal, A., Mukhopadhyay, T., & Krishnan, M. S. (2002). The role of software processes and communication in offshore software development. *Communications of the ACM*, *45*(4), 193–200.

Herbsleb, J. D., & Moitra, D. (2001). Global software development. *IEEE Software*, *18*(2), 16.

Hirschheim, R., & Klein, H. K. (2003). Crisis in the IS field? A critical reflection on the state of the discipline. *Journal of the Association for Information Systems*, *4*(5), 237–293.

Hirschheim, R., & Lacity, M. (2000). Information technology insourcing: Myths and realities. *Communications of the ACM*, *43*(2), 99–107.

Hirschheim, R., Leobbecke, C., Newman, M., & Valor, J. (2005). Offshoring and its implications for the information systems discipline. *Proceedings of Twenty-Sixth International Conference on Information Systems*, Las Vegas.

Hirschheim, R. A. (1998). Backsourcing: An emerging trend? *Infoserver*, http://www.infoserver.com/sep1998/html/academic.html, September 1998.

Indian firms get a phoren touch. (2005, February 23). *The Times of India*.

Indiatimes. (2006). Break a bone in NY, see X-ray in B'lore. http://infotech.indiatimes.com/BPO__ITES/Outsourcing/Break_a_bone_in_NY_see_X-ray_in_Blore/articleshow/1849304.cms

Jones, W. (2004). Offshore outsourcing: Trends, pitfalls, and practices. *Sourcing and Vendor Relationships*, *4*, 4.

Karamouzis, F. (2002). Debunking the myths of offshore IT service offerings. Note number: DF-15-5315, Gartner Research.

Kern, T., Lacity, M. C., & Willcocks, L. (2002). *Net sourcing: Renting business applications and services over a network*. Upper Saddle River, NJ: Prentice-Hall.

Khan, N., Currie, W. L., Weerakkody, V., & Desai, B. (2002). Evaluating offshore IT outsourcing in India: Supplier and customer scenarios. *Proceedings of the 36th Hawaii International Conference on System Sciences*.

Krishna, S., Sahay, S., & Walsham, G. (2004). Managing cross-cultural issues in global software outsourcing. *Communications of the ACM*, *47*(4), 62–66.

Kumar, K., & Willcocks, L. (1996). Offshore outsourcing: A country too far? *Proceedings of the 4th European Conference on Information Systems,* 1309–1325.

Kumar, N., & Palvia, P. (2004). A framework for global IT outsourcing management: Key influence factors and strategies. *JITC.*

Lacity, M., & Hirschheim, R. (1993). *Information systems outsourcing: Myths, metaphors and realities.* Chichester: Wiley.

Lacity, M., Hirschheim, R., & Willcocks, L. (1994). Realizing outsourcing expectations: Incredible expectations, credible outcomes. *Information Systems Management, 11*(4), 7–18.

Lacity, M. C., & Willcocks, L. P. (2001). *Global information technology outsourcing: In search of business advantage.* Chichester: Wiley.

Linder, J. (2004). *Outsourcing for radical change.* New York: AMACOM.

Markus, L. M. (1996). The futures of IT management. *The DATABASE for Advances in Information Systems, 27*(4), 67–84.

McFarlan, F. W. (1995). Issues in global outsourcing. In: P. Palvia, S. Palvia & E. Roche (Eds.), *Global information technology and systems management: Key issues and trends* (pp. 352–364). Nashua, NH: Ivy League Publishing.

Mohnot, N. (2003). Why "India Inside" spells quality? *Dataquest,* October 2003; accessed from http://www.dqindia.com

Morstead, S., & Blount, G. (2003). *Offshore ready: Strategies to plan & profit from offshore IT-enabled services.* Houston, TX: ISANI Press.

NASSCOM (2004). Business in India: Quality. http://www.nasscom.org (August 15, 2004).

Nicholson, B., & Sahay, S. (2001). Some political and cultural issues in the globalization of software development: Case experience from Britain and India. *Information and Organization, 11,* 25–43.

Offshore IT Outsourcing. (2004). IT leading as most active area of outsourcing. http://offshoreitoutsourcing.com/Pages/outsourcing_statistics.asp (August 10, 2004).

Overby, S. (2003a). Bringing I.T. back home. *CIO, March*(1).

Overby, S. (2003b). The hidden costs of offshore outsourcing. *CIO Magazine.*

Pruitt, S. (2004). Survey: 275,000 telecom jobs to go offshore by 2008. *Computerworld.*

Qu, Z., & Brocklehurst, M. (2003). What will it take for China to become a competitive force in offshore outsourcing? An analysis of the role of transaction costs in supplier selection. *Journal of Information Technology, 18*(1), 53–67.

Rajkumar, T. M., & Dawley, D. L. (1998). Problems and issues in offshore development of software. In: L. P. Willcocks & M. C. Lacity (Eds.), *Strategic Sourcing of Information Systems.* Chichester: Wiley.

Ramanujan, S., & Lou, H. (1997). Outsourcing maintenance operations to off-shore vendors: Some lessons from the field. *Journal of Global Information Management, 5*(2).

Ramarapu, N., Parzinger, M., & Lado, A. (1997). Issues in foreign outsourcing. *Information Systems Management,* 7–31.

Rapoport, R. (1996). Bangalore. *Wired,* Issue 4.02, February 1996.

Reingold, J. (2004). A brief (recent) history of offshoring. *FastCompany,* Issue 81, April 2004. http://www.fastcompany.com/magazine/81/offshore_extra.html

Robinson, M., & Kalakota, R. (2004). *Offshore outsourcing: Business models, ROI and best practices.* Alpharetta, GA: Milvar Press.

Rottman, J., & Lacity, M. (2004). Twenty practices for offshore sourcing. *MISQ Executive, 3*(3), 117–130.

Sabherwal, R. (1999). The role of trust in outsourced IS development projects. *Communications of the ACM, 42*(2), 80–86.

Sahay, S., Nicholson, B., & Krishna, S. (2003). *Global software work: Micro-studies across borders*. Cambridge: Cambridge University Press.

Sheshabalaya, A. (2004). *Rising elephant: The growing clash with India over white collar jobs*. London: Common Courage Press.

Sobol, M. G., & Apte, U. (1995). Domestic and global outsourcing practices of America's most effective IS users. *Journal of Information Technology*, *10*(4), 269–280.

Susarla, A., Barua, A., & Whinston, A. B. (2003). Understanding the service component of application service provision: An empirical analysis of satisfaction with ASP services. *Management Information Systems Quarterly*, *27*(1), 91–123.

Terdiman, R. (2002). Offshore outsourcing can achieve more than cost savings. Note number: CS-16-3520, Gartner Research.

Ventoro Institute. (2006). Offshore outsourcing research report 2005. January 22, 2005. http://www.ventoro.com (May 15, 2006)

Westerman, G., & Ross, J. (2003). Utility computing and the future of IT outsourcing. *IBM Systems Journal*.

www.NeoIT.com. (2004). *The captive ownership option in offshoring — Challenges & opportunities*. San Ramon, CA: NeoIT.

Chapter 14

Information Technology Sourcing: Reflections and Lessons 1991–2007

Leslie Willcocks, Mary Lacity and Sara Cullen

ABSTRACT

IT outsourcing practice has matured over the last 16 years. This chapter details the learning that can lead to more effective outsourcing in the future. It finds a learning curve in outsourcing, and recommends a risk mitigation approach to outsourcing, warning practitioners not to take on more objectives and outsourcing than they can manage. We suggest that IT needs to be managed as a portfolio of capabilities and that certain, distinctive retained management capabilities are the key to successful outsourcing. The chapter provides a guide to navigating a range of market and contracting options, and gives research-based evidence on the capabilities needed to ensure effective relationships. Finally, we provide a checklist of seven key practices, and challenge practitioners to face the neglected issue of what happens to knowledge when they outsource IT.

Introduction

The information technology outsourcing (ITO) and business process outsourcing (BPO) services markets, together with more recent offshore variants, have been dynamically expanding revenues, capabilities and associated rhetoric, in equal measure, for over a decade. On our estimates, ITO global revenues exceeded $200 billion per year at the end of 2005. After, and indeed partly because of, the slowdown between 2001 and 2004 this figure will rise by at least 7% per annum for the next 5 years. Use of external IT/BP services combined is likely to move from a 2005 average of 12% to 20% of the corporation's total costs by 2009 (Willcocks & Lacity, 2006). For many organizations, then, outsourcing is well above the parapet in sheer expenditure terms. However, much of this has been happening incrementally, as a response to immediate market conditions and specific opportunities to cut costs, rather than through long-term strategic thinking. Moreover, despite the accumulated experience, learning has been painfully slow; there has been mixed success, and much conflicting advice.

This chapter identifies the findings from a limited but coherent and internally consistent stream of studies the authors have been conducting since the early 1990s (see Cullen, 2005; Cullen & Willcocks, 2003; Lacity & Willcocks, 2001; Lacity, Willcocks, & Cullen, 2008; Willcocks & Lacity, 2006). One key feature of this body of research is that we measured actual outcomes compared to expected outcomes in our 600 plus longitudinal case studies and 6 surveys. This enables us to draw conclusions as to the practices associated with success and failure and to analyze results over time. Based on this extensive research, the rest of the chapter summarizes the findings. First we will comment on the degree of learning experienced in the 15 years under study. Next we organize the research findings under four headings: assessing the portfolio, evaluating market options, crafting deals, and managing relationships.

The Outsourcing Learning Curve

Most of our participants were from large North American, European, and Australian companies and few approached outsourcing from a strategic perspective at the outset. Most organizations initially engaged in outsourcing for tactical reasons, such as seeking lower labor rates for staff augmentation on specific projects. Only after pilot tests were complete, supplier relationships established, and viability proven, did senior executives seek more radical and strategic uses of global resources. This incremental approach, we found, allowed organizations to gain experience with outsourcing options at an operational level before seeking more strategic objectives.

Figure 14.1 illustrates the typical customer learning curve for ITO and BPO approaches and more recent offshore variants. The learning curve is demonstrated

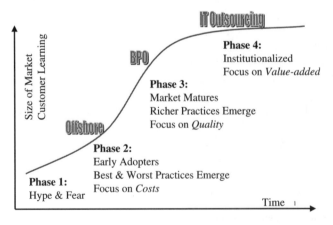

Figure 14.1: The outsourcing learning curve.

through the typical learning of one particular outsourcing model, namely offshore outsourcing. The general mass of organizations using ITO are weighted toward phase 3 and 4, with some organization on their third or fourth generation ITO, while most BPO and offshore clients, as at 2007, were much further down the learning curve.

During Phase I, senior executives we interviewed became aware of offshore outsourcing through marketing hype ("you'll save 60% off your costs") or irrational propaganda ("Software: Will Outsourcing Hurt America's Supremacy" — see McGee, 2003; Hof & Kerttetter, 2004). Senior executives quickly learned about potential benefits, costs, and risks by talking to peers, consultants, and reading research. During pilot testing, senior executives learned about the immense amount of in-house management required to effectively work with global suppliers and to achieve real cost savings. Phase II saw a focus on cost. As learning accumulated, some senior executives moved to Phase III when they exploited global sourcing for quality as well as cost reasons. One phrase we heard over and over again from participants was, *we went for the price, we stayed for the quality.*

More mature adopters in Phase IV used offshore outsourcing to strategically enable corporate strategies, such as increasing business agility, bringing products to market faster and cheaper, financing new product development, accessing new markets, or creating new business. These strategic initiatives often evolved over time. Customers continually learned how to assess better their own service portfolio, evaluate suppliers' capabilities, craft contracts, and manage supplier relationships. Let us look at these issues in detail.

Assessing the Back-Office Portfolio

IT as a Portfolio of Capabilities

We have increasingly found sourcing strategies beginning with the assumption that back-offices should be treated as a portfolio of activities and capabilities. Some IT activities must be kept in-house to ensure current and future business advantage and flexibility, while others may be safely outsourced. This portfolio perspective is empirically supported by our research findings that selective outsourcing decisions had a higher relative frequency of success than total outsourcing decisions. We defined the scope of sourcing options as either "total outsourcing" (80% plus of IT budget with third parties), "total in-house sourcing" (80% plus of IT budget delivered internally), or "selective outsourcing" (between 20 and 80% sourced externally, usually with several providers).

Selective outsourcing decisions have been generally successful during the past 10 years, with 85% successes reported by 1995 and 77% reported by 2001 (Lacity & Willcocks, 2001). This relates to the finding that selective outsourcing is also the most common sourcing practice. In most cases, suppliers were judged to have an ability to deliver these products and services less expensively than internal managers. The ability to focus in-house resources to higher value work also justified selective outsourcing.

Participants frequently encountered one or more of the following problems with total outsourcing:

- Excess fees for services beyond the contract due to increase in user demand
- Excess fees for services participants assumed were in the contract
- "Hidden costs" such as software license transfer fees
- Fixed prices that exceeded market prices 2–3 years into the contract
- Inability to adapt the contract to even minor changes in business or technology without triggering additional costs
- Lack of innovation from the supplier
- Deteriorating service in the face of patchy supplier staffing of the contract.

In-house sourcing has remained generally successful (67% up to 1995, 76% up to 2001). We found, however, that success stemmed from the potential threat of outsourcing. Once empowered through the threat of competition, internal managers often had cost advantages over suppliers (such as no marketing expense, no need to generate a profit). In addition, they often had service advantages, such as knowledge of idiosyncratic business applications (see also Willcocks & Lacity, 2006; Lacity et al., 2008).

Core In-House IT Capabilities

There are many frameworks and theories to help managers assess core capabilities to keep in-house. The most popular portfolio assessment models are based on theories such as resource dependency theory, agency theory, auction theory, game theory, institutional theory, and, by far the two dominant theories: transaction cost economics (TCE) and the resource-based view (RBV). In many ways, TCE is the ideal theoretical foundation because it specifically addresses make-or-buy decisions based on generic attributes of assets and describes appropriate ways to govern customer–supplier relationships. For example, TCEs posits that transactions with high asset specificity (essentially customization), high uncertainty, and/or occur frequently are best managed internally, while the rest should be more efficiently outsourced (Williamson, 1991). Indeed, a number of empirical outsourcing studies have found that asset specificity, the degree to which assets can be redeployed elsewhere without losing value, has been a significant factor (Ang & Straub, 1998; Lacity & Willcocks, 1996; Nam, Rajagopalan, Rao, & Chaudhury, 1996). RBV has been the second theory most widely applied to the outsourcing context. RBV suggests that managers keep valuable, rare, non-imitable, and non-substitutable strategic assets in-house, while potentially outsourcing the rest. TCE and RBV are both valuable perspectives. They also guide managers to treat the entire business functions as a portfolio of transactions/capabilities — some which must be kept in-house, some which may be outsourced (Barney, 1991; Straub, Weill, & Stewart, 2002).

Our most direct assessment of IT as a portfolio has been the model developed by Feeny and Willcocks (1998). By synthesizing research findings this suggests four broad categories which customers must keep in-house, even if they intend to

BUSINESS and I.S. VISION

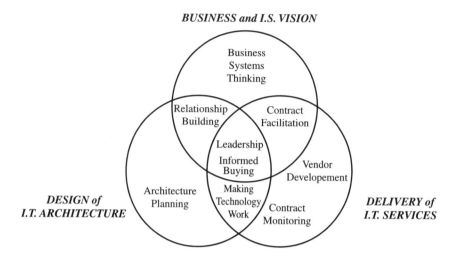

Figure 14.2: Core in-house IT capabilities.

outsource nearly all of the IT (or another — e.g., human resources, legal, procurement, accounting) function:

- Governance
- Eliciting and delivering business requirements
- Ensuring technical ability and architecture
- Managing external suppliers.

These four in-house functions need to be underpinned by the nine core in-house IT capabilities shown in Figure 14.2.

"Best-Sourcing" of Non-Core Capabilities

Once organizations identify core IT capabilities, it does not automatically follow that the remaining "non-core" capabilities will be outsourced. We found that customers who considered additional business, economic, and technical factors relating to non-core capabilities were most frequently happy with their sourcing decisions.

A much more complex picture of "best-sourcing" practice emerged. From a business perspective, some capabilities that are non-core today could become core in the future. Outsourcing this non-core function could well impede strategic exploitation in the future. From an economic perspective, some non-core activities may well be more efficiently kept in-house. For example, several of our case study participants were willing to outsource their large data centers but could not find suppliers who could do it cheaper. From a technical perspective, some non-core capabilities are highly integrated with other core activities. This makes outsourcing extremely difficult, and we have many examples of organizations that run into difficulties as a result.

Assuming non-core capabilities pass these tests, we found clients still needing to evaluate the market options, in order to further validate an outsourcing model and to identify viable suppliers.

Evaluation of Market Options

An important and ongoing sourcing process we identified was to keep abreast of market options. We identify four: fee-for-service (time and materials or exchange based), netsourcing, joint ventures, and enterprise partnerships. These models are often blended, such as having a joint venture component to structure a shared risk and reward and a traditional outsourcing component for operational delivery. In general, we found each model most suited to particular types of activities, as discussed below.

Time and Materials Model

Here, supplier capabilities are bought-in to supplement in-house capabilities under in-house management. A typical example is hiring consultants to help in-house teams implement customer relationship management (CRM) systems. Because requirements are uncertain, the customer cannot negotiate a detailed contract, and thus the variable price based on time and materials emerged as more appropriate. We found this time and materials model as the most common, and posing the least risk to customers.

Exchange-Based or Traditional Outsourcing Contracts

Here, the customer pays a fee to the supplier in exchange for a customized product or service. In this model, the customer typically transfers its assets, leases, licenses, and personnel to the external supplier. The supplier manages the resources and provides back to the customer a set of products and services governed by a one-to-one contract.

In our early studies of IT outsourcing, we found that customers often had naive expectations about this model. For example, many customers expected to save 25% on IT costs by signing 10-year, fixed-price contracts for a set of baseline services they assumed would remain stable for the duration of the contract. Many customers subsequently re-negotiated, terminated, or switched suppliers midstream. For example, one 2000 survey found that 32% of respondents had terminated at least one IT outsourcing contract. Of those, 51% switched suppliers, 34% brought the function back in-house, and the remainder eventually reinstated their initial suppliers due to prohibitively high switching costs (Cullen & Willcocks, 2003).

Survey respondents generally provided a healthy report card for exchange-based outsourcing. These results may be explained by the common practice of selective outsourcing of stable, non-core IT activities rather than of, for example, IT development or IT strategy (Lacity & Willcocks, 2001).

Netsourcing

Here, the customer pays a fee to the supplier in exchange for a standard product or service delivered over the Internet or other networks. Netsourcing promises to deliver best-of-breed, scalable, and flexible business applications to customer desktops for a low monthly fee based on number of users or number of transactions at the customer site. Customers can rent nearly all popular independent software vendor (ISV) products from netsourcing providers, including enterprise resource planning (ERP), CRM, personal productivity and communications, e-commerce and e-business packages. Our early research (Kern, Lacity, & Willcocks, 2002) shows that this model is suited for customers wanting lower back-office costs at the expense of accepting standardized solutions. The revenues generated in this space are still modest, less than $3 billion annually in 2005. Our preliminary research on this space found that early adopters were mainly small to mid-sized enterprises.

Customer–Supplier Joint Ventures

In the joint venture model, the supplier and customer create a new company. Deals are typically structured so that the customer investor provides personnel, becomes the venture's first major customer, and shares in future profits if the venture can attract external customers.

In the past, we found joint ventures between customers and suppliers often failed to attract external customers and the relationships were redefined as exchange based. Examples include Delta Airlines and AT&T, Xerox and EDS, and UBS and Perot Systems. But in the offshore outsourcing space, joint ventures have been the preferred vehicle for large organizations to create a large offshore facility without the risks with a fully owned captive center. Customers, such as MasterCard, CSC, Perot Systems, and TRW chose this model over a fully owned model to trade off some control in exchange for less risk.

Enterprise Partnerships

The goal here is often to transform the back-offices of large organizations that have grown through mergers and acquisitions. We have tracked how old ITO and new start-up BPO suppliers have entered the new market space from 1999 offering to transform their larger customer's back-offices through leadership, streamlined processes, and new technology (see Willcocks & Lacity, 2006).

For example, the UK-based company Xchanging created three joint ventures with customers, beginning in 2001. The first was a joint venture with British Aerospace (BAe) called Xchanging HR Services for BPO of human resource management. Becoming the venture's first customer, BAe signed a 10-year contract worth £250 million and transferred 430 HR employees to the venture. The second joint venture named Xchanging Procurement Services, also with BAe, provided BPO for procurement. Again, the venture's first customer was BAe, which signed a £800 million, 10-year contract. The third joint venture, with Lloyd's of London and the

London insurance market generally, originally called Ins-sure, as at 2006 continued to provide policy and claims processing BPO. Lloyd's signed a 10-year contract worth £400 million with Ins-sure. In these three ventures, BAe and Lloyd's were guaranteed an undisclosed amount of cost savings on the business process and share in the ventures' future profits. In these deals, success will depend partly on Xchanging's ability to deliver on the contracts while simultaneously attracting external customers beyond BAe and the London insurance market.

Comparing Request-For-Proposal to Internal Bids

During the last 15 years, organizations that invited both internal and external bids had a higher relative frequency of success than organizations that merely compared a few external bids to current performance (89% by 1995, 83% by 2001 successful — see Lacity & Willcocks, 2001). We believe that this was because formal external supplier bids were often based on efficient managerial practices that could be replicated by internal managers (Hirschheim & Lacity, 2000).

In some cases, internal managers could not implement cost reduction tactics because the internal politics often resisted cost reduction tactics such as consolidating departments, reducing headcount, and standardizing processes and technology. Based on 85 case studies, we found that when customers allowed internal bid teams to compete with external suppliers, 83% of those decisions were successful. When no in-house bid was invited and existing costs were compared with 1 or 2 supplier bids, only 42% of those decisions were successful. The use of an internal bid team served to provide a baseline on what could be attained internally if the in-house staff was empowered to behave like a supplier, such as proposing unfavorable consolidation and standardization of technology (Lacity & Willcocks, 2001).

Senior Management and Sourcing Decisions

Our case study and survey data both suggest that multiple stakeholder involvement and strong outsourcing performance are correlated. In our 2001 survey data, 68% of respondents had at least two stakeholders driving the decision, most frequently the back-office manager and lawyers or the back-office manager and senior executives. Our case study data shows that joint senior executive/back-office manager decisions or back-office managers acting alone had higher relative frequencies of success than senior executives acting alone (Lacity & Willcocks, 2001).

It appears that successful sourcing decisions require a mix of political power and technical skills (Beath, 1996). Political power helped to enforce the larger business perspective — such as the need for organization-wide cost cuts — as well as the "muscle" to implement such business initiatives. Domain expertize on back-office services, service levels, measures of performance, rates of service growth, and price/performance improvements were needed to develop requests-for-proposals, evaluate supplier bids, and negotiate and manage sound contracts.

The Crafting of Outsourcing Arrangements

This section looks at how organizations craft outsourcing contracts, and with what results.

Exchange-Based Contracts Revisited

The exchange-based model is still the most common model. But our data reveals there are several types of exchange-based contracts:

Standard Contracts: The customer signed the supplier's standard, off-the-shelf contract. This is primarily restricted to the netsourcing space.

Detailed Contracts: The contract included special contractual clauses for service scope, service levels, measures of performance, and penalties for non-performance.

Loose Contracts: The contract did not provide comprehensive performance measures or contingencies but specified that the suppliers perform "whatever the customer was doing in the baseline year" for the duration of the contract at 10–30% less than the customer's baseline budget.

Mixed Contracts: For the first few years of the contract, requirements were fully specified, connoting a "detailed" contract. However, participants could not define requirements in the long run, and subsequent requirements were only loosely defined, connoting a "loose" contract.

Detailed contracts achieved expectations with greater relative frequency than other types of contracts (75% of detailed contracts were successful). These organizations understood their own functions very well, and could therefore define their precise requirements in a contract. They also spent up to 18 months negotiating the details of contracts, often with the help of outside experts.

From our 2001 survey, customers included the following clauses in their detailed contracts:

- costs (100%),
- confidentiality (95%),
- service level agreements (88%),
- early termination (84%),
- liability and indemnity (82%),
- change contingency (65%), and
- supplier non-performance penalty (62%).

Increasingly, contracts have also included responsibility matrices which outline the responsibilities for both customers and suppliers. This innovation recognizes that suppliers sometimes missed service levels because of their customers' inaction.

No matter how detailed contracts become, changes in requirements occur. As at time of writing, many detailed contracts now have mechanisms of change, including:

- planned contract realignment points to adapt the contract every few years,
- contingency prices for fluctuation in volume of demand,

- negotiated price and service-level improvements over time, or even
- external benchmarking of best-of-breed suppliers to reset prices and service levels.

In contrast to the success of the detailed contract, all seven of the loose contracts we studied were disasters in terms of costs and services. Two of these companies actually terminated their outsourcing contracts early and rebuilt their internal departments. Another company threatened to sue the supplier. Six of the eleven "mixed" contracts we studied achieved expectations. The contracts contained either shared risks and rewards or significant performance incentives (Lacity et al., 2008).

Length of Contract

From the customer perspective, there is clear evidence that short-term contracts have higher frequencies of success than long-term contracts. From 85 case studies we studied, 87% of outsourcing decisions with contracts of 3 years or less were successful, compared to a 38% success rate for contracts 8 years or longer. Short-term contracts involved less uncertainty, motivated supplier performance, allowed participants to recover from mistakes quicker, and helped to ensure that participants were getting a fair market price. Participants also only outsourced for the duration in which requirements were stable. Thus they could articulate adequately their cost and service needs. Some participants noted that short-term contracts motivated supplier performance because suppliers realized customers could opt to switch suppliers when the contract expired (Lacity et al., 2008).

In contrast, long-term contracts have remained troublesome, with failure to achieve cost savings as the primary reason. As at 2006, we found that few total outsourcing mega deals had reached maturity without a major stumbling block. Conflicts are increasingly being resolved through contract re-negotiations. Suppliers, however, have a clear preference for long-term relationships to recoup excessive transition and investment costs. Clearly, the customer's incentives for short-term deals must be balanced with the supplier's incentives for long-term deals.

The Management of External Relationships

As Kern and Willcocks (2001) detail, even under the most favorable circumstances, relationship management in outsourcing has emerged as difficult. Here we will mention from our consolidated research three areas where customers and suppliers found ways of improving the relationship dimension in their outsourcing arrangements.

Core Capabilities for Managing External Supply

In Figure 14.2 we listed nine core capabilities needing to be retained in-house. Of these, five are orientated toward managing external supply, including Leadership and

Informed Buying. These two tend to be more strategic in orientation, but require relationship skills for dealing with senior executives and negotiators within suppliers. The remaining three involve key tasks, but also major skills in relationship management.

Thus *contract facilitation* is the capability to provide a vital liaison role between the supplier and the customer's user and business communities to ensure supplier success. We found the role arising for a variety of reasons, for example, to provide one-stop shopping for the business user; the supplier or user demanded it; users were demanding too much and incurring excessive charges.

Contract monitoring is the capability to ensure that the supplier delivers on the contract. While the contract facilitator is working to "make things happen" on a day-to-day basis, the contract monitor is ensuring that the business position is protected at all times.

Vendor development is the capability beyond the legal requirements of a contract to explore increasing ways the customers and suppliers can engage in win–win activities. It is in the customer's interest to maximize the contribution of existing suppliers and guard against what we call "mid-contract sag" where minimal contractual commitments are met, but little else.

Relationship Dynamics

Even with these capabilities in place, we found customer and supplier relationships sometimes troublesome, but the parties still tended to have a good relationship overall. Rather than seek to extinguish such troubles, the best relationships embraced the dynamics of these quite complex interactions. We identified four common types of customer–supplier interactions: adversarial, tentative, cooperative, and collaborative (Lacity & Willcocks, 2001). These are based on the extent of goal alignment for the task at hand:

- Tentative interactions occurred when goal alignments are unknown, such as during the bidding process. At such times, each side tended to exaggerate their strengths and hide their weaknesses.
- Adversarial interactions occurred when goals were conflicting, such as interpreting which party should pay for something ambiguously stated in the contract.
- Cooperative interactions occurred when goals were complementary, such as the customer wanted the service, the supplier wanted the payment.
- Collaborative interactions occurred when both sides had shared goals, such as educating the user community on what they could expect from the contract.

By attending to the expectations and goals of many outsourcing stakeholders, apparent anomalies in relationships could be clarified. Why, for example, did customer contract managers and supplier account managers *collaborate* to mediate user expectations, then feel perfectly comfortable *fighting* over a monthly bill? Quite simply, the dynamics of stakeholder relationships vary with the task.

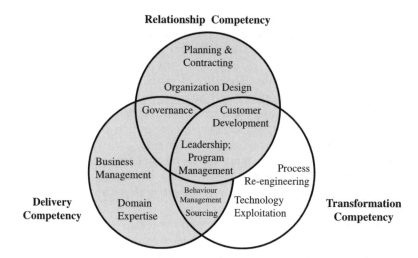

Figure 14.3: Core capabilities in the outsourcing services provider.

Supplier Capabilities

A major recent stream of our research has focused on an area much neglected in academic studies of outsourcing, namely supplier core competencies. *Delivery* competency encompasses how well a supplier can respond to the client's requirement for day-to-day operational services. *Transformation* competency represents how well a supplier can radically improve and even transform cost, quality, and functionality in line with the client's formal and informal expectations. *Relationship* competency relates to the supplier's motivation and ability to align with client needs over time. If a customer is looking mainly for lower costs on baseline services then the Delivery competency will be prioritized. The Relationship competency will be primary if business development with the supplier is the target, while the Transformation competency is key for radical improvement of the IT function. Our ongoing work points to 12 capabilities needed to underpin these competencies (see Feeny, Lacity, & Willcocks, 2005 for details). These are shown in Figure 14.3 and as can be seen, many overlap. These six capabilities are needed to deliver the Relationship competency, seven to support any Transformation agenda, and seven to underpin the Delivery competency.

Conclusion

We have consolidated our findings into a rich picture of evolution over 15 years, from its origins as a relatively small IT services market in some sectors, through to the rise of selective multiple supplier sourcing as the consistently dominant approach in IT to the present day. We conclude that organizational learning on outsourcing has on the whole been quite slow. It may well be that a lower risk approach, and a safer way to accumulate learning has been through incremental outsourcing, and that customers have adopted this outsourcing strategy precisely to develop in-house knowledge about outsourcing.

Having said that, we regularly find that organizations do not apply their learning well until their third or even fourth generation deals. While client organizations may have a history of outsourcing experiences to draw upon, the problem is change. First generation outsourcing clients often changed what they outsourced and how they outsourced the second and third times around. Each time, they found themselves in a relatively new situation, having to learn anew. Furthermore, if their knowledgeable people had left and had not been replaced, organizational learning could not occur until sometimes the fourth generation deal. At the same time people providing the service to a client also move on, and take with them valuable knowledge that cannot easily be replaced, and will no longer be applied to improving the specific outsourcing arrangement.

The practical point is to adopt a risk mitigation approach to outsourcing and not take on more than you can manage. Thus Phase II customers in particular (see Figure 14.1) are advised to:

1. Selectively outsource stable, non-core discrete activities that they understand and can write detailed contracts for.
2. Make sure outsourcing decisions are made by both the IT function and the business.
3. Invite internal and external competitive bids for all large outsourcing contracts.
4. Not over-focus on costs alone. Pick a limited number of objectives, make sure they are consistent and not conflicting, and make sure your expectations are realistic.
5. Ensure the supplier has the capabilities needed to deliver the objectives you have decided upon.
6. Make sure that it is a win–win contract across its lifetime. A key part of this is ensuring that the supplier makes a reasonable profit. The research shows that if the supplier has a bad experience, you are very likely to have one too.
7. Build the nine core retained capabilities — if possible before you outsource. They have proved to be the ultimate way of dealing with what can be a very risky business.

A final point on knowledge. Although customer and supplier maturity definitely looks set to evolve further in the next 5 years, we have seen few signs of the knowledge issues inherent in outsourcing IT and other back-office functions being addressed in the strategies and practices that these parties brought to bear in the outsourcing arena. By 2007 there were promising signs of some studies in this area appearing in the academic journals. But it remained to be seen whether practitioners themselves would, beyond intellectual property issues, start recognizing knowledge issues implicit in the act of outsourcing large parts of the back-office, let alone standardizing practices on ensuring key retained knowledge, and on suppliers possessing and fully deploying complementary knowledge in the service of their customers.

References

Ang, S., & Straub, D. (1998). Production and transaction economies and information systems outsourcing — A study of the US banking industry. *MIS Quarterly, 22*(4), 535–552.

Barney, J. (1991). Firm resources and sustained competitive advantage. *Journal of Management, 17*(1), 99–121.

Beath, C. (1996). The project champion. In: M. Earl (Ed.), *Information management: The organizational dimension*. Oxford: Oxford University Press.

Cullen, S. (2005). *Reframing outsourcing: A study of choices regarding processes, structures and success*. Unpublished PhD thesis, University of Melbourne, Melbourne, Australia.

Cullen, S., & Willcocks, L. P. (2003). *Intelligent IT outsourcing: Eight building blocks to success*. Chichester: Elsevier.

Feeny, D., Lacity, M. C., & Willcocks, L. P. (2005). Taking the measure of outsourcing service providers. *Sloan Management Review, 46*(3), 41–48.

Feeny, D., & Willcocks, L. P. (1998). Core IS capabilities for exploiting information technology. *Sloan Management Review, 39*(3), 9–21.

Hirschheim, R., & Lacity, M. (2000, February). Information technology insourcing: myths and realities. *Communications of the ACM, 1*, 99–107.

Hof, R., & Kerttetter, J. (2004, March 1). Software: Will outsourcing hurt America's supremacy? *Business Week*, 84–95.

Kern, T., Lacity, M. C., & Willcocks, L. P. (2002). *Net sourcing: Renting business applications and services over a network*. Upper Saddle River, NJ: Prentice-Hall.

Kern, T., & Willcocks, L. P. (2001). *The relationship advantage: Information technologies, sourcing and management*. Oxford: Oxford University Press.

Lacity, M., & Willcocks, L. (1996). Interpreting information technology sourcing decisions from a transaction cost perspective: Findings and critique. *Accounting, Management and Information Technologies, 5*(3/4), 203–244.

Lacity, M., Willcocks, L., & Cullen, S. (2008). *Global IT outsourcing: 21st century search for business advantage* (2nd ed.). Chichester: Wiley.

Lacity, M. C., & Willcocks, L. P. (2001). *Global information technology outsourcing: Search for business advantage*. Chichester: Wiley.

McGee, M. (2003, August 25). Offshore outsourcing drags down U.S. bonus pay. *InformationWeek*, 23.

Nam, K., Rajagopalan, S., Rao, H., & Chaudhury (1996). A two-level investigation of information systems outsourcing. *Communications of the ACM, 39*(7), 36–44.

Straub, D., Weill, P., & Stewart, K. (2002). *Strategic control of IT resources: A test of resource-based theory in the context of selective IT outsourcing*. Working Paper, Georgia State University and MIT Sloan School of Management.

Williamson, O. (1991). Strategizing, economizing, and economic organization. *Strategic Management Journal, 12*, 75–94.

Willcocks, L., & Lacity, M. (Eds.) (2006). *Global sourcing of business and IT services*. Chichester: Wiley.

Chapter 15

ICT-Outsourcing: A Resource-Based Information Management Perspective

Bjorn Cumps, Guido Dedene and Stijn Viaene

ABSTRACT

The increased use of ICT outsourcing requires a deeper analysis of interorganizational information management practices. In this chapter this strategic role of ICT for the organization is used to determine two leading outsourcing scenarios. Using transaction cost theory (TCT) and the resource-based view (RBV), alignment practices are proposed for both scenarios. The role of service level contracts, and the interfaces in terms of processes, structures and roles are discussed, using the integrative framework for information management of Maes (2007). In the conclusion, a summary of the best practices is presented.

Introduction

The integrative framework for information management (Maes, 2005, 2007) is a well-established framework for studying best practices in information management. The focus in many publications using this framework is on business — ICT alignment issues. Originally, these alignment practices were mainly studied from an *intraorganizational* point of view. However, the increased use of insourcing and outsourcing requires *interorganizational* alignment, which has not been studied extensively so far in the literature. In a lot of the current literature on outsourcing the focus is on finding the determinants for outsourcing decisions (Gonzalez, Gasco, & Llopis, 2006; Hirschheim, 1995; Hirschheim, Heinzl, & Dibbern, 2002; Hirschheim & Lacity, 2000). In this chapter these studies will be used and extended with best practices for interorganizational information management, once the outsourcing decision is taken. For example, one important management factor is complexity, which rapidly increases in outsourcing situations, in particular in multiple sourcing situations. In this chapter, the integrative framework for information management (Maes, 2007) will be used as a roadmap for better managing the relations with outsourcing ICT suppliers. The interfaces that need information management attention are clearly determined. This results in practical guidelines for better managing outsourcing situations.

So, the essence of this chapter is a mapping of outsourcing and interorganizational alignment issues on the integrative framework for information management (Maes, 2007). The starting point is a theoretical foundation (Watjatrakul, 2005), in which transaction cost theory (TCT) and the resource-based view (RBV) are combined to give fairly strong and clear indicators for an outsourcing (versus insourcing) decision. The choice for this theoretical foundation is manifold:

- The RBV on the firm has a natural linkage to the integrative framework for information management (Truijens, 2004).
- The RBV adds additional arguments to the TCT (in particular regarding asset specificity).
- Most studies suggest that outsourcing doesn't make sense in the case of strategic resources. In this study, it is shown how scenarios may exist where outsourcing still makes sense in the case of strategic resources.
- The results of this theoretical foundation can be used as characteristics of client organizations that go for an outsourcing decision.

In this chapter, two major scenarios are selected from the recommendations in the theoretical foundation to go for outsourcing. The first scenario is the situation in which nonstrategic resources are outsourced. The second (and quite particular) situation deals with the outsourcing of strategic resources. Strategic resources yield sustainable competitive advantage by exploiting market opportunities (imperfections) and by neutralizing competitors' threats (Barney, 1991).

To link the outsourcing scenarios to an empirical study on best practices on alignment (Cumps, Viaene, Dedene, & Vandenbulcke, 2006), the scenarios are characterized in terms of the *strategic importance of ICT*. In case when ICT is of low strategic importance, contracts (including service level agreements) are the leading alignment mechanism. When ICT is of high strategic importance, process, structure and role interfaces (such as described in the RBV (Peppard & Ward, 2004)) are the instruments for interorganizational alignment. In both situations, the best practices are positioned on the components of the integrative framework for information management (Maes, 2007).

In the last section of the chapter, the situation of multiple internal and external suppliers is considered. Client organizations increasingly use this type of *multi-sourcing* to reduce the risks involved with uncertainties in the outsourcing relations. In this situation, a well-elaborated enterprise architecture is crucial. Once again, enterprise architecture turns out to be a communication vehicle (Bryant & Maes, 2005), in this case mainly to integrate multiple suppliers.

In the conclusion, an overview is given of the interorganizational information management practices that are relevant for dealing with outsourcing situations successfully.

Foundations for the Outsourcing Decision

In the literature there are two major theories that explain in which situations outsourcing is a relevant decision. The combination of these two theories allows developing two major scenarios for outsourcing. The interorganizational alignment issues for these two scenarios will be explored in the rest of the chapter, using the integrative framework for information management as a roadmap for the best practices that are applicable in the two scenarios. This section will discuss the theoretical foundations for the outsourcing scenarios that are considered in this chapter.

Since sourcing decisions are often related to costing or cost-transformation issues, TCT is one of the explaining frameworks for outsourcing decisions. Basically, when confronted with sourcing decisions, organizations will attempt to minimize their transaction costs. When transaction costs are already low, the organization will use the market according to economies of scale and economies of scope may exist. If transaction costs are high, the organization has little or no production cost advantages in the market, and will prefer internal sourcing (Leiblein, 2003).

TCT considers several characteristics of interorganizational transactions. Two of these factors have a clear influence on sourcing decisions, and can be summarized as follows:

- *Asset specificity:* This is the extent to which investments made to support a particular transaction have a higher value to that particular type of transaction in contrast with the value when these investments are used for another purpose. It is very risky for a client organization to outsource its highly specific assets, because in this way the supplier company gains control and power over the client organization (mainly due to switching costs). Transactions with high asset specificity will typically drive insourcing, as organizations attempt to protect their resources themselves. Transactions with low asset specificity may lead to outsourcing. Furthermore, outsourcing supplier firms can lower their costs by pooling demand across multiple customers and services, and by utilizing excess capacity in a more efficient way (Aubert, Rivard, & Patry, 2004). That gives them an advantage when client organizations are looking for the least costly market options (Koh, Ang, & Yeo, 2007).
- *Uncertainty:* There are two forms of uncertainty in TCT: behavioral and environmental uncertainty. In case of behavioral uncertainty, the client organization is not sure about the strategic behavior of the supplier company for outsourcing. This would lead to higher contract enforcement and monitoring costs, which ultimately drive the client organization toward insourcing. Environmental uncertainty exists when the client organization has limited possibilities to predict future outcomes. To anticipate opportunistic behavior of supplier companies, such as dealing with possibly changing circumstances, the client organization will have to write more complete contracts. These higher transaction costs will drive organizations again toward insourcing.

The influence of asset specificity can be explored deeper by adding the RBV on organizations. Resources may be very specific, when they cannot be redeployed or transferred without a reduction of value. *Strategic resources* yield — by definition — sustainable competitive advantage to organizations. Strategic resources exploit market opportunities (imperfections) and try to neutralize competitive forces (Barney, 1991). *Nonstrategic resources* are operational resources, which are more oriented toward day-to-day continuity of the operations, without giving sustained competitive advantage. The two characteristics should not be confused: even strategic resources may be nonspecific, for example, if they are strategic in many scenarios.

Combining these two characteristics (specific and strategic) leads to the following resource classification (Watjatrakul, 2005):

- *Low-specific nonstrategic resources (LSNR):* Examples are generic (nonspecific) operational management skills.
- *High-specific nonstrategic resources (HSNR):* Examples are highly technical customized skills (e.g., to administer an internal groupware system tailored to the specific needs of the organization).
- *Low-specific strategic resources (LSSR):* Examples are generic collaboration skills that can make a management team a strategic asset for sustainable value.
- *High-specific strategic resources (HSSR):* Examples are highly specialized software teams that create sustainable strategic advantage, which is difficult to imitate (due to, e.g., dependency on specific data of the organization and its customers).

When using this classification of assets specificity, the combination with uncertainty leads to an integrated schema that predicts sourcing decisions, based on either TCT or RBV (Watjatrakul, 2005), as shown in Table 15.1. There are some

Table 15.1: Sourcing decisions (Watjatrakul, 2005).

		Behavioral or Environmental Uncertainity	
		LOW	HIGH
Low specificity, Non-Strategic	TCT	OUTSOURCING	INSOURCING
Resources (*LSNR*)	RBV	OUTSOURCING	OUTSOURCING
Low specificity, Strategic	TCT	OUTSOURCING	INSOURCING
Resources (*LSSR*)	RBV	INSOURCING	INSOURCING
High specificity, Non-Strategic	TCT	INSOURCING	INSOURCING
Resources (*HSNR*)	RBV	OUTSOURCING	OUTSOURCING
High specificity, Strategic	TCT	INSOURCING	INSOURCING
Resources (*HSSR*)	RBV	INSOURCING	INSOURCING

interesting observations to discuss relating to these results:

- Risks (uncertainty) apparently do not influence the sourcing decision in most of the cases, except for the TCT view on low-specific resources. In fact, higher risks will almost never stimulate outsourcing.
- Based on RBV, one will never outsource strategic resources, although TCT suggests differently in case of low specificity and low uncertainty. This is an interesting exception, which will be studied further in this chapter.
- Many situations suggest not to go for outsourcing, in fact 10 of the 16 recommendations in Table 15.1 go for insourcing.

In this chapter, the impact of the decision to outsource for interorganizational alignment practices is investigated. The outsourcing decision will be linked to best practices in business–ICT alignment, for which a recent European study gives significant empirical material (Cumps et al., 2006). In this survey study, two categories of respondents were identified: organizations for which ICT has a high strategic importance, and organizations for which ICT has a rather low strategic importance. The degree of strategic importance can be operationalized by considering the ICT investment portfolio of an organization (Weill & Broadbent, 1998). The investments can be allocated to four categories:

1. Legal or compliance mandated ICT investments.
2. Continuity (maintenance and infrastructure) ICT investments (keep up and running).
3. ICT investments that have an impact on the *current* competitive performance of the organization.
4. ICT investments that have an impact on the *future* (prospective) competitive performance of the organization.

Organizations for which the first two categories are dominant in the ICT portfolio, are indicated as *organizations with ICT low strategic importance*. Otherwise, when the last two categories are dominating the ICT portfolio, the organization is indicated as an *organization with ICT high strategic importance*. The European study mentioned before, confirmed that this characterization coincides with a self-positioning of the participants to the study with a correlation of 89% (Cumps et al., 2006).

Organizations, for which ICT has low strategic importance, have — by definition — no strategic resources. High-specific resources, even if they are nonstrategic, may easily lead to lock-in (hold-up) situations with the outsourcing supplier. Therefore, TCT advises insourcing in that case, and this situation will not be considered further in this study. The outsourcing scenario of organizations for which ICT has low strategic importance will be indicated as *Scenario 1*.

Organizations, for which ICT has high strategic importance, use ICT as low-specific strategic resources, in a context of low uncertainty. This is the *only* scenario where Table 15.1 suggests outsourcing for strategic resources. All the other combinations, and in particular high-specific strategic resources, strongly suggest insourcing. The particular interesting situation where low-specific strategic resources are outsourced will be indicated as *Scenario 2*. The following shows the scenarios in Table 15.2.

Table 15.2: Sourcing scenarios.

		SCENARIO 2	SCENARIO 1	
			Behavioral or Environmental Uncertainity	
			LOW	**HIGH**
Low specificity, Non-Strategic	TCT		OUTSOURCING	INSOURCING
Resources (*LSNR*)	RBV		OUTSOURCING	OUTSOURCING
Low specificity, Strategic	TCT		OUTSOURCING	INSOURCING
Resources (*LSSR*)	RBV		INSOURCING	INSOURCING
High specificity, Non-Strategic	TCT		INSOURCING	INSOURCING
Resources (*HSNR*)	RBV		OUTSOURCING	OUTSOURCING
High specificity, Strategic	TCT		INSOURCING	INSOURCING
Resources (*HSSR*)	RBV		INSOURCING	INSOURCING

Scenario 1: ICT with Low Strategic Importance

As discussed in the previous section, outsourcing client organizations for which ICT has a low strategic importance use ICT as low-specific, nonstrategic resources, in a context of low uncertainty. This is the only scenario where both TCT and RBV predict outsourcing. A typical example is using highly standardized desktop (client) computers, networks and databases, and having basic, off-the-shelf ERP-systems for their transaction support.

Given the uniform suggestion for outsourcing, from TCT and RBV, such a client organization may be stimulated to outsource the entire technological services to an external supplier. The client organization buys technology capacity and services from the external outsourcing supplier company, and keeps little or nothing in-house. This view is sometimes referred to as the *utility view on ICT* or *on-demand computing*. The organization pays the service supplier for the use of the network capacity, data storage volumes, application services (e.g., in application service provider (ASP) or software as a service (SAAS) mode). Increasingly, small and midsize enterprises are choosing for this type of outsourcing.

The supplier company is responsible for the hardware and software investments, and the client organization pays for the computing power that it uses from the supplier company. This means that the supplier has autonomous freedom to develop its own technology strategy, as long as the demands from the client organization can be fulfilled. So, the client organization buys computing power just as it buys electricity, or pays for a telephone service, without having any interference with the strategy and the structure of the service supplier organization.

Consequently, this type of outsourcing has a particular representation in the integrative framework for information management (Maes, 2007). For this type of client organization, the entire right column (the technology column) is outsourced. The client will pay for services and will not be involved in the technology strategy and organizational structure of the supplier. From the above schema, it is clear that the client and the supplier company only meet each other at the operational level in the integrative framework for information management, putting a strong emphasis on *operational alignment* issues.

One of the success factors for operational alignment is activity-based costing (ABC), applied to ICT services (Dedene, Viaene, Cumps, & De Backer, 2004). In this type of outsourcing, the client organization will define its *business activities* (purchase orders, customer accounts and so on). Next the client organization will determine which type of I/C services are needed. These are *I/C service activities* (such as messages, transactions, database queries, internet queries, etc.). The client organization will express the translation of business activities into service activities in the form of micro-economical production functions, called *business profiles*. Fortunately, the operational laws of performance management (such as Little's Law) indicate that these production functions are basically linear functions.

It is the responsibility of the supplier company to deliver the necessary *technology activities*, say the technology "power", to realize the ICT-services that the client organization needs. The translation is again done by means of production functions, called *service profiles*. The mathematical formulation of this mapping on the integrative framework for information management goes beyond the scope of this chapter (Dedene et al., 2004). One detail is very relevant: the production functions can only be optimized when their mathematical boundary values are fixed. This is precisely the role of the *service level Agreements*.

So, in this case, the best practices for operational alignment are the following key practices:

- Align the business activities with the service activities using the business profiles.
- Align the service activities with the (outsourced) technological activities using the service profiles.
- Negotiate for the best possible profiles by fixing the service level agreements (Figure 15.1).

A simple example may illustrate the above practices. Assume that the core activity of the client organization is order taking, whereby, when serving a customer, web forms are completed with the customer specifications, next the web forms are transmitted to a server application to calculate the offer costs, and finally the tailor-made offer is e-mailed to the customer in pdf format. Hence, the core business activity is *customer order taking*, which is measured in terms of numbers of concurrent customers served.

The service activities are threefold in this case:

- Filling in a (web-)form. This is a web server-based activity.
- Calculating the costs of the offer and write the result as a tailor-based order to a pdf file. This is a typical server software transaction.
- E-mail the offer to the customer. This is a standard e-mail service.

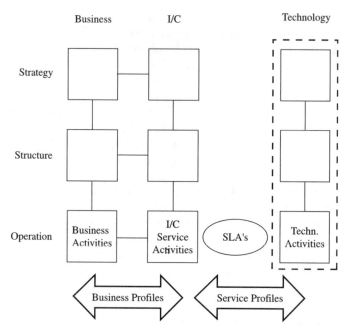

Figure 15.1: Outsourcing when ICT has low strategic importance.

While serving its customers, the client organization discovered that they typically use one fill-in form, do three offer calculations and e-mail two pdf files. This is an example of how the profiles can be determined in practice.

This client organization is using outsourced technological resources to realize these services. The technological resources are CPU power and disk storage. The negotiation of the service profiles is driven by the service level agreements. For example, the client organization may want to optimize the response times of the service activities, and has chosen for not optimizing disk storage. The supplier could propose (cheaper) alternatives, which use less disk space, but may take more CPU power and longer response times to execute the same service activities. Other service level agreement aspects may focus on the availability of the services activities, and require adequate backup facilities and nondestructive computation techniques.

In conclusion, there is a strong focus on the outsourcing contract issues. The formal contract is the main relationship with the supplier company. The focus is on maintaining consistency in the delivery of the services, by monitoring it in terms of performance metrics, and raise sanctioning when the service levels are not met. After all, this is still a relative simple procedure, in contrast with the situation when ICT has a high strategic importance.

One remark regarding the situation of high-specificity, nonstrategic resources in Table 15.1 remains. TCT suggest no outsourcing in this case, primarily due to potential lock-in situations with the supplier organization. The RBV suggests outsourcing, in which case, the service level contract is again the primary alignment instrument. However, in this case, the contract must be extended to include a clause that prevents hold-up practices by the supplier organization.

Scenario 2: ICT with High Strategic Importance

Outsourcing is a nontrivial decision in the situation when ICT has high strategic importance. Based on Table 15.1, client organizations where ICT has high strategic importance will only outsource low-specific, strategic resources, in a context of low uncertainty. This is the only scenario where outsourcing is predicted, and only by TCT.

A client organization with low-specific but strategic ICT resources typically uses only standard, of-the-shelf ICT to support its key business activities, but in such a way that they use innovation in the processes as a basis for sustainable competitive advantage. An example is a financial institute that uses standard web-based technology, which allows its customers to upload a picture that can be printed on their loyalty bank card. This institute creates customer affinity and product differentiation, based on standard ICT techniques. Furthermore, this organization hopes to gain younger customers, and uses standard analysis tools to extract strategic customer profiles for this market segment. Other examples include government institutes, such as ministries, which use standardized nonspecific ICT, but in a very information-intensive way. The Flemish government in Belgium is a case where this type of outsourcing is put into practice for several years now.

In this section, it will be assumed that the client organization only wants to outsource part of its ICT activities. Indeed, if ICT is critical to the organization's core business processes, it probably wants to retain some control over it. The client organization may be willing to outsource the operational/technological aspects of the ICT activity, without completely loosing control over the strategic and some of the structural aspects. In the integrative framework for information management (Maes, 2007), typically the right lower half is, more-or-less, subject of outsourcing (Figure 15.2).

Client organizations may outsource the entire lower right half, or less, as the dashed line in the framework suggests. The line is actually the border line between the client (demand) organization, and the supplier outsourcing company. To be successful in this scenario, the client–supplier relationship should be much more elaborated than in the previous section, where there was only a relationship at the operational level.

Typically, when ICT is of high strategic importance, the supplier company will have to align and change according to the client organization's strategy and structures. This is much more than just transferring technology operations from one organization to another (the outsourcer). Understandably, the term *strategic outsourcing* is sometimes used for this situation.

Therefore, if an organization outsources parts of its strategically important ICT, it will only do this with outsourcing organizations that it *trusts*. This is a *partnership*

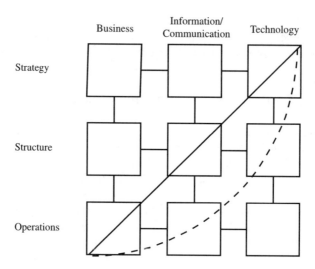

Figure 15.2: Outsourcing when ICT has high strategic importance.

relationship rather than a formal client–supplier relationship. Consequently, there is a stronger focus on coordination and integration on the strategic and structural levels (Beulen, Ribbers, & Roos, 2006; Lacity, Hirschheim, & Willcocks, 1994). Rather, in this case, the client organization has to integrate the supplier's strategic and structural skills and expertise in its own structures, roles and processes.

A RBV of the business — ICT alignment issues requires a precise distinction between the resources, the competencies and the capabilities (Caldeira & Ward, 2003; Peppard & Ward, 2004; Truijens, 2004). Peppard and Ward (2004) propose the following definitions for the key concepts in the RBV.

- *Resources* are stocks of available factors that are owned or controlled by the organization. The data, information, knowledge, systems and technology owned or available to the organization are examples of resources. The integrative framework for information management (Maes, 2007) considers three types of resources: business, information/communication and technological resources.
- *Competencies* refer to an organization's capacity to deploy resources, usually in combination, using organizational processes, to affect a desired end. They refer to the organization's ability to deploy bundles of specific resources to accomplish a given task.
- *Capability* refers to the strategic application of competencies, i.e., their use and deployment to accomplish given organizational goals.

Put differently, *resources* are what an organization has under its control or at its disposal; *competencies* are the abilities of the organization to develop, mobilize and use those resources; *capability* is what the business can achieve through focused investments and deployment of competencies. ICT value is not only created just by the ICT resources, but rather by the organization's ability (competence) to utilize or mobilize those resources.

Peppard and Ward (2004) focused on the links between these concepts in RBV. According to their model, resources are transformed into competencies through the interplay of organizational *processes, structures* and *roles*. These are the mechanisms to leverage the resources and build competencies. In the situation of outsourcing when ICT has high strategic importance, the resources of the supplier company must be integrated with the (strategically important) resources of the client organization. Figure 15.3 shows an application of the model of Peppard and Ward (2004) to this scenario.

From this model, it becomes clear that the success of the outsourcing decision is more about building collaborative relationships/structures and internalizing external knowledge and expertise than it is about integrating technology operations.

In the integrative framework for information management (Maes, 2007), the information and communication column plays a pivotal role in realizing this success. Part of the ICT function remains in the client organization, and is often referred to as the *retained ICT organization* (Mani, Barua, & Whiston, 2006). The role of the retained ICT organization is to create interfaces with the supplier company. As such, the retained ICT organization has to focus on the processes, structures and roles that can act as alignment enhancing interfaces between the two partners. Coordination, integration and relationship management are its main responsibilities. The retained ICT organization can be mapped on the framework of Maes, 2007 (Figure 15.4), showing that the "what" aspects cannot be outsourced, while the "how" aspects may be outsourced in this scenario.

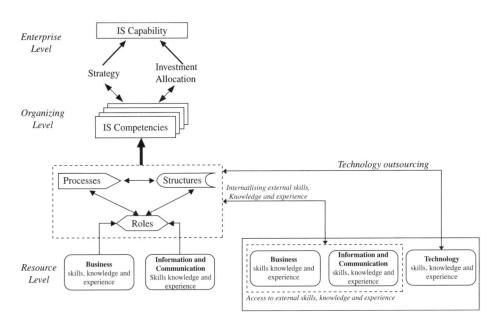

Figure 15.3: RBV model for outsourcing when ICT has high strategic importance.

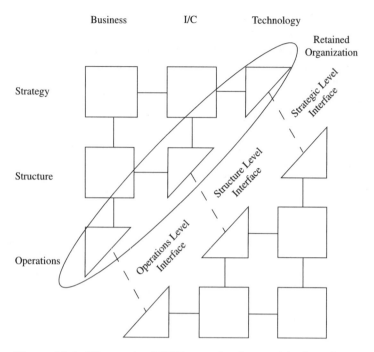

Figure 15.4: The retained ICT organization and its interfaces.

At the *strategic level*, only part of the technology strategy can be outsourced, due to its strategic importance. An organization will almost never outsource business strategy or information/communication strategy (Lacity et al., 1994; Mc Farlan & Nolan, 1995). The client organization will retain control over the role of ICT in their organization, and the objectives and plans that define how ICT will support the business goals. However, part of the objectives and plans on how technology will be used, i.e., technology strategy, may be outsourced.

When part of the technology strategy is outsourced, there is a need for a strategic level interface to make sure that the technology, I/C and business strategies are well aligned. The CIO and senior executives from both the client and the supplier organization are required to explore how both parties can benefit from the relationship. This focus in both organizations is necessary to ensure a long-term partnership in which both are willing to invest. For example, a joint executive steering committee can be established to commit and communicate shared goals, objectives, core competencies and discuss how the outsourcer's technology strategy can leverage innovations in technology to support the client's business and information strategies. To apply the RBV, according to the model of Peppard and Ward (2004), the processes, structures and roles that make up the strategic level interface must be defined for the client organization as well as the supplier organization. This has been shown in Table 15.3.

Table 15.3: Processes, structures and roles for the strategic level interface.

	Client	**Joint**	**Supplier**
Processes	Determining business strategy	Determining technology strategy	Innovative use of IT
	Determining I/C strategy		Industry trend analysis
			Gaining business insight
Structures	Executive committee	Joint executive Steering committee	Executive committee
	CIO office — ICT board		
Roles	CIO		Senior Executive

The *structural level interface* mainly relies on enterprise architecture practices. The retained organization needs to have a clear overview of the business processes as well as the business and information requirements. Furthermore, a clear vision of how the core business processes will evolve in the future to support the business strategy will help to formulate future requirements. Working out the information and technology architectures together with the outsourcing partner ensures that the outsourced systems and technology serve the necessary information needs to feed the core business processes of the client organization. Furthermore, project portfolio management needs to be a joint responsibility as the outsourcing organization needs to have a clear overview of the portfolio of business projects to assess the impact on the systems and technology architecture (Table 15.4).

Enterprise and technology architects are the crucial liaison roles at the structure level interface. The service and contract review groups make sure that the overall ICT service and projects are delivered to the client's satisfaction, and that the outsourcing organization can give input of ICT potential and constraints in the planning of new business activities and the corresponding projects.

Finally, the *operations level interface* can be used for service management and problem management between both organizations. The operational alignment focuses on service levels and operational performance. Service and performance quality monitoring are the main joint responsibilities together with problem management and process improvements. The process and delivery managers are the key liaison roles that need a direct line of communication at this interface level (Table 15.5).

It is clear from the discussion in this section that a contract alone will not suffice as an interface to make the outsourcing a success. Joint processes, structures and liaison roles are the interfaces that the retained ICT organization uses to ensure that the outsourcing organization is supporting the client's business operations, processes and strategy.

Table 15.4: Processes, structures and roles for the structure level interface.

	Client	Joint	Supplier
Processes	Determining business processes	Information and technology architecture planning and integration	Defining and managing technology architecture
	Determining business and information requirements	Project portfolio management	Infrastructure solution design
	Business program management	Contract compliance monitoring	Requirements management
	Enterprise architecture vision	Business portfolio impact analysis	
Structures	Activity committees	Service review groups Contract review groups	Activity committees
Roles	Enterprise architect		Technology architect

Table 15.5: Processes, structures and roles for the operational level interface.

	Client	Joint	Supplier
Processes	Business project management	Service level management	Technology, applications and infrastructure, development, maintenance and monitoring
	Business process execution	Change management	
	Business process monitoring	Problem management	Technology project management Manage service levels Deliver ICT service
Structures	Domain councils	Project groups	Technology project groups
	Business project groups	Organizational performance groups	
Roles	Business process managers		Delivery managers
			Business analysts

Multisourcing Arrangements

A recent development seen in practice is the combination of multiple outsourcing suppliers, also called *multisourcing* arrangements. Multisourcing is often considered to be a primary instrument to reduce behavioral and environmental uncertainty, and may lead organizations into applying Scenario 1 or Scenario 2, or a combination of both.

Multisourcing is the disciplined provisioning and blending of business and ICT services from the optimal set of internal and external providers in the pursuit of business goals (Cohen & Young, 2005). This means that organizations have to manage multiple suppliers both internally (such as shared service centers) as well as external. The advantages are that the client organization spreads its risks over multiple suppliers, stimulates competition between the outdoor ICT providers and can create best-of-breed solutions with each supplier focusing on what he does best. One of the most important dangers of multisourcing is the potential *interdependency of the suppliers*. Therefore, again, the creation of a good process, structure and role interface by the retained ICT organization is crucial for the outsourcing supplier orchestration and to resolve responsibility issues. So, what was discussed in the previous section becomes even more important in multisourcing settings.

As emphasized in the literature, if an organization is outsourcing different parts to different suppliers, enterprise architecture becomes a key success factor. The different outsourced parts need to be described in a formal way, such as the *sourceable unit* concept (Delen, 2005). A sourceable unit may be a process, but also a set of processes, application components or infrastructure components for which the *interfaces* to other internal or external components are well defined. Inspired by the integrated definition (IDEF)-style of methodologies, this means that each unit is described in terms of

1. IN: What goes into the unit.
2. The resources that are used.
3. OUT: What comes out of the unit, what are the deliverables.
4. How is the unit managed, governed.

Optimized sourceable units should be modular, and have maximal cohesion and minimal coupling to each other. The way and the precision by means of which organizations define interfaces have an important impact on multisourcing. Only those parts of the organization that have clearly defined interfaces can be taken out and transferred to supplier organizations. Organizations that invest in enterprise architecture, clearly defining and mapping out their business structures, will have much more flexibility in multisourcing arrangements. Finding the appropriate granularity, for example, by applying service-oriented architecture, may significantly drive the multisourcing flexibility.

Consider the following example, in which an organization is using only high-level, black-box views on its business activities, such as shown in Figure 15.5.

Such an organization has little or no knowledge of and insight into the structure of its business processes. Therefore, multisourcing these monolithic processes to

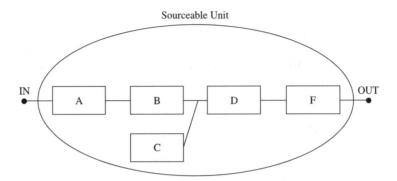

Figure 15.5: Large monolithic sourceable units.

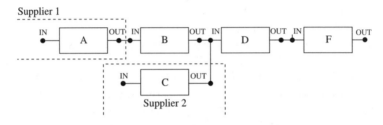

Figure 15.6: Small atomic sourceable units.

multiple vendor becomes an almost impossible task. If the organization had invested in defining the structural components of the business activities, together with their interfaces, much more flexibility in multisourcing options would have been generated. It turns out, for example, that in this case two input components, at the beginning of the activity, can be outsourced to different suppliers, as becomes clear in the finer granularity analysis (see Figure 15.6).

It shows how the finer granularity is required to generate sufficient flexibility for an organization. The degree of architecturization of the business and information processes, the systems and the technology are key to enable various multisourcing options. The finer the granularity of the component and interface definitions of business processes, the more possibilities an organization has to multisource specific activities to both internal as well as external suppliers.

Multisourcing is complex, also from an information management perspective. Consider an example, in which an organization has outsourced two business operations to two different suppliers A and B, while the organization retains its core business operations. Furthermore, assume that two technological activities are outsourced to suppliers C and D, while the organization retains its core technology infrastructure. This is a typical multisourcing situation: the organization externalizes a number of focused activities, processes or systems to specialized outsourcing companies, while keeping control on its core activities. This results in more specific, smaller contracts with multiple suppliers, that each delivers very specific services. In order to manage the possible interdependencies amongst the outsourcing companies, as well as potential responsibility overlaps, the organization may want to use an *integrator* (Beulen et al., 2006; Cohen & Young, 2005). This integrator can be an external supplier that only acts as an integrator between the organization and all of its different suppliers (see Figure 15.7). However, the retained ICT organization may also choose to perform this function itself. It is obvious that an integrator must have deep skills in enterprise architecture, to deal with the risks of the multisourcing integration.

Cohen and Young (2005) argue that the three core competencies for successful multisourcing are *communication, coordination* and *integration*. This maps exactly to what has been discussed in the previous sections of this chapter. A contract alone, as often used for large, single sourcing, monolithic outsourcing deals is not a sufficient interface between a client organization and its multiple outsourcing companies to provide sufficient communication and coordination. Strong process, structure and role interfaces are required to create dedicated peer-to-peer communication channels, and to facilitate coordination processes and structures between the multiple sourcing suppliers and the organization. Moreover, the retained organization should rely on enterprise architecture to clearly define the structural components and interfaces in

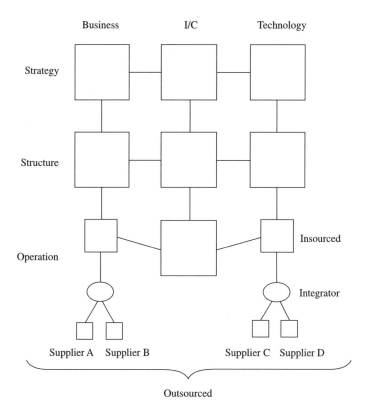

Figure 15.7: An example of multisourcing arrangement.

its business activities, to determine the sourceable units. It is clear how architecture fulfils its role as a communication instrument, and an enabler for good integration (Bryant & Maes, 2005).

Conclusions

The goal of this chapter was to explore the impact of various outsourcing scenarios on information management, using the RBV as a guidance instrument (in particular because of its emphasis on structures, processes and roles). In particular, it was illustrated how different forms of outsourcing have a different impact on alignment issues, with a positioning on the framework of Maes (2005). In the case of low ICT importance organizations, where complete outsourcing may become feasible, alignment problems reduce mainly to operational alignment issues with the external outsourcing company. The operational alignment is established in an analytical way by means of (optimized) production functions and contracts, in which service level agreements play a crucial role. Strategic outsourcing, in the case of high-ICT importance organizations, is more challenging. The resource-based theory helps to determine the necessary process, structure and role interfaces that must exist to ensure the success of the strategic outsourcing. In the case of strategic outsourcing, the client organization and the outsourcing company cooperate as an *extended enterprise* in which relationship building and collaborative issues are crucial. Collaborative routines and learning structures are needed to internalize the external knowledge and expertise from the outsourcing company. Further research is needed to understand and measure how this precisely works. Table 15.6 summarizes the two major outsourcing scenarios.

The RBV brings more structure in managing multisourcing situations. Additionally, the role of enterprise architecture is stressed in such situations, to determine in a

Table 15.6: Best practices for the outsourcing scenarios in this chapter.

	Low Strategic Importance (Scenario 1)	High Strategic Importance (Scenario 2)
Goal	Efficiency improvements Cost reductions Variable capacity	Business expansion Competitive advantage Effectiveness improvement
Key metrics	Bottom line impact	Quality, project success
Alignment	Operational alignment	Strategic, structural and operational
	Contract management	Relationship and interface management
	Service level monitoring	Mutual goal attainment
Relationship	Client – supplier	Partner

precise way the sourceable units, and to function as a communication language between the various outsourcing suppliers and the integrator(s). This makes it clear again that enterprise architecture can hardly or never be outsourced. Otherwise unacceptable dependencies will exist between the client organization and its outsourcing suppliers.

References

Aubert, B., Rivard, S., & Patry, M. (2004). A transaction cost model of IT outsourcing. *Information & Management, 41.*

Barney, J. B. (1991). Firm resources and sustained competitive advantage. *Journal of Management, 17*(1).

Beulen, E., Ribbers, P., & Roos, J. (2006). *Managing IT outsourcing: Governance in global partnerships.* UK: Routledge.

Bryant, T., & Maes, R. (2005). *Information architecture: From structural notion to meaningful communicative concept, Critical Management Studies Conference, Cambridge, U.K. 2005.* Also available as PrimaVera working paper 2005–09.

Caldeira, M. M., & Ward, J. M. (2003). Using resource-based theory to interpret the successful adoption and use of information systems and technology in manufacturing small and medium-sized enterprises. *European Journal of Information Systems, 12.*

Cohen, L., & Young, A. (2005). *Multisourcing: Moving beyond outsourcing to achieve growth and agility.* Boston, MA: Harvard Business School Press.

Cumps, B., Viaene, S., Dedene, G., & Vandenbulcke, J. (2006). An empirical study on business/ICT alignment in European organizations. In: *Proceedings of the 39th Hawaiien International Conference on System Sciences (HICSS 39),* Kawai, HI.

Dedene, G., Viaene, S., Cumps, B., & De Backer, M. (2004). An ABC-based approach for operational business/ICT alignment. In: *Proceedings of the 11th European Conference on Information Technology Evaluation (ECITE),* Amsterdam, The Netherlands.

Delen, G. (2005). *Decision en controlfactoren voor IT sourcing.* Zaltbommel, The Netherlands: Van Haren Publishing.

Gonzalez, R., Gasco, J., & Llopis, J. (2006). Information systems outsourcing: A literature analysis. *Information and Management, 43*(7).

Hirschheim, R., Heinzl, A., & Dibbern, J. (Eds.) (2002). *Information systems outsourcing. Enduring themes, emergent patterns and future directions.* Berlin: Springer.

Hirschheim, R., & Lacity, M. (2000). The myths and realities of information technology insourcing. *Communications of the ACM, 43*(2).

Koh, C., Ang, S., & Yeo, G. (2007). Does IT Outsourcing Create Firm Value? In: *Proceedings of the 2007 ACM SIGMIS CPR Special Interest Group on Computer Personnel Research,* St. Louis, MO.

Lacity, M. C., Hirschheim, R., & Willcocks, L. P. (1994). Realising outsourcing expectations. *Journal of Information Systems Management, 1*(4).

Leiblein, M. (2003). The choice of organizational governance form and performance: Predictions from transaction cost, resource-based, and real options theories. *Journal of Management, 29*(6).

Maes, R. (2005). Information Management: A roadmap, 1st European Conference on IS Management, Leadership and Governance, Reading, U.K. 2005. Also available as PrimaVera working paper 2004–13.

Maes, R. (2007). An integrative perspective on information management. In: A. Huizing, & E. J. de Vries (Eds.), *Information management: Setting the scene: Book series Perspectives on Information Management* (vol. 1). Oxford: Elsevier Scientific Publishers.

Mani, D., Barua, A., & Whiston, A. (2006). Successfully governing business process outsourcing relationships. *MIS Quarterly Executive, 5*(1).

Mc Farlan, F. W., & Nolan, R. L. (1995). How to manage an IT outsourcing alliance. *Sloan Management Review, 36*(2).

Peppard, J., & Ward, J. (2004). Beyond strategic information systems: Towards an IS capability. *Journal of Strategic Information Systems, 13*(2).

Truijens, O. (2004). *Towards a theory of information strategy: Exploiting market opaqueness in search for infoRent*, PhD thesis, University of Amsterdam, Universal Press, Veenendaal, The Netherlands.

Watjatrakul, B. (2005). Determinants of IS sourcing decisions: A comparative study of transaction cost theory versus the resource-based view. *Journal of Strategic Information Systems, 14*(4).

Weill, P., & Broadbent, M. (1998). *Leveraging the new infrastructure: How market leaders capitalize on information technology*. Boston, MA: Harvard Business School Press.

Chapter 16

Operational Pitfalls and Opportunities in Offshore Software Development

Guido Dedene and Aimé Heene

ABSTRACT

Offshore software projects are a major segment in the outsourcing business sector. In this chapter a number of operational issues in offshore projects are discussed. On the one hand it becomes clear how other quantitative factors than cost reductions contribute to the success of offshore projects. The role of time zones, and the explicit evaluation of risks in testing procedures are typical examples. On the other hand, global issues, such as intercultural factors, the inclusion of learning curve structures in contract payments and concerns about global ICT competencies require management focus. This chapter can be used as a practical guideline for offshore software projects.

Introduction

In many publications the strategic factors which lead to an offshore outsourcing decision have been studied (Hirschheim, Heinzl, & Dibbern, 2002; Hirschheim & George, 2007; Willcocks, Lacity, & Cullen, 2007). In publications on best practices for successful offshore outsourcing, it becomes clear how frequently non-strategic issues are the drivers for failing offshore projects (Rottman & Lacity, 2004). In this chapter, these non-strategic, or operational factors are discussed in detail. Some of the arguments are briefly illustrated by two case study experiences from one of the authors, on which specifics are provided in the Appendix.

The success factors that will be discussed are as follows:

- The inclusion of human resource value restructuring elements to obtain the total cost of offshoring for the projects.
- Considering the impact of differences in time zones.
- Responsibility for defect removal, including testing.

Information Management: Setting the Scene
Copyright © 2007 by Elsevier Ltd.
All rights of reproduction in any form reserved.
ISBN: 978-0-08-046326-1

- The consideration of cultural differences.
- The inclusion of (rewarding) structures in offshore contracts.

Applying the recommendations that are discussed in this chapter may lead to a more sustained success in offshore software development activities.

From Costs to ICT Competencies

Very often a major operational factor in outsourcing is the cost savings issue, due to the significantly lower wages for equivalent ICT professionals in offshore development countries. Typical salaries for good ICT professionals vary between 5,000 and 10,000 $ per year, in contrast to the equivalent salaries of 50,000–80,000 $ in the United States (Robinson & Kalakota, 2004). Despite these enormous salary differences, the overall cost savings for outsourcing projects are only up to 30%, in the majority of the cases (Ventoro Institute, 2005).

Increasingly, companies no longer use offshore projects to replace the existing ICT staff at lower cost. They focus on handling project backlogs which could not be handled with the existing ICT head count. The lower salaries in the outsourcing countries can also be taken advantage of in a radically different way, namely to *train* ICT professionals in skills and capabilities that are rarely available in typical US and European ICT teams. Typical examples are legacy mainframe related capabilities (see Case I, and Dedene, 1995). Once the training is completed, the best professionals can be selected based on exam tests, and engaged in the offshore outsourcing contract. This, in turn, leads to higher quality staff for specific technologies. This type of upfront training also ensures that the necessary competencies are indeed available offshore.

The higher quality of work is a typical outcome that is rarely explicitly anticipated in offshore projects. The working distance of an offshore relationship forces the offshore workers to document very precisely the artifacts that are involved in the outsourcing contract. As a result, client organizations receive back artifacts with a significantly higher quality of documentation. Observe that often this aspect was not explicitly mentioned in the outsourcing contract.

The use of offshore teams allows application of *value restructuring* to the current ICT staff in the client organization. Indeed, less motivating tasks, such as maintenance and routine programming tasks can be outsourced, removing the maintenance pressure from the internal ICT staff. This may become an important incentive for an internal ICT team that is reluctant to engage itself for offshore outsourcing activities: in this way offshore outsourcing is not taking away jobs internally, but even allows to increase the value of the existing internal ICT jobs in client organizations (Lim, Richardson, & Zmud, 2007).

In recent studies it is shown how the current outsourcing models may dramatically be impacted by the worldwide availability of ICT skills and competencies. Today, the potential supply of low-wage ICT talent is still greater than the likely demand. This situation may change rapidly. In a McKinsey Global Institute Analysis document

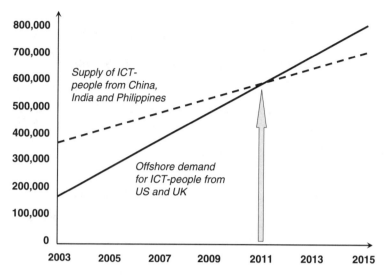

Figure 16.1: Demand versus supply for offshore talent.

(McKinsey & Company, 2005) it is anticipated that the United States and the United Kingdom together alone can absorb *by 2011* the *entire supply* of suitable young professional engineers from the major offshore countries: India, China, and the Philippines (see Figure 16.1).

This reality calls for dramatic actions by policy-makers and educational institutions worldwide. Educational capacity must be increased, and the United States as well as Europe both should increase their investments in local as well as offshore ICT education and training. Outsourcing countries can benefit by not only increasing the number of students, but also their quality.

Increasingly, Western education institutes should equip their students to work effectively and efficiently with their peer equivalent students in today's outsourcing countries. Of course, there is an impact on the cost issue: average wages will raise in the ICT community, although it is expected that the wages will stabilize around 30% of the level of wages for equivalent jobs in the United States (McKinsey & Company, 2005). Apart from the labor costs, other cost factors will influence the choice of location for offshore activities, such as the quality of the local talent, the market orientation (and potential), the intrinsic risks and stability of the location, and the quality of the ICT infrastructure. Client organizations need to weigh these criteria according to their specific requirements, and obtain in this way the *Total Cost of Offshoring* for their particular projects.

Time Zones: ICT Around the Clock

The time zone factor is often disregarded in the choice of offshore locations. For offshore software development activities, choosing the right time zone may have a

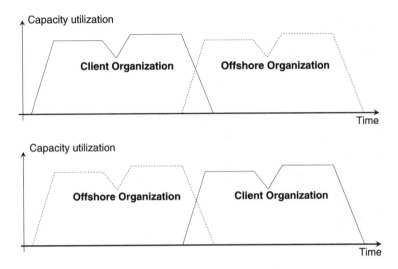

Figure 16.2: Ideal time zones for offshore software development.

significant impact on the success of the offshore project. In the ideal situation, the software teams of the client organization and the offshore outsourcing company should create a *tandem* effect, with a minimal overlap of the time zones. The small overlapping can be used for short management briefings, or development (de-)briefings on specific deliverables in the project. In Figure 16.2, an ideal time zone situation is given.

As is suggested in Figure 16.2, a slightly overlapping time zone setup is giving an ideal capacity utilization. This is particularly important in situations where the offshore software team must use shared resources with the client organization's team. In Figure 16.2, the lower setup is the easiest to establish, for example, when the client organization is a typical Western Europe organization, and the offshore country is the Philippines (Pepito, 2005), or the east area of China.

Having large time zone overlaps creates another drawback. It is well-known in software engineering that larger teams are less productive than smaller teams (Jones, 1998). In the case of significant overlapping, *de facto* a larger software team is established, which may suffer from decreasing returns to scale.

Another factor related to the time zone is the peak utilization of the worldwide Internet infrastructure. It is well-known that the peak utilizations and slowest response times (at least, today) occur in the time period when the United States users are massively waking up and start their Internet activities. For Western Europe organizations, this implies again that the time zone of the offshore outsourcing organization precedes the one of the client organization.

Finally, this element may explain why some projects that are successful as United States offshore projects (e.g., with India) may not share all of the same benefits when the same offshore country is used in Europe. The very far East Asia offshore areas (such as the Philippines, Australia, Shanghai,...) can be more attractive for European client organizations to create the desired tandem effect. The tandem effect may allow the teams to do the work "around the clock" with significantly less stress that such a schedule would involve if the internal staff were attempting to do so. Everyone is essentially working regular hours.

Observe again how all these remarks are typical for software projects. In particular in conversion projects, the offshore team may benefit from the availability of the unconverted system, for example, to understand better the system functionality. Other types of outsourcing activities (e.g., helpdesk support) may indeed be more suited for nearshoring because other time zone issues are involved.

Errors and Testing: The Risk Factor

Many offshore software development projects are related to conversions of systems, whereby (legacy) systems are reengineered to new platforms. An aspect that is often neglected in offshore contracts is the responsibility for testing and defect removal activities. In the software literature, it is known that the industry average defect removal efficiency is approximately 85% (Jones, 1998). The offshore outsourcer should be obliged to apply a mix of defect removal and defect prevention techniques to achieve at least this efficiency (or preferably higher). Postponing testing completely to the end of a software project, and/or letting the testing responsibility to the client organization leads to unacceptable additional costs (Verhoef, 2005). Especially in software reengineering projects, testing is a major part of the effort because the code has already been developed, the documentation may be spotty, and often the software is likely to be proprietary and non-standard, so default testing tools cannot be used.

Research showed that for outsourced software that ends up in court litigation because of quality problems, the number of testing stages is around three, and formal inspections were almost never used (Jones, 1998; Verhoef, 2005). Performing three stages of testing typically accumulates the defect removal efficiency only to approximately 70%.

A mistake that is often made, is to base the delivery conditions for offshore-developed software on so-called production–acceptance tests: if the system passes the tests when it is installed in the production configuration, it is accepted. Experience (Jones, 2001) reports show how only between 25 and 35% of the defects are found during such acceptance tests. So, acceptance of offshore-developed software should be based on a diversified set of testing procedures, including production–acceptance tests, but also other tests during the offshore development.

Another issue related to this is the application of the Capability Maturity Model (CMM) in the offshore relationship. The client organization has in many cases a lower CMM level than the offshore outsourcing organization. In practice, the lowest CMM level dominates the outsourcing relationship because the practices and processes of the higher CMM level have no counterpart in the client organization. So, the client organization can only benefit from the stricter testing and quality control procedures of the higher CMM levels by increasing its own CMM level. In the other cases, the client organization should negotiate a flexible application of the (higher level) CMM practices to avoid unnecessary costs (Rottman & Lacity, 2004).

The Intercultural Factor

Intercultural issues and cultural differences can drain the productivity in offshore projects. Typical United States or Western Europe trained developers cannot be replaced overnight by offshore workers. Their perceived values and attitudes may be very different. These are some examples (Vonsild & Jensen, 2005):

- Workers in the client organization may feel more comfortable to speak up and make suggestions. Offshore developers may keep these feelings rather to themselves, for example, because they think they cannot contradict the client.
- Conflict handling models may be dramatically different in various cultures. Recognition of the early symptoms of emerging conflicts is an important intercultural success factor. This may affect transaction costs of offshoring.
- Procedures that systematically log all the activities may seem provocative in some cultures.
- Hierarchical ordering may have a big impact in offshore organizations. This in turn can have an impact on flexibility and changes during the project.
- Speaking a common language fluently is crucial to bridge intercultural issues. Often, an English language training focusing on the specific vocabulary of the client organization's business is needed. The impact of Spanish is growing too.
- A common religion (or, at least, an avoidance of conflicting religions) may smooth intercultural relations. This gives the Philippines a unique position in far Asia, with respect to United States and Western Europe offshore outsourcing.

Lags in productivity due to cultural differences may add as much as 20% of additional costs to offshore projects, at least in the first years. Some of the intercultural issues can be addressed by some simple, but effective measures:

- Define peer-to-peer project management responsible persons within the client as well as the offshore organization. Conflicts at lower levels can be solved at higher levels, in a peer-to-peer way, without intervening directly at the lower levels in an intercultural way.
- Organize frequent (de-)briefings and face-to-face interaction (using video-conferencing and other Internet technologies). The right time zone selection may turn out to be crucial, as was discussed earlier in this chapter.
- Share risks and benefits in the contract, which is always an excellent way to create peer-to-peer responsibility and pride on the results of the offshore project.
- In case the client organization as well as the offshore outsourcing organization have relations with higher education institutes, such as universities, it may help to involve the mutual academic expertize, again, in a peer-to-peer mirror structure. This can also contribute to the educational issues mentioned before in this chapter.

Intercultural differences may sometimes be reduced by *captive offshore* constructions. In this case, the offshore company is a joint venture, or even a wholly owned subsidiary of the client organization. Major technology providers and consultants established this type of companies in offshore countries (e.g., IBM, Accenture, ...). By definition, the mother company most often has a high impact on the captive offshore construction, for example, by establishing most of the high-level management structure. In this way, intercultural issues may be reduced somewhat. Captive offshore companies may contribute less to the local economies, depending on the contractual relation with the mother company.

Learning Curve Payment Structures

Most Western software houses work under *time-and-material* contracts. The client organization is billed for the resources consumed, even if these exceed the budgetary estimates that were initially defined in signing the contract. A client organization can always pay extra for a guarantee against the risk of overrunning the schedule and the budget, but this implies typically an additional cost of 50% to the contract. Moreover, typical time-and-material contracts require a significant upfront payment at the start of the project, or shortly thereafter, which means that the client has invested a great deal before a substantial amount of development is completed. And if the results go wrong, it is too late to pull out.

An alternative arrangement, which may turn out to be more satisfactory to smaller projects is a *no-cure-no-pay* contract. In this contract, the intended results, the objectives, and major milestones are clearly described upfront, and the offshore organization is signing for a rather fixed price. Of course this seems the cheapest way to cover the contract risks. However, and merely due to the significant salary differences between the client organization and the offshore outsourcing organization, this can still go wrong if the initial payments are too high (and cover, e.g., already all the costs on the side of the offshore company). Therefore, it is advised to build a *learning curve structure* in the payment scheme. In such a structure, the initial down payments are very low (not higher than the salary and infrastructure costs for the offshore company). Additional payments are introduced for every major milestone that is reached. Every milestone could be a substantial part of the required system, fully accepted by the client organization. In such a learning curve structure, every major milestone is an insurance that the project is likely to be completed successfully. It is a practical way to distribute the risks as well as the rewards for success equally amongst the client organization and the offshore outsourcing organization.

Conclusions

In this chapter, some practical, operational success factors for offshore outsourcing of software projects have been reviewed. First of all, the typical cost reduction arguments for offshore projects are gradually replaced by human resource value restructuring arguments. One major observation in this chapter is a fast growing bottleneck in the available ICT competencies worldwide. Together with the intercultural issues, it becomes clear how offshore outsourcing is globalizing the ICT culture on this planet. A careful choice of time zones can facilitate a global workforce around the planet. Finally, it was discussed how risk factors can be controlled by including clear testing procedures, as well as a motivating payment scheme in the offshore outsourcing project contract.

It is obvious that a lot of these practicalities become natural best practices in long-term offshore relationships. The key message remains: problems cannot be outsourced, only shared solutions...

References

Boesmans, P. (2001). Amicus live at National Library of Hungary, available at http://www.biblio-tech.com/BTR900/December_2000/elias_2000_12.html

Dedene, G. (1995). Realities of off-shore reengineering. *IEEE Software, 12*, 35–45.

Hirschheim, R., & George, B. (2007). Three waves of information technology outsourcing. In: A. Huizing & E. J. de Vries (Eds.), *Information management: Setting the scene. Book series: Perspectives on information management* (Vol. 1). Oxford: Elsevier Scientific Publishers.

Hirschheim, R., Heinzl, A., & Dibbern, J. (Eds.) (2002). *Information systems outsourcing. Enduring themes, emergent patterns and future directions.* Berlin: Springer.

Jones, C. (1998). *Estimating software costs.* New York: McGraw-Hill Companies.

Jones, C. (2001). *Conflict and litigation between software clients and developers.* Working Paper, Software Productivity Research, Inc., Burlington, MA.

Lim, J. H., Richardson, V. J., & Zmud, R. W. (2007). *Value implications of IT outsoucing contextual characteristics.* Working Paper, available at http://misrc.umn.edu/workshops/2007/spring/Bob.pdf

McKinsey, & Company. (2005, June), *The emerging global labor market.* McKinsey Global Institute Analysis Report.

Pepito, W. (2005, March 24). Philippines catching up with India in the outsourcing industry. *EzineArticles*, available at http://ezinearticles.com/?Philippines-Catching-up-with-India-in-the-Outsourcing-Industry&id=23319

Robinson, M., & Kalakota, R. (2004). *Offshore outsourcing: Business models, ROI and best practices.* New York: Milvar Press.

Rottman, J., & Lacity, M. (2004). Twelve practices for offshore sourcing. *MIS Quarterly Executive, 3*, 117–130.

Ventoro Institute. (2005). *Offshore Outsourcing Research Report 2005*, available at http://www.ventoro.com

Verhoef, C. (2005). Quantitative aspects of outsourcing deals. *Science of Computer Programming, 56.*

Vonsild, S., & Jensen, L. B. (2005). Outsourcing projects between Europe and India – bridging the cultural divide. In: *Proceedings of the 2005 International Project Management Association*, New Delhi, India, available at http://www.ipmacourse.com/articles/c/DELHI_outsourcing.pdf

Willcocks, L., Lacity, M., & Cullen, S. (2007). Information technology sourcing: Reflections and lessons 1991–2007. In: A. Huizing & E. J. de Vries (Eds.), *Information management: Setting the scene. Book series: Perspectives on information management* (Vol. 1). Oxford: Elsevier Scientific Publishers.

Appendix: Case Experiences

Case 1: Sidmar and K. U. Leuven/LIBIS Offshore Software Reengineering

This is an early case study on offshore outsourcing during the period 1992–1993 (Dedene, 1995). The projects were executed simultaneously (to share a dedicated satellite communication line) in the Philippines. The results of these offshore software development projects turned out to be of high quality. The intercultural issues and contract issues were addressed according to the practices described in this chapter. Cost savings were in the order of magnitude of 35%. In many of the software modules, testing took up to 80% of the resources, and was explicitly addressed in the contract. This case study was awarded by an IEEE Software Best Practice Paper Award in 1995.

Case 2: Offshore and Nearshore Multisource Development: ELiAS Library Systems

ELiAS was a Belgian University Spin-off focusing on large-scale multi-library software systems (Boesmans, 2001). At some point, ELiAS was contractually forced to speed up the development of a new library database kernel, requiring a redevelopment of a multi-library model in ORACLE/UNIX, with intelligent search algorithms to be developed in C/UNIX, and a new user interface for the library search facilities. The project had to be finished in 5 months. A multisourcing approach was taken, using three partners:

- The database development was done in the Philippines.
- The development of the search algorithms was outsourced to Moscow, Russia, mainly because of the rich availability of C/UNIX skills.
- The development of the user interface was nearsourced to Dublin, Ireland. This location was also used as the mean seat for the project, for example, for tax reasons. So this partner was an early example of captive nearshoring.
- The overall project management was in the hands of ELiAS, with three project managers forming the management team for this project.

This case study, at the end of the 1990s in the previous century, ran successfully, by applying the practices described in this chapter, with a particular focus on the intercultural issues.

SECTION V:

CUSTOMER ORIENTED INNOVATION

Innovation has always been a key subject in information management. Especially the impact of ICT on organizations and society at large and the translation of new technological concepts into customer-oriented entrepreneurial initiatives have been central to the field. The last two chapters in this section should be placed in this tradition. Rolf Wigand contributes to our thinking about the impact of ICT on organizations and society by providing insights into the emerging second generation Internet technology, the so-called Web 2.0. Wigand points out that Web 2.0 should be seen as a participatory medium, as a social phenomenon instead of a technology *per se* and shows the different ways in which companies use Web 2.0 for their business. Slagter et al. zoom in on the entrepreneurial challenges of a particular instance of Web 2.0 technology: virtual worlds in 3D Internet, Second Life in particular. They show some examples of early 'Second Life presence' and consumer and business motives for being alive virtually; and compare early Second Life business models with traditional 2D Internet business models. Both contributions indicate the interesting phenomenon of citizens already possessing information on the use context of a new trend, where companies have yet to find out what to do with it.

The first two chapters of this section take a somewhat alternative route. In the information management field the concept of innovation has always been closely related to that of ICT and therefore the prevalent conceptualization of innovation is that of technological innovation, implicating quite linear ways of thinking like research-development-market trial-diffusion-adoption-implementation with the invention of new technology as the main driver for innovation, thus rather technology/supply push ideas.

Although this is certainly one way of looking at innovation, the vast literature on service innovation of the last two decades leads to a more differentiated approach. Technology is not the only driver, many service innovations start at the customer interface, are by no means (semi) linear processes and R&D as such is hard to recognize in the service industry. Service companies do innovate, although in different ways. Understanding service innovation has become a major topic now that services account for a large share of developed countries' economies; many information managers are working in the service sector (including public services); ICT has become the most important technology to build service innovation on; and the ICT industry is beginning to view itself as a service industry (take for instance IBM's Service Science program, the Software as Service movement and concepts like

Service Oriented Architecture). The first two chapters in this section add to that understanding.

Segers et al. question how service firms deal with service innovation and related R&D in the first chapter. By doing so, they address important societal and business questions. Service innovation tends not to be very visible in macro-economic statistics, mainly because service firms report low investments on R&D, and national innovation stimulation programs seem not to be very focused on service innovation. Furthermore, we know that service firms innovate, but how do they organize it, who is in charge, and who takes initiative? Last but not least, do service firms innovate on their own and if not, which other parties do they involve? In the second chapter Erik de Vries addresses the question how service innovation is related to the strategic positioning of services on the market. Three generic service positioning strategies and the distinctive characteristics of service innovation are introduced and some interesting patterns on how service providers innovate in relation to these strategies are discussed. The chapter ends by drawing practical implications for information management. Both chapters build on case studies of leading Dutch service firms.

The overall picture that evolves from this section is that information management certainly has a role in technology trend watching and transforming technological concepts into entrepreneurial initiatives but also should pay attention to the non-technological drivers of service innovation, its distinctive characteristics and the rather organic way in which service firms organize innovations. Furthermore, information management should be aware of the effects of service innovation on the positioning of services on the market, the different management trade-offs that need to be made in this regard and their role in developing and implementing service concepts.

Chapter 17

The Organisation of Innovation in Service Firms: Evidence from Four Dutch Service Firms

Jeroen Segers, Pim den Hertog and Harry Bouwman

ABSTRACT

The objective of this paper is to understand how Dutch firms currently are dealing with service innovation. Based on a multiple case study in which the service innovation in four companies is analysed in detail, as well on the basis of a broader study (Hertog et al., 2006), we have found that the nature of service innovation is diffuse. The organisational embedding and motivation for service innovation tend to be market driven, service innovation is not very formalised, it is distributed within the organisations, and it is less explicitly managed and funded. A systematic approach based on a service innovation strategy, formalised decision-making processes regarding service innovation, a bundling of resources within service firms and collaboration of service firms with relevant service innovation research centres, is rare. Service innovation is clearly a process in which many parties within and outside companies have to share resources and capabilities, knowledge, and learning experiences. This type of collaboration is still relatively hard to find.

Introduction and Background

Against the background of increasing competition, successful companies no longer try to achieve decisive advantages through cost leadership or advances in quality or technology alone. They tend to differentiate themselves through innovative services that give them a decisive unique selling proposition compared to their competitors. The crucial challenges are, above all, to continuously offer enhanced or new services to the market, to be quicker than the competition, and at the same time meet customers' needs and expectations. In light of the widely acknowledged importance of service innovation, it is striking to see that, although 50% of value added in the EU economies stems from services, service innovation accounts for only 13% of R&D expenditures (EU, 2005). Service innovation tends to be ill structured; it takes more

Information Management: Setting the Scene
ISBN: 978-0-08-046326-1

often than not place under high time pressure, and customer orientation is hard to guarantee (Simons & Bouwman, 2005). Therefore, we address the following research question:

How are Dutch service firms currently dealing with service innovation?

Service innovation is more than R&D. It is about new concepts, new ways of interacting with clients and new service delivery organisations. That is why our focus is on (1) how firms conceptualise service innovation, (2) what their motives for R&D in services are, (3) how service firms deal with service innovation on a managerial and a process level, i.e. what the organisational arrangements are with regard to service innovation, the embedding in decision-making processes, and formalization of the service innovation process, and (4) how service firms collaborate with others in service innovation.[1] In the next sections we discuss these four questions in greater detail, based on a broader study on service innovations (Hertog et al., 2006). We will illustrate our findings in more detail on basis of four specific Dutch cases.

Conceptualisation of R&D

Despite the growing importance of services in many companies, existing corporate structures and processes are not designed for an efficient development and market positioning of professional services. In particular, there are no appropriate tools for the strategic and operational planning of innovation processes for services. Problems often start because the services offered by companies are not clearly defined.

Although all the companies we surveyed are familiar with the term "R&D", only about half of them use it routinely. Most of them associated R&D, above all, with technological R&D, rather than with creating new services or new service development. This implies that, in practice, the R&D and innovation activities of important

---

[1]We used a semi-standardised interview framework in the Reneser study (Hertog et al., 2006). When we selected the companies to survey, the sample was clearly confined to firms that were already engaged in service innovation and that had many years of experience. No further restrictions were applied to the selection of companies, for instance on the basis of sector or company size. The four Dutch case studies concentrated on major services firms in different industries:
- *Ahold*: Royal Ahold is a group of leading quality supermarket and foodservice companies
- *Océ*: A major manufacturer and provider of digital document management technology and services. The firm now realises most of its turnover in services
- *Rabobank*: Rabobank Group, founded as a cooperative of Dutch agricultural banks, is owned by about 259 member banks, and focuses next to private banking, on the food and agribusiness industry, and
- *Randstad*: The Randstad Group is one of the largest temporary and contract staffing organizations in the world.
- Each case study includes desk research and at least three or four interviews, which were conducted between December 2005 and March 2006. Members of management responsible for R&D within the companies were addressed as the target group. Based on extensive literature research (Tidd and Hull, 2003; OECD, 2005) a semi-standardized interview guide was developed, as well as an analysis protocol. This approach allowed us to obtain clear statements regarding strategic and operational questions in relation to service innovation and the organisational embedding. The case studies are exploratory and illustrative in nature, and are not claimed to have any external validity.

Box 17.1: Services R&D and innovation at Randstad.

Innovation and new services are important to Randstad. How they emerge and are managed cannot be compared to common practices in manufacturing. Innovation in an organisation like Randstad means enriching, blending, and customising the company's basic ingredients into well defined, profitable, and specific service concepts. Innovation is embedded in various activities and is therefore best viewed as a scattered activity. Innovation is embedded in the business culture (entrepreneurial, open-minded), in the fine-tuning of massive administrative and ICT systems (scope for predominantly incremental innovations) and the combined central/decentralised marketing resource management. Innovation is most visible in business concept development (codifying and diffusing best practices), co-innovation with strategic international accounts, and the practice of portfolio management at top management level.

Box 17.2: How Océ is gradually developing into a service firm.

Although generally known, organised, and managed as a goods-oriented manufacturing company, Océ over the years has added a large variety of services to its portfolio. Océ is currently dependant on revenues generated through its various services (some 50% of which are product related) for more than 70% of its turnover. In fact this shift has the character of a complete (paradigm) shift, from a hardware or product-based business model towards a (much more) customised services business model. It is no longer the machines or number of copies that count, but the profit made on client-specific service contracts.

---

services are hidden behind labels like *business development, service improvement, customisation*, etc., rather than being seen as service-related R&D. Much of this type of R&D is also concealed in client-specific solutions (which later on may serve as a basis for the development of more standardised service products) (Box 17.1).

Finally, it should be pointed out that the boundary between hardcore technical R&D and service innovation seems to be blurring more and more, as is illustrated by the Océ case (Box 17.2). At Océ the borders between R&D for material goods, ICT, and services are less and less clearly defined.

Motivation for Service-Related R&D

The companies included in our study only began dealing with service-related R&D in recent years. The question as to what motivated the companies to become more active in this field is a highly relevant one. The reasons often cited are "to preserve or boost their own competitiveness", "customer wishes", "cost reductions and/or efficiency improvements", and "the use of new technical capabilities". We see that

---

Box 17.3: What market trends drive Océ towards client-specific solutions?

Apart from the switch to digital printers, digital documents, and colour printing machines, Océ's shift towards a customised services business model is motivated by two major related market trends. In the first place, a trend towards increasing service content and what used to be labelled as higher *customer intimacy* can be identified. Customers demand complete solutions, i.e. combinations of hardware, software, and services. They increasingly want integrated solutions to manage their office documents. Consequently, key accounts are increasingly offered additional services, such as output management and document management solutions, fleet management archiving and scanning services, in addition to printing services that help control their costs (e.g. by using more centralised printers, web-based ordering, print job management). A second development is the trend among clients towards reducing the cost of ownership, document process outsourcing and hence, for Océ, a more service-based business model. There is a gradual development from merely supplying the machine and the related maintenance services and supplying paper, toner and supplies, towards additionally offering financial services, taking over people from the reproduction and related service departments, and eventually exploiting an infrastructure in-house with a certain functionality. Increasingly, large accounts want to be able to purchase printing and related services without having to purchase or lease the actual systems. Eventually they are interested in buying a specific functionality, which is why they increasingly outsource document handling processes. In fact, this development requires a complete shift from a hardware or product-based business model towards a customised services business model in which it is not the machines or even the number of copies that matter, but the profit made on client-specific service contracts.

---

among the companies we investigated there is a blend of proactive and more defensive considerations (Box 17.3).

Important obstacles to systematic service innovation that were cited frequently were *insufficient support by top management*, followed by *inadequate resources*. Other reasons that were mentioned included an overriding preoccupation with day-to-day business, an unwillingness on the part of customers to pay for new services, an insufficiently innovation-oriented corporate culture, inadequate exchange of R&D knowledge within the company, and a lack of organisational infrastructure to carry out R&D tasks.

Organisational Arrangements

There appears to be no "one best way" when it comes to the organisational arrangements being made for services innovation. In practice this means that there is a variety of arrangements. Moreover, it should be mentioned, that the creation of a service innovation culture (and an open management style), or at least a corporate culture where innovation is valued, was used in a number of the firms we investigated to support service innovation on a company-wide basis and to trigger bottom-up innovation.

The degree in which the innovation function is organisationally embedded in a company is an essential issue in the case studies. In almost all the companies we surveyed, service R&D is supported by project teams. In some cases these teams are cross-divisional, i.e. they include employees from various business units. In most cases, central responsibility is in the hands of departments that have relatively high levels of contact with customers, such as marketing, product management, or sales. It is also noticeable that IT Departments are represented relatively heavily in the project teams of the companies we examined (Box 17.4).

Box 17.4: Ahold's R&D function: Centralised versus decentralised.

Thus far, Ahold's R&D function is not designated or fully formalised within the organisation. No employees are assigned with specific R&D tasks in their job description. Nevertheless, the increasing (global) competition and consumer wishes have resulted in an increasing need for a more coherent view on R&D processes and innovation. Most of Ahold's R&D is decentralised, which means that most of it is performed by several hundreds of employees in the subsidiary companies. Within Ahold there is no strict hierarchy, and it can be seen as a management holding structure with different arenas supported by central units. The bottom-up approach used at Ahold has grown historically. Ninety percent of its new products, concepts, ICT and logistic improvements are developed at Ahold. R&D can be broadly divided into 10% product development, 50% new shop concepts and 40% ICT/logistics. Market leaders Albert Heijn (the Netherlands) and ICA (Sweden) serve as examples. Their successful innovations will diffuse into other parts of the Ahold organisation. The remainder of Ahold's R&D (10%) is centralised and carried out by (several) dozens of employees. At a corporate level there is no development of new shop concepts, with 20% being allocated to new product development and 80% to the development and implementation of new ICT systems and logistic solutions. Less developed parts within the arenas are picked up at corporate level. Criteria (to be formalised) for the development of innovations or projects at the centre are: (1) requirement of economies of scale, (2) requirement of a certain level of standardisation, and (3) distribution requirements, such as exchanging ideas and managing knowledge flows between the arenas. At a corporate level the first moves in facilitating the synergy between the relative autonomous arenas are taken mainly by the Ahold leadership team (ALT) and the business support office (BSO). To conclude the organisational arrangements, we point out that Ahold's historically developed decentralised approach on the one hand has certain advantages (regional specific, more creativity), but that there are also disadvantages in terms of efficiency and speed. The strength and efficiency of Ahold's competitors, for instance WalMart, are to an extent the result of their central and hierarchical organisation. However, WalMart's market strength makes it possible to impose their preferences (and e.g. set the standards) at their suppliers and thus reinforce the efficiency gains.

The fact that service R&D is carried out in a large number of cross-divisional projects running side-by-side must be one important reason why most companies are unable to provide precise information on the extent and scope of their service R&D activities. Interviewees often report "hidden R&D", i.e. nobody in the company knows who exactly deals with service R&D. In some companies, it is even reported that several hundred employees are active in projects involving R&D tasks, but they are not regarded as such within the company.

The main drawback of R&D teams that work together on temporary basis and with shifting responsibilities is that the knowledge acquired at the end of a project is often lost because the employees involved move on to other tasks (Box 17.5).

The disappearance of the embodied knowledge is the reason why companies have already opted in favour of assigning service R&D to existing organisational units as an ongoing ancillary task. When asked which organisational unit was entrusted with service R&D, the companies responded that they usually opt in favour of business development, marketing, product management, or the specialised departments that most come into contact with customers. This is yet more evidence that the level of customer contact seems to be an important criterion for companies when it comes to allocating service R&D (Box 17.6).

An important aspect of organisational arrangements is the decision-making process regarding service R&D. Although there is no clear R&D strategy in this area, services R&D projects are controlled by top management. Most of these firms realise the necessity of such a strategy. With respect to the decision-making process regarding new service R&D projects, the following practices were mentioned. Some of these practices are followed in parallel:

- Decision making is part of the wider overall R&D strategy and budget cycle,
- Decision making is based on a form of dedicated portfolio management,

---

Box 17.5: Cosmopolites play an important role in Rabobank services' R&D and innovation process.

Service R&D can be found in a number of places within the Rabobank organisation. Basically, innovations are pushed by actors who are conceptualised in social network analysis as cosmopolites. *Cosmopolites* are persons who have creative new ideas, act like a kind of free agents within an organisation, are part of extensive networks outside — in this case — the Rabo organisation with strong ties to (technology) providers and universities, as well as with market parties, local banks, and strategic key informants within the central Rabobank. *Cosmopolites* are consulted and asked to invest in new concepts and technologies. Based on these proposals, the cosmopolites develop new service concepts. To develop these concepts further, they bypass the regular decision-making processes, and use their network to find funding and marketing support, inside or outside the Rabo organisation. They act as intrapreneurs within the organisation. After successful completion, pilot projects can gain formal status within the Rabobank.

Box 17.6:   Role of co-innovation at Randstad.

A key characteristic of innovations at Randstad is that most of them involve clients. It is hard to pilot a new service without clients. This is most visible at the group that is responsible for major international accounts. This group deals with major clients operating in Europe, the US, and Asia. The international accounts group is organised along industries (telecom, food/pharmaceuticals, logistics, finance, etc.). A differentiation is made between international top accounts with high volumes of (Randstad) services and a wide geographical scope, international clients with either lower volumes or a more limited international representation, and accounts with more limited international activities. The first group consists of a limited number of businesses that are open to new service concepts and in practice function as launching customers. Randstad and these top accounts co-innovate, effectively in a risk-sharing partnership. The clients benefit most by gaining competitive advantage *vis-à-vis* major competitors. New services are initiated in a sort of open or proactive dialogue with key accounts. The act of piloting new services is mostly a matter of smart organisation and low-key experimentation rather than massive investments in new service concepts.

- Decision making is delegated to committees or the departmental heads who are most involved,
- Decision making takes place on a case-by-case basis (e.g. sound business cases),
- Decision making depends on priorities of clients,
- Development of new ideas takes place under the radar of senior management.

In most cases there was some mechanism for joint decision making involving priorities concerning service R&D, although not necessarily at the highest management levels. Also, case-by-case decision making was quite prevalent, leaving professionals dealing with service innovation with considerable room to manoeuvre. Sometimes the role of entrepreneurial employees or free agents was seen as crucially important. However, the scope to play around and really experiment varied considerably (as customers need to be involved) (Box 17.7).

Companies were not always able to provide detailed information to another question concerning the exact budgets involved in-service innovation. In a few cases budgets are clearly defined and, as a rule, they are allocated from one project to the next. Consequently, generally speaking there is insufficient overarching control of service R&D activities. It is rare that investments in service R&D are evaluated and conclusions drawn for future service R&D activities. There is definitely a trend towards or need for formalising service R&D strategies, budgets, and organisational embedding, as well as for planning, managing, and assigning and controlling budgets in a more structured way.

To make the R&D processes transparent and reproducible, to avoid duplication of work and to recycle existing knowledge (including mistakes), and to meet quality standards, efforts are made to describe R&D processes and standardise individual

---

Box 17.7: Decision making regarding the Rabobank's R&D activities — shift from a business centric towards a customer-oriented view.

Proposals for innovative hard or soft R&D projects are judged like any other project. There are some budgets available for out-of-pocket costs or projects for innovative projects. The board of executives of Rabobank keeps a distance, which makes it possible for employees to work on innovative projects that are not under the board's direct control. There is no direct involvement or active interest in service innovation from the board of directors. Decisions concerning projects are made every six months when portfolios are defined. It is important that projects be supported by local banks or other business units. Basically, funding of projects is based on a 50–50 basis (marketing and IT). Half the funding is provided by the innovation team within the ICT department, the other half by marketing, local banks or interested business units. An important criterion is a proper fit with the core strategy of the Rabobank, i.e. a focus on customer value. The Rabobank will always look at customer value first. Technical conditions and the business case are important criteria.

R&D tasks. This "formalisation" ranges from fixed preset processes on one hand to flexible, situation-specific procedures on the other. Based on the Reneser study (Hertog et al., 2006), three levels of "formalisation" can be identified.

First level companies use virtually no set guidelines for developing services. In these companies, most new services come into being on an *ad hoc* basis or on the initiative of individual employees. At best, people resort to general project management rules to shape the development workflow.

At the second level, although the development of services follows predefined workflows, it is often documented only in a rudimentary way. Experience and knowledge from previous development projects is only available in the form of tacit knowledge. In addition, some methods are used to develop new services, i.e. portfolio management, trend analysis, scenario analysis, SWOT analysis, quality function deployment (QFD), and failure measurement and effects analysis (FMEA). The main focus is on systematic portfolio management.

Third level companies had definitively defined and comprehensively documented their R&D processes in writing. Detailed specifications and guidelines for the development of new services were worked out to this end. The advantage of this is that knowledge of service development is available to all the employees that are involved, rather than being confined to individual experts (Box 17.8).

R&D Co-operation

Working together with external partners is important to almost all the companies we surveyed. An open collaborative network model seems to be the standard when it comes to service R&D. The most important partners are customers who co-operate

Box 17.8: Ahold attempts to standardise the methods of working in a four phases *service engineering model.*

As part of its innovation strategy development, Ahold is standardising its operational methods, although a formalised organisational structure for service innovation is lacking. This standardisation process relates to different areas and levels throughout the organisation, such as corporate brand development, local brand development, Ahold sustainable brand development, category profitability improvement method, and functional food as part of the healthy living programme. In these areas Ahold has developed a four phases *service engineering model* for strategic initiative development:

Desk research is carried out mainly by the BSO at corporate level, albeit under the radar of the executive board.

If the desk research turns out to be promising, a more formal initiative is taken. Further exploration by SWOT analysis is centralised.

Next, a thoroughly worked-out business plan must be approved by the ALT.

The final phase involves piloting and feedback rounds and a rollout throughout the organisation.

In addition to streamlining the working processes, Ahold puts a great deal of effort into measuring the output of its innovative activities. The value provided to the customers needs to be substantial, specific, and measurable. A variety of methods are used, from business impact analysis to customer satisfaction measurements.

in R&D projects as lead users or development partners. Suppliers, ICT companies, and consultants are also mentioned frequently (Box 17.9).

Although co-operation is seen as very important, there is no distinctive co-operation with universities and scientific establishments, which are regarded as suitable places for talent scouting and personnel recruitment or as partners for creating an innovation culture, but which rarely are invited to participate in actual R&D projects. The companies we surveyed indicated that they felt there was insufficient practical relevance, an excessively abstract method of working, a strong focus on manufacturing and technologies, and a "lack of innovative drive". At the same time, many of the companies claimed they were interested in working together more closely.

Another area of great interest in the investigation involved the participation of business-related service firms in publicly funded R&D programmes. Although some of the companies claimed they had already participated in publicly funded R&D projects, the number and scope of the projects varied enormously. Most of the interviewees — who were, after all, predominantly persons responsible for R&D — were unable or found it difficult to cite examples of such R&D projects, a fact that underscores the hitherto subordinate role of this type of R&D support (Box 17.10).

Box 17.9: Linkages and collaboration for R&D at Océ.

Océ is best known as one of the major R&D-oriented manufacturing companies, and as such the company cooperates with other businesses, universities, and other research organisations. However, in the area of service R&D there is as yet much less co-operation with other companies, universities, and research organisations, although some co-operation exists. Océ indicated that it would like to learn more from and share experiences with similar industrial companies, and more specifically companies from capital goods industries, with medium-sized production runs and an important service component, e.g. manufacturers of medical equipment and service industries that provide secondary or facilitating/enabling service functions to other industries. Océ would like to intensify co-operation with firms that possess the necessary process and business knowledge, and the creation of a community of interest/practice was seen as helpful. Additionally, there is an interest in working closely with universities and other research organisations. One of the problems mentioned with regard to cooperating — on services and services R&D — with the knowledge infrastructure is that there are only a few individuals at best that have relevant knowledge.

Box 17.10: Randstad's participation in (government-funded) research programmes.

As Randstad typically starts from its own strengths and R&D and innovation are mostly hidden (at least not managed as a major R&D or innovation effort), the company is not a regular user of R&D and innovation programmes. Although there are incidental examples of R&D or innovation support through government, e.g. when developing innovative ICT applications, participation in these programmes is not centrally managed and it is not dealt with *in the field*. For example Randstad does not participate in the Telematics Institute, one of the leading technological institutes, in which some major Dutch service enterprises do participate.

The companies we surveyed made the following statements in response to the questions regarding their generally speaking inadequate participation in existing research programmes that are subsidised by governments:

- The contents of programmes are insufficiently geared towards the needs of service companies (in fact almost all programmes mentioned by the companies have a strong technological bias).
- The application processes are described as being too bureaucratic, too costly, and too time consuming. In some cases there are also reservations concerning the participation of service-only companies in research projects.

In general, it would appear that the opportunities offered by fund providers are still insufficiently tailored to match the needs of service providers. On the other hand, there is undoubtedly room for improving the ability and willingness of companies to participate in service-innovation programmes.

Conclusions

Our study is a first step in understanding the management issues, both at a strategic and at an operational level, involved in service innovation. As far as we know, no similar studies are as yet available. Our study shows that service firms have begun to respond to the need for a more formalised approach to service innovation by tackling service innovation more energetically. Nevertheless, the main emphasis of service innovation and the way service innovation activities are organised, budgeted, and managed differ from what we see in manufacturing firms, and there is also considerable variety among the particular service firms in this study. Based on the cases we investigated, as well as on the four Dutch illustrative cases, the following conclusions can be drawn:

- Although most service firms pay some form of structured attention to service R&D, it is in most cases less formalized, more widely distributed, and less explicitly managed and funded, than technology driven R&D.
- Increasing competitiveness and customer needs are important drivers for service R&D.
- A dedicated long-term service R&D and innovation strategy (and hence management) at the level of the board of management is rare. Formalised approaches to service R&D strategies are limited.
- Some service firms show high levels of technological R&D as well as technology-enabled innovation, in addition to service delivery and organisational innovation.
- Formalised, service-only R&D is the exception rather than the rule. However, in practice important service R&D activities are hidden behind labels like *business development, service improvement,* etc., without actually being identified as service R&D. A great deal of service R&D is also hidden in client-specific solutions.
- More formal methods for managing services' R&D and innovation portfolios were used only in about half of the cases, and at the project level about half of the firms involved used more formalised (mostly rudimentary) models for new service development.
- Although open innovation models feature quite prominently in most cases, there is considerable room to improve R&D collaboration between service firms and research organisations. In most cases co-operation on service R&D is poorly developed.
- Most large service firms are not well connected to the R&D and innovation policy scene (apart from the few that perform extensive technological R&D themselves).

- To most service firms existing R&D schemes are of limited value, and most of them find it hard or unappealing to try and gain access to or participate in them. At the same time, almost none of the companies we analysed has an internal structure designed to support the systematic acquisition of funded R&D projects.
- There is a whole array of innovation and non-innovation policies that could help service firms become more innovative and eventually more competitive.
- There is huge potential for cross-firm and cross-industry (lateral) learning.
- Creating an innovation culture suited to service R&D and innovation (in firms, in industries, society-wide) is seen as the key factor to successfully growing competitiveness through service R&D and innovation.

These conclusions should be considered with some care. Although the cases studies involves some prominent and highly visible companies, the number of cases is limited. The companies involved in the study are all major companies. They focus on food, financial services, HRM, and document management. It is possible that a focus on, for instance, the ICT service industry would have yielded a slightly different picture. Our selection of the four companies is furthermore biased towards the *best kids in class*. All cases involve Dutch companies, and in that sense one might argue that our conclusions only applies to the Netherlands. Moreover, in view of the fact that service innovation is becoming a more prominent item on the agenda of the management boards of companies, the picture presented here may change quickly and only have a temporary validity.

Based on the study we would like to discuss some practical implications. First of all, an awareness of the relevance of service innovation has to be stimulated among board members of companies, as well as being engrained in the company culture, creating an open culture aimed at service innovation. The design and development process of services, as well as the allocation and sharing of resources, financial as well as with regard to sharing tacit knowledge on service innovation, requires full management attention. Managers need to organise the service innovation process and to institutionalise service innovation within their organisations. Awareness of the material and immaterial consequences of service innovation needs to be stimulated.

In practice, service innovation appears to be a bottom-up, market-driven process. However, a more rational approach, based on a combination of business intelligence and practical market know-how, as well as the availability of tools that have been tested, may be an important driver when it comes to service innovation. Close collaboration between marketing, information management, and ICT departments is important in the development of new services.

Needless to say, government can create favourable conditions for service innovations, not only by stimulating centres of excellence where business, research, and government meet, discuss, and research the management, operational, and practical issues at stake, but also by creating awareness of the societal and economic relevance of service innovation, as well as by opening up its more traditional hardcore technology programmes for service R&D. If there is one thing that this study has made clear, it is that service innovation has to be made more visible.

Acknowledgements

The case studies on which this chapter is based are part of the so-named RENESER study performed over 2005 and 2006 for the European Commission (DG internal market and services). We like to express our gratitude to Mr. Ronald Mackay and Mr. Jean Bergevin who as officials supported the project. We like to thank the various professionals at Ahold, Océ, Rabo, and Randstad and the other firms participating in the RENESER project who invested their valuable time in giving an insight into the ways in which service innovation is brought about and managed in their companies.

References

EU. (2005). *Key figures on Science, Technology and Innovation. Towards a European knowledge area, 19/07/05*, European Commission DG Research, p. 37.

Hertog, P. den, Meiren, T., Rubalcaba, L., Segers, J., & Tether, B., et al. (2006). *Research and Development Needs of Business Related Service Firms*. RENESER Project. Utrecht: Dialogic. http://www.dialogic.nl/modules/document/bestand.aspx?BID = 275

OECD. (2005). *Enhancing the performance of the services sector*, OECD, Paris. [Chapter 9: Case studies of successful companies and lessons for public policy].

Simons, L., & Bouwman, H. (2005). Multi channel service design processes: Challenges and solutions. *International Journal of Electronic Business*, *3*(1), 50–67.

Tidd, J., & Hull, F.M. (2003). *Service Innovation. Organizational responses to technological opportunities & market imperatives*. Series on technology management — Vol. 9. London: Imperial College Press.

Chapter 18

Service Innovation and Service Positioning Strategies

Erik J. de Vries

ABSTRACT

In this chapter, service innovation is related to the concept of service positioning. Services are seen as processes carried out on behalf of customers and therefore the positioning of services on the market is based on the degree of customer influence on these service processes (low in standardized services, medium in mass customization and high in customization). Three service positioning strategies are presented. Innovation takes place within the scope of these strategies but three case studies show that innovation could also lead to oscillation between two strategies and to incremental migration or radical migration from one strategy to the other. Service positioning strategies, innovation patterns related to these strategies and characteristics of service innovation are important reference frameworks for information management and several management implications are drawn upon these concepts and the case studies.

Introduction

Innovation is one of the central issues in information management. As services account for approximately 70% of employment in most developed countries (Drejer, 2004; Gallouj, 2002) and 50% of value added in the EU economies stems from services (EU, 2005), the innovation of services has become especially important. Although several studies have been done on the distinctive characteristics of service innovation and what can be learned from it for other fields in the economy, the majority of innovation studies have been focused on innovation within manufacturing or study service innovation from a typical technological perspective and tend to focus on the impact of technology on services, with ICT as one of these technologies (Drejer, 2004; de Vries, 2006). In this chapter, I build on those studies that developed insights into the characteristics of service innovations.

Information Management: Setting the Scene
Copyright © 2007 by Elsevier Ltd.
ISBN: 978-0-08-046326-1

Services are generally defined as sets of processing operations carried out by a service provider on behalf of a client, in a medium held by the client, and intended to bring about a change in this medium (Hill, 1977). Services are thus seen as processes and therefore services need to be positioned in the market in such a way that clients recognize the kind of processes and activities they need. In the literature this is generally called a service positioning strategy (Shostack, 1987).

In this chapter, I relate the concept of service innovation to the concept of service positioning strategy and come to implications for information management. The chapter unfolds as follows. At first I present three general service positioning strategies and some main characteristics of service innovation that differentiate service innovation from traditional product and manufacturing innovation. Then I describe three case studies in which different and somewhat unexpected patterns of service innovation in relation to service positioning are analyzed. In the last section I present the implications for information management. The methodological aspects of the case studies are shortly described in the Appendix.

Service Positioning Strategy

Service positioning is based on the nature of the service process and traditionally has been understood as a trade-off between standardization and customization (Levitt, 1976; Shostack, 1987; Sundbo, 1994). Over the last decade however many authors paid attention to a service strategy which combines the mass production capabilities of standardized services with the customization capabilities of customized services, which became known as mass customization (Pine, Victor, & Boynton, 1993). I differentiate three generic service position strategies, which are labeled as *mass orientation, scope orientation and partnership orientation*. The three generic service positioning strategies and their organizational design characteristics are depicted in Table 18.1 and elaborated in the next paragraphs.

Mass Orientation Strategy

In this service positioning strategy the service is of the 'product' type and service delivery processes are standardized, non-varying processes suited for mass production. Shaw (1990) differentiates services based on whether the value adding focus is on sources from suppliers, the production process, the interaction with the customer or the customer himself. In this strategy the value adding focus is mainly built upon sources from suppliers (e.g. ICT or logistical equipment) and on the (production) process. The interaction governance (the customer contact strategy) is of the selling type. The customer faces a 'take it or leave it' situation in which she is unable to influence the specifications of the service (de Jong & van Bemmel, 1992). In standardization strategies behavior can be controlled by mechanistic means such as rules, regulations or 'script based' approaches (Smith & Houston, 1983). This management approach is characterized as the production-line approach (Levitt, 1976; Pine et al.,

Table 18.1: Three generic service positioning strategies.

Service positioning strategy → Organizational design characteristics:	Mass orientation	Scope orientation	Partnership orientation
Service type	Product (standardized)	Service/product (mass customized)	Pure service (customized)
Nature of the service process	Standardized	Modular/component based	Professional knowledge based and interconnected with customer processes
Value adding focus	Process and source	Process, interactive, and client	Client and interactive
Interaction governance	Selling	Sparring	Partner role
Management approach	Production-line perspective	Empowerment perspective	Empowerment perspective
Marketing approach	Transaction marketing	Relationship marketing	Relationship marketing
Economies	Economies of scale	Economies of scope	Economies of relationships

1993). Transaction marketing is the most appropriate marketing approach for standardized services. In transaction marketing the relationship is limited to the product itself and the image of the seller (Grönroos, 1990). In mass orientation, service providers profit primarily from economies of scale.

Scope Orientation Strategy

This strategy is based on the concept of mass customization. *Mass customization* is the ability to serve a wide range of customers and meet changing demands through service variety against low costs (Pine et al., 1993). Services are customized within a predetermined range of variety and assembled out of standardized modules that can be combined for individual customers at the interface with the customer (Sundbo, 1994). The value adding focus is on the process and customer interaction. This interaction is of the sparring type in which governance is shared/negotiated (de Jong & van Bemmel, 1992). Customers can influence the specification of the service to the extent to which the service company is willing to provide. The server's role is one of configuring available, standardized components to meet individual customer needs.

For strategies of mass customization a management approach of empowerment is seen as most appropriate (Bowen & Lawler, 1995). As the complexity of services rises, customers expect high levels of expertise and decision making from contact employees. Empowerment is based on the insight that decisions should be made at the most appropriate level to avoid time and resource consuming channels of decision making (Quinn & Paquette, 1990). Mass customization is related to relationship marketing (Glazer, 1991) because a certain level of relationship is needed to recognize the customer's individual needs and because interactive configuration provide opportunities for relationship building. Service providers with a scope orientation profit from economies of scope which are associated with the delivery of a high variety of services to a large market scope through modularized processes.

Partnership Orientation Strategy

This strategy is based on service delivery processes with high degrees of freedom for adaptation and tailoring to the needs of individual customers. The service type is that of pure services, unique solutions to complex problems, in which the value adding focus is on the customer and the interaction with the customer (Shaw, 1990). Interaction governance is of the partner role type and is negotiated with the customer based on the service professional's diagnostic skills and his strive for partnership with the customer. Such partnership is characterized by mutual dependency, bilateral decision making and cooperation and the aim of the professional is to provide permanent solutions (Block, 2001). For customization strategies a management approach of empowerment and a relationship marketing approach is seen as most appropriate for the same reasons as in scope orientation strategies.

Partnership oriented service providers primarily profit from what I call '*economies of relationships*'. These economies are based on close partnerships with customers, resulting in high levels of knowledge about the customer's processes, employees and organizational culture. This knowledge and the trust of the customer provide the service company with a special kind of economies: recognizing the needs of the customer at first, even before the customer recognizes his own needs. This early recognition enables them to design service concepts together with their customers, often resulting in short payback periods of new service designs and a price premium. Recognition, dissemination and codification of these service innovations might lead to reproduction at lower cost. Similar to every kind of economies, economies of relationships have its drawbacks as well. Full exploitation of new service concepts needs a broad market (as in scope strategies), but serving a broad market contrasts with building close partnerships with customers.

Service Positioning Strategies from the Resource-Based Perspective

The idea of service positioning through positioning service delivery processes is congruent with the resource-based perspective on strategy. The resource-based view is paramount in services (de Jong & van Bemmel, 1992). The resource-based view contends that sustainable competitive advantage results from the possession of key resources explaining firm heterogeneity and imperfect competition (Fahy & Smithee, 1999). The source of uniqueness is not seen as the uniqueness of the resources itself but as the uniqueness of the services these resources render. Service processes can be seen as configurations of resources aimed to produce services, which are of value to customers (Grönroos, 1998). Resources that service companies drive on are routines, processes, skills, customer and process knowledge, a culture of customer orientation, customer co-production abilities, relationship networks and information technological infrastructures (Shaw, 1990; de Jong & van Bemmel, 1992; Schneider & Bowen, 1995). Resources are developed over time through innovations and by continuously responding to market needs. Building critical resources is path dependent and requires learning processes and sometimes involves accidental rather than rational events (Hunt & Morgan, 1996; Barney, 1999). Internal resource configurations facilitate or limit the company's abilities on the market.

Service Innovation

Service innovations are changes in processes and activities performed for the customer or changes in the competencies put to production in these processes and therefore are related to service positioning in the sense that service innovations could lead to refinements in existing service positioning strategies or could lead to migration from one strategy to another.

Service innovation has specific characteristics that are different from traditional manufacturing innovation (de Vries, 2006). Several of these characteristics become apparent from Segers, den Hertog, and Bouwman (2007) in this volume as well. Service innovation is interactive with suppliers, competitors, ruling organizations and with customers who often have a co-production role in innovation processes (Drejer, 2004; Gallouj & Weinstein, 1997). Service innovation could be both technological and non-technological (Djellal & Gallouj, 2001; Drejer, 2004; Gallouj & Weinstein, 1997). The distinction between product and process innovation is difficult in service innovation because services are acts or processes instead of products (Gallouj & Weinstein, 1997). Service innovations are not just radical or incremental but could be as well a result of evolution, disappearance, appearance, association and disassociation mechanisms (Gallouj & Weinstein, 1997). *Recombinative* or architectural innovation (Henderson & Clark, 1990) for instance is the systematic reutilization of components of the service system creating new outcomes by combining characteristics or by splitting a service into two or more new ones (bundling and unbundling) and is typical for service innovation. Another kind of innovation typical for services is *ad hoc* innovation, the interactive (social) construction of an original solution to a particular problem put forward by a client, ideally followed by *a posteriori* recognition, dissemination and codification of new built competencies to make the innovation recombinant for exploitation on a broader market. *Ad hoc* innovation is par excellence a type of innovation with high customer involvement.

The next three paragraphs show three case studies with three different innovation patterns in relation to the three service positioning strategies.

The Unique Case: Innovation Through Oscillation

Unique Nederland (part of the United Services Group) provides flexible work services in the Dutch marketplace. By the time of the study, Unique's strategy *oscillated* between scope and partnership orientation.

A large proportion of its turnover came from its scope orientation with basic services like temporary employment, recruitment, selection and payrolling. Unique depended on a broad reach in the market, in which different groups of customers were served with services that had modular characteristics, denoted as the existing arsenal of instruments.

Unique however followed a partnership strategy as well and saw itself 'not so much as a supplier of individual services and products, but more as a partner in lengthy and business critical processes'; as *'advisor during the concept phase, followed by active support during the implementation phase of developed flex-models'*. *'A trend is visible in the direction of more customization and longer relationships'*. The following citation shows a case of interactive and recombinative service innovation in which existing service modules are combined with new service elements into a new service concept.

> There are also services for which Unique designs new procedures and instruments to provide a new service. There is an existing arsenal of instruments available to help evaluate if the temporary employee is the right person (for a recruitment and selection trajectory or the pre-trajectory of a match). If you want to develop new services because the customer requires them, then you develop new instruments like in the case of insurance company De Amersfoortse. The initiative came from both De Amersfoortse as well as from Unique. It's about a re-integration service. The arsenal of resources applied to determine a person's re-integration degree is in fact all new instruments. After implementing these, the service returns to the formal operational circuit, temporary employment, secondment or recruitment and selection.

This next citation shows an *ad hoc* innovation in which services are customized for the customer and the core process of the customer (providing logistical services) became highly dependent on Unique's process to provide the customer with the human resource capacity needed. Unique's customer even considered moving its operations to regions where Unique had a better chance of recruiting human resources.

> We are involved in a customizing trajectory for Banta, a computer company. This customer requires solutions that deviate from standard solutions. For this you design new instruments. A customer of Banta, an American company, continually asks for new things, which means that Banta's work and consequently our work is continually changing... Their customer requires a service for which 2/3 temporary employees and 1/3 permanent employees are

necessary. They ask us to think with them on how the level of quality of both the permanent employees as well as the temporary employees can be raised. In this case we are a sort of pool manager, where in fact you take over 2/3 of the personnel management...They don't only require production workers but also quality managers, shift managers and production managers. Part of the labor logistics process is carried by Unique...Unique's role keeps increasing. The question is how it's going to end...A problem is that this customer is continually on the move, so that the form of service never stabilizes. Banta has three customers on the waiting list. They want a guarantee on how many employees we can supply...The customer wonders if it can take on one of their customers or not, then asks Unique if they must relocate some of their activities elsewhere, and if so, where, because they do need the people...The company keeps insisting: tell us Unique, because we depend on your reasoning.

The cases show a value adding focus on the client and customer–supplier interaction and an interaction governance of the partner role type. Unique used an empowerment management approach with relationship marketing to retain its customers. Unique needed these customization initiatives to stay in the market. This resulted in an *oscillation* between a scope and partnership strategy. Unique deliberately innovated through customized services for specific customers (*ad hoc* innovations) and tried to standardize new service elements to make these recombinant for future service provision in a mass customization mode...

A package of services has been customized with the customer, and that was really 'playing'...You penetrate deeper and deeper into the customer's process and are able to finalize the project from A to Z. You enter at the customer at a certain management level and gradually rise to higher levels. This gives you insight into the customer's decision-making processes. Internally, I had commitment to invest in a project office...Unique supplies the employees. A manual for the project has been designed for the branch offices, containing procedures, methods and function profiles. A whole range of new instruments has been developed that are partly reusable for other projects, because the manual systematically deals with the various parts. A similar manual has also once been written for the outplacement service. This has by now grown into a standard concept that is offered on the branches' own initiative to customers.

The oscillation pattern in which two generic service positioning strategies are followed in the same business unit is contrary to Shaw's (1990) line of thinking that business units often have trouble in focusing on more than one positioning strategy. This is not to say that companies could not serve different market segments, but the best way to do so would be by different business units.

I explain the oscillation pattern by the resource-based view and the need to extend resources to react on market heterogeneity through innovation. Especially through ad hoc and recombinative innovations, specialized resources are developed or recombined to offer a diversified set of related services to the market.

Combinations of scope and partnership orientation in one business unit seem to make sense in three situations.

- The business unit wants to continuously enhance its existing base of modules. Experimenting with new service elements in ad hoc innovations and a posteriori recognition, dissemination and codification of new built competencies, forms an alternative for traditional new service development in which the costs are (partly) covered by the customer who receives a unique service outcome.
- The business unit has (large) customers, which need to be retained, and which now and then have service requests beyond the scope of current customization options, thus driving the supplier towards customized solutions.
- The business unit's emphasis is on partnership orientation and pure customization, but it sees a market opportunity to standardize part of its service into standardized modules to serve a larger market without giving signals to the market that services are just mass customized.

As with many management decisions a trade-off needs to be made between the advantages and disadvantages of combining two generic strategies. The danger of the first above-mentioned situation is that customers who co-produce in ad hoc innovations might come to view themselves as guinea pigs after it becomes clear to them that these innovations are used by their supplier to serve a larger market. This will be especially painful if the customer perceived the relationship with the supplier to be a good one (a prerequisite to innovate together) or if the customer paid a premium price for the unique service outcome. Clear agreements between both parties seem advisable. The drawback of the second situation is 'drifting strategy'. Too many requests for pure customized solutions from a (ever-increasing) set of perceived valuable customers might erode the business logic of the business unit. Premium pricing of customized solutions and clear criteria for customer valuation are needed in such situations. The danger of the third situation is obviously that it becomes visible to the market that the solutions provided are mass customized instead of customized and that the price is too high. In this situation the service provider's reputation of premium priced customized solution provider is damaged. To circumvent this situation, the service provider might start service specification always in the partnership mode (having both mass customized and customized solutions available). When it becomes clear that the customer's request could be served with a mass customized solution, the service provider might lower its price, because costs are lower.

Oscillation between scale and scope orientation seems plausible if higher prices and a certain volume for mass customized solutions or shortening time to market for standardized solutions outweigh the costs of building a modular organization.

The Interpolis Case: Incremental Migration Through Innovation

Interpolis is a general insurance company providing a broad range of insurance services. I specifically studied Interpolis' employee benefits service offering to SMEs by the business unit Employment Benefits (EB). Interpolis provided quite customizable EB solutions to large enterprises as well. By the time of the study, Interpolis was a 100% subsidiary of the Rabo Groep, belonging to the top five in the financial services industry in the Netherlands.

The Rabo Groep already supported its SME clients in the financial aspects of their business (through financial products) and in the physical aspects of it (through insurances), but not in the human resource aspects. Absenteeism and dropout of human resources had become a serious risk for SMEs because of changing social security legislation. Rabo Groep as being one of the most important financers of SMEs wanted to protect its clients from these risks. The Rabo Groep had another reason to invest in its employee benefits business as well. As Interpolis stated in its yearly report: *There were disappointments as well, mainly with the illness absenteeism insurances....*

EB module one (a service package) focused on building relationships with customers through anchoring the relationship marketing model in the EB formula; by building relationships with Rabo Banks (the primary distribution channel for the SME market); through developing assurance and self-confidence in the sales of EB products by providing relevant, just-in-time support; and by building relationships with suppliers through simplifying and bundling of coherent products into packages. *The BU EB is a content organizer, contrary to the other business units that are content providers* . An 'convenience proposition' had to be offered: *It is clear that the strongest side of the service needs to be convenience for the supplier, the intermediary and the customer.* Several instruments to sell module one were developed, like business processes; commercial instruments; CRM tools, training programs; an intranet application to support Rabo Banks and to support knowledge building through a learning community and a help desk.

The service positioning strategy of Interpolis' EB module one showed both characteristics of a mass oriented strategy and of scope orientation (see Table 18.2).

Rabo and Interpolis planned to arrive at a service proposition to SME's that would be (mass) customizable based on collective labor agreements, requirements of the employer and in the end the employee's wishes. The first step Interpolis took with its module one, however, was a clear *standardization* one. It standardized services into a package with limited possibilities to leave out components or to customize it. It standardized its former basic employee benefits product, which had too many options (up to 83 different combinations). Because of all these options the product required too much data collection from the customer and the offering of the product took Rabo employees/the distribution channel too long. Many clients who considered an offer never signed it.

Interpolis standardized the interaction governance as well into a 'take it or leave it' selling one. But this did not mean that the value adding focus was on the process and source only. A considerable part of the value adding focus was on the interaction with customers to create awareness of the risks and challenges associated with employing people.

The module one service package contained two service elements that were mass customizable during service delivery but were presented at the level of the package (during the sales process) as quite standardized. A data roundabout made it possible

Table 18.2: Interpolis' combination of mass orientation and scope orientation.

Service positioning strategy→ Organizational design characteristics:	Mass orientation	Scope orientation	Partnership orientation
Service type	Product (standardized)	Service/product (mass customized) ←——— Module one ——→ Next modules	Pure service (customized)
Nature of the service process	Standardized	Modular ←——— Module one ——→ Next modules	Professional knowledge based and interconnected with customer processes
Value adding focus	Process and source	Process, interactive, and client	Client and interactive
Interaction governance	Selling	Sparring	Partner role
Management approach	Production-line perspective	Empowerment perspective	Empowerment perspective
Marketing approach	Transaction marketing	Relationship marketing	Relationship marketing
Economies	Economies of scale	Economies of scope	Economies of relationships

for employers to electronically supply data on, for instance tenures and salaries and to report illness directly from their HRM systems; and the Compaan service provided intermediation between ill employees and a large network of reintegration companies.

Interpolis based its introduction of EB modules on relationship marketing, to strengthen the advice relation with customers. '*With module one Rabo and Interpolis implement a relation focused advising and sales approach around the most important business capital: people.*' The introduction of EB module one focused on empowerment initiating instruments to enable Rabo employees to close contracts independently. Economies in Interpolis EB services had to come from standardization and scale in its operations on the one hand and a variety in services on the other hand. Scope was looked for by offering parts of the EB module one to certain industry members as well as through specific industry arrangements. These services were processed in the same way, but premiums, commissions, distribution and marketing differed.

The case of Interpolis shows a service positioning pattern towards the SME market in which characteristics of *mass orientation* (a standardized service type and a selling interaction governance) are *combined with* characteristics of *scope orientation* (an empowerment management approach, relationship marketing and economies of scope). Interpolis faced the challenge to introduce quite complex EB services to a market, which was unaware of its HRM risks and opportunities, and through a distribution channel, which showed limited readiness for these services. They deliberately chose a migration strategy towards more complex services (module two/three) by first introducing a standardized package but did so without compromising their relationship marketing intention and the need to advise their customers. To a certain extent, they built modular processes to enable recombinative and *ad hoc* innovations to large employers, but standardized their sales offering towards the SME market. The whole concept of EB module one was a recombinative innovation in the sense that existing elements of the business, for example service elements delivered by supplying business units, were recombined into a package by the BU EB. The Compaan and data roundabout were elements of the package that in itself was again a recombination of existing services.

The Gak Case: Radical Migration Through Innovation

Gak Nederland was the largest Dutch social security administration agency, administering all social security laws in the Netherlands for 193,000 employers and 3,782,000 tenures, collecting 13 billion Euro premiums and paying 8.3 billion Euro benefits with approximately 12,000 employees.

During the period of research the service positioning strategy of Gak *moved from a mass oriented strategy to a scope oriented one*. At the start of the study, Gak's business was one of mass transactions along standardized processes with limited market segmentation and service differentiation. An external consultancy bureau characterized the situation as efficiency oriented, standard products and a hierarchical, functional partitioned organization with central decision making. Gak changed its strategy towards scope orientation, in which different customer groups would be served with mass customized services and with a relationship marketing approach.

> The larger the customer the more we think in packages that are built in a modular way. The strategy that will be applied for SMEs (80%) will be focused on low costs, run-in procedures, convenience for customers and standard products, eventually with some cosmetic customization. For large accounts (20%), we will deliver mass customization...Gak uses the BarbaPappa model:

a metaphor for a flexible organization with a solid back office surrounded by bulgings that might disappear.

The marketing strategy is focused on retention of customers and enlarging the turnover per customer.

The change from mass orientation towards scope orientation was organized in an ambitious change program anticipating market changes and rising competition, which resulted from new legislation on social security administration allowing new entrants to the market and targeting full competition. The program was ICT driven, focused on process innovation (to arrive at modular services) and can be characterized as a typical business reengineering endeavor. The change program included the implementation of modular processes (mass customization); the establishment of a marketing and sales function; customer-focused data acquisition, processing and storage and the implementation of supply chain integration. The ambition of the program was reflected by its cost (295 million euros) and its time frame (4 years).

During the period of change several ad hoc and recombinative innovations already took place and could have supported the overall change program, but clear a posteriori recognition, dissemination and codification of new built competencies was not organized.

At the moment several customization initiatives are running in the operations and data supply for different sectors, for example for the temporary employment sector. Other initiatives led to concentration of case processing on district offices, as for example for the sector Merchant Marine, Akzo Nobel, NS, etc. There is no coordination recognizable over these different initiatives.

To deliver customization, you have to get together the right people in a working group, who study, together with the customer, what is possible. Although things changed the last two years, still too little time is made for working group members to engage themselves continually with development and conceptualization of customization applications. If Gak sees customization as a product, resources should be made free to analyze patterns over customization initiatives.... Nowadays, when we want to customize, we always have to search for product components. The wheel gets reinvented all the time because internally we don't have sufficient run-in procedures.

The mass oriented strategy of the past years had resulted in an operations oriented organization in which protection of standardized operations ('the factory') made innovation and customization hard to realize...

Customers find it incomprehensible that the factory is protected that way. Gak is not very customer oriented in this regard.

...and marketing and sales competencies were underdeveloped.

The problem is that we target too low from the idea 'then we're in', but in the end we don't meet the right persons. We have to go to the right decision-making unit the first time. Gak doesn't know the decision-making unit structure of its customers.

... why don't I [EdV: an account manager] know the industry? Because I have to scrape that information together. I have to pay an enormous amount of money to let someone do that for me and if I want that information structurally, things become very difficult.

The Gak case tells a story of 'contra' resources (resources that limit the company's abilities given a new market situation). The tremendous change program was intended to bring about major organizational, informational, technical and marketing changes. The change program however was never finished because only 3 years later the Dutch government changed its strategy towards the organization of social security again quite radically.

Implications for Information Management

The three cases show patterns of innovation and service positioning which are of interest to information management.

Service Positioning

The patterns of mass, scope and partnership orientation are a reference frame for information management to analyze one's own service positioning and that of suppliers and information management is clearly involved in the implementation of service positioning strategies. Generally speaking, in mass orientation information management focuses on standardization, in scope orientation on modularization and in partnership orientation on supporting professionals. The service positioning strategies are assumed to hold for different kinds of services, including ICT services, and thus are a reference for ICT departments and ICT suppliers as well. ICT departments with a mass orientation strategy, for example might expect outsourcing considerations from their management, while ICT departments with a clear partnership orientation find in their economies of relationship an advantage over general ICT suppliers.

Service Innovation and Its Drivers

As services are defined as processing operations carried out on behalf of customers in a medium held by customers, service innovation brings about changes in processing operations, customers or market segments or in the medium held by customers. As information management is the field of expertise on information, processes, technology and media, service innovation belongs almost by definition to this field. Information management therefore should be aware of the specific characteristics of service innovation as mentioned above and recognizable in the cases. These characteristics are fundamentally different from innovation in manufacturing or traditional models of technology-driven innovation (de Vries, 2006).

To play a role in service innovation, information management needs to recognize the different drivers for service innovation, like changing regulation, specific customer requests, interactivity with business partners, market opportunities or current business problems. The cases show that technological developments are by no means the only drivers that trigger innovation. The association of information management with ICT seems to have led to a focus on translating ICT into business opportunities (e.g. technological trend watching), whereas the cases as well as the service innovation literature tell us that the driver of innovation often comes from ruling organizations, partners, customers or needs in business processes.

Innovation in Relation to Service Positioning

The cases show three patterns in the relationship between innovation and service positioning that go beyond the obvious pattern of innovation within the context of the business' current service positioning strategy: oscillation, incremental migration and radical migration. The concept of mass customization not only implies an alternative strategy for pure standardization or pure customization, but offers opportunities to oscillate or to migrate as well.

The management trade-offs in oscillation as mentioned in the Unique case have implications for information management. Large investments and control obviously should be focused on the core positioning strategy (supporting the prevalent business logic), but to leverage from oscillation between scope and partnership for instance, implies learning how to interpret information coming from customers in *ad hoc* innovations and learning how to recognize, disseminate and codify new built competencies *a posteriori*.

The combination between mass and scope orientation at Interpolis and their thoughtful migration strategy carries an important lesson for information management. Although a technology oriented vision would hold that mass customization was possible (and indeed had been tried by Interpolis), it however turned out to be not feasible because the market and distribution channel were not ready for it and sales time and costs in the distribution channel became too high. What we learn from this is that it is the whole service concept that counts (of which ICT is just a part). Pine et al.'s (1993) imperative *anything that can be digitized can be customized* does not mean that the market is ready for it or that the selling could be done economically efficient. Here's another management trade-off that needs to be made: between market readiness/customer's knowledge, distribution and sales costs on the one hand and low production costs on the other. Mass customization leads to more service options implicating a growing need for customer advice and interactional configuration, leading to a demand for more highly educated front office employees (which are scarce and thus expensive), in the end resulting in lower margins. The margin for SME oriented EB products at Interpolis became that small that they had to standardize their service and tried to do so without compromising their relationship marketing intentions. One of the solutions to this trade-off, might be to distribute modular products by rich self service distribution channels like the Internet to knowledgeable (more highly educated) customers. The problem however is that technological media/channels have an easily accessible, low cost, less time consuming, commodity-like image to many people. This is not an image naturally compatible with high end, modular-based products or advice sensitive distribution. I do not say that for some services this solution is impossible (and indeed it has been shown to be possible), but there are considerations to be made.

The GAK case shows that huge investments need to be made to radically migrate from mass orientation to scope orientation to resolve contra-resources. Large parts of this investment needed to be made in fields related to information management: business processes, CRM, supply chain integration, ICT and employee training. The contradiction in such situations is that management, coming from a situation of tight control of mass production, needs to manage a large change process towards a situation requiring more open organizational boundaries, where customer wishes will penetrate deeper into business process and more enactment on the environment is required. The chance is high that management in itself is the contra-resource, not being able to lead such change programs, to intervene on large scale and/or not being familiar with how to manage beyond mass production control. Such situations might not get any better if the change is based on new technological opportunities and gets controlled by traditional ICT management related change tools like classical project management. Then there is a fair chance that the introduction of new technology enlarges the gap between the existing situation and the future (making the future even more unclear for large groups within the organization) and that the fall back on traditional control related change instruments (project management) reinforces management's contra-resources. Here the trade-off seems to be: investment in one self as management versus investment in organizational (infra)structures, processes and employees. A de-mystifying and learning oriented role taking by information management might be more advisable in such situations than that of technology propagator.

Function of ICT in Service Innovation

Gak shows a typical technology-driven Business Process Redesign innovation program with quite some adherence to the technological hypes of that moment. Unique on the other hand shows almost no technology at all. Their innovations were non-technological recombinations and renewals of human skills and procedures that needed codification efforts to be scaled. These innovations were informational in nature but without technology as a driver. At Interpolis, technology was certainly involved but not as driver or cult, but as an integral part of a new service concept in which organizational issues, human resource development, marketing, distribution and the application of ICT were balanced and aligned on the level of the service concept. The cases suggest at least three roles for information management. The role of de-mystifier in cases of technology hyphenation and/or adherence. The role of emancipator in the case of technology unawareness (in the sense of fertilizing awareness and facilitating codification). The role of co-designer of new service concepts in cases where technology awareness is mature and technology is seen as 'part of the deal'.

References

Barney, J. B. (1999). How a firm's capabilities affect boundary decisions. *Sloan Management Review*, *40*(3), 137–145.

Block, P. (2001). *Feilloos adviseren, een praktische gids voor adviesvaardigheden*. Schoonhoven: Academic Service.

Bowen, D. E., & Lawler, E. E. (1995). Empowering service employees. *Sloan Management Review*, *36*(3), 73–84.

de Jong, M. W., & van Bemmel, L. P. (1992). *De systematische ontwikkeling van diensten. Een klantgerichte benadering*. INRO-TNO-rapport.

de Vries, E. J. (2005, May 25–28). Epistemology and methodology in case research: A comparison between European and American IS journals. In: *Proceedings of the 13th European Conference of Information Systems*, Regensburg.

de Vries, E. J. (2006). Innovation in services in networks of organisations and in the distribution of services. *Research Policy*, *35*, 1037–1051.

Djellal, F., & Gallouj, F. (2001). Patterns of innovation organisation in service firms: Portal survey results and theoretical models. *Science and Public Policy*, *28*, 57–67.

Drejer, I. (2004). Identifying innovation in surveys of services: A Schumpeterian perspective. *Research Policy*, *33*, 551–562.

EU. (2005). Key figures on science, technology and innovation. Towards a European knowledge area, 19/07/05, European Commission DG Research, p. 37.

Fahy, J., & Smithee, A. (1999). Strategic marketing and the resource based view of the firm. *Academy of Marketing Science Review* [Online] *99*(10), 1–20. Available at http://www.amsreview.org/amsrev/theory/fahy10-99.html

Gallouj, F. (2002). Innovation in services and the attendant old and new myths. *Journal of Socio-Economics*, *31*, 137–154.

Gallouj, F., & Weinstein, O. (1997). Innovation in services. *Research Policy*, *26*, 537–556.

Glazer, R. (1991). Marketing in an information-intensive environment: Strategic implications of knowledge as an asset. *Journal of Marketing*, *55*(4), 1–19.

Grönroos, C. (1990). *Service management and marketing*. Lexington, MA: Lexington Books.

Grönroos, C. (1998). Marketing services: The case of the missing product. *Journal of Business and Industrial Marketing*, *13*(4/5), 322–338.

Henderson, R. M., & Clark, K. B. (1990). Architectural innovation: The reconfiguration of existing product technologies and the failure of established firms. *Administrative Science Quarterly*, *31*(1), 9–30.

Hill, P. (1977). On goods and services. *Review Income and Wealth*, *4*, 315–338.

Hunt, S. D., & Morgan, R. M. (1996). The resource-advantage theory of competition: Dynamics, path dependencies, and evolutionary dimensions. *Journal of Marketing*, *60*(4), 107–114.

Levitt, T. (1976). The industrialization of service. *Harvard Business Review*, *54*(5), 63–74.

Miles, M. B., & Huberman, A. M. (1994). *Qualitative data analysis*. Thousand Oaks, CA: Sage Publications.

Pine, B. J., Victor, B., & Boynton, A. C. (1993). Making mass customization work. *Harvard Business Review*, *71*(5), 108–119.

Quinn, J. B., & Paquette, P. C. (1990). Technology in services: Creating organizational revolutions. *Sloan Management Review*, *31*(2), 67–78.

Schneider, B., & Bowen, D. E. (1995). *Winning the service game*. Boston, MA: Harvard Business School Press.

Segers, J., den Hertog, P., & Bouwman, H. (2007). The organisation of innovation in service firms. Evidence from four Dutch service firms. In: A. Huizing & E. J. de Vries (Eds.), *Information management: Setting the scene. Book series: Perspectives on information management* (Vol. 1). Oxford: Elsevier Scientific Publishers.

Shaw, J. C. (1990). *The service focus.* Homewood, IL: Dow Jones-Irving.

Shostack, G. L. (1987). Service positioning through structural change. *Journal of Marketing,* *51*(1), 34–43.

Smith, R. A., & Houston, M. J. (1983). *Script-based evaluation of satisfaction with services.* Chicago, IL: American Marketing Association.

Sundbo, J. (1994). Modularization of service production and a thesis of convergence between service and manufacturing organizations. *Scandinavian Journal of Management,* *10*(3), 245–266.

Yin, R. K. (1994). *Case study research, design and methods.* Thousand Oaks, CA: Sage Publications.

Appendix: Methodology

The case studies are conducted according to generally accepted guidelines as discussed in Yin (1994), Miles and Huberman (1994) and de Vries (2005). The case study method is appropriate when dealing with questions regarding contemporary events, over which the researcher has little or no control and in which the borders between the phenomenon of interest and its context are not clear, as is the case with questions regarding service innovation in relation to service positioning strategies. This study is exploratory, for which the case study method is a well-accepted strategy. The study is a multiple case study with three cases in which the units of analysis are business units. I used multiple data sources for data collection: interviews (approximately 15 in each case), documents and artifacts, like ICT applications which allowed for triangulation. In the data analysis I made use of pattern matching, content analysis and conceptually ordered data displays. In every case several opportunities have been used to get feedback on the data analysis by interviewees and management. The studies are conducted following a case study protocol and data is recorded in a case study database.

Chapter 19

Web 2.0: Disruptive Technology or is Everything Miscellaneous?

Rolf T. Wigand

ABSTRACT

This chapter explores various Web 2.0 developments. The author defines Web 2.0, views it as a paradigm shift and examines how the vast amount and huge variety of information on the Web is attempted to be organized, sorted, ordered, tagged and classified. The nature and role of social networking sites is addressed, especially asking how businesses might find a role here. Moreover, the author asks how one might reach and connect with Web 2.0 customers and what strategy businesses might pursue. Online shopping communities are explored and some opportunities for retailers are identified. Lastly, questions and issues are raised with regard to the implementation of Web 2.0 and the bottom line, i.e., an attempt to see what some businesses are doing in this context and how they embrace Web 2.0 technologies and applications. Conclusions are offered.

Over the last few years several books have been published that address in part or indirectly aspects of Web 2.0 developments and have influenced our thinking in this area. First of all, one must recognize Chris Anderson's (2006) *The Long Tail*, with the author recognizing that the future of business and culture is not in big hits (the high-volume head of the traditional demand and diffusion curve) as in the past, but the endless long tail of that same curve with demand being splintered into ever more media outlets. Yochai Benkler's (2006) *The Wealth of Networks: How Social Production Transforms Markets and Freedom* addresses the restructuring and reconfiguration of power and knowledge derived from the tightly knit and complex interactions among as well as impact of business, public, nonprofit, educational and amateur media producers. Tom Malone's (2004) *The Future of Work* addresses how such changes alter and reshape the management needs and practices of major corporations. Henry Jenkin's (2006) *Convergence Culture: Where Old and New Media Collide* addresses this currently evolving world in which every story, image, sound, brand and relationship find new traction and uses across an ever-increasing number of media platforms. In this he recognizes that the flow of media content is shaped just as much by decisions made in teenagers' bedrooms as by decisions made in corporate boardrooms. The last book to be mentioned in this context is David Weinberger's (2007) *Everything is Miscellaneous: The Power of the New Digital Disorder*. The author identifies and charts new principles of digital order that are remaking business, education, politics, science and culture. In doing so he views these developments within a chart of a new world order (or better, disorder).

The authors of these influential books approach these intertwined topics from very different disciplinary perspectives and, interestingly, most did not know of each other until their respective books appeared. When these books are examined together though, we can recognize an emerging paradigm shift in our understanding of business, political economy, media, culture and society. This paradigm shift can be viewed under the label of Web 2.0.

Thomas Kuhn (1962) is credited with addressing the notion of paradigm shift in the context of scientific revolution. Although we are certainly not observing a scientific revolution in the context of Web 2.0, yet the paradigm, in Kuhn's view, is not simply the currently prevailing theory, but the larger picture, even the entire worldview in which it exists as well as all of the implications coming with it. It is often this final comprehension, the result of the long process of change, that is understood when the expression *paradigm shift* is used colloquially, i.e., the change of worldview, without reference to the specificities of Kuhn's historical argument.

Web 2.0 is a somewhat misleading term, as it may suggest ideas about a new technology, but what has abruptly changed is something very different: what has drastically changed is common every-day as well as business life, simply by being online in some fashion, has become interwoven, linked and in part enabled by the Internet. More than ever we realize that the media shapes and reconfigures society not only through their content, but also through their form. Although it is difficult at this stage, maybe even impossible, to provide a precise picture of what this shift looks like and to determine where these developments are precisely headed. Here the author will address several manifestations of this paradigm shift and demonstrate through examples how these changes are unfolding. An attempt is made to reflect on the implications and the impact these developments may have on companies and how companies should position themselves strategically in light of these developments.

With such reshaping and reconfiguration, however, we can observe how the media and tools used in people's interaction and communication are utilized and that a restructuring and regrouping of their real relations to each other is occurring. Such a shift is never possible without consequences. Along come of course concerns about excesses and extreme behaviors [various forms of addiction (e.g., Internet gambling, excessive gaming), choosing the internet as an exclusive means of communication, etc.], such as when parents are concerned with their children's missing the *real life*. But such concerns had arisen with the introduction of any new medium. One only needs to recall parents' concerns about excessive television viewing in the past. Even Socrates envisioned the sad possibility that the sheer practice of writing and scripting may push aside or bypass the lively exchange of ideas, an early form of disintermediation. Gutenberg's printing presses disseminated not only the idea of freedom of choice, but they enabled the technical free choice of ideas. Similar concerns were also raised when silence permeated in 17th century English coffee houses as the visitor mostly heard the rustling of newspapers instead of the twitter of patrons. Here, too, concerns about *real and actual life* were expressed. This cycle repeated itself with the introduction of the telephone as well. It seems that what is happening on the Internet and with Web 2.0 is not any less real.

1.1 billion people use the Internet (Internet World Stats, 2007). In that sense the behavior of embracing Web 2.0 capabilities has become a mass phenomenon. Some skeptics argue that if of the 1000 users of an interactive Web site merely one is making a contribution to the site's content then this is not very exciting and meaningful. Yet if this very same site enjoys overall several millions of users, this, in turn, does result in thousands of authors (*The Long Tail* economics phenomenon).

What is Web 2.0?

Although the precise demarcations and delineations of Web 2.0 are still somewhat cloudy, one thing is clear: Web 2.0 is not a creation by business or the economy, it is being created by millions of users. Web 2.0 is a participatory medium. We may loosely understand Web 2.0 as the second or new Internet. There is some debate on how new Web 2.0 really is. Tim Berners-Lee for one, the creator of the WWW, views Web 2.0 merely as the logical next development. In that sense there is no new software or application with the name of Web 2.0. And yet what we observe with Web 2.0 is a paradigm shift in how users use the Web, a development that questions everything that has been developed and applied so far. Many agree that Web 2.0 is woven from a fabric of technologies designed to enable collaboration and break down information silos in an effort to aggregate and to publish information. In that sense Web 2.0 is a social phenomenon, not a technology *per se*. New in the Web 2.0 era is that anyone can explore, join, build or depart any Web community and can create and post content onto the Internet without requiring extensive technical know-how. In a nutshell, Web 2.0 is a broad range of Web sites that encourage interaction and collaborative work. Users do not just consume content, but they create and produce content as well. Obvious examples along this line of thinking are YouTube and the family photo album Flickr. YouTube reported uploads of several million videos within a few short months and functionally has become indeed the *tube of the chip culture*. When everyone can produce one's own video program, in the long run, this may become a threat for traditional television (see e.g., The Future of Television, 2007).

Although there is no hard-and-fast definition of Web 2.0, the concept of Web 2.0 is generally attributed to Tim O'Reilly (2007) coining the phrase in 2004, stating that "One of the key lessons of the Web 2.0 era is this: Users add value....Therefore, Web 2.0 companies set inclusive defaults for aggregating user data and building value as a side-effect of ordinary use of the application." In general, Web 2.0 is a broad concept that has been subdivided into three anchor points: technology, community and business. The challenge is that Web 2.0 is more than just a set of technologies. It also incorporates attributes with a social dimension including new business models, user-contributed content and user-generated metadata, relatively open and transparent business processes, increased simplicity in design and features as well as decentralized and participatory products and processes. The three anchor points for Web 2.0 are (Smith, 2006; Wigand, 2006; and others):

- Technology and architecture — consisting of the infrastructure of the Web and the concept of Web platforms. Examples of specific technologies include Ajax, Representational State Transfer (REST) and Really Simple Syndication (RSS). Technologists tend to gravitate toward this view.
- Community and social — looks at the dynamics around social networks, communities and other personal content publish/share models, wikis and other collaborative content models. Most people tend to gravitate toward this view; hence, there is much Web 2.0 focus on "the architecture of participation."
- Business and process — Web services-enabled business models and mashup (i.e., a Web site or Web application that combines content from more than one source)/ remix applications. Examples include advertising, subscription models — software as a service (SaaS) — and long-tail economics. A well-known specific example is connecting a rental-housing Web site with Google Maps to create a new, more useful service that automatically shows the location of each rental listing — of course, business people tend to zero in on this angle.

These three anchor points are fully applied with another Web 2.0 phenomenon: Second Life. Second Life is an excellent example of a Web 2.0 application with which we are still exploring and discovering business appropriate roles (see Chapter 20 of this book). Google, BMW, Adidas, IBM and numerous other companies do have a presence on Second Life today. Various business processes and business solutions can be explored here. Mr. Martin Jetter, CEO of IBM Germany, e.g., has a personal presence on Second Life in the form of his own avatar.

Table 19.1 shows the results from a study looking at what roles businesses envision Web 2.0 technologies to have in the future. One should note that a whopping 25% believe that Web 2.0 technologies will not play a role in their business, yet one wonders if this finding would be the same if the survey were repeated in a year or two.

Politicians, firms and various entrepreneurial forms represent and construct themselves on the Internet within an artificial world. Similarly blogs and Wikipedia help shape Web 2.0. Firms — not just virtual or newly created entrepreneurial firms but the BMWs, Dells and IBMs of the world — ask themselves how traditional Internet-based offers can be integrated with those of the Web 2.0 development. Even though no one at the present time is completely sure of what Web 2.0 fully comprises and exactly how to deploy its elements, it has become clear that the Internet demands evermore powerful networks. In spite of these uncertainties, we may agree that Web 2.0 is a very heterogeneous child, yet we will have to wait and see what it might look like as an adult.

There is considerable discussion about Web 3.0, the next step after Web 2.0, largely comprising the semantic realm of the Web (the Semantic Web) and finding

Table 19.1: What role will Web 2.0 technologies play in business?

Roles businesses envision	Respondents (%)
Web 2.0 technologies will play no role in my business	25
Communicating with customers	22
Providing customer service	15
Improving productivity	14
Sharing employee knowledge	9
Communicating with employees	8
Reducing costs	8
Obtaining customer feedback	3

Source: CIO INSIGHT (November 2006) (based on $N = 179$).

new ways to mine human intelligence. The goal is to insert a layer of meaning on top of the existing Web that, in turn, would make the Web less of a catalog and more of a guide. Moreover, such efforts would even provide the foundation for computing and systems to reason in human fashion. This challenge, i.e., machines doing the thinking instead of simply following commands, has eluded computer scientists and researchers for the last 50 years and may be viewed analogous to the pursuit of the Holy Grail. Such a system, in contrast to today's search engines, would be capable of providing a reasonable and complete response to a question like: "I'm looking for a place to vacation in a warm climate and I have a budget of $2000. Oh, I also have a dog and 12-year-old daughter." Given the vast number of searches necessary (choosing a location, flight, hotel, available entertainment, kennel, etc.), under Web 3.0 the same search would ideally deliver a complete vacation package that was planned in detail as meticulously as if it had been put together by a human travel agent. Early forms of such systems are under development (e.g., KnowItAll, Radar Networks, Metaweb) and when they become available they will be commercially more valuable than today's Web 2.0 search engines.

Is Everything Miscellaneous? Making Sense of Web 2.0 Developments

Making sense out of the Web and what it offers is a daunting task and somewhat analogous to scientists' efforts to classify the living world 300 years ago. Carl Linnaeus, a Swedish naturalist, born at that time is remembered for devising the system to classify living organisms. Linnaeus pursued what he thought to be the divine order of the natural world in order to exploit it for human benefit. At that time exploration and trade brought new specimens to be classified to European scientists. Toward the end of the 17th century there was no sense of how creatures were related to each other and it was common that descriptions and classifications were unsystematic. Accordingly, and reflective of the belief at the time, Linnaeus offered an organizing hierarchy with kingdoms at the top and species at the bottom. This system created by Linnaeus turned out to be robust and flexible and even survived the emergence of evolution. Moreover, it survived even the discovery of entire categories of organisms, such as bacteria, that Linnaeus never even suspected. A similar daunting task is faced today by those trying to make sense out of the massive and rapid developments observable on the WWW and the Internet. Here, too, we would benefit from a comprehensive effort to describe, sort and classify — and eventually understand — these observations.

David Weinberger (2007) in his book, *Everything Is Miscellaneous: The Power of the New Digital Disorder*, struggles with similar issues: Bringing order to the Web, i.e., to provide a new world order or, according to Weinberger, a world disorder. He questions if the chaos of the information society could not be viewed as a creative chaos that is observable in the tectonic shifting on the map of knowledge. The underlying task to make sense out of these observations in the form of *tag clouds*, e.g., is as challenging as making sense and bringing mental order to a large newspaper and magazine kiosk in a large city. Here, too, creative chaos seems to prevail and in this analog world no Dewey Decimal System is of any help. Linnaeus would have enjoyed this sorting and bringing-order challenge. A generation of bookkeepers and library scientists is growing up in our Web 2.0 world; they write blogs and are experiencing a deliberate collecting and sorting of various articles and literature online. In doing so they categorize, group, etc. their material and label their contents. The Pew Internet centers found that 7% of U.S. Internet users devote themselves to daily activities such as tagging, digging or social bookmarking. They label their own or others' documents, photos or videos or sort online text into ever new contexts.

At first glance this reminds us of philately — stamp collecting. But according to Weinberger (2007), this is more than a hobby of some eager geeks on the Internet. These individuals on the one hand consider the history of traditional classification systems (using the alphabet to Melvin Dewey's Decimal System from 1876, still used by most libraries today) that appear nearly useless in today's information chaos. On the other hand, Weinberger demonstrates the shortcomings of these classification schemata. They become obvious when asking what the perfect order for a record collection might look like. The resulting mixed order transforms not only the economy but also how we think about the organization of the world itself, but — maybe even more importantly — who in our opinion has the authority to tell us what to think on this. This may create strange classifications or groupings or tag clouds: The photo portal Flickr offered 167,643 pictures on the theme of "decay" on July 1, 2007: rusting cars, damaged statues, etc. YouTube offered over 22,200 hits on the search term *invisible*.

Such collaboratively generated folksonomies are one form of organizing knowledge. This may be appreciated, but when the readers of news media decide themselves which news are important to them they compete with the expertise of news professionals, editors, etc. This is already being practiced with digg.com and yigg.com where news stories from the Internet are being chosen, earmarked and are being recommended to others. On the other hand, many newspapers make it a common practice to inform their readers of the most downloaded articles. When examining the topics and themes of these articles however, there is considerable variability: from terrorist attacks to the relative unimportance of penis size and the Apple iPhone. Maybe David Weinberger is right: Everything is indeed (at least somewhat) miscellaneous?

Social Networking Sites are Not Just for Teenagers

A central component and anchor point of Web 2.0 are communal and social aspects that group, organize and aggregate people, but also business customers. The phenomenal growth of social networking sites has become legendary. The social community site MySpace is growing at 375,000 new registrants per day and will soon enjoy 1 billion members. MySpace.com increased 183% from 16.2 million unique visitors in July 2005 to 46 million in July 2006 (Social Networking Sites, 2006). The average stay for MySpace users is 29 min each time they log on and the average number of pages viewed by each user is 75.6 (Compete, Inc., 2007). Over a million enthusiasts work and live in the virtual online community Second Life. During the month of February 2007 the online Encyclopedia, Wikipedia, had become 12 times larger than the *Encyclopedia Britannica*. On February 4, 2007 Super Bowl viewers watched a Frito-Lay chips advertisement that was created and chosen by its customers on the Internet. A new blog is being created at the rate of 1 per s day-in and day-out. Web portals such as Edmunds.com and Carspace.com have created their own social networks.

The phenomenal success of YouTube is now legendary. YouTube was acquired by Google for $1.6 billion in October 2006. At the time of the acquisition, Google had about 50 million users worldwide, a purchase price amounting to about $32 a user. One million videos are dished up by YouTube daily. There are many YouTube videos uploaded each day that are socially and otherwise utterly useless, if not dysfunctional. What is the importance of "flipping butter to the ceiling," to see if the butter sticks or not or what is the redeeming social value of the instructional video on how to pick locks by the Boston Lockpick Society (Open Organization of Lockpickers)? On the other hand, there are many videos that are funny and entertaining of course as well as there are videos that are indeed informative, helpful and socially relevant, if not even taking on a democratization role within society. One citizen produced video depicting the handling of a suspect by Los Angeles police on a Hollywood street on August 11, 2006 yielded over 200,000 views. Under the search term *police brutality* one finds over 500 amateur videos, not just from the U.S. but also Egypt and Hungary. Videos are being used as evidence in police reviews.

The fundamental question that many businesses are asking themselves today is: Could there be a role for business on YouTube, MySpace or Second Life? One wonders if the following YouTube scenario is all that far-fetched:

> Imagine that a person is experiencing a leaking faucet at home and would like to fix it. He chooses not to call a plumber and tries to do this himself. He searches on YouTube and finds a video describing in detail how to repair his leaking faucet as well as which tools and parts are needed. Would this person be

willing to pay $5, $3, $1 or 50 Cents for downloading this video? Or would the downloading be free, but the video would be produced and sponsored by Home Depot or OBI, respective hardware store chains in the United States or Germany? Or would the downloading be free and a brief message appears that all the parts and tools needed are available at Home Depot or OBI and, if you feel you cannot do the repair yourself, here is a toll-free national number to call to make an appointment for a Home Depot or OBI repairperson?

How can business reach these potential customers? There is a fine line when approaching these mostly younger people. Blatant advertising will not work. Many teenagers are likely to be fickle and could potentially switch to another social networking site at a moment's notice, if their friends were likely to do the same. The underlying technology platform is not proprietary and could be reconstructed elsewhere with relative ease.

How to Reach and Connect with Web 2.0 Customers: What is a Business to Do?

Throughout the economy these Web 2.0 developments are creating new modes of connecting, transaction, innovation and production. Google has embraced these developments and has become a digital conglomerate with a capitalization of $150 billion by entering not just the media industry, but retail, software, networking, telephony, payment systems, hardware and soon television. The underlying technologies also enable forms of mass collaboration to design, conceive and distribute products in innovative ways.

Individuals post blogs and other messages on the Internet and this has become an increasingly popular way for sharing information among people about products. In turn, they offer companies a treasure of voluntary and non-intrusive consumer feedback without having to administer cumbersome, expensive and slow surveys. Approximately 1.4 million Internet blog messages were posted each day in March 2007, up from 600,000 a day 2 years ago, according to Technorati (Patrick, 2007).

Yes despite these intriguing developments, what is a company to do, if it wants to embrace Web 2.0 developments? Visitors to video-sharing Web sites, e.g., have demonstrated that they watch almost anything, from flipping butter to the ceiling, cats chasing mice and people singing in the shower. This may be fine and also funny, but would people tune in to see and hear things about Coca-Cola or Hellmann's mayonnaise? Although the author cannot provide generalized prescriptions to answer these questions, the following deliberations and examples may suggest approaches and some solutions.

The Coca-Cola Company created a cell phone-only virtual teenager hangout like MySpace and Facebook in the U.S. and China to attract more young people to its soda and flavored drinks (Coca-Cola Sets up Social Web Site for Teens to Access via Cellphones, 2007). This is just one example of companies eyeing the success of teen social sites, such as News Corp.'s MySpace, and here Coca-Cola created on a mobile phone network under its Sprite brand on June 22, 2007 where members can set up profiles, post pictures and meet new friends. A somewhat parallel effort in China was started during the week of June 4, 2007 and the company is looking at markets in such regions as Latin America. MySpace is available on some mobile phones, but most of its nearly 67 million monthly unique visitors in the U.S. access the site on computers. Cellphone use has been hampered by relatively small screens. Coca-Cola hopes to overcome this limitation by tailoring the format of the service and by offering free content to promote Sprite through free music and video clips to visitors who type in a number found under bottled lids.

Unilever, the manufacturer of Hellmann's mayonnaise launched on Yahoo's Food section an entertainment and video series on June 28, 2007 intended to subtly promote this condiment. The series is part of a multimillion dollar marketing and advertising campaign Unilever started in April 2007 to promote the freshness of ingredients in Hellmann's mayonnaise. The series is entitled, "In Search of Real Food," scheduled for 12 weeks and starred by David Lieberman, chef and host of the popular Food Network television show. Mr. Lieberman will travel throughout the country looking for interesting recipes. In some cases these recipes will call for Hellmann's mayonnaise (Yahoo Food Section, 2007).

The Hellmann case is a fitting example in terms of Web 2.0 applications. The generation of entertainment television shows, movies and videos to subtly advertise and promote a product has enjoyed increasing popularity and as a marketing technique is labeled "branded entertainment". They enable advertisers to reach consumers who deliberately avoid traditional advertising. No doubt, this technique is challenging in that if the advertising message is too pushy and overt, these potential consumers might leave the channel.

Yet the Hellmann show is light on subtlety. One notices, e.g., that the phrase *Real Food* in the program's title is identical to Hellmann's advertising slogan. Moreover, Hellmann's logo also appears on Yahoo's Food Web page alongside videos. In addition, the Hellmann product itself appears occasionally in actual cooking scenes.

After various difficulties of attempting to air the show on the Food Network (Vranica, 2007), Hellmann turned to the Web, an effort that is increasingly seen by advertisers as an alternative distribution network for programs. Advertisers and marketers have realized that content for broadband (or the Web) costs significantly less than television productions and it enables them to distribute the show to a much broader audience. Access to Yahoo's portal and traffic is guaranteed by Hellmann linking up with Yahoo and can thus capitalize on that portal's audience. Yahoo Food, just about one year old, attracted 4.3 million people in May 2007, making the site the fifth largest food Web site in the U.S. according to comScore (Shields, 2007).

Advertisers and marketers producing content for the Web are more and more linking with a portal rather than creating their own respective sites. This suggests a recognition that drawing traffic to a stand-alone site can be demanding and challenging. Beer producer Anheuser-Busch was disappointed with the numbers of users visiting its recently launched entertainment Web site Bud.TV. Yet when Procter & Gamble started Capessa, a Web site for women to discuss topics such as parenting, it joined with Yahoo's health section. Portals just like Yahoo can enjoy deals with advertisers that deliver access to well-produced content but also assured advertising revenue. The latter should be especially attractive to Yahoo, as the company is facing and struggling with considerable competition from Google and similar competitors. Unilever is said to have committed between $1 and $2 million in advertisements on Yahoo to promote the "Real Food" show. Moreover, Hellmann — spending about $30 million on advertising space and time in 2006, according to TNS Media Intelligence — will refer to the show in print advertisement and on jar caps, which, in turn, should direct and drive consumers to Yahoo Food (Vranica, 2007).

Online Shopping Communities

Increasingly retailers and designers (including Nordstrom, Gap, Lisa Klein, Ron Herman and online discounter Bluefly.com) are trying to tap into "social-shopping" sites where ardent shoppers gather to chat and exchange ideas. Social shopping sites give shopaholics the opportunity to gather and swap ideas about choices, prices, looks, quality and the like. Among these sites enabling such shopping chatter, many barely 1-year old and untainted by retailers pushing or nudging the user into liking or buying anything, are Glimpse.com, Kaboodle.com, Meosphere.com, Shopstyle.com, Stylehive.com, Stylediary.net and Thisnext.com. Table 19.2 shows various features and capabilities these sites offer and that most of the sites do not (yet?) give retailers the opportunity to pay for prominent placement.

For many users these sites have been perceived as a true and rich source of creativity and support. The essential feature of a social networking site is exhibited when the site offers the highly desirable and handy feature to "follow" a fellow shopper whose style or person, maybe even a celebrity, is admired by the focal shopper. Being associated with, linked to or a "friendster" of such leading shoppers and trend setters can have considerable appeal not only to the user/shopper, but to retailers as well. This gives retailers the potential to engage in a dialogue with these social shopping communities. Whenever the shopper raves about the dress she just purchased, the linked fellow shopper receives an alert offering this shopper the opportunity to check out this latest acquisition. Embedded in this feature is the capability to launch products, to initiate trends, new styles, etc., a feature that potentially can be carried out subtly and without intruding on the delicate sensitivities with regard to reaching the potential shop through other, more traditional and intrusive forms of marketing and advertising. Unquestionably, the retailer's presence blurs the line between sheer information shopping chats and having a retailer push a particular item. Here again we encounter the delicate demarcation line between plain old advertising and independent social shopping chats, as social shopping is only appealing if people perceive the site they are using to have legitimacy. Thus the decision to offer retailers a paid presence of social shopping sites is a complicated, nested and delicate decision. Not all of these sites are likely to survive in the long run, as some of these efforts and features may fizzle with shoppers.

Table 19.2: Social shopping sites: Web 2.0 features and user features.

Website name	Paid retailer presence	User features
Climpse.com	No	Facebook users can create, upload and share shopping lists of products, including professionally shot pictures and information, from over 100 retailers and brands.
Kaboodle.com	No	Users can discover new things from people with similar taste and style; recommend, share, discover and discuss favorite products and stores; create wish lists and shopping lists.
Meosphere.com	No	Users check lists (over 2500) related to topics ranging from cars they have owned to former hairstyles to countries they have visited. When the answers from these lists are compiled, a mesosphere is created (emphasis on "me") which then can be shared.
Shopstyle.com	Yes	Users can create "stylebook" pages featuring items they desire and covet, recently purchased and exchange comments and recommendations on products.
Stylehive.com	Yes	Users can create "hives", i.e., pages, lists, featuring items they like; the site allows users to "follow" a shopper whose style they like and receive alerts whenever he/she adds new products on his/her respective page.
Stylediary.net	No	Users mostly post photos of themselves wearing their favorite outfits, dresses and items form their own wardrobe.
Thisnext.com	No	Users recommend or pan clothing, outfits, accessories or home items on pages they create.

Note: Social shopping sites typically receive about 5% of each purchase occurring as a result of a click-through from the site.

Implementing Web 2.0 and the Bottom Line: What Some Businesses are Doing

Web 2.0 has been relabeled within the information systems (IS) and information technology (IT) implementation world as Enterprise 2.0, unfortunately yet another trendy term in spite of the already prevailing ambiguousness of Web 2.0. No one in the industry seems to like this label and some suggest that one should find a better name. Yet there seems to be real meaning behind the 2.0 tag, giving business people and consultants a way to talk about the kind of collaboration and information sharing they will have to embrace. Most likely there will be a future point in time when Enterprise 2.0 will lose its meaning entirely similar to e-business when Internet commerce became less of an innovation and was absorbed as standard fare and folded into several functional organization areas.

Various surveys by McKinsey and Company (2007), *Information Week* (Hoover, 2007), CIO INSIGHT (2006) (see Table 19.1) and others show that more than half of the participating firms are either skeptical about tools such as blogs, wikis and online social networks or they are rather reluctant of adopting them. "Web 2.0 creep" in the form of real-time demands and the bursty nature of the latest collaboration and social networking software are frequently identified as problem children by IT and IS managers. Yet others question the role of social networking in the workplace and its value to the bottom line, even though they acknowledge and do not deny the popularity of social networking. Cisco CEO John Chambers famously quipped when stating that Web 2.0 software, such as blogs, chat, Web video and other tools, have "been a way that people kind of communicated in spite of the IT department" inside large organizations. "Now the IT department has to lead (Hochmuth, 2007, p. 1)."

More than half of the companies do not use blogs at all, while 41% do not use wikis. More than 20% make these tools available, but they are not much used (Hoover, 2007, p. 40). Following are a few selective experiences and Web 2.0/ Enterprise 2.0 applications that companies have experienced:

- *Boeing*: Web 2.0, collaboration, etc. have been strongly embraced since 2000. LabNet, a subset of the larger corporate IT/network group, connects over 700 of the company's laboratories worldwide using an array of real-time technologies: VoIP, instant messaging (IM), real-time video and digital whiteboarding are some of the tools engineers use to collaborate. An example application is testing Boeing's 787 aircraft, involving a wind tunnel facility in England, streaming video, real-time telemetry, voice and two-way text chat to Boeing sites in Seattle and elsewhere. The challenge is said to be the tuning of the network to deliver real-time voice, video and data to the point where users feel comfortable with the IT and are more productive using it. Often this involves wringing those last tenths of a second of delay out of the environment and doing so in real time (Hochmuth, 2007, pp. 1, 41).
- *Procter & Gamble*: At P&G, the Web 2.0 emphasis is on speed: the enablement of effective collaboration is being compared to adding a sixth gear to a race car. In order to accomplish this, the 140,000 employee company is using Microsoft SharePoint and Office Communicator while adopting blogging and video

conferencing in critical niche roles. P&G seeks to make it easier for employees to connect to each other and to outsiders and the effort will be measured to the extent to which the undertaking helps to get smart products to shelves faster in a world where competition gets tougher each day and where differences in minutes count (Hoover, 2007, pp. 33–34).

- *DuPont*: DuPont examines the productivity value of Web 2.0 technology where the network team is being challenged by taking on new roles beyond just managing LAN ports, QoS and SLA. It is now being asked to build social networks to solve business problems that, in turn, transform businesses. While doing all of this, the team is expected to reduce costs. Younger people may enjoy collaboration software and tools, but the bottom line payback of such technology is significantly more important than any feel-good factor the technology may deliver. It is nearly impossible to sell a project migrating 60,000 employees based on the soft benefits associated with the effort. Upper management expects and requires demonstrable savings directly linked to the solution (Hochmuth, 2007, p. 41).
- *Wells Fargo*: This bank is using blogs to provide executives with an informal channel for employee and customer discussions and RSS feeds funnel news into a CRM system (Hoover, 2007, p. 34). The company's effort to build a presence inside Second Life called Stagecoach Island, designed to attract young people involved with the brand and learn about personal finance, had merely 11 people signed in on a July 2007 afternoon.
- *T. Rowe Price*: This financial services company embraces numerous Web 2.0 applications, from wikis to blogs, widespread use of IM and chat applications. Part of its Web 2.0 initiatives is the Confluence enterprise wiki software enabling users to add searchable tags and comments to the library of documentation and policies. This platform lets 1500 call center employees shave off 2 min from customer calls. Content in wiki-based systems can be changed in 30 min as opposed to 24 h in the past. Moreover, the company will expand the platform to include RSS aggregation, persistent IM and blogging features inside the fabric of the platform. T. Row Price is carefully monitoring the growth of XML-based traffic, RSS streams and IM (Hochmuth, 2007, p. 41).
- *Motorola*: This company has 3900 active blogs, 3300 separate wikis, 3600 "project workspaces," and 12 million daily instant messages in addition to enormous e-mail's use. This array of information channels is organized into the OpenText's knowledge management platform. It contains some 16 million documents and is getting bigger by 100 Gbytes a day. It is accessible via mobile devices and much of this information can be retrieved outside of the firewall as well (Hoover, 2007, p. 39).
- *Disney*: This company, an early adopter of virtual worlds like Second Life, built a virtual world for would-be Disneyland visitors with its Virtual Magic Kingdom. This is a community where people can tour and play games within a digital mockup of Disneyland and Walt Disney World's Magic Kingdom. Visitors can talk with one another as well as to employees Disney hired to work as virtual tour guides in the system. Disney reports 2.2 million users having signed up but is unwilling to reveal how many people are using the system on a daily basis (Hoover, 2007, p. 40). When compared to Wells Fargo's experience with Stagecoach Island

Table 19.3: Which tools are very useful?

Technology/application	Respondents (%)
Instant messaging	69
Collaborative content tools	61
Integrated search tools	56
Unified communications	49
Wikis	47
Mashups	43
Ajax-powered Web portals	39
RSS feeds	38
Blogs with partners or customers	31
Presence awareness	31
Business social networks	30
Click-to-call communication	27
Blogs among employees	26

Note: Based on a 1–5 scale where 4 and 5 are very useful. Survey based on 250 business technology professionals.
Source: Hoover (February 26, 2007).

mentioned above, this suggests that indeed few companies have the impressive Disney-like power to attract visitors to their respective virtual worlds.

Information Week conducted a survey of 250 business technology professionals (Hoover, 2007) to find out which Enterprise 2.0 tools and applications are considered useful. The results are presented in Table 19.3 below.

Aside from providing employees with the right tools for more effective and efficient communication (see Table 19.3), the IT/IS department must find a way to integrate and pull all of these technologies and applications together into a coherent whole. In that sense Enterprise 2.0 clearly goes beyond the mix of Web 2.0-inspired technologies by providing truly unified communications. Some have predicted that identity services, i.e., directories that recognize and know who an individual is, what access rights he/she has and where the person is located, will emerge as the unifying factor across all Enterprise 2.0 technologies. This, in turn, will permit employees to connect when and how they want to. Integrating these technologies with legacy systems is not an easy task and has been mentioned by more than half of the companies interviewed in the *Information Week* survey (Hoover, 2007). Lastly, Enterprise 2.0 can be challenging to manage and support, particularly as most IT/IS departments do not have much experience with these new tools.

Summary and Conclusion

This chapter explored various Web 2.0 developments. The author defined Web 2.0, views this development as a paradigm shift and examined how the vast amount and huge variety of information on the Web is getting organized, sorted, ordered, tagged and classified. The nature and role of social networking sites was addressed, especially asking how businesses might find a role here. Moreover, the author asked how one might reach and connect with Web 2.0 customers and what strategy businesses might pursue. Online shopping communities were explored and some opportunities for retailers were identified. Lastly, questions and issues were raised with regard to the implementation of Web 2.0 and the bottom line, i.e., an attempt to see what some businesses are doing in this context and how they embrace Web 2.0 technologies and applications.

When reflecting on these Web 2.0 developments and the issues addressed here, the author believes that what we observe is not the emergence of a new theory or fundamental concept within a theory, but it may well be described as a shift in how we view the Web. This paradigm shift forces us to take a new look recognizing innovative opportunities and challenges while it crosses a number of dimensions, including media, the Web, organizations, economics, society and culture.

Today the World Wide Web no longer serves the mere acquisition of information or for the sheer purpose of communication. Users have taken on the role of being the producer of their own content. Moreover, users tend to react interactively to the content produced by other users. Their participation in social networks, formed *via* Web 2.0 applications, has become common practice. Users leave MySpace and Facebook windows open all day such that they may receive alerts from these and other sites. More than 80 percent of the time U.S. adults spend on the Internet, they are involved in another activity at the same time.

Today Internet users are more active and longer online and their use behavior is often changing from that of a consumer to a producer of information. They discuss, debate and argue on Weblogs and distribute information faster, more comprehensively and more personalized *via* the RSS format than *via* the classical and traditional media from the past. Users are networked millionfold *via* online offers such as Windows Life Spaces with such services as mail, spaces, instant messaging or search as expressions of Web 2.0 in order to exchange pictures, videos and text. Services offered within the Web 2.0 framework are now part of the evolutionary history of the World Wide Web. This implies that if a firm today wants to be active on the Internet, it has no choice but to find its appropriate role *via* Web 2.0. Most major firms, including Adidas, BMW, IBM, Google and many others, are positioning themselves to find their strategic place and fit within these developments.

In some ways, we may argue that this is just another beginning as the waves of IT cost performance inexorably continue. This is expected to impact interactive applications in the living room and the office alike, and will find parallel manifestations in the mobile communications area, resulting in many subsequent development and evolutionary stages.

These advances imply that those who choose to participate and help shape the Internet, have no choice but to keep in step with these developments. The challenges for firms and users will be to blend, merge and consolidate these developments into an integrated and comprehensive concept such that users enjoy a best possible experience.

Acknowledgments

The author gratefully acknowledges the comments and suggestions received from Mr. Martin Jetter, General Manager and Chairman of the Board, IBM Germany GmbH; Professor Robert I. Benjamin and Ms. Johanna L. H. Birkland, both with Syracuse University, Syracuse, NY.

References

Anderson, C. (2006). *The long tail*. New York, NY: Hyperion.

Benkler, Y. (2006). *The wealth of networks: How social production transforms markets and freedom*. New Haven, CT: Yale University Press.

CIO INSIGHT. (November, 2006). What role will Web 2.0 technologies play in business? *CIO INSIGHT*, p. 20.

Coca-Cola sets up social Web site for teens to access via cellphones. (2007). *The Wall Street Journal*, June 8–10, *250*, 7.

Compete, Inc. (2007). Attention 200 (A Report). Boston, MA: Compete, Inc.

Hochmuth, P. (2007, May 28). Web 2.0 apps exact a toll on enterprises. *Network World*, p. 1, 41.

Hoover, J. N. (2007, February 26). Enterprise 2.0. *InformationWeek*, pp. 23–34, 38–42.

Internet World Stats. (2007). http://www.internetworldstats.com/stats.htm, last accessed on August 26, 2007.

Jenkins, H. (2006). *Convergence culture: Where old and new media collide*. New York: New York University Press.

Kuhn, T. S. (1962). *The structure of scientific revolution* (3rd ed.). Chicago: University of Chicago Press.

Malone, T. W. (2004). *The future of work*. Boston, MA: Harvard Business School Press.

McKinsey & Company. (2007). How businesses are using Web 2.0: A McKinsey Global Survey. New York, March 2007.

O'Reilly, T. (2007). What is Web 2.0? http://oreillynet.com/pub/a/oreilly/tim/news/2005/09/30/what-is-web-20.html?page=2, last accessed on August 26, 2007.

Patrick, A. O. (2007, May 28). Tapping into customers' online chatter. *The Wall Street Journal*, *250*, B3.

Shields, M. (2007). Yahoo, Hellmann's launch entertainment series. *Mediaweek*, June 27-007 (http://www.mediaweek.com/mw/news/recent_display.jsp?vnu_content_id=1003604398, last accessed on August 26, 2007).

Smith, D. M. (2006). Web 2.0: Structuring the discussion. *Gartner Research*, 2006.

Social Networking Sites. (2006). *PC Today*, November, 2006, p. 8.

The Future of Television. (2007, February 10). What's on next? *The Economist*, p. 65.

Vranica, S. (2007, June 27). Hellmann's targets yahoo for its spread. *The Wall Street Journal*, *250*, B4.

Weinberger, D. (2007). *Everything is miscellaneous: The power of the new digital disorder*. New York, NY: Times Books.

Wigand, R. T. (2006). The long road toward evolving Internet business models: Long-tail economics, mass participation and social value networks. Presentation to the Seminar, "*Business Model Innovation: Trapped between Theory and Practice*," November 27, 2006, Technical University Delft, Delft, The Netherlands, 2006.

Yahoo Food Section. (2007). http://food.yahoo.com/realfood, last accessed on August 26, 2007.

Chapter 20

Real Business in Virtual Worlds: First Insights

Robert Slagter, Erwin Fielt and Wil Janssen

ABSTRACT

Virtual worlds, such as Second Life and Entropia, have attracted enormous attention in the last few months. Many people try them, a limited number stays, and numerous organizations start business there. However, there is little understanding of what business in virtual worlds should be. In this chapter we identify different business models in virtual worlds, both "pure virtuals" (analogously to pure plays on the internet) as well as "inter-reality models" combining presence in virtual worlds and other forms of economic activity. Moreover, we give an outlook of prerequisites for sustainable business and services in virtual worlds.

Virtual Worlds

A virtual world is a computer-based simulated environment intended for its users to inhabit and interact *via* avatars. Typically, virtual worlds are represented as a 3-D environment similar to the real world where multiple people can log in and, *via* their avatars, perform actions and communicate. Examples of virtual worlds that currently attract a lot of attention are Second Life, Active Worlds, Entropia Universe, and There. Although sometimes referred to as massive multiplayer games, these worlds lack an important ingredient of games: there is no defined purpose, no levels, no winning or losing; instead, these worlds form a place where people can interact in a 3-D environment, communicate, and for instance create and sell virtual objects.

The current examples of virtual worlds can be considered early experiments with 3-D internet. The internet evolved from a text-only environment, *via* text and images to a multimedia 2-D environment where users can create, share, and consume content — referred to as Web 2.0 (O'Reilly, 2005). Extrapolating this trend, we see the 3-D internet as the logical successor: the internet is more and more becoming a social place that resembles the real world, where people can interact, create, and share virtual objects and go through experiences (Benkler, 2006; Lessig, 2003;

Information Management: Setting the Scene
Copyright © 2007 by Elsevier Ltd.
All rights of reproduction in any form reserved.
ISBN: 978-0-08-046326-1

Pine & Gilmore, 1999). All this in 3-D with a rich user interface, similar to game environments.

As virtual worlds become populated places where people spend a considerable amount of time, they also become more interesting for organizations. Second Life, for instance, was populated by more than 5.6 million inhabitants by mid-April 2007, and experienced a steady growth of population of more than 30% per month for the last 9 months. From these, about 10% is active, spending more than 18 million hours per month Second Life (Second Life, 2007a). By leveraging the social aspect, organizations can use virtual worlds not only as a 3-D extension of their website, but also a place where they can interact with their customers, where customers can interact with each other and, for instance, a place where they can recruit new employees.

The question now arises what type of activity takes place in virtual worlds, how this relates to business in the real world, and what types of business strategies are possible regarding virtual worlds. In other words: what are current business models in virtual worlds and to what extent do they differ from well-known (2-D) internet business models (Magretta, 2002; Weill & Vitale, 2001)? Around the turn of the century, there was a lot of attention in research on new internet-based business models (Pateli & Giaglis, 2003; Sarkar, Butler, & Steinfield, 1995; Seddon & Lewis, 2003; Timmers, 1998). In later work, the relation between the internet channel and physical channels in business models was discussed, emphasizing sources of synergy between the two (see e.g., Preissl, Bouwman, & Steinfield, 2004; Steinfield, 2002).

In this chapter we investigate current business models in virtual worlds, or 3-D internet, and we come up with a preliminary classification. We illustrate this with early evidence from, primarily, Second Life. We conclude with a number of first insights on the sustainability of the business models presented, based on a comparison with current business models. The research was done in two ways: first of all, an extensive study of current literature and background of virtual worlds, especially Second Life, was done. Thereafter, we conducted a number of interviews within Second Life, specifically questioning companies on their strategies in Second Life and effects. These interviews were complemented by interviews with a limited number of experts and participants in the real world. Next to this, the authors explored Second Life by being active users and visiting businesses there in the last year.

What do People do in Virtual Worlds?

In order for companies to decide on their strategy regarding virtual worlds, it is important to understand who are the people inhabiting these worlds and what do they do there. Currently, becoming an inhabitant of a 3-D virtual world involves a learning process in which you have to learn how to navigate, communicate, act, and have to understand the local norms. As such, there is a considerable threshold for new users. Looking at the statistics provided by Linden Lab (Second Life, 2007b), we see that the Second Life population consists of about the same numbers of males and females. In Second Life, 39% of the people is between 25 and 34-years old, and only

27% under 25; teenagers are not included in these metrics: they reside in a separate teen grid. The users mostly originate from the US (31.2%), France (12.7%), Germany (10.5%), the United Kingdom (8.1%), and The Netherlands (6.6%). Research by De Nood and Attema (2006) under the Dutch population in Second Life shows that the vast majority of these inhabitants has a high education (higher vocational education, university, or PhD) and is frequently working in the creative sector or in the information technology sector. As motives for their presence in Second Life a wide range of reasons are mentioned; the most frequently mentioned ones are: fun, making friends, becoming inspired, doing things one cannot do in real life, learning, and as a pastime. Notably, shopping was not highly ranked in this list. So, organizations should be aware that users are typically looking for *experiences* and adjust their online strategies to that.

It is interesting to see that the behavior of people in virtual environments appears not to be very different from what they do in real life. We expect that the same human motivators that steer our actions in real life determine our actions in virtual worlds. People seem to visit virtual worlds for the same reasons why they live in a city:

• It provides easy access to friends, teachers, and the opposite sex.
• It provides easy access to goods, services, and entertainment.
• Like in a big city you will find brilliance and sleaze.
• There is good paying, interesting work to be done there.

We want to ensure our place as a live node on the network, we feel alive when we are connected. To be busy and to be connected is to be alive. Being present in virtual worlds allows us to meet friends, stay on top of trends and scan for new opportunities.

Business Models in Virtual Worlds

In 2-D internet, a distinction is often made between "pure play" internet companies and "click and mortar" companies that combine a physical presence with a virtual presence (e.g., Steinfield, 2002). Also, some applications of the internet emphasize external use (business-to-consumer/business) while others emphasize internal use by companies (business-to-employer). We take these two dimensions also as a starting point for 3-D internet or virtual worlds (Figure 20.1). We can position the strategies (business models) of organizations within Second Life as either focusing on Second Life itself or as supporting their real life activities. This dimension is indicated along the x-axis of Figure 20.1. Along the other axis are the main purposes why organizations are present in Second Life. This ranges from pure commerce, *via* customer interaction, to using Second Life as an environment for collaboration and simulation. Note that these are not the business models of virtual world providers, such as Linden Labs. Their business model is relatively straightforward, based on subscription fees, fees for the use of virtual land, fees for currency exchange, and uploads of external data. Notably, their business models are not based on advertisements.

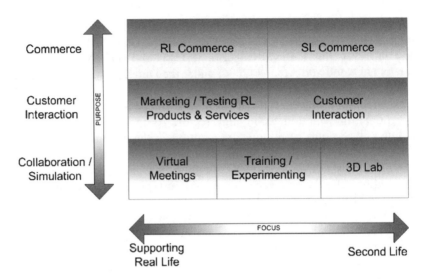

Figure 20.1: Business model classification for virtual worlds.

The Intellectual Property Right (IPR) model that is applied in Second Life is the reason for the existence of business models *enclosed* in Second Life. Users retain full intellectual property protection for the digital content they create in Second Life, including avatar characters, clothing, scripts, textures, objects, and designs. This right is enforceable and applicable both in Second Life (referred to as "in-world") and in real life, both for nonprofit and commercial ventures. So, if you create a virtual object, you own it — and you can for instance sell it for real money outside the Second Life environment. As a result, the Second Life world is entirely build and owned by its inhabitants. This IPR model not only stimulates users to invest time and money in their virtual creations, it also allows companies to create and sell virtual products and services for real currency. It is interesting to note that this model was enforced by Second Life users in winter 2003, protesting against Linden taxation activities (Rymaszewski et al., 2006). Other virtual environments, such as World of Warcraft, do not have such an IPR model and therefore attract less commercial ventures.

Each of the purposes along the *y*-axis can be focused on real life or on Second Life. For instance, commerce in Second Life can both be aimed at selling real-life products and services and aimed at selling services or virtual objects within Second Life. Customer interaction within Second Life can be a goal in itself, or it can be applied for marketing, or testing of real-life products and services together with potential customers. Finally, using Second Life as an environment for collaboration and simulation may be done by supporting real life meetings, by training people, or experimenting with designs, to using it as a 3-D simulation environment.

In the top-right corner we have Second Life-commerce models: business completely within the virtual world, albeit that the actual revenues do flow to the real world; these are so-called "pure virtuals." When combining virtual worlds and normal business, we get a situation comparable to that of the normal internet business: inter-reality models.

Example of a pure virtual: Electric Sheep

Electric Sheep is an example of a pure virtual. They build a virtual presence (buildings, avatars, functionality) for other organizations in Second Life and make a profit out of that. Electric Sheep, for example, developed the Reuters headquarters in Second Life and they constructed the virtual Starwood Hotels.

In general, many of the organizations we interviewed indicated that they see Second Life as an example of a 3-D internet environment. As they assume, such 3-D social environments will become more important in the future, they see this as a good moment to gain experience with virtual worlds, 3-D internet, and how this can provide real benefit for their organizations. While some organizations use Second Life as a showroom for their real-life products and services, others link their real-life products to their virtual products.

Example or supporting real-life commerce: Dell

Dell has created an environment in Second Life where (potential) customers can obtain information about their products and even configure their own laptop on a virtual drawing board. The resulting laptop can then be ordered for delivery to your home. Additionally, your avatar obtains a virtual version of the laptop. Dell explicitly also aims at new users of Second Life and even provides a training garden to learn the basic skills of an avatar.

Just like Dell, Adidas aims at strengthening its normal business by a presence in Second Life. Adidas sells sneakers for avatars that can be ordered in real-life as well. Another example of blending the real world and virtual worlds is American Apparel: they offer customers a 15% discount in their real-life boutiques, after buying virtual merchandise. Companies like SLexchange and SLboutique can be found in the top right corner of Figure 20.1: they offer a marketplace where people can buy and sell virtual objects. A pure virtual strategy.

Companies such as ABN AMRO and Philips do not have a direct relation with normal sales, but use Second Life primarily as a means to have a different style of interaction with (potential) customers or employees: they are positioned in the middle row in Figure 20.1.

Example of supporting customer interaction: ABN AMRO

ABN AMRO was the first European bank in Second Life. They have created an environment where (potential) customers can get some information about their products, where they host virtual seminars, for instance around investing in stocks and shares, and where they offer an additional means of communication for their "young professional" customers. Interestingly, they do not offer banking products in the virtual environment. This also has to do with the liability aspect.

ABN AMRO uses an avatar hostess, Amber Jung, to welcome new visitors and to help them find their way on the island. She can also make sure customers are contacted about questions they may have that she cannot answer directly. ABN AMRO uses a group of people to control this avatar by turns.

Yet another approach is taken by organizations that use Second Life primarily as a communication and simulation environment: these organizations can be found in the bottom row of Figure 20.1. Starwood hotels is a good example of this (see the following box). A completely different strategy has been taken by Xerox. They developed a number of closed sites in Second Life that are used for internal (Xerox) meetings and have report a positive experience in this. This business strategy aims at supporting the "real" Xerox organization only, and has no relation with Second Life as an open community.

Example of a 3-D lab: Starwood hotels
Starwoord hotels uses Second Life as an environment to experiment with new hotel designs. They construct a virtual version of a hotel and organize sessions with avatars to obtain feedback, before the real hotel is constructed. This way, they can for instance test whether customers will be able to find their way in the hotel and whether the lay out of the rooms matches the customers' demands. The virtual environment allows Starwood hotels for instance to switch between alternative lobby designs and observe the behavior of the virtual visitors.

In Figure 20.2 we positioned the primary strategies of a number of companies in the framework.

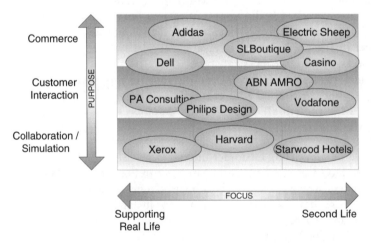

Figure 20.2: Primary company strategies in Second Life.

Discussion and Conclusion

Generally speaking, we see initial evidence of success in two areas: real-life collaboration, and Second Life commerce. As a collaborative toolset, Second Life gives an enhanced experience: it is richer than voice conferencing, as avatars allow one to provide additional cues and help focus attention, without the intrusiveness of video conferencing. Also, it is easy to give presentations and show videos. Quite a few tools are becoming available in Second Life, but it is still cumbersome to do so.

Second Life commerce is becoming a success. The flow of money within Second Life is growing, and quite a few individuals and smaller companies have serious turnover through Second Life commerce: buying and selling land, creating and selling virtual content (fashion, real-estate), or helping others to move into Second Life. Given the overall turnover of Second Life, it is clear that success is relative: it is not a breeding ground for new multimillion multinationals. In April 2007, there were 810 users that had a positive flow of more than $1000 into their accounts, of which 139 earned more than $5000 (all in USD). In September 2006, these numbers were 239 and 37, respectively (Second Life, 2007b). What is more substantial is the turnover that some Second Life developers make in real dollars. For example, Electric Sheep gets between $10,000 and $200,000 for developing an average Second Life presence (Business Week, 2006).

Many strategies take a possible synergy between Second Life and real world commerce or customer interaction as a starting point. In this area, the situation is comparable to the early days of the World Wide Web, in the nineties of the previous century. Organizations were struggling with their web presence. Should it be purely informative, or also transactional? What people visit the World Wide Web, and what do they seek? Virtual worlds such as Second Life are forms of 3-D internet, and the question arises whether or not the lessons learned from the 2-D internet can be transferred to the 3-D internet. It is clear that early adopters, such as ABN AMRO and Randstad, will profit substantially from the news triggered by their presence. This advantage is temporary. After this first wave, a clearer understanding of what people do in Second Life, beyond leisure within the virtual environment, should be available.

We compare the strategies of inter-reality models with the framework of Steinfield (2002) targeted at synergy between physical and virtual, 2-D channels. Steinfield identifies a number of sources of synergy: infrastructure, operations, marketing, and customers. Up till now customers are the main synergy source with virtual business leveraging the customer relationships of the traditional business and/or the traditional business gaining access to new customers *via* the virtual business. Synergy can result in benefits with respect to cost savings, value-added services, trust, or market extension. It is too soon to see cost savings, albeit that the investments in virtual worlds are relatively low. Costs can be saved when virtual worlds, to some extent, replaces other, more expensive channels. Value added services are starting to develop in the virtual world in the area of customer participation in product development and viral marketing. The virtual business can benefit from the established trust in the traditional business, such as the brand name. However, a synergy strategy is not without danger. For example, the presence of a Dutch municipality (Zoetermeer) in Second Life lead to substantial public indignation.

Larger organizations that think of moving to virtual worlds should have limited expectations with respect to sales. The revenues are still limited. Virtual worlds provide an interesting field of experimentation to learn about new forms of inter-action with customers. Here, the same lessons hold as for 2-D internet: the experience should add value, reflect topical matters, and should allow to interact with the organ-ization representatives (as virtual world inhabitants, not by e-mail). An additional complexity is that different virtual worlds are not interoperable. Think of it as an internet divided in several disjoint subnets that cannot interact or share resources. This leads to fragmentation of attention and of markets.

If training and simulation are objectives, 3-D worlds provide a compelling environment. At a low cost, they provide an interesting experience. Also for pure virtuals, 3-D internet can provide a sustainable business, delivering in-world services. The scale, however, is limited, and especially interesting for small and medium-sized enterprises (SMEs) that have the knowledge and flexibility to attack niche markets. Once interoperability of virtual worlds appears on the horizon, this will change, but not within the coming 2–3 years.

Acknowledgments

We would like to thank Rogier Brussee for his inspiring analogies about virtual worlds and living in cities.

References

Benkler, Y. (2006). *The wealth of networks*. New Haven, London: Yale University Press. Also available through www.benkler.org

Business Week. (2006). Second Life Lessons. http://www.businessweek.com/innovate/content/oct2006/id20061030_869611.htm

De Nood, D., & Attema, J. (2006). *Second life: Het tweede leven van virtual reality*. The Netherlands: EPN, (in Dutch).

Lessig, L. (2003). *Free culture*. New York: Penguin Press.

Magretta, J. (2002). Why business models matter. *Havard Business Review, May*, 86–91.

O'Reilly, T. (2005). *What is Web 2.0 — Design Patterns and Business Models for the Next Generation of Software*. Retrieved April 27, 2006 from: http://www.oreillynet.com/pub/a/oreilly/tim/news/2005/09/30/what-is-web-20.html

Pateli, A. G., & Giaglis, G. M. (2003). A framework for Understanding and Analysing eBusiness Models, 16th Bled Electronic Commerce Conference eTransformation, Bled, Slovenia.

Pine, J., & Gilmore, J. (1999). *The experience economy*. Boston: Harvard Business School Press.

Preissl, B., Bouwman, H., & Steinfield, C. (Eds.) (2004). *E-Life after the dot com bust*. Heidelberg: Springer.

Rymaszewski, M., Au, W. J., Wallace, M., Winters, C., Ondrejka, C., & Batstone-Cunningham, B. (2006). *Second life: The official guide*. Hoboken, New Jersey: Wiley.

Sarkar, M. B., Butler, B., & Steinfield, C. (1995). Intermediaries and cybermediaries: A continuing role for mediating players in the electronic marketplace. *Journal of Computer-Mediated Communication* [On-line]. Available: http://jcmc.indiana.edu/vol1/issue3/sarkar.html

Second Life. (2007a). May 2007 Key Metrics Published, http://blog.secondlife.com/2007/06/12/may-2007-key-metrics-published/. Visited June 18th 2007.

Second Life. (2007b). Economy Statistics, http://www.secondlife.com/whatis/economy_stats.php. Visited June 1, 2007.

Seddon, P. B., & Lewis, G. P. (2003). Strategy and business models: What's the difference? In: *The proceedings of the 7th Pacific Asia Conference on Information Systems*, Adelaide South Australia, pp. 236–248.

Steinfield, C. (2002). Understanding click and mortar E-commerce approaches: A conceptual framework and research agenda. *Journal of Interactive Advertising*, 2(2).

Timmers, P. (1998). Business models for E-commerce. *Electronic Markets*, 8(2), 3–7 (www.electronicmarkets.org).

Weill, P., & Vitale, M. R. (2001). *Place to space: Migrating to eBusiness models*. Boston, MA: Harvard Business School Press.

SECTION VI:

DESIGNING INFORMATION AND ORGANIZATIONS

It is hard to imagine organizations with no information systems and it is unlikely that information technology could have been developed as it has without the support of organizations that have embraced it. The lion's share of IT expenditures is invested in organizations and in the past few decades information technology has become part of every organization's infrastructure. Organizations and their information systems are inextricably coupled, and to study one without the other would be myopic. The following section includes four chapters that explore the complementary relationship between information and organization and focus on their design.

Dick Boland explores some of the perplexing issues in the design of management control systems that emerge when the familiar boundaries of information and organization are blurred, especially as found in inter-firm relationships that are associated with joint ventures and multiform projects. Next, *Uri Gal, Youngjin Yoo* and *Kalle Lyytinen* continue with the cross-boundary relationship motif and propose a model that outlines the relationships among boundary objects, the information infrastructures within which they are embedded, and the identities of the organizations that use them.

Turning to design of flexible systems, *Dirk Hovorka* and *Matt Germonprez* theorize about the design of tailorable technologies, that is technologies that can be modified in the context of use and be customized to fit with the continuously changing needs of the users. Finally, building on the concept of generative design, *Michel Avital* explores the desirable features of IT-based systems that are conducive to innovative processes and proposes that such systems should be evocative, adaptive and open-ended. Generative design refers to the design considerations in developing systems or platforms that are conducive to one's ability to produce new configurations and possibilities, to reframe the way we see and understand the world and to challenge the normative *status quo*.

Chapter 21

Blurring the Boundaries of Information and Organization: Morphogenesis in Design

Richard J. Boland

ABSTRACT

Information system designers increasingly confront situations that display new mixtures of market and hierarchy in organizational forms, as part of the hybrid structures associated with joint ventures and multi-firm projects. Traditional approaches to information system design are not adequate for these hybrid organizations and may even increase the difficulty of achieving management control, especially in large, multi-firm projects of architecture, engineering and construction. Instead, designers should recognize that there is a blurring of the familiar boundaries of information and organization in such hybrid settings, and incorporate an explicit attempt to reshape the form of organization itself, or morphogenesis, as part of designing its information system. Examples from the building projects of Frank O. Gehry are used to highlight this required expansion of information system design in hybrid, project organizations.

Introduction

In this chapter, I will explore some of the perplexing issues in the design of information systems for controlling emerging forms of hybrid organizations composed of multiple autonomous firms. The types of multi-firm organizations that I will consider here include joint ventures as well as multi-year, multi-firm projects. I will focus my discussion on the problems of designing information and control systems in the type of large, multi-firm projects that we have encountered during our research in the American construction industry.

When architects, engineers, construction managers, construction contractors and myriad consultants come together for a complex, long-term, construction project, a unique hybrid form of organization is created in which management control for each member firm and for the project as a whole are equally important, yet often at odds

Information Management: Setting the Scene
Copyright © 2007 by Elsevier Ltd.
ISBN: 978-0-08-046326-1

with each other. These project organizations are hybrid forms in the sense that they are a mixture of traditional hierarchical firms along with elements of market-based forms of organizing. It may at first seem as if this mixed market/hierarchy aspect of project organizations parallels the decentralized, divisionalized structure adopted by many large firms whose units interact in producing common products. If that were the case, the design of transfer pricing and reward systems in such decentralized firms could serve as a model for the design of information and control systems in project-based hybrid firms. Although there may be a resemblance between the two design problems, the underlying issues for creating a management control system are fundamentally different. In fact, I will argue, the design problems of the mixed market/hierarchy form of project organizations are unique and require morphogenesis, or a change of relational form, in order to design a management control system, whereas decentralized or divisionalized firms do not require morphogenesis. Why morphogenesis is required in designing information systems for multi-firm project organizations and some examples of efforts to create morphogenesis in them that we have observed in our research on the construction industry will be the major focus of my chapter.

As for why morphogenesis, or a change in organizational forms, not just information systems, is necessary in designing for project organizations, my argument centers on the fact that the sequence of mixing market and hierarchy elements that characterizes the project forms of organization differs from the sequence of mixing market and hierarchy in a decentralized single enterprise. The sequence of mixing market and hierarchy makes a fundamental difference between the two. In other words, history matters. Designing an information system for an enterprise that has been decomposed into autonomous units is fundamentally different from designing an information system for a project organization created by bringing separate autonomous enterprises together. The first sequence is a movement from a hierarchy to a market (creating market elements within a pre-existing organization) and the second sequence is a movement from market to hierarchy (creating an organization from pre-existing market elements).

This difference in sequence is all important, and a system-theoretic approach to the problems of decomposition *versus* synthesis is the way I will frame my discussion of it. Simply put, the logic of breaking a system down into component parts (decomposition) is distinct from the logic of putting parts together to form a system (synthesis). Even though, at the end, a similar mix of market and hierarchy may appear to be in place. The diagram of Figure 21.1 portrays the distinction in system-theoretic relations that I will explore in this chapter.

In the first instance, depicted at the top of Figure 21.1, the decomposition takes place in a multi-leveled system that has a history which is "taken for granted" by the information system designers. The history of the system is the history of the firm that serves as supra-system for the decomposition into the mixed market/hierarchy hybrid relations. They, in turn will influence the operating logics of the decentralized operating units. The firm as an historical entity is imbedded in our understanding of this multi-leveled system since it serves as the supra-system that is being decomposed. Our ideas about what the system is, how it came to be, what its missions are, how its

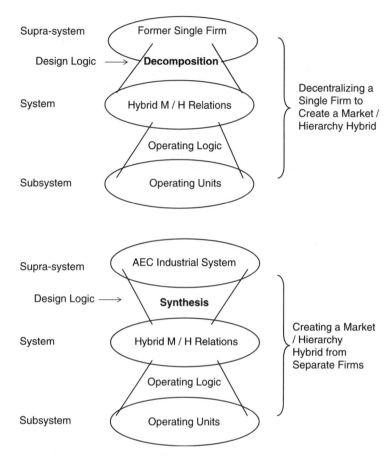

Figure 21.1: Design logic of system decomposition *versus* system synthesis.

cultures operate, why its routines are the way they are, its current situation and trajectory, etc. are all ways in which its history is manifest to us at a given moment in time. Designing its information system takes place within this understanding of the organization system, and although it is not always perfect, that pre-understanding shapes the problem space and the logic of its information design, as reflected in the mix of its market/hierarchy relations.

In the second instance, depicted at the bottom of Figure 21.1, the hybrid organizational form is synthesized from pre-existing, independent elements, which have multiple, diffuse histories, into an industrial supra-system with its own history, not necessarily tied to any coherent logic of operations. The histories that the constituent firms carry with them in the form of work practices, origins, routines, cultures, situations, trajectories, etc. are in a sense "hidden" from the information designers. The logic of synthesis does not take place within their subsystem level of operating units, but instead takes place within the supra-system into which they are being synthesized: in our case, the architecture, engineering and construction industries. The difference in the form of logic could not be more profound. Decomposition employs the logic of a firm as a system to create market/hierarchy relations among subsystems, whereas synthesis uses the logic of a supra-system to create the market/hierarchy relations among pre-existing system level components.

I realize that this is all quite abstract — simple, but abstract — and that is the nature of using system-theoretic constructs. So now, I would like to ground this argument in concrete examples from the hybrid organizational forms found in the American construction industry on large, complex projects. First, I will give a brief overview of the way that architecture, engineering and construction firms come together in order to complete a project. The important point is that these individual firms (hierarchies) come together in a temporary arrangement through a bidding process (market) in order to coordinate their separate operations in designing and constructing a building, bridge or other structure. The way that they come together does not flow from a logic of internal operations, as in the single firm being decomposed, but from the historical, path dependent practices of contracting and risk allocation that happen to be in place in the industry. The structural relations that result from these practices are where an effort at morphogenesis must take place, if an information system is to be effective. In other words, the institutional level of formal and informal contracting and the many practices, routines and communication patterns which are the history of the AEC industry should be subject to conscious redesign as part of establishing an information system that has a chance of helping the project succeed for the participating firms and also succeed in their combined objective of constructing a building.

Traditions Forming a Structured Set of Relations in the AEC Industry

The mix of market/hierarchy forms in large projects in the AEC industry is largely taken for granted by its firms as just being "the way things are". They are traditional practices that have taken shape over decades and in some cases, centuries. AEC companies "know how to go on", in Wittgenstein's sense, because their skillful activity is grounded in the form of life that characterizes their niche in the AEC industry, be it architect, construction manager, contractor, subcontractor or consultant. Bidding and contracting processes, patterns of information exchange and roles of actors in a typical building project are all formally specified or informally implied and understood in standardized contracts that are interdependent and mutually reinforcing. Competitive bidding calls for restricted communications among parties, in order to avoid collusion. Contracting is structured in specific ways in order to distribute risk among the parties, thus further shaping allowable and required communications. Contracts define the scope of specific work and the responsibility for each party. Expected patterns and formats of information exchange are specified in contracts, and the sequence and timing of messages to resolve ambiguities in those documents are also specified.

We can briefly summarize the standard practices of a traditional, design/bid project in the AEC industry as follows. An owner selects an architect who works with the client to identify their requirements and create a design as a set of drawings, which indicate the intention of what is to be built. Standard contracts assume that these drawings will be paper based and two-dimensional. The drawings do not show every detail of the construction that is required, but instead suggest typical ways in which details are to be handled. They leave it to the discretion of contractors and subcontractors to identify a suitable method of constructing the intended elements in a workman-like way, following accepted practices. Contractors and subcontractors who are successful in bidding for a job, take the architects' drawings and use them as a basis for creating their own documents for the architect's approval, showing how they intend to fabricate and install their part of the overall building. In preparing these "shop drawings", contractors ask architects questions by submitting RFIs (requests for information) or RFCs (requests for clarification). In all projects of reasonable complexity RFIs and RFCs are to be expected, and contracts specify the sequence of reviews and timing of responses for them. But they can also serve as the basis for declaring a change order and requesting more compensation.

Our research on Frank Gehry followed his firm (Gehry Partners LLP) as they adopted three-dimensional software tools for documenting the exceedingly complex surface geometries of his designs. We used the concept of path creation to guide our research, tracing the mindful deviations from established practices that a shift to three-dimensional representations entailed. We found that the changes in practice that accompanied adoption of three-dimensional representations were very broad and included innovations in organization structures and strategies, work practices and a range of technologies.

Contracts and accepted practices on an AEC project have evolved with the assumption that design and construction information will be represented with two-dimensional images and associated text documents (e.g. component and material lists). Standards have evolved in which the two-dimensional drawings are expected to contain enough information for the contractor to apply their trade specific knowledge to complete the work. In this way, responsibility for errors can be traced to either the architect or the engineer for having specified a design that was inherently inadequate, or to the contractor for having failed to apply the correct workman-like expertize. Contracting also assumes that the sequencing of the design, bidding and construction will be in discrete stages, with a full set of design documents put out for competitive bidding by contractors.

Even from this brief overview, we can see that a path creating change from two- to three-dimensional representations has the potential to be a significant disruption in the established pattern of relations among the actors in a large and complex project. What I will discuss below are some unique issues related to information and control which we encountered in our study of Gehry Partner projects that incorporated three-dimensional representations in design and construction. Their innovations with representational forms bring into relief the way that morphogenesis of the structural relations in the industry as a whole, including its contracting, risk allocation, scope of work, communication patterns and work practices, is required for effective information design, and some of the ways that Gehry Partners LLP sought to effect those changes.

The Anomalies of Risk Reduction in the Project Organization of the AEC Industry

The contracting arrangements, including both formal and informal aspects, of the AEC are supposedly intended to balance the tensions of a hybrid project organization, and reduce overall risk. But in the environment of changing technologies and practices that we observed in our study of Gehry Partners' projects, we repeatedly saw contracting and risk control strategies creating increased risk for the project and its participants. Gehry Partners and other member firms of the project organization struggled to deal with these anomalies and achieve effective management control through efforts at morphogenesis of the industrial structures themselves, rather than redesigning their information systems.

Let us first look at the management control elements that are imbedded in the contracting practices of the AEC industry, and the way they are intended to reduce risk:

a. Open bidding with contracts awarded to the lowest, competent bidder is intended to reduce the risk of overpaying.
b. Change orders being tied carefully to contract language and to the representations of the design that it includes is intended to reduce the risk of cost overruns by isolating responsibility among parties and assigning liability for errors.
c. Minimum communication among parties before bidding is intended to avoid the risk of favoritism or collusion in the bidding process.
d. Delay in payment of contractor invoices from 45 to 60 or more days is intended to assure an audit function can reduce the risk of overpaying and loss of the time value of money made available to owner by industry practice.
e. Control system managers being in place at the building site is intended to minimize the risk of scope creep, cost overruns, unauthorized activities, etc.
f. A system of layers of approval that include communication exchanges between owner, contractor, architect and consultants is intended to avoid the risk of unauthorized decisions that result in costly changes or elaborations of the design.
g. Professional liability contracts for each firm that participates in the project is intended to minimize the risk of being unprotected from the negligence or failed judgment of professionals.
h. Established risk recognition/risk mitigation procedures are intended to guide identification of high-risk situations, making of go/no-go decisions, and assuring appropriate responses to potential risks.
i. Financing break points for go/no-go decisions being tightly defined at early stages of project planning is intended to reduce the risk of over investing in unfeasible projects by the financing sources.

All of these practices seem at face value to be sensible, and have come to be accepted practice because they proved to be so over time. They were, in a sense, results of earlier morphogenesis in designing project organizations. But when the technologies change, when representational practices change, and when work practices change, as is increasingly the case in all industrial sectors, these tradition bound elements of an information control system cease functioning as intended. The open bidding system becomes a game in which contractors rely on ambiguities in the contract documents and changing representational forms to make claims for extra payments (change orders) during construction — which can be significant. Minimizing communication slows learning and insures that new circumstances will be approached with inappropriate, older construction techniques. Delays in making disbursements create a space in which the change order gaming can take place by building arguments and collecting data for supporting contentious claims. Spreadsheet wielding managers on site can inhibit collaborative communications among the project team by focusing energy on building arguments to support change order requests. Layers of approval with contractually explicit patterns for exchanging communications and obtaining signatures from the hierarchy of each firm involved predictably slow the problem solving process down and increase the risk of cost overruns.

Having separate professional liability policies for each type of professional adds motivation to game project communications to assign blame for change order requests to other team members. Risk recognition and mitigation procedures are inevitably based on historical experience, which is inherently more linear and less complexly interconnected that a present project, resulting in decisions that can potentially increase risk instead. Finally, enforcing very short go/no-go decision timelines for projects means that less time will be spent on planning and designing before "firm" construction estimates are committed to by the funding agencies, thereby increasing the risk that less costly or alternative designs or materials will surface.

In short, the design setting we observed in the AEC industrial complex is that the success of the hybrid organization is dependent on communication among all participants with the intent to collaborate in a joint problem solving effort. Team building exercises among firms are increasingly standard in these large hybrid project organizations. But, the information control systems that are employed mimic those of a system that has been decomposed, rather than one that has been synthesized. Their logics do not match those of the types of hybrid being controlled. The result is forms of management control in hybrid relations that are intended to decrease the risk of an overall project, but serve to increase the project risk instead. In a nicely balanced paradoxical equation, I will argue that the morphogenic innovations that we observed often included practices that increased project risks in order to decrease them. I will also argue that in the absence of morphogenesis at the institutional (supra-system) level of hybrid organizational forms, the chances of having effective information control systems are minimal.

Some Examples of Morphogenesis in the Hybrid Organization of AEC Projects

Below I will briefly recount a number of instances in which we observed Gehry Partners or other members of one of their project teams take a path creating action intended to change the form of relations that characterize large AEC projects. These are morphogenic in the sense that they are intended to stimulate an enduring change in the industry (supra-system) level, and that management control was improved in those projects because of the morphogenic quality of these innovations.

Example 1: The Fish Sculpture Project — Avoiding Management Control Over the Project in Order to Increase Chances for Project Success

Gehry Partners' first use of three-dimensional software tools in design and construction was a Fish Sculpture that Frank Gehry proposed for the Barcelona Olympics. Jim Glymph, Frank Gehry's senior partner tells it best:

> The first project (using 3-D) was the most successful we may have ever had. It was the Fish Sculpture and was relatively simple because it was just two sub-trades. All we had was a Frank Gehry model and it was supposed to be finished by the Olympics, and at the time we decided to do it there was only nine months to the Olympics. So we decided what tool we needed, what software, we got the contractors to agree we wouldn't be drawing, and we did that project paperless. And what convinced us was we got the job done a month early. Everybody made money, there were no extras — that never happens.
>
> That convinced us that 'wait a minute, what we just did because we had to, maybe we should be doing this all the time, it worked'. But the other thing that happened was a lot of rules were suspended in order to allow that to happen.... We literally agreed to attempt it only if the project managers were left out of it and the whole management process was abandoned because it was too slow. We made some deals with the city on approvals, a lot of deals were made to operate outside the rules and basically, most of the deals had to do with peeling away layers of oversight and management and getting down to just the people that are doing the work. And then putting only the absolute minimum amount of management back on top of that to keep it from going off the rail.
>
> And in construction, well like anything else, but in construction, you know, there's been a tradition built up about paper and a paper process, an approval process for everything you do that is very complicated. We didn't sacrifice any quality control measures, we clearly didn't sacrifice any management. We just eliminated management where it wasn't necessary, which was most places. ... We haven't done a paperless project again, because we've not had that environment where we were committed to suspend all the rules. And so that still remains the most efficient, the most successful use and it was the first use.
>
> (Jim Glymph, November 9, 2002).

The Fish Sculpture had another morphogenic feature that they have not been able to duplicate, but serves as an ideal institutional change toward which they continue to strive. That feature was an agreement between the architect and the contractor, Permasteelisa, to hold each other harmless if the paperless experiment of design and construction were to go bad. In two ways, then, they increased risk by eliminating management control oversight, and by eliminating standard contractual arrangements for attaching responsibility for failure, in order to reduce the risk of not achieving the project goal.

Example 2: Replacing Managers and Information Systems with Builders in Order to Increase Project Control

Two Gehry Partners projects with radically different approaches to management control illustrate a recurring theme in their efforts at morphogenesis in the AEC industry. Both were large, complex projects of comparable size. One had an experienced builder and two assistants running the job from their construction trailers, another had eight managers working spreadsheets to control the project from their construction trailers. The former project went smoothly, the latter went poorly. The builder and his assistants created cost and schedule reports as needed for milestone meetings, but focused on orchestrating the project team members and on collaborative problem solving. The managers and their spreadsheets spent energy on tracking deviation in performance and allocating blame when problems arose. One project employed intensive risk control strategies in the field, focusing on the financial aspects of the daily work activity, only to experience financial difficulties, finger pointing and gaming of the requests for change orders. The other project minimized management control in the field, allowing it to take place behind the scenes, while focusing on coordination and collaboration of the work. They experienced a more successful, well-controlled project.

Example 3: On the Experience Music Project, Layers of Decision Oversight are Removed in Order to Improve Decisions

On the Experience Music Project (EMP) in Seattle, the construction company, Hoffman Construction, organized construction teams in a unique way. Normally, teams would include contractor, owner and architect representatives who, when a problem was encountered, would discuss issues, identify alternatives, return to their respective firms to make engineering studies, have further discussions and approvals before the next scheduled team meeting or preset deadline. This standard procedure in the AEC reduces the risk that suboptimal actions will be taken or that actors would make agreements that their superiors would later undo. But it also increases the time required for making a decision and draws out the problem solving process. On the EMP project, Hoffman responded to the high levels of complexity on the project by forming the teams to include all the usual actors, plus any advisors, engineers and fabricators who would eventually be involved in the decision process. They then set as a goal that all decisions were to be made in the team meetings.

This was a major change in the coordination mechanism, and increased the risk that a decision may lead to a costly error, but it also created an atmosphere of genuine collaboration, intense creativity, and one of the most memorable and exciting project experiences that many of the highly seasoned participants had ever encountered.

Example 4: Eliminating Professional Responsibility (Oversight and Omissions) Insurance Policies

Each professional firm on a large construction project (architect, engineer, consultants, etc.) buys a professional liability policy, in order to have protection from liability for oversights and omissions. The policy also ensures the owner that funds will be available to rectify problems or damages that may result from one of the professional's actions or inactions. This is an eminently sensible idea, but rather than stimulate collaboration in a hybrid relationship, it encourages strategic behaviors that will tend to protect one professional group from liability and point blame toward another. On the MIT Stata center project, one insurance company was enticed to write a single professional liability policy for the entire project, covering all architects, engineers, and specialized consultants involved in the project. The ability to assign blame for any mistakes was reduced, which increased the risk that errors might occur, but this innovative insurance policy encouraged all professionals to collaborate, reduced strategic behaviors, and resulted in lower than normal claims.

Example 5. Accounts Payable Disbursements within 24 H Instead of 45 Days

Traditionally, the multiple firms on large construction projects submit invoices for work to date on a monthly basis. The invoices will include request for additional payments, based on "change orders", or claims by the contractor that a change in the scope of work from what was depicted in the contract drawings and specifications has occurred, and the billing party has suffered additional expenses that should be reimbursed over and above the fees specified in the contract. The owner, in turn, traditionally paid progress invoices 45 or more days after they were submitted. The total elapsed time between the submission of an invoice, resolution of change order disputes and final payment could be substantial. On the MIT Stata Center project, the university changed its progress payment policy, and agreed to pay invoices within 24 h if there were no open disputes concerning change order requests. This morphogenic restructuring of their organizational practices increases the risk that a proper approval could not be performed on the invoiced amounts and that an inappropriate payment could be made. It also reduced the school's ability to gain the advantage of the time value of money. Nonetheless, it changed the relational structure of the hybrid organization that was constructing the Stata Center and dramatically reduced requests for change orders, which allowed more of the project communication to be about solving construction problems and less spent on assigning blame and making claims.

Concluding Thoughts

These examples show the importance of morphogenesis at the supra-system level as key elements in an information system design that provides management control in the hybrid organizational form of a large construction project. Morphogenesis is important because the elements of practice, including routines, industry standards, histories and trajectories of individual firms and traditional practices are forming a hybrid through synthesis rather than decomposition. As a result, design elements that seem perfectly sensible when the hybrid form was achieved by decomposing an existing hierarchy in order to infuse market elements can be counter-productive for a hybrid organization that is being formed by adding elements of hierarchy to a market-based industrial system.

As these examples show, the implications can be disturbing for information system designers for several reasons. It presents the designers with a richly paradoxical situation in which: control is enhanced by reducing the number of controllers; financial efficiency is found by doing financially inefficient things; and overall professional liability risk is reduced by losing the ability to assign responsibility for individual errors to the professionals who "caused" them. One message that comes through in our study of the hybrid forms of market/hierarchy relations in the construction industry is that the mix of market and hierarchy that has evolved traditionally may itself have to be redesigned, through a process of morphogenesis, which will include a change in the set of formal and informal contracting procedures of the industry, in order to create an effective management control system. And, that increasing the attention to information systems procedures that are borrowed from our familiar set of management control techniques, is probably not a viable approach.

Chapter 22

Boundary Matters: Boundary Objects, Boundary Practices, and the Shaping of Organisational Identities

Uri Gal, Youngjin Yoo and Kalle Lyytinen

ABSTRACT

We propose a model that outlines the relationships among boundary objects, the information infrastructures within which they are embedded, and the identities of the organisations that use them. We illustrate the dynamics of the model by presenting two vignettes that describe the introduction of three-dimensional (3-D) modelling technologies into the architecture, engineering, and construction (AEC) industry, and the accompanying organisational changes. Based on the vignettes we suggest that boundary objects are used not only to facilitate cross-organisational communication, but also as a resource to form organisational identities. We further propose the occurrence of a dynamic process whereby changes in boundary objects enable changes in information infrastructures and identities in one organisation. These changes, in turn, create the conditions for change in bordering organisations through shared boundary objects and boundary practices. We conclude by drawing implications for designing and implementing inter-organisational information systems.

Introduction

Information technologies (IT) are used increasingly in inter-organisational contexts where they mediate interactions among multiple organisations and may be associated with changes in some, or all of them simultaneously. Existing work on the use of IT in inter-organisational settings tends to draw on information processing and transaction cost theoretical approaches and typically emphasises the effect of IT on the efficiency of inter-organisational coordination and communication sharing. Interestingly, researchers have paid less attention to the interrelationships between IT and the social processes within and across the organisations that use them.

Information Management: Setting the Scene
Copyright © 2007 by Elsevier Ltd.
ISBN: 978-0-08-046326-1

To address this gap, we conceptualise IT as boundary objects; conceptual or physical artefacts that reside in the interfaces between organisations and that help bridge their cognitive and practical differences to facilitate common understandings and co-operation (Star & Griesemer, 1989). Examining boundary objects can be useful in understanding how IT, as boundary objects, are used by organisations as they interact, and how changes in them may relate to changes in interacting organisations.

Past work on boundary objects has highlighted their role as translation devices that enable collaboration and knowledge sharing across diverse organisations (Carlile, 2002; Henderson, 1991). We expand this view by examining the dynamics of interacting organisations and the ways that these dynamics shape and are shaped by the use of IT as boundary objects. To this end, we analyse IT-based boundary objects in the context of the information infrastructures in which they are embedded and the identities of the organisations that use them. We define *information infrastructure* as a system of standardised practices and modes of communication that emerge in relation to a set of IT that are deployed within organisational boundaries. An *organisational identity* is defined as a symbolic representation of the organisation that is commonly and continually negotiated among organisational members.

We propose a model that outlines the relationships among boundary objects, organisational identities, and information infrastructures, and the way they interact during a process of organisational change. We illustrate the dynamics of the model by analysing an IT-generated change process in the AEC industry wherein 2-D modelling technologies — computer aided design (CAD) models and paper drawings — which served as boundary objects, were replaced with 3-D technologies. Additionally, we examine the implications of these changes for the information infrastructure and identity of one organisation in the industry.

The model we develop addresses the following aspects of IT-enabled organisational change processes: (1) the way boundary objects (in this case, IT-based boundary objects) shape and are shaped by organisational practices and patterns of communication; (2) the way IT-based boundary objects shape and are shaped by the identities of the organisations that use them; and (3) the implications of changes in IT-based boundary objects for the identities, practices, and interactions of the organisations that use them.

In what follows, we introduce the theoretical constructs that inform our study: information infrastructures, organisational identities, and boundary objects. Next, we present the model and describe the research setting, methodology, and results. This is followed by a discussion of the main findings and their implications for designing and implementing inter-organisational information systems.

Theoretical Foundations

Information Infrastructures

The term *infrastructure* generally refers to any substructure or underlying system. It denotes the basic physical and organisational structures needed for the operation of a society or enterprise (Oxford Dictionary). Information infrastructure refers to a system of standardised practices and modes of communication that emerge in relation to a set of IT within organisational boundaries. Such practices are acquired when actors are inducted into a community and undergo a process of socialisation whereby they internalise local knowledge, practices, language, and values. Over time, such artefacts and associated organisational practices become taken for granted, at which point they recede into the background and become part of the infrastructure (Star & Ruhleder, 1996).

Although they function in relation to communal standards, no community or organisation exists in isolation. Multiple organisations always coexist and interact and therefore do not have clear definitive boundaries (Ciborra, 2000). Hence, infrastructures always overlap to create interfacing areas. These areas depend on reciprocal evolution of practices, discourses, and artefacts across interacting organisations. Therefore, an important aspect in the constitution of information infrastructures involves organising practices, meanings, and roles that form and articulate organisational identities at the interfacing areas.

Organisational Identities

Organisational identity is understood to be organisational members' collective understandings of the features that are presumed to be essential, distinctive, and relatively permanent about the organisation (Albert & Whetten, 1985). Central to most accounts is the recognition that organisational identity is rooted in a deep cultural level of the organisation (Gioia, Schultz, & Corley, 2000). That is, identity resides in interpretive schemes that organisational members collectively construct to provide meaning to their shared history, experience, and activities.

We emphasise the *relational* and *dynamic* nature of organisational identity. In this perspective, identity is constructed not only against a backdrop of organisational members' shared histories and experiences, but also in the context of multiple interactions in which the organisation engages with a variety of outsiders such as costumers, competitors, and suppliers. Identity emerges in a dynamic context where multiple organisations interact and is therefore reflective of the circumstances in which such interactions are situated.

Because an organisation's identity is tied to the dynamic environment from which it materialises, it will vary with the context for which it is expressed (Gioia et al., 2000). Since organisations interact with multiple organisations simultaneously, organisational identity is not uniform but multifaceted; and not singular but multiple across different, intersecting practices and discourses; and not stable but constantly in the process of change (Hall, 1996). Accordingly, identity is best understood as a verb rather than a noun, and is better conceptualised as a 'work-in-progress' rather than a finished product (Gioia et al., 2000): Organisational identity is an ongoing enactment that unfolds as organisations interact with each other. This interaction is constituted through the engagement of organisations in mutual practices. Therefore the articulation of identities takes place in the interfaces among organisations. We next suggest that interfaces are populated by boundary objects, which thus form a critical element in the process of identity formation.

Boundary Objects

Boundary objects are conceptual or physical artefacts that reside in the interfaces between organisations. On the one hand they are flexible enough to contain varying meanings, which arise from multiple organisations. On the other hand they are robust enough to serve as a common reference point to members of the organisations that use them as they engage in mutual practice. Therefore they can serve as a means of translation and facilitate collaboration between diverse organisations (Star & Griesemer, 1989). For example, a contract is a boundary object that is used by multiple parties as a regulating mechanism that defines roles, allocates responsibilities, and lays out activity plans. The contract acts as a 'social lubricant' that enables the disjointed parties to work together. While it is recognised as a contract to all the parties involved, it is sufficiently ambiguous so that multiple views and interpretations of it can coexist.

Previous studies have examined the types and use of boundary objects in multiple organisational settings and typically attempted to establish different categories of boundary objects (Garrety & Badham, 2000) or determine the usefulness of different types of boundary objects in different organisational or boundary conditions (Carlile, 2002). However, most research on boundary objects has examined them in a context of relatively stable settings and/or for short periods of time. A few studies hint at the potential for change in boundary objects, but do not explore that process and its possible implications. In addition, previous research has not looked at the social dynamics within interacting organisations, namely, the changing identities and infrastructures that are associated with dynamic boundary objects. In short, the relationship between information infrastructures, organisational identities, and the creation, maintenance, and change of boundary objects has remained unexplored. To address this gap, we next outline a model that juxtaposes boundary objects, organisational identities, and information infrastructures, and captures their relationships.

The 'Butterfly' Model: The Interrelationships of Boundary Objects, Organisational Identities, and Information Infrastructures

The model, which resembles the shape of a butterfly, represents an ideal-type situation where two organisations are engaged in mutual practice that is mediated by one or several boundary objects (Figure 22.1).

The practices and identity of each organisation are reciprocally shaped in process that crosses organisational boundaries. In this process, organisation A's identity is predicated not only on its members' shared experiences and history, but also on the organisation's interactions with organisation B, that is, on the boundary practices that are common to organisations A and B (a similar argument can be made for organisation B's identity). These practices, however, involve the use of certain

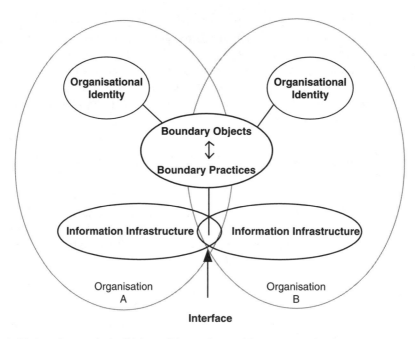

Figure 22.1: . Interrelationships of boundary objects, organisational identities, and information infrastructures.

boundary artefacts, which on the one hand facilitate inter-organisational collaboration, and on the other carry different meanings and inform different standardised practices in each organisation. Therefore, the interaction, or the interface, between organisations A and B involves the engagement of the two organisations in mutual practice along with their common use of shared objects.[1] Such objects and practices, in turn, play an important role in the articulation of the identities of both organisations. A change in boundary objects is likely to modify the conditions for the interaction of organisations A and B, reconfigure the interface between them, and therefore enable new organisational identities to be enacted.

The three elements in the model have previously been extensively researched. Furthermore, some of the relationships between them have been examined, although not in a way that connects all three constructs together (e.g., Bowker & Star, 1999; Lamb & Davidson, 2005; Levina, 2005). Earlier studies have not systematically looked at the relationships among boundary objects, information infrastructures, and organisational identities. Moreover, they have not explored *changes* in boundary objects and their implications for the organisations that use them. Therefore the model we present supplements past studies by suggesting that information infrastructures, boundary objects, and organisational identities constitute a dynamic system whose constituent

---

[1]In Figure 22.1, the oval containing boundary objects and boundary practices should have been the same area signifying the interface. We kept them graphically separate to prevent from cluttering the model.

elements cannot be understood in isolation from each other. Furthermore, it provides a framework for examining the dynamic relationships among these elements and delineates the consequences of changes in boundary objects for the identities and infrastructures of the organisations that share them. To illustrate the dynamics of the model, we next present vignettes from our research in the AEC industry, which depict an ongoing transformation process in an IT-based boundary object, and the changes in organisational practices and identities associated with it.

Illustrative Vignettes: Changes in Modelling Technologies in the AEC Industry

Our research focused on the replacement of 2-D modelling technologies by 3-D technologies by various organisations in the AEC industry, and the way these technologies were used as a new form of boundary object to facilitate collaboration during construction projects. We additionally observed the associated changes in the infrastructural practices and identities that these organisations have experienced.

We utilised data from two case studies that focused on one organisation, Hoffman Construction Company (hereafter Hoffman), a general contractor, and its involvement in two construction projects. The vignettes below demonstrate the transitions the company has experienced when it started to incorporate 3-D technologies to replace 2-D technologies in its construction practice. Data were collected using 18 semi-structured interviews with five Hoffman employees over a period of 6 years (2002–2007). The interviews were analysed using established methods for handling qualitative data (Eisenhardt, 1989; Yin, 2003).

The AEC industry encompasses tens of thousands of organisations whose main undertaking is the construction of civic structures. The successful completion of construction projects requires extensive cooperation among these organisations, which may have different technical expertise, business practices, and ways of representing their work and themselves. In other words, they may have different information infrastructures and identities. Given this diversity, boundary objects are an important means for maintaining effective collaboration during construction projects.

A prominent boundary object in the AEC industry comes in the form of 2-D representations such as CAD models and paper drawings. Modelling technologies are a central element in the coordination efforts during construction projects and play a critical role in structuring construction activities. Paper and CAD models constitute the basic component of communication, shape the structure of the work, which may participate in the work, and the final products of design (Henderson, 1991). While the models are shared by multiple organisations and used by them in common practice, different organisations may have their own specified language and practices in light of which they interpret and use the models.

In the last decade a growing number of organisations in the AEC industry have started to use 3-D modelling technologies to replace 2-D technologies. The first to extensively use 3-D technologies was Frank Gehry, a renowned architect who is internationally recognised for his exceptional building designs. Gehry's buildings are characterised by unstandardised curvilinear shapes that are designed with 3-D modelling software called CATIA. CATIA was introduced into the AEC industry by Gehry Partners (Gehry's architectural firm) in the early 1990s. Since then, the use of CATIA and other 3-D modelling tools in the industry has grown significantly. Given the importance of visual models, as boundary objects, to the organisation of construction projects, a move to using 3-D models can have vast repercussions to the way construction projects are managed, and to the way organisations interact and construct their identities.

As noted, we focus on one general contracting company, Hoffman. Regarded as one of the leading and most experienced general contractors in the AEC industry, Hoffman has been operating for 85 years. It has a rich experience in using conventional 2-D technologies and, as of the late 1990s, it has used 3-D technologies in its high-end construction projects. As a general contractor, Hoffman is responsible for ensuring effective collaboration among the various stakeholders during construction projects and for mediating communications between subcontractors and the architectural team. Overall, Hoffman's example reflects the organisational transitions associated with the move from using 2-D technologies to 3-D technologies.

Findings

The cases below depict a path of transformation in Hoffman's information infrastructure and identity as the company starts using 3-D modelling technologies. The first case describes Hoffman's infrastructural practices and identity prior to using 3-D technologies. The second case demonstrates how Hoffman's infrastructure and identity start changing when it partakes in a project where the use of 3-D modelling technologies was mandated by the architect.

The Poker Dealer: Hoffman in Typical 2-D Construction Projects

The use of 2-D models in the AEC industry is an established aspect of the relationships among architects, general contractors, and subcontractors. In this traditional organisation of the building process, construction activities are mostly separated from the preceding planning and design activities. The 2-D contract documents that are created in the earlier stages by the architects only schematically convey the design of the building. They do not refer to specific construction methods and leave the selection of these and the solution of related field engineering problems to the subcontractors working on-site. The architects deliver the contract documents to Hoffman, which reviews and distributes them to the subcontractors. Each subcontractor then translates the documents into shop drawings, which contain their detailed work plans and construction methods and materials. Therefore, different subcontractors end up using distinct models to support their respective construction activities. This tends to generate a loosely coupled system of communication flows among these heterogeneous organisations that, nonetheless, have to maintain high level of coordination. Furthermore, while interdependent, the construction processes of multiple subcontractors are likely to conflict with each other as they represent their unique professional, practical, and financial interests. Therefore, Hoffman's role in 2-D-based projects consists primarily of ensuring that collaboration takes place among these organisations. Accordingly, Hoffman's infrastructural practice relies on the use of 2-D contract documents and shop drawings, as boundary objects, to coordinate construction activities, inform subcontractors about other subcon-tractors' activities, and reconcile various, and at times, conflicting perspectives that subcontractors have.

Figure 22.2 below illustrates the established pattern of relationships among different organisations in 2-D-based projects. It reflects Hoffman's central position in this network of relationships and the extensive use that is made of 2-D models to coordinate the construction process. The arrows denote the transfer of information across organisations through 2-D models.

Hoffman's identity is predicated upon the interactions in which it is involved. In 2-D-based projects, the nature of these interactions noticeably resembles those that characterise a poker game. Each actor's actions are calculated based on the anticipated actions of other actors in an effort to increase their own benefits and minimise their costs. Furthermore, each subcontractor is reluctant to share its shop drawings with other subcontractors as they may contain proprietary knowledge. Similarly, architects are reluctant to release fully detailed information in their contract documents to avoid contradicting their own modelling and measurements. Hoffman is the only party that has access to everybody else's information bases: it is the only one to receive all the

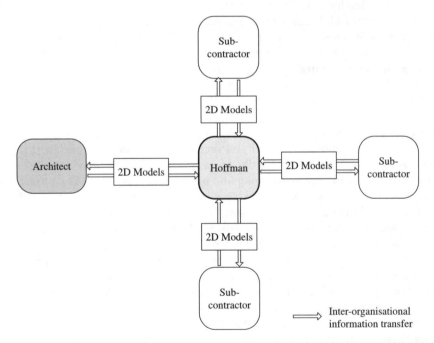

Figure 22.2: A process model of relationships in 2-D-based construction projects.

architect's contract documents and all the subcontractors' shop drawings. Thus, Hoffman is situated at a central node in a system composed of itself, the architects, and the subcontractors. Much like a poker dealer, Hoffman sits at a table while each party lays out their cards for construction. Each player keeps their proprietary information to themselves and tries to negotiate the sequence of construction and the location of their components for their own benefit.

The Dispersed Collaborator: Using 3-D Technologies with Gehry Partners

In the summer of 1997, Hoffman became involved in the construction of the Experience Music Project (EMP) in Seattle, Washington, which was designed by Frank Gehry. As noted, Gehry started using CATIA in his practice in the beginning of the 1990s. The EMP building was one of the first projects in which Gehry used 3-D CATIA models as contract documents, and insisted that all the main subcontractors adopt this technology.

During the construction process, the established loosely coupled inter-organisational system associated with the 2-D construction process was reshaped into a more tightly coupled and interdependent system. In this system, new levels of knowledge sharing and communications were reached among the participating organisations. One reason for these changes involved the overarching use of CATIA. 3-D CATIA models are rich digital representations of the building that embed multiple layers of information. Therefore, the same model can be used by multiple subcontractors to support their construction activities, thereby eliminating the need to create separate shop drawings. Also, 3-D models are transparent such that changes that are made in one portion of the model are visible to other users of the model, thus enhancing inter-organisational coordination. Another reason for the emergence of a tightly coupled system during EMP concerns the nature of the task. The high complexity of the building combined with the fact that most participants had not been previously involved in similar projects or used CATIA facilitated tighter collaboration.

In this newly formed interdependent system, Hoffman's infrastructural practices and role changed. Instead of managing a linear 2-D-based process, the company became more involved in the construction process and stepped out of its traditional organisational bounds. One example of this involves the use of CATIA by the subcontractors. On EMP, the use of 3-D contract documents by all the main subcontractors was demanded by Gehry. However, since most of the subcontractors were not familiar with CATIA, Hoffman hired CATIA operators and placed them in the major subcontractors. This was unusual as the general contractor now had its own employees in the subcontractors whereas usually the parties remain separated.

Another way Hoffman became more involved in the construction process concerns the design of the 3-D models. The 3-D contract documents produced by Gehry Partners often were not sufficiently accurate to support construction. Therefore, Hoffman had to step in to further develop these models, frequently in collaboration with the subcontractors. Changing the architects' contract documents by the general contractors is unusual. Typically, due to liability issues, the general contractor does

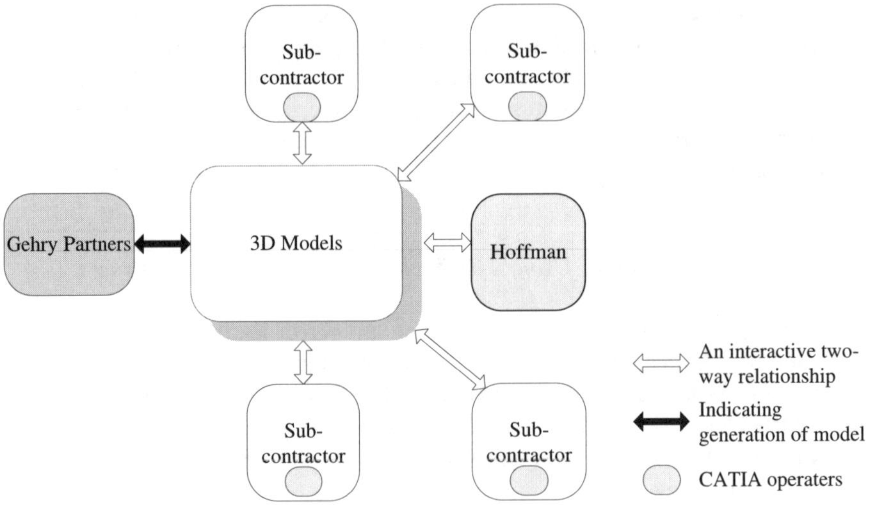

Figure 22.3: A process model of relationships on the EMP project.

not meddle with the documents and instead receives them from the architects and sends them to the subcontractors.

Figure 22.3 below illustrates the pattern of relationships among the different organisations during EMP. The grey areas in the subcontractors' rectangles denote the CATIA operators that were hired by Hoffman. The bold arrow signifies that the 3-D model was initially created by Gehry Partners. The double-headed arrows signify the transparency and interactivity that were allowed by CATIA. The figure also reflects the centrality of the 3-D model as a key coordinating mechanism.

As Hoffman's infrastructural practices and interactions changed, so did its identity. Hoffman's poker dealer identity drew on the central position that the company had in 2-D settings, and on the relationships with other organisations associated with this position. On EMP, Hoffman's interactions changed as the company became more involved in the construction process and as boundaries between Hoffman and the subcontractors blurred. Accordingly, Hoffman was now characterised as a dispersed collaborator rather than a poker dealer.

Discussion

Prior to working with Gehry Partners, Hoffman's organisational identity reflected a traditional general contracting company. This identity was defined by the company's use of 2-D models as boundary objects, and its engagement in associated infrastructural practices. The use of 2-D boundary objects in conjunction with carrying out institutionalised boundary practices such as sequentially managing communication channels between subcontractors and architects and coordinating the subcontractors' work, manifested in an inter-organisational system whose nature resembled that of a poker game. These relationships constituted the interface between Hoffman and its adjacent organisations and provided the context for the ongoing enactment of the company's poker dealer identity.

This identity began to change when the company started interacting with Gehry Partners during EMP. The use of 3-D tools as boundary objects and the change in Hoffman's infrastructural boundary practices associated with it, reconfigured the interface between Hoffman and its adjacent organisations, and changed the conditions for the enactment of the company's identity. Hoffman was no longer able to draw on 2-D boundary objects to form its relationships (i.e., its boundary practices) with architects and subcontractors in a way that would reaffirm its poker dealer identity. The previously established loosely coupled construction process was reshaped into a tighter collaborative system. In this system, traditional organisational responsibilities shifted, organisational boundaries blurred, and consequently, existing identities were renegotiated. Rather than having a distinct position in the construction process, Hoffman now played a more involved role. This was manifested in the company having its own CATIA operators embedded in the subcontractor's offices, in it taking a hands-on approach with the 3-D contract documents, and in its intensified collaboration with subcontractors. These newly formed practices provided the context for the enactment of Hoffman's dispersed collaborator identity.

The two cases illustrate the validity of the model outlined above and of the relationships it depicts. First, with regard to boundary objects and organisational practices, the cases demonstrate the tight connection between the objects that are jointly used by multiple organisations and the practices that connect these organisations. In each of the cases one would be hard pressed to describe the interface shared by the multiple organisations without taking into account both the boundary practices and the objects that constitute it. For example, understanding the poker game inter-organisational environment requires more than analysing the features of 2-D CAD and paper models and examining the linearity of inter-organisational practices. It is the interlacing of 2-D models and linear coordination, which makes up the interface that is shared by organisations. On the one hand, the restricted capacity of 2-D models to hold rich information limits the ability of organisations to directly interact with or be aware of the activities of other organisations. This in turn supports sequential interactions that are mediated by a 'governing hand,' or rather, a 'dealer'. On the other hand, such sequential interactions that are characterised by interdependency, mutual suspicion, and strategic sharing of information, encourage the use of technologies that limit the degree of inter-organisational visibility and that enable organisations to keep private their proprietary knowledge and processes.

Second, with regard to boundary objects and organisational identities, the cases demonstrate the importance of the technologies organisations use to communicate with each other and the mutual practices through which such communications unfold in the development of organisational symbolic representations. In each of the case studies, Hoffman's identity was intertwined with the nature of the company's relationships with other organisations, which in turn were associated with the use of particular IT-based boundary objects. For example, Hoffman's poker dealer identity was based on the nature of inter-organisational relations, which resembled those that characterise a poker game. However, these relations were in turn associated with the use of 2-D models as boundary objects.

Third, concerning the consequences of changes in boundary objects, the cases illustrate that a change in technologies that are shared by multiple organisations is likely to be associated with changes in these organisations' boundary practices, and therefore with modified conditions for enacting their identities. This was evident when Hoffman's poker dealer identity, which was based on the use of 2-D models and engagement in sequential construction processes, was going through transformations when the company started working on EMP. The use of a new IT-based boundary object in conjunction with the involvement in different boundary practices altered the interface between Hoffman and its neighbouring organisations and enabled the company's dispersed collaborator identity to emerge.

Finally, the cases highlight that organisational changes associated with dynamic boundary objects can cross-organisational boundaries. For example, the introduction of 3-D technologies by Gehry Partners and their use as boundary objects instigated a cascade of changes in other organisations that interacted with Gehry Partners. The use of 3-D tools by Gehry Partners changed not only their internal practices, but also their boundary practices — the way they communicated and cooperated with general contractors and subcontractors. Gehry's ability to impose the use of 3-D tools on the construction team and change mutual boundary practices consequently changed the conditions for the ongoing enactment of other organisations' identities, as was evident in Hoffman's case whose identity changed when it started interacting with Gehry partners during EMP. Accordingly, our model suggests that boundary objects are part of a dynamic system whose elements are bound up in reciprocal relationships. When change occurs in one of the elements, it will carry over to the others generating cascading transformations. Notably, these changes are not always accommodated within a single organisation and can carry over to neighbouring organisations through shared boundary objects and practices.

Implications and Future Research

Our study suggests a number of implications. The first stems from our finding that boundary objects have greater significance than previously indicated. Past research has primarily focused on boundary objects as translation devices that facilitate cross-organisational knowledge sharing and communication. Our study, by highlighting the social dynamics of the organisations that use boundary objects, illustrates that boundary objects are also used as an essential resource for the symbolic structuring of organisations. This is due to the role boundary objects play in the formation of organisational identities. This suggests that the adoption of new boundary-crossing IT could not only improve the efficiency of inter-organisational information sharing or coordination, but also lead to fundamental changes in the identity and practices of the adopting organisations. Therefore, organisations that implement inter-organisational IT need to be strategic about the possible consequences of such technologies, not only for their relationships with other actors, but also for their own identity and practices.

Second, our study suggests that the design and choice of boundary objects to mediate between organisations can be used to purposefully influence the shaping of practices and identities of adjacent organisations. Organisations may position specific types of objects at their boundaries with different actors in an effort to influence their pattern of relationships with these actors (i.e., their boundary practices) and consequently, these actors' institutionalised practices and identities. In our research we witnessed such a situation when a large manufacturing firm implemented a new web-based supply-chain management system to replace its previous phone and fax-based system of managing its relationships with its suppliers. The purpose of the new system was not only to improve the firm's supply chain efficiency, but also to deliberately instil significant changes in their suppliers' institutionalised practices, and in the manner in which the suppliers perceived their work, their relationships, and themselves.

Third, although the idea that IT artefacts form an important class of boundary objects has been previously discussed (e.g., Karsten, Lyytinen, Hurskainen, & Koskelainen, 2001), their relation to the organisations that draw upon them, in particular to their identities and practices, has remained largely unexplored. Our study suggests that the use of IT goes beyond sheer instrumental considerations of efficiency or effectiveness and cannot be fully comprehended when such logic is applied. IT should be understood not only as physical objects that can enter an organisation and change it in any number of ways. IT also needs to be construed as an element around which organisations develop institutional practices and patterns of inter-organisational relationships, which serve as the basis for the enactment of their identity. Therefore they have a significant symbolic importance for organisational members. When dealing with resistance to IT-based change, managers need to be aware that organisational actors' reluctance to use the new technology may have to do not only with the necessity of having to change their work routines or acquire new expertise, but possibly also with the difficulties of having to change their established identities.

Finally, our study implies that organisational change associated with mobilising new IT artefacts can be fruitfully understood in the context of reciprocal and dynamic inter-organisational relationships that are constituted through the use of shared objects and engagement in mutual practices. Some organisational change literature has suggested are the ways to improve the change process and its organisational consequences (Labianca, Gray, & Brass, 2000). Process-oriented studies have examined the actual process of organisational change (e.g., Van De Ven & Poole, 1995). Information systems researchers have examined the ensuing contradictory impacts of IT artefacts (e.g., Robey & Boudreau, 1999). What is striking in the extant literature is the scant attention paid to the fact that organisations are situated within dynamic and reciprocal social systems that are mediated and supported by boundary objects. Understanding organisational change in such dynamic context is particularly important given that contemporary organisations are increasingly connected through a myriad of IT that serve as boundary objects. Our theoretical perspective complements existing theories of organisational change by explicitly incorporating such dynamic and reciprocal inter-organisational contexts.

The model and cases we presented suggest that attempts to initiate IT-enabled organisational changes are likely to instigate further changes in neighbouring organisations through mutually shared boundary objects, which could have unexpected consequences. Therefore, managers of organisational change initiatives should take into account the broader socio-technical ecology that may be affected as a result of the initial change. Furthermore, anticipating and mitigating resistance to change within the implementing organisation may be insufficient when a change in technology is likely to instigate a cascade of changes in neighbouring organisations, and when those organisations are not ready to embrace such changes. In such cases, an organisation's efforts to minimise internal resistance to change are likely to be futile as the source of resistance may lie beyond that organisation's boundaries and reach. Therefore, management may need to enlist the cooperation of neighbouring organisations and develop systemic approaches to technology-enabled organisational change.

Our findings suggest several paths for future research. First, modelling and representational technologies are just one IT tool that can be employed to facilitate communications in inter-organisational environments. There is a need to examine the role of other mediating devices, and in other contexts, to assess the soundness of the model proposed here. Second, boundary objects are part of a system whose elements are connected in reciprocal relationships. When change occurs in one of the elements it will carry over to the others, spanning multiple organisations. In an increasingly inter-connected world, studies that follow the trajectory of such processes and examine their pattern can be particularly relevant. Finally, efforts by organisational groups to retain their identities can play a significant role in shaping their adoption and use of new technologies. Future studies could illustrate how this process unfolds, and identify conditions that generate different patterns of this process.

References

Albert, S., & Whetten, D. A. (1985). Organisational identity. In: L. L. Cummings & B. M. Staw (Eds.), *Research in Organisational Behaviour*. Greenwich, CT: JAI Press.

Bowker, G. C., & Star, S. L. (1999). *Sorting things out: Classification and its consequences*. Cambridge, MA: MIT.

Carlile, P. R. (2002). A pragmatic view of knowledge and boundaries: Boundary objects in new product development. *Organisation Science, 13*(4), 442–455.

Ciborra, U. C. (2000). *From control to drift: The dynamics of corporate information infrastructures*. Oxford, UK: Oxford University Press.

Eisenhardt, K. M. (1989). Building theories from case studies. *Academy of Management Review, 14*(4), 532–550.

Garrety, K., & Badham, R. (2000). The politics of socio-technical intervention: An interactionist view. *Technology Analysis & Strategic Management, 12*(1), 103–118.

Gioia, D. A., Schultz, M., & Corley, K. G. (2000). Organizational identity, image, and adaptive instability. *Academy of Management Journal, 25*(1), 63–81.

Hall, S. (1996). Who needs social identity? In: S. Hall & P.D. Gay (Eds.), *Questions of Cultural Identity*. London, UK: Sage Publications

Henderson, K. (1991). Flexible sketches and inflexible data-bases: Visual communication, conscription devices and boundary objects in design engineering. *Science, Technology & Human Values, 16*(4), 448–473.

Karsten, H., Lyytinen, K., Hurskainen, M., & Koskelainen, T. (2001). Crossing boundaries and conscripting participation: Representing and integrating knowledge in a paper machinery project. *European Journal of Information Systems, 10*, 89–98.

Labianca, G., Gray, B., & Brass, D. (2000). A grounded model of organisational schema change during empowerment. *Organisation Science, 11*(2), 235–257.

Lamb, R., & Davidson, E. (2005). Information and communication technology challenges to scientific professional identity. *The Information Society, 21*, 1–24.

Levina, N. (2005). Collaborating on multiparty information systems development projects: A collective reflection-in-action view. *Information Systems Research, 16*(2), 109–130.

Oxford Dictionary: www.askoxford.com

Robey, D., & Boudreau, M. C. (1999). Accounting for the contradictory consequences of information technology: Theoretical directions and methodological implications. *Information Systems Research, 10*(2), 167–187.

Star, S. L., & Griesemer, J. R. (1989). Institutional ecology, 'translations' and boundary objects: Amateurs and professionals in Berkeley's museum of vertebrate zoology, 1907–1939. *Social Studies of Science, 19*, 387–420.

Star, S. L., & Ruhleder, K. (1996). Steps toward an ecology of infrastructure: Design and access for large information spaces. *Information Systems Research, 7*(1), 111–134.

Van De Ven, A. H., & Poole, M. S. (1995). Explaining development and change in organisations. *Academy of Management Review, 20*(3), 510–540.

Yin, K. R. (2003). *Case study research: Design and methods.* Thousand Oaks, CA: Sage Publications.

Chapter 23

Design Theorizing: A Kantian Inquiring Approach

Dirk S. Hovorka and Matt Germonprez

ABSTRACT

Design theorizing is a research activity that provides functional, goal oriented, and pragmatic principles, which if embedded in an artifact, will create and support a desirable phenomenon. Through the application of the Kantian inquiry approach, we theorize about the design of tailorable technologies — technologies modifiable in the context of use. The Kantian approach is based on the synthesis of concepts from multiple sources and differs from other methods of theorizing by providing a thought process in which theory precipitates out of the convergence of diverse perspectives. The approach was used to survey a broad set of literature across computer science, information systems, and architecture to identify definitional characteristics and corresponding principles necessary in the design of tailorable technology. This research contributes to the approaches toward design theorizing and proposes a design theory for tailorable technologies that can be further tested and refined.

Introduction

Design theorizing is a research activity intended to provide functional, goal oriented, and pragmatic principles, which if embedded in an artifact, will create and support a desirable phenomenon. This approach is described as a *design science mode* of research. Rather than producing general theoretical knowledge, the design science paradigm seeks to produce and evaluate novel artifacts that can improve individual, organizational, and societal capabilities. Design science theories operate in an ill-defined problem space that may not be fully anticipated by the original designer. We contend that the focus on performance tends to miss the "multigenerational and emergent aspects of technological artifacts that arise as designers, developers, users, and other stakeholders engage with evolving artifacts over time and across a variety of contexts" (Orlikowski & Iacono, 2001, p. 132). Therefore, there is a need for design theory that can create and support a class of *tailorable technology* — information systems (IS) that are intended to be modified in the context of use. Tailorable technologies represent one form of the mutable nature of IS artifacts (Gregor & Jones, 2007) where artifacts may have an evolutionary trajectory that emerges from versioning or customization. Tailoring is specifically a user-initiated process where ideas regarding the configuration, aesthetics, and uses of the technology arise from the interactions of the user with the technology itself.

In this paper we explore the value of a Kantian Inquiring System of cross-disciplinary research as a method of *design theorizing*. There is little consensus or detail regarding methods of design theorizing and this approach is particularly suited because the phenomena supported by innovative technologies are not unique to IS. A broad set of literature from diverse disciplines is examined to find recurring principles that define a particular phenomenon (i.e., tailoring) and to identify the theoretical principles used in the design of tailorable IS. The Kantian approach embraces the diverse definitions, principles, kernel theories, and perspectives of the problem space and allows for the precipitation of new theory. We do not believe that a single discipline can provide for the range of thought required to develop theories of technology design in a world where the desired artifacts themselves are mutable, environments change and desired outcomes are unknown (Germonprez, Hovorka, & Collopy, 2007).

Design Theory

Extensive reviews of design science literature illustrate the role that theory plays in this domain. Design theory is necessary to add new knowledge to a community and to address domains that do not yet have established design practices. Design theory must provide novel values and goals because ill-defined problem spaces do not contain sufficient information to enable designers to create systems by manipulating extant information (Archer, 1984). Theory provides identification of the class of artifacts and the principles that support the goals of those artifacts rather than a solution to a specific problem or situation. Theories themselves may be demonstrated to be incorrect and theory choice is based on the standard evaluative criteria of accuracy, consistency, scope, simplicity, and fruitfulness (Kuhn, 1977). We emphasize that design theory can range from approximations, to mid-range theory, to strong theory (Weick, 1995, 2001; Gregor & Jones, 2007). Therefore a design theory can be considered a starting point from which testing and refinement may flow. "Good theories contribute to knowledge for the sake of action" (Romme, 2003) and are "interesting rather than obvious... a source of unexpected connections... high in narrative rationality... and aesthetically pleasing" (Weick, 2001, p. 517). The construction of a theory does not guarantee its verification or validity and testing of design science theory requires pragmatic, action-oriented experimentation and observation, which tests the propositions presented by the theory.

Romme (2003) suggests meta-requirements for design science theories, which include descriptive, function-oriented, normative, and prescriptive aspects. Rather than focusing on the structural components of design theory proposed in prior research (Walls,

Widmeyer, & El Sawy, 1992; Markus, Majchrazak, & Gasser, 2002; Gregor & Jones, 2007), we are concerned with the *method of design theorizing*. Common approaches to design theorizing include action research, case studies, and prescriptions for building-specific applications (Gregor, 2006). Romme (2003) traces organizational design methodologies from early technical and instrumental concepts through more recent interventionist views in which the human being is a designer of action. Other design science research specifies a need for grounding design theories in multiple other theory types. Hevner, Ram, March, and Park (2004) propose interactive develop/build and justify/evaluate theories/artifacts based on the contribution of behavioral theory and empiricism. However as noted by Venable (2006), *methods* of design theorizing are not well developed or defined. This provides a primary motivation for examining and applying a Kantian Inquiring System as a method of design theorizing.

A Kantian Inquiring System for Design Theorizing

Our approach to design theorizing relies on a Kantian Inquiring System to produce knowledge (Churchman, 1971; Mason & Mitroff, 1973). The Kantian Inquiring System is based on the synthesis of concepts from multiple sources and differs from other methods of theorizing by providing a thought process in which theory precipitates out of the convergence of diverse perspectives. A Kantian Inquiring System juxtaposes at least two alternate theories on any phenomenon, which provide different explicit views of the problem. In this case the theories from different researchers or research domains provide design principles that support the desired phenomenon and permit the extraction of a set of design propositions that best addresses the scope of the tailoring. The propositions include kernel theories, design practices, and methodologies and comprise approximation or mid-level theory. The Kantian approach differs from the optimizing decision tree design model of Simon (1981) by moving beyond the designer focus and incorporating multiple views of the same situation. In addition, the Kantian approach also allows us to incorporate and extend the Hevner et al. (2004) definition of IT artifacts to explicitly include the process of how technologies change over time. The Kantian Inquiring System also provides design integrity (Swanson, 1994) by incorporating propositions that the design is teleological, has an environment, and has a designer who can modify performance measures (Churchman, 1971).

Design Theorizing of Tailorable Technology: A Kantian Approach

We apply a Kantian Inquiring System to develop a design theory[1] of tailorable technology (Germonprez et al., 2007). The general concept of tailorability is found in

---

[1]Information systems themselves are frequently characterized in terms of Chruchman's (1971) inquiring systems. In this application, we use the Kantian Inquiring System to identify the defining characteristics and propositions of a theory for a specific class of information systems (tailorable technology).

numerous disciplines including architecture, cybernetics, computer science, IS, and is reflected in the design ontology of Winograd and Flores (1986). Tailorable technologies are IS where the designers and users are not necessarily concerned with the traditional IS utility or performance goals (e.g., performance, satisfaction, productivity, efficiency). Instead, designers of tailorable technologies produce systems intended for users to modify them to achieve intentional processes, functions, and perceived value. Tailoring occurs when a user encounters a *breakdown* or mismatch between the IS and the intentions or goals of the user. Tailorable technologies represent a shift in the design of IS from a fixed external physical object to design of "a space of potential for human concern and action" (Winograd & Flores, 1986, p. 37). To address this, we must understand how to design tailorable technologies to encourage the achievement of numerous, unforeseen goals, such as improving one-time task-oriented communication, or creating a metaphorical or aesthetically pleasing interface. A theory of tailorable technology design is based on the idea that users of technology are *designers of action* and that through tailoring technology, this action can be supported (Romme, 2003). MacLean, Carter, Lovstrand, and Moran (1990, p. 175) note that it is "impossible to design systems which are appropriate for all users and all situations." Tailorable technologies are systems where end-users' actions are not dictated through predefined rules on how the technology should be used or by structural limitations on the system's coupling with the world — what it is intended to do and the consequences of its use. Instead, users of tailorable technologies create specific forms and functional systems by tailoring characteristics of the technology. There is a large literature in human computer interaction (HCI), IS, architecture, and design that describes the relationship between human cognition and technology. In a broad set of domains, studies suggest that users play an integral role in the modification of the technologies in the context of their use.

The design ontology of Winograd and Flores (1986) provides a representation of the often ill-defined problem-space of designing for diverse and changing tasks, environments, and users and recognizes that IS will be used in unexpected ways. A design approach that provides possibilities for action is in contrast with the structurally oriented guidelines proposed by Hevner et al. (2004) and Gregor and Jones (2007). By comparing and contrasting the definitional characteristics and design principles of Gordon Pask (1971) (cybernetics), Christopher Alexander (1979) (architecture), Greg Gargarian (1993) (music), and Kim Madsen (1989) (IS) we gain a broad perspective on the phenomenon of tailoring and how tailorable technologies can be built. Other disciplines and domains may need to be consulted to refine the theory but these represent a sufficient scope and diversity to provide accuracy and consistency of principles. From these different domain perspectives, we extract the design principles that provide support for propositions about tailorable technology design.

Possibilities for Action

When applied to the design of IS, the phenomenon of tailoring requires a shift in design ontology. When engaged with tailorable technologies, the user can initiate innovations in the structural coupling between the artifact's function, aesthetics, and operation and the user's goals and interpretation of what the IS can accomplish. The phenomenological concept of "possibilities for" encompasses the linkages between the users' cognitive domain and the designer's structural domain that accompany the continuous redesign of the artifact by the user in the context of changing uses. Consequently the design of tailorable artifacts is concerned with the design of the *potential for action*, which can accommodate new forms of a technology that did not exist in the initial design and new actions that would not formerly have made sense (Winograd & Flores, 1986). There is a complex referential whole and set of "possibilities for" created when a user interacts with, and modifies, a technology. Designers align the IS with the general structure of the task domain and allow reflective action to tailor the system to generate new coupling with the world. This perspective is in contrast to structure-determined system design in which designers define structural/functional mechanisms for the IS. The biological analogy of a baby nursing provides an example of a complex set of reflex behaviors (e.g., crying, "rooting" reflex, sucking) that are mechanistic but do not depend on analysis, representations, or planning (Winograd & Flores, 1986). These actions could be programmed in terms of a simple set of goals and operations. But if these actions do not fulfill the goal, there is no ability for the baby to develop other ways to eat. The structural coupling to the world limits the available courses of action. In the same way, mechanistic design may fulfill task-specific goals or operations but will be limited if users have different representation or the task/environment of the IS changes. This mechanistic-structural design ontology is focused on the *outcome* of the design rather than the process of redesign by the user.

If we submit these two perspectives on the ontology of design theorizing to a Kantian Inquiring System, we can see that the seven-step design science approach of Hevner et al. (2004) does not fully support the design goals of tailoring. Not all of the stages apply in the same way that they apply to systems that are intended to address-specific problems and produce quantifiable business outcomes. Table 23.1 illustrates the modification of the Hevner et al. (2004) model necessary to support the design of tailorable technologies.

Designers of tailorable technologies recognize that the system will be used to address problems and goals unique to each user and that it is impossible for designers to articulate what intentions all users have for a system. All task domains are contained within a larger context and it is not possible to anticipate every user's concerns and goals in every context. This makes the requirement of problem relevance problematic if one is designing in an ill-defined problem space. Our proposed alternative, "possibilities for action and tailoring" allows our theory to accommodate the uncertainty in task, problem, environment, and user preference faced by many designers. Designers are also presented with limited information about the system to be designed and must rely on assumptions in first identifying a general task domain and the general actions to achieve meta-level goals. This limitation restricts the search process aspect of the seven steps proposed by Hevner et al. (2004). Instead, we adopt a dual-phase design phase in which the designer initially creates the *initial state* that provides functional components and an environment in which the user may

Table 23.1: A theory of tailorable technology design (Germonprez et al., 2007) with respect to Hevner et al. (2004) model.

Design as artifact	Tailorable technologies are a specific, tangible class of technology.
Problem relevance	A tailorable technology is not specified for any particular problem. It is specified to be tailorable and provide for possible action. Although tailorable technologies may be used in their initial or default state, they are tailorable to address problems not anticipated by the designer as the user creates secondary and tertiary versions of the technology.
Design evaluation	As a function of not being specified for a problem, evaluation of the technology, in the form of organizational outcomes, utility, quality, and efficacy would not occur until the secondary or tertiary states of the technology. The tailorable technology could be evaluated at the level of supporting tailoring but value judgments are not placed on this evaluation.
Research contributions	Tailorable technologies are designed to be modifiable in the context of use, not solve unsolved problems. Because of this, tailorable technologies only address two of the three requirements to make a research contribution as proposed by Hevner et al. (2004). However, this research contributes to design theory (not mentioned by Hevner et al., 2004), foundations of principles, and a method of design theorizing.
Research rigor	The application of the Kantian Inquiring System to design theorizing provides rigor.
Design as a search process	The only differentiation with tailorable technologies in this step is that tailorable technologies are not focused on a specific problem. Because of this, the generate/test cycle is never completed. The technology is in a constant cycle from its original design to later user constructions. This, however, does not preclude the use of design as a search process within tailorable technology design.
Communication of research	This research and Germonprez et al. (2007) provides communication that permits the design of tailorable technology as specified by the theory.

tailor the technology. The second phase is the ongoing act of *tailoring* or the user-defined design of the technology during its use and during this phase, specific problems may be addressed. Through this process of participation and interaction, the artifact is shaped to take on various forms across various environments (Romme, 2003). This design ontology results in a shift away from the computational metaphor of mechanism in a structure-determined system to a cognitive domain in which flexibility of purpose and coupling with the world "allow for modification and evolution to generate new structural coupling" (Winograd & Flores, 1986, p. 53). As user-tailored artifacts are created, the relevant domains of action may change and the IS's ability to execute multiple courses of action, as determined by the user, may increase. Winograd and Flores (1986, p. 177) state this eloquently as "the world determines what we can do, and what we do determines the world".

A Design Theory for Tailorable Technology: Design Principles

Design principles from the four stream of literature were identified and mapped to the Romme (2003) design model and serve as the propositions of a design theory. In the Kantian style, we identified nine principles that support the phenomenon of tailoring and represent concepts that are generalizable and operational in designing tailorable technologies, and are unique and mutually exclusive. The Romme model acts as a framework of two design environments for designers: the reflective and the active environments. The reflective environment describes how knowledge and content are used in the *service of action*. This is similar to Heidegger's (1927) *ready at hand* where the technology acts as an extension of the users actions. A web browser is an example of a technology in the service of action. When a user seeks information, the browser simply acts as portal to a desired search space. Consideration is placed on the goal and not on the technology. The reflective environment supports tailoring through encouraging environments and recognizable design spaces. The active environment employs knowledge and content in the *form of action*. The form of action supports tailoring through practical and functional design principles similar to Heidegger's (1927) *present at hand* where technology is evident as a tool for user actions. The design of tailorable technology relies on the support of two environments that are designed into the technology. The first is an environment that supports a natural use of the technology to extend functionality such as user searching, communicating, and computing. The second is an environment that allows the user to realize the tailorable technology as a technology that can be manipulated to serve changing uses (Table 23.2).

Table 23.2 defines the nine principles identified from the literatures and their relationship to the reflective and active environments, and illustrates at least two authors who evidenced the principle. The different literatures were used to identify recurring design principles that could be taken into the field for further validation and are not intended to illustrate tested and implemented principles. Instead they represent a first step in identifying design principles for tailorable technologies.

Discussion

This research makes three contributions to the literature. First, we demonstrate how the Kantian Inquiring System is a viable approach to design theorizing. Although the

Table 23.2: Nine principles in the design of tailorable technologies (Germonprez et al., 2007).

Environment	Principle	Principle definition	Evidenced by
Reflective	Task setting	The technology supports variable tasks and problems.	Gargarian (1993) and Madsen (1989)
	Recognizable components	The technology supports components from existing technologies.	Alexander (1979) and Pask (1971)
	Recognizable conventions	The technology supports use patterns from existing technologies.	Alexander (1979) and Pask (1971)
	Outward representation	The technology supports the context that it will likely be used in.	Alexander (1979) and Madsen (1989)
	Metaphor	The technology supports symbolic representation.	Madsen (1989) and Pask (1971)
Active	Tools	The technology supports existing design tools.	Gargarian (1993) and Pask (1971)
	Methods	The technology supports existing design methods.	Gargarian (1993) and Pask (1971)
	Functional characteristics	The technology supports functional requirements.	Alexander (1979) and Pask (1971)
	User representation	The technology supports the representation of users.	Alexander (1979) and Pask (1971)

structure of design science theory has received significant attention, less research has examined methods of theorizing. Design theorizing can greatly benefit from explicit comparison and contrast of principles that support the desired phenomenon from different perspectives.

Second, we represent tailorable technologies as a class of IS intended to be modified by individual, group, or organizational users in the context of use (Germonprez et al., 2007). These systems are a cognitive-technological assemblage embodying the principles outlined in Table 23.2 which provide for a cognitively based referential whole and set of "possibilities for." Although tailorable technology design has been a characteristic of practice, this paper provides a design theory for this practice. We argue that our tailorable technology design theory is an important theoretical contribution because the design principles address developmental meta-requirements for tailorable technology. Users tailor technologies in the context of use for a wide variety of reasons and some tailoring may be beneficial from the perspective of traditional measures of utility.

This design theory addresses an important class of human-IS interaction. The theory of tailorable technology design can explain why there is a need for tailorable technology. In addition to proposing design principles for tailorable technologies, we emphasize that design of tailorable systems requires a shift from the metaphor of IS as external artifact to a cognitive-technical set of possibilities for action. The key to tailoring is the plasticity of coupling between the structure of the IS and the user's cognitive domain of task, environment, metaphor, competencies, representation, and goals. This theory also illuminates the possibility that some IS need to be nontailorable (e.g., financial systems within an organization).

The principles of a theory of tailorable technology design are similar to those in more traditional design approaches. What differs is the way that the principles are handled. In the case of tailorable technology, the active and reflective environments are built into the technology for use in the ongoing tailoring of the system as well as used to design the default state. This perspective allows designers to recognize the distinction between the reflective environment, an environment where users recognize and imagine uses for the technology, and the active environment in which the technology is redesigned in accordance with user-constructed parameters. Designer awareness of the principles in the active environment (tools, method, functional characteristics, and user representation) will allow designers to effectively apply the principles and constraints of task setting, components, conventions, representation, and metaphor in the reflective environment. We are critical of the *activity-centered design* (Norman, 2005) approach however, because our design theory suggests that users' are crucial in the ongoing redesign of tailorable technologies and are supported through the use of metaphor, recognizable components, and conventions. While the user is not directly interacted with, they are critical participants in the design of tailorable technology as they envision possibilities for action. The ability of users to modify the technology requires that the designer decouple the system structure from a predetermined function set and allow users to determine what classes of functions go together to fill a user niche (Hovorka, 2005). Incorporating the potential for action component into the theory is beneficial as such efforts could explore the relationship and interaction between principles and activities as well as the mix of applied research methods needed to study these technologies in practice. Being mindful of activities may affect degrees to which tailorable technology design principles are evident and others are hidden from users.

Conclusions

A Kantian Inquiring System provides a novel and rigorous approach to design theorizing for the class of tailorable technologies in IS. The theory itself explicates the defining characteristics of a broad class of IS artifacts and provides guidance to developers and outlines an agenda for future research. By incorporating a broad set of literature, delineating the active and reflective environments, and providing principles for developers, we narrow the development process into a manageable set of parameters. This design theory provides a generalized set of principles to solve design issues for a class of IS rather than a solution to a specific problem or specification of a unique set of system features. This theory also articulates a set of principles in distinct design environments that are subject to empirical and pragmatic validation and refinement. The proposed design theory provides opportunity for future work in a variety of areas: (1) Use of case study data from a design team and users to validate the proposed design principles, (2) Software engineering principles which will support the meta-requirements of the theory, (3) Determination of degrees of tailoring, (4) Implications and evaluation of tailoring, (5) Design principles for systems that are intended to be nontailorable, (6) Whether tailorable technology is necessarily tailored in practice, and (7) the role of task, context, environmental factors, or design-evaluation interaction on tailoring in action.

References

Alexander, C. (1979). *The timeless way of building*. New York, NY: Oxford University Press.

Archer, L. B. (1984). Systematic method for designers. In: N. Cross (Ed.), *Developments in design methodology*. Chichester: Wiley.

Churchman, C. W. (1971). *The design of inquiring systems: Basic concepts of systems and organizations*. New York, NY: Basic Books.

Gargarian, G. (1993). *The art of design: Expressive intelligence in music*. Unpublished Doctoral Dissertation, Massachusetts Institute of Technology, MA.

Germonprez, M., Hovorka, D. S., & Collopy, F. (2007). A theory of tailorable technology design. *Journal of the Association for Information Systems*, 8(6), 351–367.

Gregor, S. (2006). The nature of theory in information systems. *MIS Quarterly*, 30(3), 611–642.

Gregor, S., & Jones (2007). The anatomy of a design theory. *Journal of the Association for Information Systems*, 8(5), 312–335.

Heidegger, M. (1927). *Being and time*. Albany, NY: State University of New York Press.

Hevner, A. R., Ram, S., March, S. T., & Park, J. (2004). Design science in IS research. *MIS Quarterly*, 28(1), 75–106.

Hovorka, D. S. (2005). Functional explanation in information systems. In: *Proceedings of the 11th Americas Conference on Information Systems* Omaha, NE.

Kuhn, T. (1977). *The essential tension*. Chicago: University of Chicago.

MacLean, A., Carter, K., Lovstrand, L., & Moran, T. (1990). User tailorable systems: Pressing the issues with buttons. In: *Proceedings of CHI '90*, New Orleans, LA.

Madsen, K. H. (1989). Breakthrough by breakdown: Metaphors and structured domains. In: H. Klein & K. Kumar (Eds.), *Systems development for human progress*. North Holland: Elsevier Science Publishers.

Markus, M. L., Majchrzak, A., & Gasser, L. (2002). A design theory for systems that support emergent knowledge processes. *MIS Quarterly*, 26(3), 179–212.

Mason, R. O., & Mitroff, I. I. (1973). A program for research on management information systems. *Management Science*, 19(5), 475–487.

Norman, D. (2005). Human centered design considered harmful. *Interactions*, (July/August), 14–19.

Pask, G. (1971). A comment, a case history, and a plan. In: J. Reichardt (Ed.), *Cybernetics, art and ideas*. London: Studio Vista.

Orlikowski, W., & Iacono, S. (2001). Research commentary: Desperately seeking the "IT" in IT research — A call for theorizing the IT Artifact. *Information Systems Research*, *12*(2), 121–134.

Romme, A. G. L. (2003). Making a difference: Organization as design. *Organization Science*, *14*(5), 558–573.

Simon, H. (1981). *The sciences of the artificial*. Cambridge, MA: MIT Press.

Swanson, B. (1994). Information systems innovation among organizations. *Management Science*, *40*(9), 1069–1092.

Venable, J. (2006). The role of theorizing in design science research. *DESRIST*, Claremont, CA.

Walls, J. G., Widmeyer, G. R., & El Sawy, O. A. (1992). Building an information system design theory for vigilant EIS. *Information Systems Research*, *3*(1), 36–59.

Weick, K. (1995). What theory is not, theorizing is. *Administrative Science Quarterly*, *40*, 385–390.

Weick, K. (2001). *Making sense of the organization*. Oxford: Blackwell Publishers.

Winograd, T., & Flores, F. (1986). *Understanding computers and cognition: A new foundation for design*. Norwood, NJ: Ablex Publishing Corporation.

Chapter 24

Fostering Innovation Through Generative Systems Design

Michel Avital

ABSTRACT

Building on the concept of generative design, *I explore the desirable features of IT-based systems that are conducive to innovative processes and propose that such systems should be evocative, adaptive, and open-ended. I present the three design directives and take a stab at extending them into design features that can be made operational. Generative design refers to the design considerations in developing systems or platforms that are conducive to one's ability to produce new configurations and possibilities, to reframe the way we see and understand the world, and to challenge the normative* status quo. *Thereby, generative design is particularly relevant for promoting innovation.*

Introduction

The bulk of the literature that covers the conditions conducive to innovative processes emphasizes the features of a work environment that promotes one's creativity. For example, it argues that creativity is a consequence of motivation, autonomy, work settings, climate, workload, and personal characteristics (Amabile, 1983; Amabile et al., 1996; Stenmark, 2005). Considerations also include wider scope determinants of innovation such as organizational vision (Swanson & Ramiller, 1997), technological infrastructure (Broadbent, Weill, & Clair, 1999), or institutional factors (King et al., 1994). However, there is not much attention to the desirable features of IT-based systems in that context and particularly to requirements for systems that fit for innovative processes.

Building on the concept of *generative design*, I address this void by suggesting a set of considerations for designing systems that are conducive to innovative processes. More specifically, I propose that such systems should be evocative, adaptive, and

Information Management: Setting the Scene
ISBN: 978-0-08-046326-1

open-ended. This position paper presents these three design directives and takes a stab at extending them into design features that can be made operational.

Generative design refers to the design considerations in developing systems or platforms that support and enhance *generative capacity* — that is the considerations in designing systems that are conducive to one's ability to produce new configurations and possibilities, to reframe the way we see and understand the world, and to challenge the normative *status quo* (Avital & Te'eni, 2006). Thus, people's generative capacity is a key source of innovation, and by definition, generative design aims to encapsulate the design directives of systems that enhance and complement that capability.

The concept of generativity has been applied time and again in central theories of various disciplines — for example, in Psychology (Erikson, 1950), Linguistics (Chomsky, 1972), Organization Science (Schön, 1979), and Computer Science (Frazer, 2002). In general, being generative refers to having an evocative power or aptitude that can result in producing or creating something (Weick, 2007), or tapping into a source of innovation (Cook & Brown, 1999). In our context, the modifier "generative" denotes conducive to the production of something innovative. In other words, generative design refers to the design requirements and considerations in developing information systems that augment people's natural ability to innovate.

Contrary to the common 'parametric design' in which a design target is predefined and can be parameterized, generative design is focused on the generation or discovery of new design alternatives in the form of disparate sets of evolving configurations. An earlier attempt to apply the concept was made by Frazer (2002) who presented *generative evolutionary design* for computer-assisted generation of possible solutions for ill-defined or wicked problems. However, John Frazer has focused on designing computers that can generate possible innovative solutions, this paper focuses on information systems that support people who aim to innovate. With fundamentally different underlying innovative agents (i.e., a machine *vis-à-vis* a person), the consequent system design requirements and considerations take a different path in each instance.

Other attempts to approach the underlying topic in IS research fall in the domain of creativity research and focus on the effect of creativity support information systems on work in organizational settings. However, so far, in spite of the wide variety of possible tasks and desired creative outputs in organizations, their operationalization in IS studies has been often a certain decision-making task. Reducing all creative acts to decision-making tasks is problematic for two reasons. There are other kinds of task that require creativity in the organizational context, let alone outside the organizational realm (e.g., design-oriented tasks). Furthermore, analytical decision-making is merely one part of a manager's job; the other part involves idea generation, form-giving, innovation design (Boland & Collopy, 2004). Ironically, creativity support systems that one might believe are built primarily to enhance a syntactical process that resembles design thinking and attitude, have been treated in IS research as decision support systems that inherently focus on analytical processes.

Table 24.1: Generative design directives and respective features.

Generative design directive	System feature	Description
• System should be *evocative*	Visualization	Incorporate tools that enable seeing an object from multiple perspectives
	Simulation	Incorporate tools that enable testing an object or a process or part thereof in multiple situations
	Abstraction	Incorporate tools that enable examining objects or processes at multiple degrees of granularity
	Integration	Incorporate tools that enable aligning exclusive yet related domains, objects or processes in multiple overlay configurations
	Communication	Incorporate tools that enable sharing of multiple points of view and support of cross-domain exchange
• System should be *adaptive*	Customization	Incorporate tailorable facilities and customization tools that enable user-induced adaptation
	Automation	Incorporate artificial intelligence that enables system-induced adaptation
• System should be *open-ended*	Peer-production	Incorporate an extensible architecture that enables anyone to produce and share at their own volition new and useful extensions of products or services
	Rejuvenation	Incorporate open development standards, easy upgrade path and a modular architecture in support of renewal processes

Generative Design

It has been argued that people's generative capacity is a source of innovation and that generative design refers to the requirements or characteristics of (computer-based) systems that enhance and complement that capability (Avital & Te'eni, 2006). In this position paper, I share insights regarding generative design considerations and their possible operationalization, as summarized in Table 24.1. Overall, I submit that generative design should be evocative, adaptive, and open-ended.

Generative Design is Evocative

A system with a generative design inspires people to create something unique. It evokes new thinking and enables them to translate their ideas into a new context. Information technology can help toward creating the environment or conditions that are prone to those insights by generating and juxtaposing *diverse frames* that are not commonly associated with one another within an underlying context (Sternberg, 1988). There are several ways to generate or elicit diverse frames using information technology, as demonstrated below:

Visualization: Systems should incorporate human-centered visualization tools that enable seeing multiple dimensions. That is, 3-D digital images of physical objects and visual representations of various facets of less tangible parameters such as the characteristics of networks, hierarchies, processes, and the like. Visualization provides the ability to see an object from **multiple perspectives** and to search for new insightful points of view.

Simulation: Systems should incorporate human-centered simulation tools that enable testing an object or a process or part thereof in **multiple situations**. This refers to the underlying process or object's behavior, its dynamic capabilities or response to particular stimulus in different contexts.

Abstraction: Systems should incorporate human-centered abstraction tools that enable examining objects or processes at **multiple degrees of granularity**. Increasing or decreasing granularity enables one to distinguish between the situated features of a task or object and the fundamental characteristics that define it. The ability to move swiftly between levels of granularity is essential for identifying emergent patterns, commonalities, and anomalies.

Integration: Systems should incorporate human-centered integration tools that enable aligning exclusive yet related domains, objects, or processes in **multiple overlay configurations**. Integration refers to one's ability to overlay or merge views of various parallel subsystems or crosscuts of objects that are associated with different core domains, disciplines, practices, or organizational units, and which are traditionally or institutionally unrelated. Supporting the ability to overlay traditionally unrelated subsystems or objects through integrated platforms provides much insight about interoperability between heterogeneous systems and promotes system-wide boundary crossing, across-the-board sharing, and cross-fertilization.

Communication: Systems should incorporate human-centered communication tools that enable sharing of **multiple points of view**. In this case, communication refers to one's ability to talk and share information with other actors and stakeholders with no regard to institutionally imposed boundaries. Communication tools enable cross-fertilization through sharing of information, participative action, *ad hoc* and ongoing cooperation, and collaborative work practices. An extended notion of communication tools includes ubiquitous access and fast connectivity to shared knowledge-based repositories.

Generative Design is Adaptive

A system with a generative design can be used by a diverse set of people in their own respective environments and for various tasks within an intended scope. It is adaptive with respect to the type of users or groups it serves in diverse problem spaces. It is also simple to understand and easy to master by anyone. Information technology can help in creating evocative systems or platforms that are flexible yet powerful to enable the generation of new configurations. Two main IT-enabled features drive the systemic flexibility and adaptivity that are required for generative design, as follows:

Customization: Systems should incorporate tailorable facilities and customization tools that enable **user-induced adaptation**. As it is impossible to design systems that fit all users and all situations, the incorporation of tailorable facilities affords systems where one's actions are not dictated through narrowly defined rules of engagement or training on how the technology ought to be used. In contrast, using built-in customization tools allows users to play an integral role in the modification of the technology in the context of its use. Technology tailoring should be a native concept in generative design to allow users to redefine continually the services they need and to customize it according to the use patterns of their choice.

Automation: Systems should incorporate artificial intelligence that enables **system-induced adaptation**. Although customization tools provide much value, they also require users' attention in response to change in use pattern, environment and the like. Designing adaptive systems that incorporate continuous learning and improvement based on codified use patterns and other measures of performance, allows users to shift resources from system operations to generating the desired outputs.

Generative Design is Open-Ended

A system with a generative design can virtually generate an infinite number of configurations. It is inherently open-ended because it is evocative and because it is adaptive. Information technology can help to enhance regeneration and future configurations, and thus contribute further to the long-term vitality and sustainable fit of the underlying systems. Two IT-enabled features enhance open-endedness that characterizes generative design, as follows:

Peer-production: Systems should incorporate peer-production facilities; that is, the means that enable any individual or group to produce and share at their own volition new and useful extensions of products or services. Peer-production promotes innovation through collective action that yields chains of uncoordinated successive evolutionary changes in response to market demands and emerging opportunities. Peer-production becomes possible only in a technological environment that is designed *a priori* with **extensible architecture** and a social environment that affords the necessary incentives and normative support. For example, the architecture of Internet browsers encourages the development of plug-ins or add-ons by unaffiliated third parties, and the architecture of Wikipedia encourages contributions of knowledge objects and a stream of continuous updates and refinements. Both platforms are examples of an extensible architecture and a design strategy that counts on peer-production for continuous development and growth.

Rejuvenation: Systems should incorporate a **modular architecture** in support of renewal processes. Renewal refers to building an integrative path for continuous fine-tuning as well as radical innovation. The degree of modularity pertains to the embedded reconfigurable flexibility of its components and corresponds to the inherent coupling among them. For example, open-source applications are designed with a modular architecture that affords easy reconfiguration and upgrade path.

In summary, systems that are conducive to innovative processes should be evocative, adaptive, and open-ended. These design requirements and the possible operationalization thereof are summarized in Table 24.1.

Conclusion

Generative design is particularly relevant for promoting innovation — it has the potential to evoke a capacity for rejuvenation, a capacity to produce infinite possibilities or configurations, a capacity to challenge the *status quo* and think out-of-the-box, a capacity to reconstruct social reality and consequent action, and a capacity to revitalize our epistemic stance. Generative design can help ordinary people to achieve extraordinary results.

Acknowledgement

This chapter was presented in the Design Requirements Workshop, Cleveland, Ohio (2007). It is part of a larger body of work that has been developed with Dov Te'eni.

References

Amabile, T. M. (1983). *The social psychology of creativity.* New York: Springer-Verlag.

Amabile, T. M., Conti, R., Coon, H., Collins, M. A., Lazenby, J., & Herron, M. (1996). Assessing the work environment for creativity. *Academy of Management Journal, 39,* 1154–1184.

Avital, M., & Te'eni, D. (2006). From generative fit to generative capacity: Exploring an emerging dimension of information systems fit and task performance, *Proceedings of the 14thEuropean Conference on Information Systems,* Göteborg, Sweden.

Boland, R. J., & Collopy, F. (Eds.) (2004). *Managing as designing.* Stanford, CA: Stanford University Press.

Broadbent, M., Weill, P., & Clair, D. S. (1999). The implications of information technology infrastructure for business process redesign. *MIS Quarterly, 23*(2), 159–182.

Chomsky, N. (1972). *Language and mind.* New York: Harcourt Brace Jovanovich.

Cook, S. D. N., & Brown, J. S. (1999). Bridging epistemologies: The generative dance between organizational knowledge and organizational knowing. *Organization Science, 10*(4), 381–400.

Erikson, E. H. (1950). *Childhood and society*. New York: W. W. Norton & Company.

Frazer, J. (2002). Creative design and the generative evolutionary paradigm. In: P. J. Bentley & D. W. Corne (Eds.), *Creative evolutionary systems* (pp. 253–274). San Francisco, CA: Morgan Kaufmann Publishers.

King, J. L., Gurbaxani, V., Kraemer, K. L., McFarlan, F. W., Raman, K. S., & Yao, C. S. (1994). Institutional factors in information technology innovation. *Information Systems Research*, 5(2), 139–169.

Schön, D. A. (1979). Generative metaphor: A perspective on problem-setting in social policy. In: A. Ortony (Ed.), *Metaphor and thought* (pp. 254–283). Cambridge: Cambridge University Press.

Stenmark, D. (2005). Organisational creativity in context: Learning from a failing attempt to introduce IT support for creativity. *Journal of Technology and Human Interaction*, 1(4), 80–98.

Sternberg, R. J. (1988). *The nature of creativity: Contemporary psychological perspectives*. New York: Cambridge University Press.

Swanson, E. B., & Ramiller, N. C. (1997). The organizing vision in information systems innovation. *Organization Science*, 8(5), 458–474.

Weick, K. E. (2007). The generative properties of richness. *Academy of Management Journal*, 50(1), 14–19.

Authors' Biographies

Michel Avital is an associate professor of information management at the Universiteit van Amsterdam Business School. Building on positive modalities of inquiry, his research focuses on information and organization with an emphasis on the social aspects of information technologies. He has published articles on topics such as information systems design, creativity, knowledge sharing, social responsibility, and appreciative inquiry. Further information about publications, research projects and editorial activities is available at http://abs.uva.nl/avital. E-mail: avital@uva.nl

Alistair Black read history at London University at both undergraduate and postgraduate levels. Having qualified as a librarian in 1982, he occupied professional posts in both academic and public libraries in the 1980s. He obtained his doctorate from the Polytechnic of North London (now University of North London) in 1989. In 1990 he became a lecturer in information studies at Leeds Polytechnic (now Leeds Metropolitan University) where he is currently professor of library and information history. He is author of numerous articles and has written four books. He is the current editor of the international journal *Library History*. E-mail: a.black @leedsmet.ac.uk

Richard Boland is professor at Case Western University, Weatherhead School of Management, Cleveland, OH. He conducts qualitative studies of individuals as they design and use information. His interest is in how people make meaning as they interpret situations in an organization, or as they interpret data in a report. He has studied this hermeneutic process in a wide range of settings and professions, but primarily he focused on how managers and consultants turn an ambiguous situation into a problem statement and declare a particular course of action to be rational. Most recently he is fascinated with narrative and design as modes of cognition, which are systematically undervalued, yet dominate our meaning making. Boland published many books and articles and fulfils several journal editorships and review board memberships. E-mail: boland@case.edu

Harry Bouwman is an associate professor and chair of the Information and Communication Technology section, Faculty of Technology, Policy and Management Delft University of Technology, and private lecturer at the Institute for Advanced Management Systems Research, Åbo Akademi University, Turku Finland. He studied political science at the Free University of Amsterdam (1979) and is specialized in research methods and techniques, statistics, information systems and advanced mobile telecommunication services. He received his PhD at the Catholic University Nijmegen in 1986 at the Faculty of Social Science. E-mail: W.A.G.A.Bouwman @tudelft.nl

Martin Brigham is a lecturer in the Department of Organisation, Work and Technology, Lancaster University Management School, Lancaster. His current research centers on the relationship between mobile information and organizational change, public sector modernization, social and organization theory for the study of information infrastructures, the natural environment, and developing countries. He is also an associate member of the Centre for the Study of Technology and Organisation, Lancaster University. He was previously at the University of Warwick, Coventry. E-mail: m.brigham@lancaster.ac.uk

Rodney Brunt graduated in modern history and politics and took his graduate diploma in library and information studies at the Queen's University of Belfast. He took his PhD at Leeds Metropolitan University, where he is currently a principal lecturer in the School of Information Management. He is author of numerous articles and contributions to books in both the cataloging and indexing disciplines in librarianship and on the indexing of military intelligence. E-mail r.brunt@leedsmet.ac.uk

Antony Bryant is currently professor of informatics at Leeds Metropolitan University, Leeds. As an undergraduate he studied social and political sciences at Cambridge, and completed a PhD at the London School of Economics. He later completed a masters in computing, followed by several years working as a systems analyst for a commercial software developer. He is also currently ASEM professor at the University of Malaya, and visiting professor at the University of Amsterdam. His recent publications include *Thinking Informatically: A New Understanding of Information, Communication & Technology* (Edwin Mellen, 2006), and a series of collaborative articles in *Theory, Culture & Society* (2007) focusing on the work of Zygmunt Bauman and Gustav Metzger, 'Liquid Arts'. E-mail: a.bryant@leedsmet. ac.uk

Chun Wei Choo is professor at the Faculty of Information Studies, University of Toronto. His recent books include *The Knowing Organization* (2006, Oxford) and *The Strategic Management of Intellectual Capital and Organizational Knowledge* (2002, Oxford). E-mail: cw.choo@utoronto.ca

Sara Cullen is a former national partner at Deloitte (Australia) and the managing director of The Cullen Group. She is one of the Asia–Pacific region's most experienced outsourcing experts, having advised on 115 outsourcing initiatives spanning 51 countries with contract values up to $1.5 billion per annum. Her doctorate is from the University of Melbourne and she is coauthor of *Intelligent IT Outsourcing* (Butterworth, 2003), many articles and refereed papers and several major reports. E-mail: scullen@cullengroup.com.au

Bjorn Cumps is a PhD candidate in applied economics at the Decision Sciences and Information Management Department of the Katholieke Universiteit Leuven (K. U. Leuven). He obtained his masters degree in commercial engineering from K. U. Leuven in 2003. His PhD research is aimed at both intra- and inter-organizational business–ICT alignment, and more specifically at the interplay of organizational processes, structures, and roles to create alignment competencies. His research interests include business–ICT alignment, ICT governance, and ICT performance management. E-mail: Bjorn.Cumps@econ.kuleuven.be

Guido Dedene holds a PhD in mathematics from the K. U. Leuven, Belgium. He is a full professor at K. U. Leuven, Faculty of Economics and Applied Economics, in the Decision Sciences and Information Systems Department. He holds the chair on "Development of Information and Communication Systems" at the Universiteit van Amsterdam Business School, where he is member of the PrimaVera research program. He has published regularly in international journals and conferences, and is member of ACM and IEEE. E-mail: Guido.Dedene@econ.kuleuven.be

Erwin Fielt is a researcher at the Telematica Instituut, The Netherlands, and is working on service innovation and business models. Erwin studied industrial engineering and management at the University of Twente, specializing in information systems, and has a PhD from the Delft University of Technology. His PhD research focused on the design and acceptance of exchanges for electronic intermediaries. Current research activities include the business use of virtual worlds, the market introduction of mobile health applications, and design approaches for service innovation. E-mail: Erwin.Fielt@telin.nl

Uri Gal is an assistant professor of information systems at the Aarhus School of Business at the University of Aarhus. He holds a PhD in information systems from Case Western Reserve University and an MSc degree in organizational psychology from the London School of Economics and Political Science. His research takes a social view of organizational processes in the context of the implementation and use of information systems. He is particularly interested in the relationships between people and technology in organizations, and the changes in the nature of work practices, organizational identities, and interactions associated with the introduction of new information technologies. E-mail: urig@asb.dk

Beena George is an assistant professor in the Cameron School of Business of the University of St. Thomas, Houston, TX. She completed her graduate studies in business administration at the Indian Institute of Management, Calcutta, India and her doctoral studies at the University of Houston, TX. Her primary research interests are the management of sourcing of information technology and business services and the acceptance and use of technology. E-mail: georgeb@stthom.edu

Matt Germonprez is an assistant professor of information systems at the University of Wisconsin-Eau Claire, WI. He received his PhD at the University of Colorado in

Boulder in 2002. His research interests are in the domain of human–computer interaction with a secondary interest in information systems theory. He has published work in *Communication of the AIS, Organization Studies, International Journal of IT Standards and Standardization Research,* and *Journal of the Association for Information Systems.* E-mail: germonr@uwec.edu

Aimé Heene holds a PhD in educational sciences and an MBA from Ghent University (Belgium). He is a full professor at Ghent University, Faculty of Economics and Business Administration, heading the Department Management and Entrepreneurship. He has published five Dutch books on strategic management in private and public organizations and has served as a coeditor of several English volumes on competence-based strategy theory. He is also a member of the editorial board of several journals. E-mail: Aime.Heene@UGent.be

Pim den Hertog is a senior researcher and codirector of Dialogic *innovation & interaction,* a research-based consultancy with specializations in innovation studies and innovation management (Utrecht, The Netherlands). Pim originally graduated as an economic geographer (Utrecht University, 1990). His research interests are in management of national innovation systems, knowledge transfer, service innovation, innovation policy making (including evaluation), and innovation governance. E-mail: denhertog@dialogic.nl

Rudy Hirschheim is the Ourso Family Distinguished Professor of Information Systems in the Information Systems and Decision Sciences Department of Louisiana State University. His PhD is in information systems from the University of London and he holds an honorary doctorate from the University of Oulu, Finland. He and Richard Boland are the consulting editors of the John Wiley Series in information systems. He is a senior editor for the *Journal of the Association for Information Systems* and on the editorial boards of the journals *Information and Organization, Information Systems Journal, Journal of Information Technology, Journal of Strategic Information Systems,* and *Journal of Management Information Systems.* E-mail: rudy@lsu.edu

Dirk S. Hovorka is currently a scholar in residence at the Leeds School of Business, University of Colorado at Boulder. He attended Williams College, MA for his BA, holds a MS in Geology, and an MS in interdisciplinary telecommunications, and received his PhD in information systems from the University of Colorado. His research includes development of design theory, the philosophical foundations of IS research, the evolving role of information systems in science and the influences of social networks on knowledge exchange. E-mail: dirk.hovorka@colorado.edu

Ard Huizing holds a PhD in Economics from the Universiteit van Amsterdam and currently works as associate professor at the information management section of the Universiteit van Amsterdam Business School. He has coauthored or edited a number of books, contributed to other books with chapters, and published in many refereed journals. His research is focused on the organization of information and learning processes in organizational and broader contexts. E-mail: a.huizing@uva.nl

Lucas D. Introna is professor of technology, organization and ethics at Lancaster University. His research interest is the social study of information technology and its consequences for society. In particular, he is concerned with the ethics and politics of technology. He is coeditor *Ethics and Information Technology*, associate editor of *Management Information Systems Quarterly* (MISQ) and a founding member of the International Society for Ethics and Information Technology (INSEIT). His most recent work includes a book *Management, Information and Power* published by Macmillan, and various academic papers in journals and conference proceedings on a variety of topics such as phenomenology of technology, information and power, privacy, surveillance, information technology and post-modern ethics, autopoiesis and social systems, and virtual organizations. He was previously at the London School of Economics, Holborn, London. E-mail: l.introna@lancaster.ac.uk

Fernando Ilharco is assistant professor of the Catholic University of Portugal, Lisbon, where he is director of the PhD and master in communication sciences programs. He holds a PhD by the London School of Economics and Political Science (LSE), Department of Information Systems (July 2002), and an MBA by the Catholic University of Portugal, Lisbon (1993). Since his PhD, Ilharco has been publishing regularly in academic journals and books. His areas of interest are communication, information and technology; and organization theory and leadership — both informed by phenomenological lenses. E-mail: ilharco@ucp.pt

Wil Janssen is a research fellow at the Telematica Instituut, The Netherlands, and involved in research into new internet-enabled business models and the integration of the internet with the real world. Wil has a background in computer science and a PhD in formal methods in computing science. Since then he worked on business process engineering, e-business, and collaborative environments. In his work he combines research and the development of new public–private research partnerships. E-mail: Wil.Janssen@telin.nl

Mary Lacity is a professor of information systems at the University of Missouri-St. Louis, research affiliate at Templeton College, Oxford University, and doctoral faculty advisor at Washington University. She has written five books and her more than 50 publications have appeared in journals such as the *Harvard Business Review*, *Sloan Management Review*, *MIS Quarterly*, *IEEE Computer*, *Communications of the ACM*, and many other academic and practitioner outlets. She is senior editor for *MIS Quarterly Executive* and US editor of the *Journal of Information Technology*. E-mail: Mary.Lacity@umsl.edu

Kalle Lyytinen is Iris S. Wolstein Professor at Case Western Reserve University, Cleveland, OH and adjunct professor at University of Jyvaskyla, Finland. He serves currently on the editorial boards of several leading IS journals including *Journal of*

AIS (editor-in-chief), Journal of Strategic Information Systems, Information & Organization, Requirements Engineering Journal, Information Systems Journal, Scandinavian Journal of Information Systems, and *Information Technology and People,* among others. He has published over 150 scientific articles and conference papers and edited or written ten books on topics related to nature of IS discipline, system design, method engineering, organizational implementation, risk assessment, computer-supported cooperative work, standardization, and ubiquitous computing among others. He is currently involved in research projects that looks at the IT-induced radical innovation in software development, IT innovation in architecture, engineering and construction industry, design and use of ubiquitous applications, and the adoption of broadband wireless services in the UK, South Korea, and the US. E-mail: kalle@case.edu

Rik Maes is professor in information and communication management at the Universiteit van Amsterdam Business School, where he is currently head of the Department of Information Management and dean of the Executive Master in Information Management program. His current research interests include the foundations of information management, innovative learning strategies and sense making in organizations. He is particularly interested in combining different disciplines, including philosophy, design, art, and architecture in the development of the field of information management. E-mail: maestro@uva.nl

Jeroen Segers is a researcher and consultant at Dialogic *Innovation & Interaction* (Utrecht, The Netherlands). He has built up experience in the field of the deployment of ICT within large organizations/SMEs/sectors or industries, measurement and evaluation of innovation processes, management of national innovation systems, knowledge transfer, and services innovation. Other research interests include user adoption/involvement and technology development within broadband/content industries. He graduated from Delft University of Technology (systems engineering, policy analysis and management) in 2003 and Utrecht University (science and policy) in 2001. E-mail: segers@dialogic.nl

Robert Slagter is a researcher at the Telematica Instituut, The Netherlands, and leading the exploration into the business uses of Second Life. Robert has a background in computer science and cognitive ergonomics and has earned his PhD based on research into adaptable groupware systems. He has been involved in research projects around collaboration, architecture, and user-oriented design. Currently he is investigating new ways of working, including knowledge work in virtual environments. E-mail: Robert.Slagter@telin.nl

Stijn Viaene is a professor at the Department of Decision Sciences and Information Management of the K. U. Leuven, Belgium, and professor at the Vlerick Leuven Gent Management School, Belgium, where he heads the Management & ICT competence unit. He holds a PhD in information management from the K. U. Leuven, Belgium. His research, teaching, and coaching build, very generally, on exploration of the managerial aspects of business–IT alignment, with a particular interest in realizing the benefits from business intelligence systems. E-mail: Stijn.Viaene@vlerick.be

Erik J. de Vries holds a Cum Laude and prize-winning PhD in economics from the Universiteit van Amsterdam and received his MSc in informatics from the same university. His research interests include the informational aspects of distribution strategies in the service sector, (ICT-enabled) service innovation, and research methods. He published several works in these fields. His research is part of the PrimaVera research program (http://primavera.fee.uva.nl/) of the Universiteit van Amsterdam Business School. E-mail: erik.devries@uva.nl

Rolf T. Wigand is the Maulden-Entergy Chair and Distinguished Professor of Information Science and Management at the University of Arkansas at Little Rock. He is the past director of the Center for Digital Commerce and the graduate program in information management at Syracuse University. His research interests lie at the intersection of information and communication business issues, the role of newer information technologies, and their strategic alignment within business and industry. Past and current research efforts have been supported by the National Science Foundation, the German Science Foundation, and other funding agencies. A three-year research project is currently being supported by NSF on the emergence of vertical industry standards in three industries. Rolf Wigand holds editorial positions with different leading journals and is an editorial board and review member of over 40 academic and professional journals, book series, and yearbooks. His publications have appeared in *MIS Quarterly, Sloan Management Review, Journal of MIS, Journal of Informantion Technology, Electronic Markets, European Journal of Information Systems* and others. Wigand is the author of four books and over 110 articles, book chapters, and monographs. E-mail: rtwigand@ualr.edu

Leslie Willcocks is professor of technology, work and globalization at the London School of Economics and Political Science. He is also associate fellow at Templeton College University of Oxford, and holds visiting chairs at Erasmus and Melbourne Universities. He has published 27 books and over 160 refereed papers in the IS field in journals such as *MISQ, Journal of Strategic Information Systems, MISQE, Harvard Business Review, Sloan Management Review, Journal of Management Studies* and *Public Administration*. His doctorate is from Cambridge University and he has been coeditor-in-chief of the *Journal of Information Technology* since 1988. E-mail: l.p.willcocks@lse.ac.uk

Youngjin Yoo is associate professor in Information Systems Department and Irwin L. Gross Research Fellow at the Fox School of Business and Management, Temple University, Philadelphia, PA. He holds a PhD in information systems from the University of Maryland. He received his MBA and BS in Business Administration from Seoul National University in Seoul, Korea. His work covers a wide range of topics broadly related to IT-enabled innovation and organization transformation.

In particular, he is interested in integrating design approaches in managing innovations and information technology, knowledge management, and ubiquitous computing. His work was published in leading academic journals such as *Information Systems Research, MIS Quarterly, Organization Science, the Communications of the ACM, the Academy of Management Journal, the Journal of Strategic Information Systems, the Journal of Management Education*, and *Information Systems Management*. He also edited two books on ubiquitous computing and wrote several books' chapters. He is an associate editor of *Information Systems Research* and on the editorial board of *Organization Science, Journal of AIS*, and *Information and Organization*. E-mail: youngjin.yoo@temple.edu

Subject Index